MEMOIRS OF
McCHEYNE

D1075716

MEMOIRS OF McCHEYNE

Including His Letters and Messages

EDITED BY

ANDREW A. BONAR

WITH A BIOGRAPHICAL INTRODUCTION
BY S. MAXWELL CODER

MOODY PRESS
CHICAGO

© 1947, by
THE MOODY BIBLE INSTITUTE
OF CHICAGO

All rights reserved

ISBN: 0-8024-5241-8

1978 Edition

Printed in the United States of America

CONTENTS

BIBLE MESSAGES

MISCELLANEOUS PAPERS

EDITORIAL PREFACE

TO REPRODUCE, in our time, a work which in some editions contained as many as 632 pages of rather fine print, is an enterprise beset with some difficulties. To make possible the present volume, set in type of such a size as to encourage the reader, it was found necessary to reduce the quantity of material found in some of the older editions of this notable compilation of the papers of Robert Murray McCheyne.

After careful study of the matter, during which a number of Christian leaders were consulted who were best in a position to evaluate the various parts which made up the original work edited by Andrew A. Bonar, it was recognized that the most valuable feature of the volume was the actual writings of McCheyne himself, rather than the somewhat lengthy biography written by Bonar about his friend.

The present edition therefore contains, unabridged except for the omission of a few fragments and two minor papers, the exceedingly rich works of McCheyne which have been treasured as one of the great heritages of the Church. The biographical introduction is largely a condensation of the original memoir by Bonar.

S.M.C.

BIOGRAPHICAL INTRODUCTION

S CARCELY once in a century does such a remarkable volume appear as this collection of the letters, Bible messages, and other papers of Robert Murray McCheyne, originally compiled by Andrew A. Bonar. First published in 1844, it has been sought after and treasured by God's people everywhere as one of the greatest and most blessed spiritual classics of all time. Within twenty-five years after its first appearance, the book was in its one hundred sixteenth English edition, and its circulation in America was likewise phenomenal.

In spite of the almost countless editions in which the volume has been published during the past century, it has been practically unobtainable for many years. There is no reason for doubting that this scarcity is the result of the fact that those who are fortunate enough to possess copies regard them as almost priceless.

Why such a collection of papers, gathered together by a friend and published after McCheyne's death, should be so cherished by so many for so long a time, while the careful life work of other men of God has quickly passed into oblivion, cannot be understood apart from some knowledge of the life of this young minister of the Church of Scotland, who died at the age of twenty-nine.

Robert Murray McCheyne was born in Edinburgh on May 21, 1813, at a time when the first evidences of a spiritual awakening in Scotland were beginning to appear, following a period when orthodoxy and piety had sunk to such a low level that "the things which remained were ready to die." Among the secret preparations of God for coming times of refreshing from on high was the birth of this youngest son of Adam McCheyne, writer to the signet, for he was destined to be recognized as one of God's greatest gifts to His Church in many generations, and to be known long after his death as "the saintly Mc-Cheyne."

That brilliance of intellect which was later to make him an accomplished Hebrew and Greek scholar was evident at the early age of four, when he taught himself to name and write all the letters of the Greek alphabet, as a means of recreation. Within the next year he achieved eminence among his school fellows because of his progress in English, and the sweetness and correctness of his powers of recitation.

McCheyne entered the high school in his eighth year, and matriculated at Edinburgh University when he was fourteen, in November, 1827. There he repeatedly distinguished himself as a versatile student, especially in poetical exercises. He was awarded a special prize by Professor Wilson for a poem, "On the Covenanters." He is described as having been of a tall, light form, full of elasticity and vigor as a young man; ambitious, yet noble in his disposition, disdaining everything like meanness or deceit. Some would have regarded him as exhibiting many traits of a Christian character; but his susceptible mind had not, at that time, a relish for any higher joy than the refined gaieties of society, and for such pleasures as the song and the dance could yield.

Although he never knew the date of his new birth, he possessed a definite assurance that it had taken place. It was characteristic of his ministry that such assurance did not prevent deep and lifelong searchings and longings for greater holiness of life.

In the winter of 1831 he commenced his studies in the Divinity Hall where Thomas Chalmers was Professor of Divinity and David Welsh, Professor of Ecclesiastical History. Those who recall the important movements within the Church of Scotland at this period, and the places of leadership these men occupied, will realize that this four-year course afforded no ordinary advantages to McCheyne for enlarging his understanding and deepening his spiritual life.

From the day of the death of Robert's eldest brother, David, his senior by eight or nine years, his friends observed a change. His diary contains numerous allusions to the effect the passing of this godly and well-beloved brother had upon young McCheyne, who was eighteen years of age at the time. One year later, he wrote, "On this morning last year came the first overwhelming blow to my worldliness; how blessed to me, Thou, O God, only knowest, who hast made it so." Again to a friend, he penned the lines, "Pray for me, that I may be made holier and wiser—less like myself, and more like my heavenly Master; that I may not regard my life, if so be I may finish my course with joy. This day eleven years ago, I lost my loved and loving brother, and began to seek a Brother who cannot die."

Together with Edward Irving, Andrew and Horatius Bonar, and other ardent young souls, McCheyne met frequently for prayer, Bible study and exercises in the Hebrew and Greek Scriptures. When Dr. Chalmers heard of the simple literal way in which the words of Scripture were taken by these young believers, he said, "I like these literalities." A study of any of McCheyne's sermons reveals how profound was his respect for the exact language of the written Word of God, whether he was speaking of the return of the Lord, or of the obligation resting upon believers to reach the lost about them for Christ. These young men also set apart an hour or two every week for visiting the careless and needy in the most neglected portions of the town. They stirred each other up to faithfulness in this ministry, in such hours as might otherwise have been given to recreation. His diary reveals the state of mind of young McCheyne during these years of preparation.

"May 21. This day I attained my twenty-first year. Oh, how long and how worthlessly I have lived, Thou only knowest! *Neff* died in his thirty-first year; when shall I?"

"October 17. Private meditation exchanged for conversation. Here is the root of the evil—forsake God and He forsakes us."

"November 21. If nothing else will do to sever me from my sins, Lord, send me such sore and trying calamities as shall awake me from earthly slumbers. It must always be best to be alive to Thee, whatever be the quickening instrument. I tremble as I write, for Oh! on every hand do I see too likely occasions for sore afflictions."

On December 31, 1832, McCheyne summed up twelve months of progress. "God has in this past year introduced me to the preparation of the ministry—I bless Him for that. He has helped me to give up much of my shame to name His name, and be on His side, especially before particular friends—I bless Him for that. He has taken conclusively away friends that might have been a snare—must have been a stumbling block—I bless Him for that. He has introduced me to one Christian friend, and seals more and more my amity with another—I bless Him for that."

The consciousness of some sin caused him to write, "Somewhat overcome. Let me see: There is a creeping defect here. Humble, purposelike reading of the Word omitted. What plant can be unwatered and not wither?"

His diary gives evidence of unsparing self judgment.

"June 4. Evening almost lost. Music will not sanctify, though it make feminine the heart."

"June 22. Omissions make way for commissions. Could I but take effective warning! A world's wealth would not make up for that saying, 'If any man sin, we have an advocate with the Father.' But how shall we that are dead to sin live any longer therein?"

"August 13. Clear conviction of sin is the only true origin of dependence on another's righteousness, and therefore (strange to say!) of the Christian's peace of mind and cheerfulness."

"September 8. Reading Adams' *Private Thoughts.* Oh, for his heart-searching ability! Ah me! On what mountains of pride must I be wandering, when all I do is tinctured with the very sin this man so deplored; yet where are my wailings, where my tears, over my love of praise?"

"November 14. I fear the love of applause or effect goes a great way. May God keep me from preaching myself instead of Christ crucified."

"February 23, (1834). Rose early to seek God and found Him whom my soul loveth. Who would not rise early to meet such company? The rains are over and gone. They that sow in tears shall reap in joy."

Wrote Andrew Bonar of his friend, "During his first years of his college course, his studies did not absorb his full attention; but no sooner was the change in his soul begun, than his studies shared in the results. A deeper sense of responsibility led him to occupy his talents for the service of Him who bestowed them. There have been few who, along with a devotedness of spirit that sought to be ever directly engaged in the Lord's work, have nevertheless retained such continued and undecaying esteem for the advantages of study. While attending the usual literary and philosophical classes, he found time to turn his attention to theology and natural history. And often in his days of most successful preaching, when, next to his own soul, his parish and his flock were his only care, he has been known to express a regret that he had not laid up in former days more stores of all useful knowledge; for he found himself able to use the jewels of the Egyptians in the service of Christ. His previous studies would sometimes flash into his mind some happy illustration of divine truth, at the very moment when he was most solemnly applying the glorious gospel to the most ignorant and vile."

His own words will best show his estimate of study, and at the same time the prayerful manner in which he felt it should be carried on. "Do get on with your studies," he wrote to a young student in 1840. "Remember you are now forming the character of your future ministry in great measure, if God spare you. If you acquire slovenly or sleepy habits of study now, you will never get the better of it. Do everything in its own time. Do everything in earnest; if it is worth doing, then do it with all your might. Above all, keep much in the presence of God. Never see the face of man until you have seen His face who is our light, our all. Pray for others; pray for your teachers and fellow students." To another he wrote: "Beware of the atmosphere of the classics. It is pernicious indeed; and you need much of the south wind breathing over the Scriptures to counteract it. True, we ought to know them; but only as chemists handle poisons—to discover their qualities, not to infect their blood with them." And again: "Pray that the Holy Spirit would not only make you a believing and holy lad, but make you wise in your studies also. A ray of divine light in the soul sometimes clears up a mathematical problem wonderfully. The smile of God calms the spirit, and the left hand of Jesus holds up the fainting head, and His Holy Spirit quickens the affections, so that even natural studies go on a million times more easily and comfortably."

Vacation time, for McCheyne and such of his intimate friends as remained in town, was not regarded as a period of complete cessation from study. Once every week they spent a morning together for the purpose of investigating some point of systematic theology, and stating to each other the amount and result of their private reading. During another summer they studied unfulfilled prophecy each week at an early morning hour. As they said, "Though our views differed much on particular points, we never failed to get food for our souls in the Scriptures we explored." These discussions were so profitable that the young men formed the habit of gathering together at half past six each Saturday morning during the school term, to study whatever might cast light on the Word of God.

A young man with such unusual intellectual powers, with which were associated a love for study and a remarkably accurate memory, might have become noted for scholarship, had it not been for the fact that he regarded the winning of souls as his chief task. He made every talent he possessed subsidiary to the single desire of awakening those who were dead in trespasses and sins. He prepared his soul for what he regarded as the terrible and awful responsibility of ministering the Word of God, "by much prayer, and much study of the Word of God; by affliction in his person; by inward trials and sore temptations; by experience of the death of corruption in his own heart, and by discovery of the Saviour's fullness and grace. He learned experimentally to ask, 'Who is he that overcometh the world but he that believeth that Jesus is the Son of God?' (I John 5:5)."

Robert Murray McCheyne was licensed to preach by the Presbytery of Annan, on July 1, 1835. After preaching in various places for several months, during which many began to perceive the peculiar sweetness of the Word on his lips, he became assistant to Mr. John Bonar in the united parishes of Larbert and Dunipace, near Stirling, on November 7, 1835. His preaching was the giving out of his own inward life, the unfolding of his own soul's experience as he grew in grace and in the knowledge of his Lord and Saviour. He began each day by singing Psalms at an early hour. This was followed by the reading of the Word for his own sanctification. He found a mine of spiritual riches in the *Letters of Samuel Rutherford.* Other favorites of his were Baxter's *Call to the Unconverted,* and *The Life of David Brainerd,* by Jonathan Edwards.

He studied both the Old and New Testaments regularly, determined to "examine the most barren chapters to collect the good for which they were intended." His desire to have every possible help to holiness led him to seek the fellowship of more advanced believers. In a letter to a friend he compared these contacts with other Christians to the necessity for keeping his pocket watch corrected by consultation with the trustworthy and proved clocks in the church steeples. He wrote, "And just so I sometimes think it may be with that inner watch, whose hands point not to time but to eternity. By gradual and slow changes the wheels of my soul lag behind, or the springs of passions become too powerful; and I have no living timepiece with which I may compare, and by which I may amend my going. You will say that I may always have the Son, and so it should be; but we have many clouds which obscure the Son from our weak eyes."

After only a few weeks of ministry, a heart condition and an irritating cough made it necessary for him to be laid aside from public duty. He said to Mr. Bonar, "I hope and pray that it may be His will to restore me again to you and your parish, with a heart tutored by sickness, to speak more and more as dying to dying." Again, "Paul asked, 'What wilt thou have me to do?' and it was answered, 'I will show him what great things he must *suffer* for my name's sake.' Thus it may be with me. I have been too anxious to do great things. The lust of praise has ever been my besetting sin; and what more befitting school could be found for me than that of suffering alone, away from the eye and ear of man?"

Those who observed Mr. McCheyne's ministry closely were aware that he gave out not merely living water, but living water drawn from the springs that he had himself drunk of. He reproached himself for what he called any bitter speaking of the gospel. "Surely it is a gentle message, and should be spoken with angelic tenderness, especially by such a needy sin-

ner." Meeting a fellow pastor on one occasion, he asked what
his friend's last Sabbath subject had been. The reply was "The
wicked shall be turned into hell." On hearing this awful text,
McCheyne asked, "Were you able to preach it *with tenderness?*"

His diary contains the cry, "Oh, when will I plead, with my
tears and inward yearnings, over sinners! Oh, compassionate
Lord, give me to know what manner of spirit I am of! Give
me Thy gentle Spirit, that neither strives nor cries. Much
weariness, want of prayerfulness, and want of cleaving to
Christ." "Since Tuesday have been laid up with illness. Set by
once more for a season to seal my unprofitableness and cure
my pride. When shall this self-choosing temper be healed?
'Lord, I will preach, run, visit, wrestle,' said I. 'No, thou shalt
lie in thy bed and suffer,' said the Lord. Today missed some
fine opportunities of speaking a word for Christ. The Lord
saw I would have spoken as much for my own honor as His,
and therefore shut my mouth. *I see a man cannot be a faithful
minister, until he preaches Christ for Christ's sake*—until he
gives up striving to attract people to himself, and seeks only to
attract them to Christ. Lord, give me this! Tonight some
glimpses of humbling, and therefore some wrestling in social
prayer. But my prayers are scarcely to be called prayers."

When a friend died, he bewailed, "Oh, how I repent of our
vain controversies when we last met, and that we spoke so
little of Jesus. Oh, that we had spoken more one to another!
Lord, teach me to be always speaking as dying to dying."

McCheyne's advice to a young man about Bible reading is
most instructive as to his own prayer life. "You read your
Bible regularly, of course; but do try and understand it, and
still more to *feel* it. Read more parts than one at a time. For
example, if you are reading Genesis, read a Psalm also; or if
you are reading Matthew, read a small bit of an Epistle also.
Turn the Bible into prayer. Thus, if you were reading the First
Psalm, spread the Bible on the chair before you, and kneel, and

pray, 'O Lord, give me the blessedness of the man'; 'let me not
stand in the counsel of the ungodly.' This is the best way of
knowing the meaning of the Bible, and of learning to pray."

After ten months' ministry at Larbert and Dunipace under
Mr. John Bonar, McCheyne was unanimously called to become
pastor of a new church, St. Peter's in Dundee, where his congregation amounted from the beginning to about eleven hundred hearers. He was ordained on November 24, 1836. From
that time on, there was abundant evidence that God had answered his prayer, "Lord, may Thy grace come with the laying
on of the hands of the Presbytery." His very first sermon as a
pastor was the means of awakening souls, as he afterwards
learned, and evidently every message he ever gave served to
deepen the impression he made upon his people.

The details of the manner of McCheyne's life, and of the
way he conducted himself as a minister of the gospel, have for
a hundred years been studied by other Christian workers who
have longed to see God's blessing resting upon them as it
rested richly upon every part of the service of this young man
of God.

He resolutely secured time for devotion before breakfast
each day, believing that three chapters from the Bible were little enough food for his soul at the beginning of each day. He
refused to give to his people on the Lord's day anything which
had not cost him much of diligent application in study, meditation, and prayer. When asked by a friend about his view of
how one should prepare for the pulpit, he called attention to
Exodus 27:20: *"Beaten oil—beaten oil for the lamps of the
sanctuary."* He greatly admired the words of Jeremy Taylor,
"If thou meanest to enlarge thy religion, do it rather by enlarging thine ordinary devotions than thy extraordinary." While
McCheyne did set apart special seasons for prayer and fasting,
the real secret of his soul's prosperity lay in the daily enlarge-
ment of his own heart in fellowship with God. On one Sunday

his diary carried the comments, "Very happy in my work. Too little prayer in the morning. Must try to get early to bed on Saturday, that I may 'rise a great while before day.' "

McCheyne introduced a regular Thursday evening prayer meeting at his church, at a time when the mid-week service was a rarity. It was his custom to begin such meetings by reading some great promise from Scripture, to be hidden in the hearts of his people. Prayer preceded and followed a twenty minute Bible study period, and then the young pastor read some history of revivals, with comments in passing.

He set apart another evening for a class for the young people of his congregation. Sunday schools he encouraged in all the districts of his parish. One of the secrets of the great success of his work among children is to be found in the qualifications upon which he insisted for every teacher. "She should be able to keep up in her scholars the fluency of reading, and the knowledge of the Bible and Catechism which they may have already acquired. She should be able to teach them to sing the praises of God with feeling and melody. But, far above all, she should be a Christian woman, not in name only, but in deed and in truth—one whose heart has been touched by the Spirit of God, and who can love the souls of little children. Any teacher who wanted this last qualification, I would look upon as a curse rather than a blessing—a center of blasting and cold-ness and death, instead of a center from which light and warmth and heavenly influence might emanate."

His method of preaching was an effort to emulate the ministry of the Apostles by expounding Scripture in his sermons. After announcing the subject of a discourse, he called attention to the context, then proceeded to bring out the doctrines of the text. A friend said, "The heads of his sermons were not the milestones that tell you how near you are to your journey's end, but they were nails which fixed and fastened all he said." He referred to himself as "just an interpreter of Scripture." Far from simply preaching Bible doctrine, he sought to preach Christ, from whom all doctrine shoots forth as rays from a center. Many spoke of the peculiar sweetness and holy unction of his preaching, which attracted visitors from far and wide.

Offers for his pastoral services which came from wealthier districts with much larger emoluments, McCheyne rejected, because he was convinced that he was in the will of God "among the noisy mechanics and political weavers of this godless town. He will make the money sufficient. He that paid His taxes from a fish's mouth will supply all my needs." It was his hope that "perhaps the Lord will make this wilderness of chimney tops to be green and beautiful as the garden of the Lord, a field which the Lord hath blessed!" God graciously fulfilled this yearning of His young servant's heart, but in an altogether unexpected way, as the fruit of much suffering and prayer.

Before the showers of heavenly blessing came which were to fall on St. Peter's Church at Dundee, McCheyne's ministry was greatly enlarged when he became, in 1837, Secretary to the Association for Church Extension in the County of Forfar, in which capacity he traveled all over that area, ministering the Word. He might have written much, and have gained a name by his writing; but he laid everything aside when put in comparison with preaching the gospel. He scarcely ever refused an invitation to preach on a weekday, and his visits were always longed for in other communities as times of special refreshment.

In our own day of laxity in church discipline, it is interesting to read a statement made by Robert Murray McCheyne at an ordination of elders. "When I first entered upon the work of the ministry among you, I was exceedingly ignorant of the vast importance of church discipline. I thought that my great and almost only work was to pray and preach. I saw your souls to be so precious, and the time so short, that I devoted all my time, and care, and strength, to labor in word and doctrine. When cases of discipline were brought before me and the elders, I regarded them with something like abhorrence. It was a duty I shrank from; and I may truly say it nearly drove me from the work of the ministry among you altogether. But it pleased God, who teaches His servants in another way than man teaches, to bless some of the cases of discipline to the manifest and undeniable conversion of the souls of those under our care; and from that hour a new light broke in upon my mind, and I saw that if preaching be an ordinance of Christ, so is church discipline. I now feel very deeply persuaded that both are of God—that two keys are committed to us by Christ: the one the key of doctrine, by means of which we unlock the treasures of the Bible; the other the key of discipline, by which we open or shut the way to the sealing ordinances of the faith. Both are Christ's gifts, and neither is to be resigned without sin."

One of the most notable characteristics of McCheyne, frequently remarked upon by his contemporaries, was the holy consistency of his daily walk. Knowing, as he did, that one idle word, one needless contention, one covetous act, could destroy in his people the effect of many a solemn expostulation and earnest warning, he was peculiarly circumspect in his everyday walk. As Andrew Bonar wrote about his friend, "We must not only speak faithfully to our people in our sermons, but live faithfully for them too. Perhaps it may be found that the reason why many who preach the gospel fully and in all earnestness are not owned of God in the conversion of souls, is to be found in their defective exhibition of grace in these easy moments of life. 'Them that honor me, I will honor' (I Sam. 2:30). It was noticed long ago that men will give you leave to *preach against* their sins as much as you will, if so be you will but be easy with them when you have done, and talk as they do, and live as they live. How much otherwise it was with Mr. McCheyne, all who knew him are witnesses."

His biographer mentions the reproach which McCheyne was obliged to bear, even while his holy walk and his heavenly ministry were manifestly raising the tone of Christians. "He was the object of supercilious contempt to formal, cold-hearted ministers, and of bitter hatred to many of the ungodly . . . . Very deep was the enmity borne to him by some, all the deeper, because the only cause of it was his likeness to his Master. But nothing turned him aside. He was full of ardor, yet ever gentle, and meek, and generous; full of zeal, yet never ruffled by his zeal; and not only his strength of first love (Rev. 2:4), but even its warm glow, seemed in him to suffer no decay. Thus he spent the first years of his ministry in Dundee. The town began to feel that they had a peculiar man of God in the midst of them."

Two deep impressions were preparing McCheyne during these years for an altogether different form of service. These were his intense interest in missions, and the decided impression on his own mind that his career would be short, often seen as he sealed his letters with this statement, "The night cometh."

At the close of 1838, his unremitting labor brought on a violent palpitation of the heart, which made it necessary for him to leave Dundee to seek rest and change of occupation. In Edinburgh, Dr. Candlish suddenly asked McCheyne one day what he would think of "being useful to the Jewish cause during his cessation from labor, by going abroad to make personal inquiries into the state of Israel?" The idea thus suddenly suggested led to the sending forth of a delegation from the Church of Scotland to the Jews of Europe and Asia, to inquire into their condition, and to report on the prospects and best means of calling their attention to the character and claims of the Lord Jesus Christ. It was a signal evidence of the high esteem and confidence in which Robert Murray McCheyne was held by his brethren that he was thus honored, in the twenty-fourth year of his age, and was chosen, in connection with three older ministers, as a member of the famous Mission of Inquiry.

The interest which this proposed journey excited in Scotland was very great. For some time, the condition of the people of Israel had been upon the hearts of godly ministers in Scotland. It was anticipated that there would be "an outpouring of the Spirit, when our church should stretch out its hand to the Jew as well as to the Gentile."

During the journey to Palestine McCheyne wrote, "For much of our safety I feel indebted to the prayers of my people, I mean the Christians among them, who do not forget us. If the veil of the world's machinery were lifted off, how much we could find is done in answer to the prayers of God's children." Although extremely weak and ill, McCheyne neglected not his own prayer life. While the tent was being erected at the end of a day's arduous journey, he would lie down on the ground under some tree, completely exhausted by the long ride. After lying almost speechless for half an hour, when the palpitation of his heart somewhat abated, he would propose that his friend Andrew Bonar, who was also a member of the party, and he should pray together. Often, at the point of death in a foreign land, feeling his faculties going, one by one, with every reason to expect that he would soon be with his God, McCheyne devoted himself to prayer for his people. He wrote to them, "When I got better, I used to creep out in the evenings about sunset. I often remembered you all then. I could not write, as my eyes and head were much affected; I could read but very little; I could speak very little, for I had hardly any voice; and so I had all my time to lay my people before God and pray for a blessing on them."

On one of those days when he was stretched on his bed, praying for his flock despite all his own suffering, a very remarkable revival began to be witnessed back in Dundee, under the preaching of Mr. W. C. Burns, who was supplying Mr. McCheyne's place in his absence. Beginning in Kilsyth, a great awakening took place which soon swept over Dundee. For some time there had been symptoms of deeper attention than usual at St. Peter's, and of real anxiety in some who had previously been careless. On Thursday evening after the usual weekly prayer meeting, Mr. Burns invited those to remain who felt the need of an outpouring of the Spirit. About a hundred remained; and at the conclusion of a solemn address to these anxious souls, suddenly the power of God seemed to descend, and all were bathed in tears. At a similar service next evening in the church, there was much melting of heart and intense desire after the Lord, and a vast number pressed into the after meeting with awful eagerness.

"It was like a pent-up flood breaking forth; tears were streaming from the eyes of many, and some fell on the ground groaning, weeping, and crying for mercy. Onward from that evening meetings were held every day for many weeks; and the extraordinary nature of the work justified and called for extraordinary services. The whole town was moved. Many believers doubted; the ungodly raged; but the Word of God grew mightily and prevailed. Instances occurred where whole families were affected at once. Other men of God in the vicinity hastened to aid in the work.

"When Mr. McCheyne arrived at the conclusion of his trip through Europe, the blessing was still continuing. He saw such evidence of the revival for which he had been praying as to make his heart rejoice. He had no envy because another instrument was so honored in the place where he himself had labored with many tears and trials. In true Christian magnanimity, he rejoiced that the work of the Lord was done, by whatever hand."

His people welcomed his arrival with the greatest joy. There was not a seat in the church unoccupied; people were crowded into every available space. Many were weeping; all were still and calm, intensely earnest to hear. On coming out of his church he found the road to his house crowded with old and young who were waiting to welcome him back. He discovered that many of those who were saved during the revival were numbered among those for whom he and others had prayed before he left them. Mr. McCheyne mentioned a pleasing result of the awakening, "I find many souls who were saved under my own ministry, whom I never knew of before. They are not afraid to come out now, it has become so common a thing to be concerned about the soul."

Robert Murray McCheyne returned from his mission to Israel at the end of the year 1839. In the spring of 1843, he visited the north of England on an evangelical mission, and made similar journeys to London and Aberdeenshire. On returning from the latter place, he was seized with a sudden illness. In visiting some people sick of the fever, he had caught the infection. The crisis came on March 24, 1843.

When it became known that his life was in danger, a weeping multitude assembled in St. Peter's. Next morning, at a quarter past nine, he expired, and all that day nothing was to be heard in the houses around but lamentation and great mourning, and, as a friend in that neighborhood wrote, "In passing along the high road, you saw the faces of every one swollen with weeping." McCheyne was buried by St. Peter's Church, where an imposing tombstone marks his grave.

Tributes to his greatness could be cited almost without number. A London pastor called him "altogether one of the loveliest specimens of the Spirit's workmanship." In the *Dundee Warder*, a tribute said, "Every note from his hand had a lasting interest about it; for his mind was so full of Christ, that, even in writing about the most ordinary affairs, he contrived, by some natural turn, to introduce the glorious subject that was always uppermost with him."

This calls attention to the greatest tribute which could ever have been paid to McCheyne, the manner in which God's people have received his collected letters and messages.

Of all the works of McCheyne,* the present collection of
papers is by far the most outstanding volume. Typical of the
high regard in which this work has always been held are these
quotations from a review of the original edition, which appeared in July, 1844, in *The Presbyterian Review and Religious
Journal,* an Edinburgh periodical.

"Such language could not have been prompted by an ordinary man. Robert Murray McCheyne! . . . That disentangled,
pilgrim look which showed plainly that he 'sought a city';—
the serene self-possession of one who walks by faith . . . that
aspect of compassion, in such unison with the remonstrating
and entreating tones of his melodious and tender voice—that
entire appearance as of one who had been with Jesus, and who
would never be right at home till, where Jesus is, there he
should also be.

"To know him was the best interpretation of any text. At
least, we have a clearer conception of what is meant by a hidden life, and a 'living sacrifice,' and can better understand the
sort of life which Enoch led, since we made the acquaintance
of Robert McCheyne.

"In his prayers he held such reverential and endearing communion with a reconciled God; he pressed so near the throne;
there was something so filial in his 'Abba, Father'; it was so
obvious even to lookers-on, that he was putting his petitions
and praises into the golden censer; so express, and urgent, and
hopeful were his supplications, that it was awakening to hear
him pray. It was enough to make some Christians feel, 'hitherto we have asked nothing in Jesus' name'; enough to prick

---

* His principal works are: 1. *Narrative of a Mission of Inquiry to the Jews*
(jointly with Andrew Bonar), Edinburgh, 1842. 2. *Expositions of the Epistles to
the Seven Churches of Asia,* Dundee, 1843. 3. *The Eternal Inheritance: the
Believer's Portion, and Vessels of Wrath Fitted to Destruction, Two Discourses,*
Dundee, 1843. 4. *Memoir and Remains of Robert Murray McCheyne* (edited by
Andrew A. Bonar), Edinburgh, 1843. 5. *Additional Remains, Sermons, and Lec-
tures,* Edinburgh, 1844. 6. *A Basket of Fragments, the Substance of Sermons,*
Aberdeen, 1849.

the hearts of prayerless worldlings. His preaching was a continuation of his prayers. In both he spoke from within the veil,
his hand on the mercy seat, and his eye fixed on things invisible.
"To give this article a practical tendency, we may be allowed
to mention what we believe to have been the secret of Mr.
McCheyne's uncommon usefulness. . . . We are persuaded
that next to his habitual dependence upon the Spirit of God,
the occasion of his uncommon success was the consistency and
conspicuousness of his Christian character. He lived in the
eye of his people. Though his house had been a glass-fronted
cabinet, they could scarcely have been more minutely cognizant
of his movements and whole manner of life. They knew that
his weekdays were but a sequel to his Sabbath. And what they
saw him in the pulpit, they found him in his study and among
his friends, by the wayside, and in their own houses."

In an American edition published in Philadelphia in 1844,
Samuel Miller, of the Theological Seminary at Princeton, New
Jersey, wrote an introduction in which he said, "Such a spirit
ought to be studied deeply and recommended as widely as possible. . . . I consider that the appearance and the popularity
of such works as this Memoir are a pledge that the gracious
King of Zion will revive us. . . . Surely the contemplation of
such a portrait as that presented in this Memoir ought to fill
us with humiliation and shame. . . . I write these lines, and
recommend this work . . . under the deep impression that we
cannot pray for a greater blessing to our beloved Church, than
that the mantle of this holy man may rest upon all our pastors
and elders, exciting them to the zeal, the unceasing diligence,
and the entire consecration to their Master in heaven which
were so conspicuous in his short course."

Alexander Whyte, in a preface to a centenary edition of this
notable work which was being published in Edinburgh in 1913,
spoke of "that great spiritual classic, Andrew Bonar's *Memoir
of McCheyne.* I am constantly hearing of the great good that

book has been the means of doing, especially to ministers, and not seldom to ministers far removed from the communion to which McCheyne and Bonar belonged. . . . Depend upon it, this wonderfully fresh and fruitful book will have a new lease of life given it from this year." There is every reason to believe that Alexander Whyte's words will find another fulfillment in our own generation, as this present edition goes forth.

S. MAXWELL CODER.

LETTERS

LETTERS

To Rev. R. MacDonald, Blairgowrie

Written when first laid aside by that illness which afterwards led him to take
a trip to Palestine.

Edinburgh, January 12, 1839

THE VERY DAY I received your kind letter, I intended to
have written you that you might provide some one to
stand in my place on Monday evening next. I am ashamed at
not having answered your kind inquiries sooner, but am not
very good at the use of the pen, and I have had some necessary
letters to write. However, now I come to you. This is Saturday, when you will be busy preparing to feed the flock of God
with food convenient. Happy man! It is a glorious thing to
preach the unsearchable riches of Christ! We do not value it
aright till we are deprived of it. Then Philip Henry's saying
is felt to be true—that he would beg all the week in order to
be allowed to preach on the Sabbath day.

I have been far from alarmingly ill; my complaint is all
unseen, and sometimes unfelt. My heart beats by night and
day; but especially by night, too loud and too strong. My
medical friends have tried several ways of removing the trouble,
hitherto without complete success. As long as it lasts, I fear
I shall be unfit for the work of the ministry. But I do hope
that God has something more for me to do in the vineyard, and
that a little patient rest, accompanied by His blessing, may
quiet and restore me. Oh! my dear friend, I need it all to keep

3

this proud spirit under. Andrew Bonar was noticing the providence of "Elijah in the wilderness" being my alloted part at
our next meeting. I read it in the congregation the Sabbath
after, with an envious feeling in my own heart, though I did
not like to express it, that I would now be sent a like day's
journey to learn the same lessons as the prophet—that it is not
the tempest, nor the earthquake, nor the fire, but the still small
voice of the Spirit that carries on the glorious work of saving
souls.

Andrew will be with you on Monday, and I am almost
tempted to send this tonight to the post office; but it is not
right to encourage the Sabbath mail, so will defer it till Monday. May you have a time of refreshing from the presence of
the Lord! May He be the third with you who joined the two
disciples on the way to Emmaus, and made their hearts burn
by opening to them the Scriptures concerning Himself. I
hope your evening meeting may be as delightful as the last.
May your mind be solemnized, my dear friend, by the thought
that we are ministers but for a time; that the Master may
summon us to retire into silence, or may call us to the temple
above; or the midnight cry of the great Bridegroom may break
suddenly on our ears. Blessed is the servant that is found
waiting! Make all your services tell for eternity; speak what
you can look back upon with comfort when you must be
silent.

I am persuaded that I have been brought into retirement
to teach me the value and need of prayer. Alas! I have not
estimated aright the value of near access unto God. It is
not the mere daily routine of praying for certain things that
will obtain the blessing. But there must be the need within,
the real filial asking of God the things which we need, and
which He delights to give. We must study prayer more. Be
instant in prayer. You will be thinking my affliction is teaching me much, by my saying these things. Oh! I wish it were so.

Nobody ever made less use of affliction than I do. I feel the assaults of Satan most when I am removed into a corner; every evil thought and purpose rushes over my soul, and it is only at times that I can find Him whom my soul loveth.

Monday, January 14, 1839—I now sit down to finish this, and send it away. I am much in my usual today, perhaps, if anything, a little better. Still I have a hope at present of resuming my labors. Will you give me a Sabbath-day's labor? I had no intention of asking you when I began this; but I feel that I had better not close it without asking this favor. I would fain be back, but I do not feel that I would be justified in so doing. When I give a short prayer in the family, it often quite knocks me up. I heard of my people today: they are going on as well as can be expected. Death is busy among them, and Satan too. I try to lean then all on Him who entrusted them to me. I did hear of your brother's illness, and sympathized with you in it, though I heard no particulars. Write me particularly how he is. I hope and believe that he has an anchor within the veil, and therefore we need not fear for him whatever storms may blow. Remember me to him when you write him or see him. May we both be made better men, and holier, by our affliction.

Take care of your health. Redeem the time, because the days are evil. Does the work of God still go on among your people? There is a decided improvement in the ministers here—more prayer and faith and hope. There are marks of God's Spirit not having left us. Remember me to Gillies and Smith, your fellow laborers. May their names be in the Book of Life.

To Mrs. Thain, Heathpark

During the continuance of the same illness.

Edinburgh, February 9, 1839

I WAS HAPPY to receive your and Mr. Thain's kind letter. It is very cheering to me, in my exile from my flock, to hear of them. I send you a short line, as I am not good at writing. I am glad you are keeping pretty well, and still more that your spiritual health seems to prosper. The spring is advancing—I feel already the softness of the wind—so that we may hope the winter is past, the rain over and gone. I know the summer revives you, and the doctor gives me good hope that it will revive me. In spiritual things, this world is all wintertime so long as the Saviour is away. To them that are in Christ there are some sweet glistenings of His countenance, there are meltings of His love, and the sweet song of the turtledove when His Holy Spirit dwells in the bosom; still it is but wintertime till our Lord shall come. But then, "to you that fear his name, shall the Sun of righteousness arise with healing in his wings." And if before He comes we should go away to be where He is, still we shall enter into a world of perpetual summer—we shall behold His glory which the Father gave Him.

I feel much better than usual today; but I have returns of my beating heart occasionally. Jesus stands at the door and knocks, and sometimes I think the door will give way before His gentle hand. I am bid to try the seawater hot bath, which I hope will do me good. I have good hope of being restored to my people again, and only hope that I may come in the fullness of the blessing of the gospel of Christ, that this time of silent musing may not be lost.

I am thankful indeed at the appointment of Mr. Lewis. I hope he has been given in answer to prayer, and then he will be a blessing. We must pray that he may be furnished from on high for his arduous work. I have great hope that he will be the means of raising many more churches and schools in our poor town—I mean poor in spiritual things.

I hope Mr. Macdonald was happy, and made others so. "Apollos watered." May great grace be upon you all.

To Mrs. Thain

Before going forth on the mission to Israel.

Edinburgh, March 15, 1839

YOU WILL think me very unkind in breaking my word to Mr. Thain, in not writing you in answer to your kind letter by him. But I did too much the week he was in Edinburgh, and fairly knocked myself up, so that I had just to lay aside my pen and suffer quietly. My friendly monitor is seldom far away from me, and when I do anything too much he soon checks me. However, I feel thankful that I am better again this week, and was thinking I would preach again. This is always the way with me. When my heart afflicts me, I say to myself: Farewell, blessed work of the gospel ministry! happy days of preaching Christ and Him crucified! winning jewels for an eternal crown! And then again, when it has abated, I feel as if I would stand up once more to tell all the world what the Lord of Glory has done for sinners.

You have sent me a pocket companion [a Bible] for Immanuel's land. I shall indeed be very happy to take it with me, to remind me of you and your kind family, at the time when I am meditating on the things that concern our everlasting peace. All my ideas of peace and joy are linked in with my Bible; and I would not give the hours of secret converse with it for all the other hours I spend in this world.

Mr. M—— is the bearer of this, and I have told him he

is to call on you with it. He is one much taught of God, and though with much inward corruption to fight against, he still holds on the divine way a burning and shining lamp.

I knew you would be surprised at the thought of my going so far away; and, indeed, who could have foreseen all that has happened? I feel very plainly that it is the Lord's doing, and this has taken away the edge of the pain. How many purposes God has in view of which we know nothing! Perhaps we do not see the hundredth part of His intentions towards us in sending me away. I am contented to be led blindfold; for I know that all will redound, through the thanksgiving of many, to the glory of our heavenly Father. I feel very plainly that towards many among my people this separation has been a most faithful chastisement. To those that liked the man but not the message, who were pleased with the vessel but not with the treasure, it will reveal the vanity of what they thought their good estate. To some, I hope, it has been sent in mercy. To some, I fear, it has been sent in judgment.

Above all, none had more need of it than myself; for I am naturally so prone to make an ill use of the attachment of my people, that I need to be humbled in the dust, and to see that it is a very nothing. I need to be made willing to be forgotten. Oh! I wish that my heart were quite refined from all self-seeking. I am quite sure that our truest happiness is not to seek our own—just to forget ourselves—and to fill up the little space that remains, seeking only, and above all, that our God may be glorified. But when I would do good, evil is present with me.

I am not yet sure of the day of my going away. There is to be a meeting on Monday to arrange matters. Andrew Bonar and Dr. Black can hardly get away till the first week of April; but I may probably go before to London next week. I know you will pray for me in secret and in the family, that

I may be kept from evil, and may do good. Our desire is to save sinners—to gather souls, Jew or Gentile, before the Lord come. Oh, is it not wonderful how God is making people take an interest in the Jews! Surely the way of these kings of the East will be soon prepared.

I shall be quite delighted if J—— is able to take a small part in the Sabbath school. She knows it is what I always told her—not to be a hearer of the Word only, but a doer. It is but a little time, and we shall work no more here for Him. Oh, that we might glorify Him on the earth! I believe there are better ministers in store for Scotland than any that have yet appeared. Tell J—— to stay herself upon God. Jesus continueth ever, He hath an unchangeable priesthood. Others are not suffered to continue by reason of death.

You expected me in Dundee before I go; but I dare not. You remember Paul sailed past Ephesus—he dared not encounter the meeting with his people. Indeed, I do not dare to think too much on my going away, for it often brings sadness over my spirit, which I can ill bear just now. But the will of the Lord be done.

Kindest regards to you all. Christ's peace be left with you. I shall remember you all, and be glad to write you a word when I am far away.

To Miss Collier, Dundee

How his silence may be useful to his people and himself.

Edinburgh, March 14, 1839

I FEEL IT very kind your writing to me, and rejoice in sending you a word in answer by my excellent friend Mr. Moody. Indeed, I was just going to write to you when I received yours, for I heard you had been rather poorly, and

I was going to entreat of you to take care of yourself; for
you do not know how much my life is bound up in your
life, and in the life of those around you who are likeminded.
I feel it quite true that my absence should be regarded by
my flock as a mark that God is chastening them; and though
I know well that I am but a dim light in the hand of Jesus,
yet there is always something terrible where Jesus withdraws
the meanest light in such a dark world.

I feel that to many this trial has been absolutely needful.
Many liked their minister naturally, who had but little real relish for the message he carried. God now sifts these souls, and
wants to show them that it is a looking to Jesus that saves,
not a looking to man. I think I could name many to whom
this trial should be blessed. Some also who were really on
the true foundation, but were building wood, hay, and stubble
upon it, may be brought to see that nothing would truly
comfort in the Day of the Lord but what can stand the hour
of trial. You yourself, my dear friend, may be brought to
cleave much more simply to the Lord Jesus. You may be
made to feel that Christ continueth ever, and hath an unchangeable priesthood; that His work is perfect, and that
infinitely; and poor and naked as we are, we can appear
only in Him—only in Him.

But if the trial was needed by my people, it was still more
needed by *me*. None but God knows what an abyss of corruption is in my heart. He knows and covers all in the
blood of the Lamb. "In faithfulness thou hast afflicted me."
It is perfectly wonderful that ever God could bless such a
ministry. And now, when I go over all the faults of it, it
appears almost impossible that I can ever preach again. But
then I think again, who can preach so well as a sinner—who
is forgiven so much, and daily upheld by the Spirit with such
a heart within! I can truly say that the fruit of my long
exile has been, that I am come nearer to God, and long more

for perfect holiness, and for the world where the people shall be all righteous. I do long to be free from self, from pride, and ungodliness; and I know where to go, "for all the promises of God are yea and amen in Christ Jesus." Christ is my armory, and I go to Him to get the whole armor of God—the armor of light. My sword and buckler, my arrows, my sling and stone, all are laid up in Jesus. I know you find it so. Evermore grow in this truly practical wisdom. You have a Shepherd; you shall never want.

What effect my long absence may have on the mass of unconverted souls I do not know. I cannot yet see God's purposes towards them: perhaps it may be judgment, as in the case of Ephesus, Revelation 2:5; perhaps it may be in mercy, as in the case of Laodicea, Revelation 3:19; or perhaps there are some who would not bend under my ministry, who are to flow down as wax before the fire under the ministry of the precious fellow laborer who is to succeed me. William Burns, son of the minister of Kilsyth, has for the present agreed to supply my place; and though there is a proposal of his being sent to Ceylon, I do hope he may be kept for us. He is one truly taught of God—young, but Christ lives in him. You know he comes of a good kind by the flesh.

Another reason of our trial, I hope, has been God's mercy to Israel. There is something so wonderful about the way in which all difficulties have been overcome, and the way opened up, that I cannot doubt the hand of Jehovah has been in it. This gives me, and should give you, who love Israel, a cheering view of this trial. The Lord meant it for great good. If God be glorified, is not this our utmost desire? Oh, it is sweet, when in prayer we can lay ourselves and all our interests, along with Zion, in the hands of *Him* whom we feel to be *Abba!* And if we are thus tied ourselves in the same bundle with Zion, we must resign all right to our-

selves, and to our wishes. May the Lord open up a way to His
name being widely glorified on the earth even before we die!

I know you will pray for us on our way, that our feet may
be beautiful on the mountains of Israel, and that we may
say to Zion, "Thy God reigneth." Pray that your poor friend
may be supplied out of His riches in glory, that he may not
shrink in hours of trial, but endure hardness as a good soldier
of Jesus Christ. I will remember you when far away, and
pray God to keep you safe under the shadow of the Redeemer's wings till I come again in peace, if it be His holy
will. Dr. Black and Andrew Bonar have both consented to go.
I shall probably be sent before to London next week, to open
the way. I am not very strong yet; often revisited by my warning friend, to tell me that I may see the New Jerusalem before
I see the Jerusalem beneath. However, I have the sentence of
death in myself, and do not trust in myself, but in God,
who raises the dead.

I saw Mrs. Coutts yesterday, in good health, and full of
spirit. She almost offered to go with us to Immanuel's Land.
I fear the Pastoral Letters are not worth printing; but I
shall ask others what they think. Farewell for the present.
The Lord give you all grace and peace.

To the Rev. W. C. Burns

On his agreeing to undertake the charge of St. Peter's, during Mr. McCheyne's
absence in Palestine.

Hill Street, Edinburgh, March 22, 1839

BECAUSE I TRUST I may now reckon you among the
number in the truest sense, I haste to send you a line
in answer to your last. I am glad you have made up your
mind to begin your spiritual charge over my flock on the first
week of April. The Committee has resolved that I leave
this on Wednesday next, so that you will not hear from me

again till I am away. Take heed to *thyself*. Your own soul is your first and greatest care. You know a sound body alone can work with power; much more a *healthy soul*. Keep a clear conscience through the blood of the Lamb. Keep up close communion with God. Study likeness to Him in all things. Read the Bible for your own growth first, then for your people.

Expound much; it is through *the truth* that souls are to be sanctified, not through *essays upon the truth*. Be easy of access, apt to teach, and the Lord teach you and bless you in all you do and say. You will not find many companions. Be the more with God. My dear people are anxiously waiting for you. The prayerful are praying for you. Be of good courage; there remaineth much of the land to be possessed. Be not dismayed, for Christ shall be with thee to deliver thee. Study Isaiah 6, and Jeremiah 1, and the sending of Moses, and Psalm 51:12, 13, and John 15:26, 27, and the connection in Luke 1:15, 16.

I shall hope to hear from you when I am away. Your accounts of my people will be a good word to make my heart glad. I am often sore cast down; but the eternal God is my refuge. Now farewell; the Lord make you a faithful steward.

PASTORAL LETTERS TO THE FLOCK OF ST. PETER'S

FIRST PASTORAL LETTER

View of what God has done, how it should affect them.

Edinburgh, January 30, 1839

TO ALL OF YOU, my dear friends and people, who are beloved of God, and faithful in Christ Jesus, your pastor wishes grace and peace from God the Father, and Christ Jesus our Lord.

As several of you have expressed a desire to hear from
me, and as He who at first sent me to you to bear witness
of the Lord Jesus has for many weeks withdrawn me, and
still lays His afflicting but gentle hand on me, it has seemed
good to me, not without prayer, to write to you from week to
week a short word of exhortation. May the Holy Spirit guide
the pen, that what is written may be blessed to your comfort
and growth in grace!

God is my record how greatly I long after you all in the
bowels of Jesus Christ; and the walls of my chamber can
bear witness how often the silent watches of the night have
been filled up with entreaties to the Lord for you all. I
can truly say with John, "that I have no greater joy than
to hear that my children walk in the truth"; and though
many of you were in Christ before me, and were living
branches of the true Vine before I was sent into the vineyard,
yet, believe me, it is true of you also, I have no greater joy
than to know that you are more and more filled with the
Holy Ghost, and bear more and more fruit to the glory of
God the Father. "Herein is the Father glorified, that you bear
much fruit."

You remember what Paul, when he was a prisoner of the
Lord, wrote to the Philippians (1:12), "I would that ye should
understand, brethren, that the things which happened unto
me have fallen out rather unto the furtherance of the gospel."
I am very anxious that you and I should understand the very
same, in the things which have happened unto me, that we
may vindicate God in all His dealings with us, and "not despise
the chastening of the Lord." I know too well that there
are many amongst you who would feel it no grievance if
all the Lord's ministers were taken out of the way. Ah!
how many are there who would rejoice if they were forever
left to sin unreproved, and to do what was right in their
own eyes! Still I am quite sure that to you, "who have ob-

tained like precious faith with us," to you who are the Lord's people, the present is a season of affliction, and you feel, as Naomi felt, that the hand of the Lord is gone out against us. My present object in writing to you is shortly to persuade you that "it is well"—"the Lord doeth all things well"—and that it may be really for the furtherance of the gospel among you. In many ways may this be the case.

First, with respect to myself. It does not become me here to show what benefit it may be to me. Suffice it to say that it has been a precious opportunity in which to reflect on the sins and imperfections of my ministry among you. A calm hour with God is worth a whole lifetime with man. Let it be your prayer that I may come out like gold, that the tin may be taken away, and that I may come back to you, if that be the will of God, a better man, and a more devoted minister. I have much to learn, and these words of David have been often in my heart and on my lips, "I know that thy judgments are right, and that thou in faithfulness hast afflicted me" (Ps. 119:75). Ministers are God's tools for building up the gospel temple. Now you know well that every wise workman takes his tools away from the work from time to time, that they may be ground and sharpened; so does the only-wise Jehovah take His ministers oftentimes away into darkness and loneliness and trouble, that He may sharpen and prepare them for harder work in His service. Pray that it may be so with your own pastor.

Second, with regard to you, my dear brothers and sisters in the Lord, this time of trial is for your furtherance. Does not God teach you, by means of it, to look beyond man to the Saviour, who abideth ever? Is not God showing you that ministers are earthen vessels, easily broken, and fit only to be cast aside like a broken pitcher out of mind? Is He not bidding you look more to the treasure which was in them, and which flows in all its fullness from Christ? It is a sad error into which I see many Christians falling, that of leaning upon man, mistaking friendship toward a minister for *faith* in the Son of God.

Remember that before Moses was sent to deliver Israel, his hand was made leprous, as white as snow, to teach them that it was not the might of that hand that could deliver Israel (Exod. 4:6, 7). It has been the fault of some of you to lean too much on man. Now God is teaching you that, though the *cistern* may break, the *fountain* abides as open and full and free as ever—that it is not from sitting under any particular ministry that you are to get nourishment, but from being vitally united to Christ. Ministers "are not suffered to continue by reason of death, but *Christ,* because He continueth ever, hath an unchangeable priesthood" (Heb. 7:23, 24).

Third, with regard to those among you who are almost, but not *altogether,* persuaded to be Christians, does not this providence teach you to make sure of an interest in Christ without delay? You thought you would have the Saviour held up to you for an indefinite number of Sabbaths, little thinking that your Sabbaths and mine are all numbered. Many a time you have said to me in your heart, "Go thy way for this time; when I have a more convenient season I will call for thee." You did not think that a time might come when you may call for your teachers, and they be silent as the grave.

I find many godly people here are looking forward to a time when God's faithful witnesses shall be put to silence, and anxious souls shall wander from sea to sea, seeking the Word of God, and shall not find it. Be entreated, O wavering souls, to settle the question of your salvation *now.* Why halt ye between two opinions? It is most unreasonable to be undecided about the things of an endless eternity, in such a world as this, with such frail bodies, with such a Saviour stretching out His hand, with such a Spirit of love striving with you. Remember you are flesh—you will soon hear your last sermon.

"I call heaven and earth to record this day against you, that I have put before you life and death, blessing and cursing: therefore choose life, that both thou and thy seed may live" (Deut. 30:19).

Fourth, there is another class who are not of you, and yet are on every hand of you, of whom I have told you often, and now tell you, even weeping, that they are the enemies of the cross of Christ, whose god is their belly, who glory in their shame, who mind earthly things. Ah! you would not believe if I were to tell you the great heaviness and continual sorrow that I have in my heart for you, and yet I hope my absence may be blessed even to you. Just think for a moment, if God were to remove your teachers one by one, if He were to suffer the church of our covenanted fathers to fall before the hands of her enemies, if He were to suffer Catholicism again to spread its dark and deadly shade over the land, where would you be?—you that despise the Sabbath, that care little for the preached Word, you that have no prayer in your families, and seldom in your closets, you that are lovers of pleasure, you that wallow in sin! You would have your wish then: you would have your silent Sabbaths indeed— no warning voice to cry after you—no praying people to pray for you—none to check you in your career of wickedness— none to beseech you not to perish. Learn from so small a circumstance as the absence of your stated minister what may be in store for you, and flee now from the wrath to come. "It may be ye shall be hid in the day of the Lord's anger" (Zeph. 2:3).

Finally, my brethren, dearly beloved and longed for, my joy and crown, abide all the more in Christ because of my absence, and maintain a closer walk with God, that when I return, as God gives me good hopes now of doing, I may rejoice to see what great things God has done for your souls. God feeds the wild flowers on the lonely mountainside, without

the help of man, and they are as fresh and lovely as those
that are daily watched over in our gardens. So God can
feed His own planted ones without the help of man, by the
sweetly falling dew of His Spirit. How I long to see you
walking in holy communion with God, in love to the brethren,
and burning zeal for the cause of God in the world! I will
never rest, nor give God rest, till He make you a lamp that
burneth—a city set upon a hill that cannot be hid. Now
strive together with me, in your prayers to God for me, that
I may come unto you with joy by the will of God.

The grace of our Lord Jesus Christ be with you. My love be
with you all in Christ Jesus. Amen.

SECOND PASTORAL LETTER

Past times of privilege reviewed—privileges still remaining.

Edinburgh, February 6, 1839

TO all of you, my dear flock, who have chosen the good
part which cannot be taken away, your pastor wishes grace,
mercy, and peace, from God our Father and the Lord Jesus
Christ.

The sweet singer of Israel begins one of his psalms with
these remarkable words: "I will sing of mercy and judgment;
unto thee, O God, will I sing." This is the experience of
all God's servants in time of trouble. Even in the wildest
storms the sky is not all dark; and so in the darkest dealings
of God with His children, there are always some bright tokens
for good. His way with us of late has been "in the sea, and
his path in the deep waters." Yet some of you may have felt
that His own hand was leading us like a flock (Ps. 77:19, 20).
One great token of His loving-kindness has been the way
in which He has supplied the absence of your stated minister.
Ordained messengers, men of faith and prayer, have spoken

to you from Sabbath to Sabbath in the name of the Lord. Awakening, inviting, comforting messages you have had; and even your meetings on Thursday evenings He has continued to you; the gates of the house of prayer, like the gates of the city of refuge, have been as open to you as ever, inviting you to enter in and behold by faith what Jacob saw in Bethel, "the ladder set on earth, and the top of it reaching into heaven," inviting you to meet with Him with whom Jacob wrestled till the breaking of the day.

Think how often, in times of persecution, the apostles were constrained to leave the seed they had sown, without leaving anyone to water it but "the Lord on whom they believed." (See Acts 13:50, 52, and 14:23, and 16:40.) How often, in times of persecution in the Church of Scotland, our faithful pastors had to leave their few sheep in the wilderness, without any human shepherd to care for their souls, commending them to God and to the Word of His grace! These times may come again. God may be preparing us for such fiery trials. But He hath not yet dealt so with us. He that tempers the wind to the shorn lamb, and "who stays his rough wind in the day of his east wind," has mingled mercy with judgment; and even when He humbles us, gives us cause for praise. "Oh, that men would praise the Lord for his goodness, and for his wonderful works to the children of men!"

Another mark of His loving-kindness to us is His suffering me to pray for you. You remember how the apostles describe the work of the ministry, Acts 6:4, "We will give ourselves continually to prayer, and to the ministry of the word." Now, God is my record that this has been my heart's desire ever since my coming among you. I have always felt myself a debtor to you all, both to the wise and to the unwise; so as much as in me is I have been ready to preach the gospel unto you; but God has for a time withdrawn me from that part of the work amongst you. To me that grace is not now

given to preach among you the unsearchable riches of Christ.
(Oh, how great a grace it is! how wonderful that it should
ever have been given to me!) Still He allows me to give
myself unto prayer. Perhaps this may be the chief reason of
my exile from you, to teach me what Zechariah was taught
in the vision of the golden candlestick and the two olive trees,
(Zech. 4:6), that it is not by might, nor by power, but by *His
Spirit,* obtained in believing, wrestling prayer, that the temple
of God is to be built in our parishes. I have hung my harp
upon the willow, and am no more allowed "to open to you
dark sayings upon the harp," nor "to speak of the things
which I have made touching the King," who is "fairer than
the children of men."

Still my soul does not dwell in silence. I am permitted to
go in secret to God, my exceeding joy; and, while meditating
His praise, I can make mention of you all in my prayers,
and give thanks for the little flock, who, "by patient continuance in welldoing, seek for glory, and honor, and immortality."
"If I forget thee, O Jerusalem, let my right hand forget her
cunning; if I do not remember thee, let my tongue cleave to
the roof of my mouth, if I prefer not Jerusalem above my
chief joy."

I feel it is another gift of grace that I am suffered to
write to you. You remember how often the apostles cheered
and strengthened the disciples, when absent from them, by
writing to them.[1] What a precious legacy of the Church in
all ages have these epistles been! every verse like a branch of
the Tree of Life, bearing all manner of fruit, and the leaves
for the healing of the nations. You remember how holy
Samuel Rutherford, and many of our persecuted forefathers
in the Church of Scotland, kept the flame of grace alive in
their deserted parishes by sending them words of counsel,

---

[1] II Corinthians 7:12; Galatians 6:11; I Thessalonians 5:27; Hebrews 13:22;
I Peter 5:12; II Peter 1:12-15; 3:1; John 1:4; Jude 3.

warning, and encouragement, testifying, not face to face, but
with ink and pen, the gospel of the grace of God. I do feel
it a great privilege that this door is open to me, and that,
even when absent, I can yet speak to you of the things pertaining to the kingdom.

"This second epistle, beloved, I now write unto you, in both
which I stir up your pure minds by way of remembrance;
yea, I think it meet, so long as I am in this tabernacle, to
stir you up by putting you in remembrance."

I. Abide in Him, little children, whom I have always
preached unto you, that when He shall appear we may have
confidence and not be ashamed before Him at His coming.
Let every new sight of your wicked heart, and every new
wave of trouble, drive your soul to hide in Him, the Rock
of your salvation. There is no true peace but in a present
hold of the Lord our Righteousness.

II. Enjoy the forgiveness of sins—keep yourselves in the
love of God. If you abide in Christ, you shall abide in His
love: your joy let no man take from you. "These things
write we unto you that your joy may be full."

III. Be ye clean that bear the vessels of the Lord. "He
that saith he abideth in him ought himself also so to walk
even as he walked." Ah, how many falls will I have to
mourn over when I return, if God send me back to you, how
many unseemly quarrellings and miscarriages among you that
are God's own, how many unlovely tempers among those who
follow Him who is altogether lovely! Oh, take heed, do not
give the enemy cause to blaspheme; naming the name of
Christ, depart from all iniquity.

IV. Continue in prayer. How many messages have been
carried to you publicly and from house to house, and yet how
little success! I bless God for all the tokens He has given
us, that the Spirit of God has not departed from the Church
of Scotland—that the glory is still in the midst of her. Still

the Spirit has never yet been shed on us abundantly. The
many absentees on the forenoon of the Sabbaths, the thin
meetings on Thursday evenings, the absence of *men* from
all meetings for the worship of God, the few private prayer
meetings, the little love and union among Christians—all show
that the plentiful rain has not yet fallen to refresh our corner
of the heritage. Why is this? This is the day of Christ's
power—why are the people not made willing? Let James
give the answer: "Ye have not, because ye ask not." "Hitherto
ye have asked nothing in my name. Ask, and ye shall receive,
that your joy may be full."

Finally, dear brethren, farewell. Day and night I long
to come to you, but still God hinders me. Do not omit to
praise Him for all the great grace He has mingled in our cup
of bitterness. "Seven times a day do I praise thee because
of thy righteous judgments." When passing through the waters
He has been with us, and in the rivers they have not over-
flowed us; and, therefore, we may be sure that when we
pass through the fire we shall not be burned, neither shall
the flames kindle upon us.

Now, may the God of peace Himself give you peace always,
by all means, and the grace of the Lord Jesus Christ be with
your spirits. Amen.

THIRD PASTORAL LETTER

How God works by providences.

Edinburgh, February 13, 1839.

TO all of you, my dear friends and people, who are and
shall ever be followers of the Lamb, whithersoever He
goeth, your pastor again wishes grace and peace from God
our Father, and the Lord Jesus Christ.

I long very much that this grace may again be given unto me to preach among you face to face "the unsearchable riches of Christ." "Oftentimes I purpose to come unto you, but am let hitherto." Still I feel it a great privilege that, even in my retirement, I can send you a word, to the end that you may be established. I feel as if one door was left open to me by the Lord. Believe me, it is the foremost desire of my heart that Christ may be glorified in you, both now and at His coming, that you may be a happy and a holy people, blessed and made a blessing. For the sake of variety, let me guide your thoughts to a passage of God's own Word, and there I will speak to you as if I were yet present with you, and half forget that you are not before me.

In Job 23:8-10 you will find these solemn words: "Behold, I go forward, but he is not there; and backward, but I cannot perceive him: on the left hand, where he doth work, but I cannot behold him: he hideth himself on the right hand, that I cannot see him. But he knoweth the way that I take: when he hath tried me, I shall come forth as gold."

You all know the afflictions which came upon Job. "He was a perfect and upright man," and the greatest of all the men of the East, yet he lost his oxen and his asses, his sheep and camels, and his ten children, in one day. Again, the breath of disease came upon him, and he sat down among the ashes. In all this Job sinned not with his lips. He blessed the hand that smote him: "What! shall we receive good at the hand of the Lord, and shall we not receive evil?"

And yet when his troubles were *prolonged,* he knew not what to think. Learn how weak the strongest believer is; a bruised reed, without Christ, we are, and can do nothing. When Job's brethren dealt deceitfully with him "as a brook," when he felt God hedging him in, and God's arrows drinking up his spirit—then clouds and darkness rested on his path, he could not unravel God's dealings with his soul; then he

cried, "Show me wherefore thou contendest with me!" He
longed to get an explanation from God: "Oh, that I knew
where I might find him! that I might come even to his seat!
Behold, I go forward, but he is not there; and backward, but
I cannot perceive Him; on the left hand, where he doth
work, but I cannot behold him: he hideth himself on the
right hand, that I cannot see him." You have here, then, in
the eighth and ninth verses, a child of light walking in darkness—an afflicted soul seeking, and seeking in vain, to know
why God is contending with him.

Dear friends, this is not an uncommon case; even to some
of you God's providences often appear inexplicable. I hear
that God has been at work among you, and "his way is in
the sea." He has tried you in different ways: some of you
by the loss of your property, as He tried Job; some of you
by the loss of dear friends; some by loss of health, so that
"wearisome nights are appointed you"; some by the loss of
the esteem of friends, aye, even of Christians. "Your inward
friends abhor you." Perhaps more than one trouble has come
on you at a time—wave upon wave, thorn upon thorn. Before one wound was healed, another came, before the rain
was well away, "clouds returned." You cannot explain God's
dealings with you, you cannot get God to explain them; you
have drawn the Saviour's blood and righteousness over your
souls, and you know that the Father Himself loveth you; you
would like to meet Him to ask, "Wherefore contendest thou
with me?" "Oh, that I knew where I might find him!"

My dear afflicted brethren, this is no strange thing that has
happened unto you. Almost every believer is at one time
or another brought to feel this difficulty: "God maketh my
heart soft, and the Almighty troubleth me." Is it in anger, or
is it in pure love, that He afflicts me? Am I fleeing from the
presence of the Lord, as Jonah fled? What change would He
have wrought in me? If any of you are thinking thus in

your heart, pray over this word in Job. Remember the word
in Psalm 46, "Be still, and know that I am God." God does
many things to teach us that *He* is God, and to make us wait
upon Him. And, still further, see in the tenth verse what
light breaks in upon our darkness: "But he knoweth the way
that I take: 'when he hath tried me, I shall come forth as gold."

Observe, *first,* "*He* knoweth the way that I take." What
sweet comfort there is in these words: *He* that redeemed me—
He that pities me as a father—*He* who is the only wise God—
He whose name is love—"*He* knoweth the way that I take!"

The ungodly world does not know it; the world knoweth
us not, even as it knew Him not. A stranger doth not inter-
meddle with the joys or sorrows of a child of God. When
the world looks on your grief with unsympathizing eye, you
feel very desolate. "Your soul is exceedingly filled with
the scorning of those who are at ease." But why should you?
He that is greater than all the world is looking with the
intensest interest upon all your steps.

The most intimate friends do not know the way of an
afflicted believer. Your spirit is lonely, even among God's
children; for your way is hid, and the Lord hath hedged you in.
Still be of good cheer, the Father of all, the best of friends,
knows all the way that you take.

You do not know your own way. God has called you to
suffer, and you go, like Abraham, not knowing whither you
go. Like Israel going down into the Red Sea, every step is
strange to you. Still, be of good cheer, sufferer with Christ!
God marks your every step. "The steps of a good man are
ordered by the Lord, and he delighteth in his way." *He* that
loves you with an infinite, unchanging love, is leading you by
His Spirit and providence. *He* knows every stone, every thorn
in your path. Jesus knows your way. Jesus is afflicted in all
your afflictions. "Fear not, for I have redeemed thee. I have
called thee by my name, thou art mine. When thou passest

through the waters, I will be with thee; and through the rivers, they shall not overflow thee. When thou walkest through the fire, thou shalt not be burned, neither shall the flame kindle upon thee."

Second, "When he hath tried me, I shall come forth as gold." This also is precious comfort. There will be an end of your affliction. Christians must have "great tribulation"; but they come out of it. We must carry the cross; but only for a moment, then comes the crown. I remember one child of God's saying, that if it were God's will that she should remain in trials a thousand years, she could not but delight in His will. But this is not asked of us: we are only called *"to suffer a while."* There is a set time for putting into the furnace, and a set time for taking out of the furnace. There is a time for pruning the branches of the vine, and there is a time when the husbandman lays aside the pruninghook. Let us wait His time; "he that believeth shall not make haste." God's time is the best time.

But shall we come out the same as we went in? Ah, no! "we shall come out like gold." It is this that sweetens the bitterest cup; this brings a rainbow of promise over the darkest cloud. Affliction will *certainly* purify a believer. How boldly he says it: "I shall come out like gold!" Ah, how much dross there is in every one of you, dear believers, and in your pastor! "When I would do good, evil is present with me." Oh that all the dross may be left behind in the furnace! What imperfection, what sin, mingles with all we have ever done! But are we really fruit-bearing branches of the true vine? Then it is certain that when we are pruned, we shall bear more fruit. We shall come out like gold. We shall shine more purely as "a diadem in the hand of our God." We shall become purer vessels to hold the sweet-smelling incense of praise and prayer. We shall become holy golden vessels for the Master's use in time and in eternity.

To the many among you who have no part nor lot in Christ, I would say, "See here the happiness of being a Christian in time of trouble." It is no small joy to be able to sing Psalm 46 in the dark and cloudy day. I have often told you, and now tell you when I am far from you, "We are journeying to the place of which the Lord hath said, I will give it you: come then with us, and we will do thee good, for God hath spoken good concerning Israel."

Finally, pray that your pastor may come out of his trials like gold. All is not gold that glitters. Pray that everything that is but glittering dross may be taken away, and that, if it be *His* will, I may come unto you like the fine gold of Ophir. "Continue in prayer, and watch in the same with thanksgiving, withal praying also for us, that God would open unto us a door of utterance to speak the mystery of Christ."

My chief comfort concerning you is, that "my God shall supply all your need according to his riches in glory by Christ Jesus." Brethren, farewell! Be perfect, be of good comfort, be of one mind, live in peace, and the God of love and of peace shall be with you.

The grace of the Lord Jesus Christ, and the love of God, and the communion of the Holy Ghost, be with you all. Amen.

FOURTH PASTORAL LETTER

God the answerer of prayer.

Edinburgh, February 20, 1839.

TO all of you, my dear flock, who are chosen in Christ before the foundation of the world, to be holy and without blame before Him in love, your pastor again wishes grace and peace from God the Father and our Lord Jesus Christ.

There are many sweet providences happening to us every
day, if we would but notice them. In the texts which ministers
choose, what remarkable providences God often brings about!
I have often felt this, and never more than now. Some of
you may remember that the last chapter of the Bible which
I read to you in the church was I Kings 19, where we are
told of Elijah's going away into the wilderness for forty days
and forty nights to the mount of God, where he was taught
that it is not by the *wind*, nor the *earthquake*, nor the *fire*,
that God converts souls, but by the still small voice of the
gospel. May not this have been graciously intended to prepare us for what has happened?

Another providence some of you may have noticed. For
several Thursday evenings before I left you I was engaged
in explaining and enforcing the sweet duty of believing
prayer. Has not God since taught us the use of these things?
"Trials make the promise sweet." "Trials give new life to
prayer." Perhaps some of us were only receiving the information into the head; is not God now impressing it on our
hearts, and driving us to practice the things which we learned?

I do not now remember all the points I was led to speak
upon to you, but *one*, I think, was entirely omitted—I mean
the subject of answers to prayer. God left it for us to meditate
on *now*. Oh, there is nothing that I would have you to be
more sure of than this, that "God hears and answers prayer."
There never was, and never will be, a believing prayer left
unanswered. Meditate on this, and you will say, "I love
the Lord, because He hath heard my voice and my supplication"
(Ps. 116:1).

*First, God often gives the very thing His children ask at the
very time they ask it.* You remember Hannah (I Sam. 1:10):
she was in bitterness of soul, and prayed unto the Lord, and
wept sore. "Give unto thine handmaid a manchild." This
was her request. And so she went in peace, and the God of

Israel heard and granted her petition that she had asked
of Him; and she called the child's name Samuel, that is,
"Asked of God." Oh, that you could write the same name
upon all your gifts! You would have more joy in them and
far larger blessings along with them.

You remember *David,* in Psalm 138: *"In the day* that I
cried thou answeredst me, and strengthenedst me with strength
in my soul." You remember *Elijah,* I Kings 17:21, 22: "O
Lord my God! I pray thee let this child's soul come into him
again. And *the Lord heard the voice* of Elijah, and *the soul
of the child came into him again,* and he revived."

You remember *Daniel,* 9:20, 21: *"While I was* speaking,
and praying, and confessing my sin, and the sin of my people
Israel, and presenting my supplication before the Lord my
God for the holy mountain of my God; yea, whiles *I was
speaking in prayer,* even the man Gabriel, being caused to fly
swiftly, touched me about the time of the evening oblation."
Oh, what encouragement is here for those among you who,
like Daniel, are greatly beloved, who study much in the
books of God's Word, and who set your face unto the Lord
to seek by prayer gifts for the Church of God! Expect answers
while you are speaking in prayer. Sometimes the vapors that
ascend in the morning come down in copious showers in the
evening. So may it be with your prayers.

Take up the words of David, Psalm 5:3: "My voice shalt
thou hear in the morning; in the morning will I direct my
prayer unto thee, and will look up." You remember, in Acts
12, Peter was cast into prison, "but prayer was made without
ceasing of the church unto God for him." And, behold, the
same night the answer surprised them at the door. Oh! what
surprises of goodness and grace God has in store for you
and me, if only we pray without ceasing! If you will pray in
union to Jesus, having childlike confidence towards God,
having the spirit of adoption, crying Abba within you, seeking

the glory of God more than all personal benefits, I believe
that in all such cases you will get the *very thing you ask, at
the very time you ask it*. Before you call, God will answer; and
while you are speaking, He will hear.

Oh, if there were twenty among you who would pray thus,
and persevere therein like wrestling Jacob, you would get
whatever you ask! Yea, the case of Daniel shows that the
effectual fervent prayer of one such believer among you will
avail much. "Delight thyself in the Lord, and he shall give
thee the desires of thine heart" (Ps. 37:4).

*Second, God often delays the answer to prayer for wise
reasons.* The case of the Syrophoenician woman will occur to
you all, Matthew 15:21-28. How anxiously she cried, "Have
mercy on me, O Lord, thou son of David! But Jesus answered
her not a word." Again and again she prayed, and got no
gracious answer. Her faith grows stronger by every refusal.
She cried, she followed, she kneeled to Him, till Jesus could
refuse no longer. "O woman, great is thy faith! Be it unto
thee even as thou wilt."

Dear praying people, "continue in prayer, and watch in
the same with thanksgivings." Do not be silenced by one refusal. Jesus invites importunity by delaying to answer. Ask,
seek, knock. "The promise may be long delayed, but cannot
come too late." You remember, in the parable of the impor-
tunate widow, it is said, "Shall not God avenge his own elect,
which cry day and night unto him, though he bear long with
them? I tell you that he will avenge them speedily" (Luke
18:1-8). This shows how you, who are God's children, should
pray. You should cry day and night unto God. This shows
how God hears every one of your cries, in the busy hour of
the daytime, and in the lonely watches of the night. He treasures them up from day to day; soon the full answer will
come down: "He will answer speedily." The praying souls
beneath the altar, in Revelation 6:9-11, seem to show the same

truth, that the answer to a believer's prayers may, in the adorable wisdom of God, be delayed for a little season, and that many of them may not be fully answered till after he is dead.

Again, read that wonderful passage, Revelation 8:3, where it is said that the Lord Jesus, the great Intercessor with the Father, offers to God the incense of His merits, with the prayers of *all saints*, upon the golden altar which is before the throne. Christ never loses one believing prayer. The prayers of every believer, from Abel to the present day, He heaps upon the altar, from which they are continually ascending before His Father and our Father; and when the altar can hold no more, the full, the eternal answer will come down.

Do not be discouraged, dearly beloved, because God bears long with you—because He does not seem to answer your prayers. Your prayers are not lost. When the merchant sends his ships to distant shores, he does not expect them to come back richly laden in a single day: he has long patience. "It is good that a man should both hope and quietly wait for the salvation of the Lord." Perhaps your prayers will come back, like the ships of the merchant, all the more heavily laden with blessings, because of the delay.

Third, God often answers prayer by terrible things. So David says in Psalm 65: "By terrible things in righteousness wilt thou answer us, O God of our salvation." And all of you who are God's children have found it true. Some of you have experienced what John Newton did when he wrote that beautiful hymn, "I asked the Lord that I might grow."[1] You prayed with all your heart, "Lord, increase my faith." In answer to this, God has shown you the misery of your connection with Adam. He has revealed the hell that is in your heart. You are amazed, confounded, abashed. You cry,

---

[1] *Olney Hymns,* Book iii, Hymn 36.

"O wretched man that I am, who shall deliver me from the
body of this death?" You cleave to a Saviour God with a
thousand times greater anxiety. Your faith is increased. Your
prayer is answered by terrible things. Some of us prayed for
a praying spirit, "Lord, teach us to pray." God has laid
affliction upon us. Waves and billows go over us. We cry
out of the depths. Being afflicted, we pray. He has granted
our heart's desire. Our prayer is answered by *terrible things*.

*Fourth, God sometimes answers prayer by giving something
better than we ask.* An affectionate father on earth often does
this. The child says, Father, give me this fruit. No, my child,
the father replies; but here is bread, which is better for you.
So the Lord Jesus dealt with His beloved Paul, II Corinthians
12:7-9. There was given to Paul a thorn in the flesh, a messenger of Satan to buffet him. In bitterness of heart he
cried, "Lord, let this depart from me." No answer came.
Again he prayed the same words. No answer still. A third
time he knelt, and now the answer came, not as he expected.
The thorn is not plucked away—the messenger of Satan is not
driven back to hell; but Jesus opens wide His more loving
breast, and says, "My grace is sufficient for thee; for my
strength is made perfect in weakness." Oh! this is something
exceeding abundant above all that he asked, and all that he
thought. Surely God is able to do "exceeding abundantly above
all that we ask or think" (Eph. 3:20).

Dear praying believers, be of good cheer. God will either
give you what you ask, or something far better. Are you not
quite willing that He should choose for you and me? You
remember that even Jesus prayed, "O my Father, if it be possible, let this cup pass from me!" That desire was not
granted, but there appeared unto Him an angel from heaven
strengthening Him, Luke 22:43. He received what was far
better—strength to drink the cup of vengeance. Some of you,
my dear believing flock, have been praying that, if it be God's

will, I might be speedily restored to you, that God's name might be glorified; and I have been praying the same. Do not be surprised if He should answer our prayers by giving us something above what we imagined. Perhaps He may glorify Himself by us in another way than we thought. "Oh the depth of the riches both of the wisdom and knowledge of God! how unsearchable are his judgments, and his ways past finding out! For of him, and through him, and to him, are all things: to whom be glory forever. Amen."

These things I have written, that you may come boldly to the throne of grace. The Lord make you a praying people. "Strive together with me in your prayers to God for me." "I thank my God upon every remembrance of you, always in every prayer of mine for you all, making request with joy."

Now, the God of patience and consolation grant you to be likeminded one towards another, according to Christ Jesus. "The God of hope fill you with all joy and peace in believing; and the God of peace be with you all. Amen."

FIFTH PASTORAL LETTER

What God has done, and the returns made: Isaiah 5:4.

Edinburgh, February 27, 1839.

TO all of you, my dear flock, who are washed and sanctified and justified in the name of the Lord Jesus, and by the Spirit of our God, your pastor again wishes grace, mercy, and peace.

This is now the fifth time I am permitted by God to write to you. If *you* are not wearied, it is pleasant and refreshing to me. I wish to be like Epaphras, Colossians 4:12: "Always laboring fervently for you in prayer, that you may stand perfect and complete in all the will of God." When I am hindered by God from laboring for you in any other way, it is my heart's joy to labor for you thus. When Dr. Scott of Greenock, a good and holy minister, was laid aside by old age from preaching for some years before his death, he used to say, "I can do nothing for my people now but pray for them, and sometimes I feel that I can do that." This is what I also love to feel. Often I am like Amelia Geddie, who lived in the time of the Covenanters, and of whom I used to tell you. The great part of my time is taken up with bringing my heart into tune for prayer; but when the blessed Spirit does help my infirmities, it is my greatest joy to lay myself and you, my flock, in His hand, and to pray that God may yet make "the vine to flourish, and the pomegranate to bud."

If you turn to Isaiah 5:4, you will find these affecting words: "What could have been done more to my vineyard, that I have not done in it? wherefore, when I look that it should bring forth grapes, brought it forth wild grapes?"

Consider these words, my dear people, and may the Spirit breathe over them that they may savingly impress your souls. These words are God's pathetic lamentation over His ancient people, when He thought of all that He had done for them, and of the sad return which they made to Him. We have come into the place of Israel; the natural branches of the good olive tree have been broken off, and we have been grafted in. All the advantages God gave to Israel are now enjoyed by us; and ah! has not God occasion to take up the same lamentation over us, that we have brought forth only wild grapes? I would wish every one of you seriously to consider what more God could have done to save your soul that He has not done. But, ah! consider again whether you have borne grapes, or only wild grapes.

First, consider how much God has done to save your souls. He has provided a great Saviour, and a great salvation. He did not give man or angel, but the Creator of all, to be the substitute for sinners. His blood is precious blood. His righteousness is the righteousness of God; and now "to him that worketh not, but believeth on him that justifieth the ungodly, his faith is counted to him for righteousness" (Rom. 4:5). Most precious word! Give up your toil, self-justifying soul. You have gone from mountain to hill; you have forgotten your resting place; change your plan: work not, but believe on Him that justifieth the ungodly. Believe the record that God hath given concerning His Son. A glorious, all-perfect, all-divine Surety is laid down at your feet. He is within your reach—He is nigh thee: take Him and live; refuse Him and perish! "What could have been done more for my vineyard, that I have not done in it?"

Second, again, consider the ordinances God has given you. He has made you into a vineyard. Scotland is of all lands the most like God's ancient Israel. How wonderfully has God planted and maintained godly ministers in this land, from the time of Knox to the present day! He has divided the whole land into parishes; even on the barren hills of our country He has planted the choicest vine. Hundreds of godly laborers He has sent to gather out the stones of it. God has done this for you also. He has built a tower in the midst of you. Have you not seen His own hand fencing you round, building a gospel tower in the midst of you, and a gospel wine press therein? And has He not sent me among you, who am less than the least of all the members of Christ, and yet "determined not to know anything among you save Jesus Christ and Him crucified?" Has not the Spirit of God been sometimes present in our sanctuary? Have not some hearts been filled there with gladness more than in the time that their corn and wine increased? Have not some hearts tasted there the "love that is better than wine?" "What could have been done more for my vineyard, that I have not done in it?"

Now let me ask, what fruit have we borne—grapes or wild

grapes? Ah! I fear the most can show nothing but wild grapes. If God looks down upon us as a *parish,* what does He see? Are there not still a thousand souls utter strangers to the house of God? How many does His holy eye now rest upon who are seldom in the house of prayer, who neglect it in the forenoon! How many who frequent the tavern on the Sabbath day! Oh! why do they bring forth wild grapes? If God looks upon you as *families,* what does He see? How many prayerless families! How often, as I passed your windows, late at eve or at early dawn, have I listened for the melody of psalms, and listened all in vain! God also has listened, but still in vain.

How many careless parents does His pure eye see among you, who will one day, if you turn not, meet your neglected children in an eternal hell! How many undutiful children! How many unfaithful servants! Ah! why such a vineyard of wild grapes? If God looks on you as *individual souls,* how many does He see that were never awakened to real concern about your souls! How many that never shed a tear for your perishing souls! How many that were never driven to pray! How many that know not what it is to bend the knee! How many that have no uptaking of Christ, and are yet coldhearted and at ease! How many does God know among you that have never laid hold of the only sure covenant! How many that have no "peace in believing," and yet cry, "Peace, peace, when there is no peace!" (Jer. 8:11). How many does God see among you who have no change of heart and life, who are given up to the sins of the flesh and of the mind! And yet you "bless yourself in your heart, saying, I shall have peace, though I walk in the imagination of my heart, to add drunkenness to thirst" (Deut. 29:19).

Ah! why do you thus bring forth wild grapes? "Your vine is of the vine of Sodom, and of the fields of Gomorrah: your grapes are grapes of gall, your clusters are bitter" (Deut.

32:32). Ah! remember you will blame yourselves to all eternity for your own undoing. God washes His hands of your destruction. What could have been done more for you that God has not done? I take you all to record this day, if I should never speak to you again, that I am pure from the blood of you all. Oh barren fig trees, planted in God's vineyard, the Lord has been digging at your roots; and if ye bear fruit, well; if not, then ye shall be cut down (Luke 13:6-9).

Now I turn for a moment to you who are God's children. I am persuaded better things of you, my dearly beloved, and things that accompany salvation, though I thus speak. Yet what need is there, in these trying times, to search your heart and life, and ask what fruit does God find in me!

What fruit of *self-abasement* is there in you? Have you found out the evil of your connection with the first Adam (Rom. 5:19)? Do you know the plagues of your own heart (I Kings 8:38)? the hell of corruption that is there (Jer. 17: 9)? Do you feel you have never lived one moment to His glory (Rom. 3:25)? Do you feel that to all eternity you never can be justified by anything in yourself (Rev. 7:14)?

Consider, again, what fruit there is of *believing* in you. Have you really and fully taken up Christ as the gospel lays Him down (John 5:12)? Do you cleave to Him as a sinner (I Tim. 1:15)? Do you count all things but loss for the excellency of the knowledge of Him (Matt. 9:9)? Do you feel the glory of His person (Rev. 1:17)? His finished work (Heb. 9:26)? His offices (I Cor. 1:30)? Does He shine like the sun into your soul (Mal. 4:2)? Is your heart ravished with His beauty (S. S. 5:16)?

Again, what fruit is there in you of *crying after holiness?* Is this the one thing you do (Phil. 3:13)? Do you spend your life in cries for deliverance from this body of sin and death (Rom. 7:24)? Ah! I fear there is little of this. The most of God's people are contented to be saved from the hell that is *without.* They are not so anxious to be saved from the hell that is *within.* I fear there is little feeling of your need of the indwelling Spirit. I fear you do not know "the exceeding greatness of his power" to usward who believe. I fear many of you are strangers to the visits of the Comforter. God has reason to complain of you, "Wherefore should they bring forth wild grapes?"

Again, what fruit is there of *actual likeness to* God in you? Do you love to be much with God—"to climb up near to God (Gen. 5:22)—to love, and long, and plead, and wrestle, and stretch after Him?"[1] Are you weaned from the world (Ps. 131)—from its praise, from its hatred, from its scorn? Do you give yourselves clean away to God (II Cor. 8:5)—and all that is yours? Are you willing that your will should be lost in His great will? Do you throw yourselves into the arms of God for time and for eternity? Oh, search your hearts and try them; ask God to do it for you, and "to lead you in the way everlasting!" (Ps. 139:23, 24).

I am deeply afraid that many of us may be like the fig tree by the wayside, on which the hungry Saviour expected to find fruit, and He found none. Ah! we have been an ungrateful vine, minister and people! What more could God have done for us? Sunshine and shade, rain and wind, have all been given us; goodness and severity have both been tried with us; yet what has been returned to Him? Have curses or praises been the louder rising from our parish to heaven? Does our parish more resemble the garden of the Lord, or the howling wilderness? Is there more of the perpetual incense of believing prayer, or the "smoke in God's nose" of hypocrisy and broken sacraments?

I write not these things to shame you, but as "my beloved sons I warn you." If there be some among you, and some there are, who are growing up like the lily, casting forth their

---

[1] See *Brainerd's Diary,* Part 2, April 4.

roots like Lebanon, and bearing fruit with patience, remember "the Lord loveth the righteous." He that telleth the number of the stars taketh pleasure in you. "The Lord taketh pleasure in his people; he will beautify the meek with salvation." Keep yourselves in the love of God. Go carefully through all the steps of your effectual calling a second time.

The Lord give you daily faith. Seek to have a large heart. Pray for me, that a door of utterance may be opened to me. Remember my bonds. Pray that I may utterly renounce myself, that I may be willing to do and to suffer all His will up to the latest breath.

May you all obtain mercy of the Lord now, and in that day to which we are hastening. The grace of the Lord Jesus be with your spirits. Amen.

Sixth Pastoral Letter

Self-devotedness—what it ought to be.

Edinburgh, March 6, 1839.

TO all my dear flock over which the Holy Ghost hath made me overseer—to all of you who are of the Church of God, which He hath purchased with His own blood—your pastor wishes grace, mercy, and peace.

I thank my God without ceasing that ever I was ordained over you in the Lord. For every shower of the Spirit that ever has been shed upon us—for every soul among you that has ever been added to the Church—for every disciple among you whose soul has been confirmed during our ministry, I will praise God eternally. May this letter be blessed to you by the breathing of the Holy Spirit! May it teach you and me more than ever that we "are not our own, but bought with a price."

The most striking example of self-devotedness in the cause of Christ of which I ever heard in these days of deadness, was told here last week by an English minister. It has never been printed, and therefore I will relate it to you, just as I heard it, to stir up our cold hearts, that we may give ourselves to the Lord.

The awful disease of leprosy still exists in Africa. Whether it be the same leprosy as that mentioned in the Bible, I do not know, but it is regarded as incurable, and so infectious that no one dares to come near the leper. In the south of Africa there is a large lazarhouse for lepers. It is an immense space, enclosed by a very high wall, and containing fields, which the lepers cultivate. There is only one entrance, which is strictly guarded. Whenever anyone is found with the marks of leprosy upon him, he is brought to this gate and obliged to enter in, never to return. No one who enters in by that awful gate is ever allowed to come out again. Within this abode of misery there are multitudes of lepers in all stages of the disease. Dr. Halbeck, a missionary of the Church of England, from the top of a neighboring hill, saw them at work. He noticed two particularly sowing peas in the field. The one *had no hands,* the other *had no feet*—these members being wasted away by disease. The one who wanted the hands was carrying the other who wanted the feet upon his back, and he again carried in his hands the bag of seed, and dropped a pea every now and then, which the other pressed into the ground with his foot; and so they managed the work of one man between the two. Ah! how little we know of the misery that is in the world! Such is this prisonhouse of disease.

But you will ask, who cares for the souls of the hapless inmates? Who will venture to enter in at this dreadful gate, never to return again? Who will forsake father and mother, houses and land, to carry the message of a Saviour to these poor lepers? Two Moravian missionaries, impelled by a divine love for souls, have chosen the lazarhouse as their field of labor. They entered it never to come out again; and I am told that as soon as these die, other Moravians are quite ready to fill their place. Ah! my dear friends, may we not blush, and be ashamed before God, that we, redeemed with the same blood, and taught by the same Spirit, should yet be so unlike these men in vehement, heart-consuming love to Jesus and the souls of men?

I wish now to mention to you a proposal which deeply involves the happiness of you and me, and of which I believe most of you have already heard something. Oh that you would trace the Lord's hand in it! Oh that you would be still, and know that He is God! Let me go over some of the ways by which God has led us hitherto. When I came to you at the first, it was not of my seeking. I never had been in your town, and knew only one family in it. I did not ask to be made a candidate. I was quite happy where I was laboring in the Lord's work. God turned your hearts to ask me to settle among you. It was the Lord's doing. Since that day "ye know after what manner I have been with you at all seasons," and how, as far as God gave me light and strength, "I have kept nothing back that was profitable unto you, but have showed you, and have taught you publicly, and from house to house." Ye know also, some of you in your blessed experience, that God has given testimony to the word of His grace, so that "our gospel came not to you in word only, but in power, and in the Holy Ghost, and in much assurance."

It is indeed amazing how God should have blessed the Word when there was so much weakness and so much sin. But "who is a God like unto our God, that pardoneth iniquity, and passes by the transgressions of the remnant of his heritage?" We planted and watered, and God gave the increase. Ye are God's husbandry—ye are God's building. To Him be the glory.

You know also that I have had some painful trials among

you. The state of the mass of unconverted souls among you
has often made my heart bleed in secret. The coldness and
worldliness of you who are God's children has often damped
me. The impossibility of fully doing the work of a minister
of Christ, among so many souls, was a sad burden to me. The
turning back of some that once cared for their souls pierced
my heart with new sorrows.

Still I have had two years of great joy among you—unspeakable joy—in seeing souls added to the Church of such as shall
be saved. I may never be honored to preach again, yet still to
all eternity I shall praise God that He sent me to you: "For
what is our hope, or joy, or crown of rejoicing? Are not even
ye in the presence of the Lord Jesus Christ at his coming?
For ye are our glory and joy" (I Thess. 2:19, 20). And should
I lightly break up such a connection as this? Ah, no! My dear
friends, I do not need all your affectionate letters to persuade
me, that, if it were the Lord's will, my own vineyard is the
happiest place in the world for me to be. Again and again
other vineyards were offered to me, and I was asked to leave
you; but I never for a moment listened to one of them, for
ye were the seal of my ministry; and where could I be happier
than where the Lord had blessed me, and was still blessing
me?

But God sent another message to me. He laid a heavy
hand upon my body. I long struggled against it, but it was
too much for me. For two months I have been an exile from
you, and I have felt all the time like a widower, or like Jacob
bereaved of his children. My constant prayer was, that I might
be restored to you, and to the Lord's service. You prayed the
same; and when it was not answered, I cried, "Wherefore
contendest thou with me?" That word was sent in answer:
"My son, despise not thou the chastening of the Lord, neither
be weary of his correction" (Prov. 3:11). God seems plainly
to shut the door against my returning to you at present. I am

greatly better, yet still I am forbidden to preach. I am not even allowed to conduct the family devotions morning and evening; indeed, whenever I exert myself much in conversation, I soon feel the monitor within, warning me how frail I am.

In these circumstances, the General Assembly's Committee on the Jews has this day resolved that your pastor, accompanied by Dr. Black of Aberdeen, and my beloved friend Andrew Bonar of Collace,[1] should travel for the next six months, to make personal inquiry after the lost sheep of the house of Israel.

They propose that we should go without delay to the Holy Land—that we should then return by Smyrna, Constantinople, Poland, Germany, and Holland. Now I did not seek this appointment—I never dreamed of such a thing. "But he that hath the key of David, he that openeth and no man shutteth, and shutteth and no man openeth," He has thrown open this door to me, while He keeps the door of return to you still shut. My medical men are agreed that it is the likeliest method of restoring my broken health, and that I have strength enough for the journey. You know how my heart is engaged in the cause of Israel, and how the very sight of Immanuel's land will revive my fainting spirit. And if it be the will of God, I shall return to you, my beloved flock, to tell you all that I have seen, and to lead you in the way to the Jerusalem that is above.

I cannot tell you how many providences have been sent to me, every one convincing me that it is God's will and purpose I should go.

The most cheering one to me is, that a young man has nearly consented to fill my place, and feed your souls during my absence, who is everything I could wish, and who will make you almost forget that you want your own pastor. Nay, what-

---

[1] Dr. Keith of St. Cyrus had not at that time joined the deputation.

ever happens, I hope you will never forget me, but remember me in your families, and remember me in your secret prayers. You are all graven on my heart—I never can forget you. How wonderful have been God's dealings with us! For many reasons He has sent this affliction on us—for sin in me, for sin in you; but also, I am persuaded, that He might seek after "the dearly beloved of his soul," that are now in the hand of their enemies. His way is in the sea; His name is Wonderful.

I grieve to write so much about myself. I had far rather speak to you of *Him* who "is fairer than the children of men." May you look beyond all ministers to *Him*—may He be your guide even unto death! Once again I hope to write before I leave my home and my country. Till then, may all grace abound toward you, and peace be upon Israel. Amen.

Seventh Pastoral Letter

Unexpected calls to labor—parting counsels to believers.

Edinburgh, March 13, 1839.

TO all of you who are my brethren, and my companions in tribulation, and in the kingdom and patience of our Lord Jesus Christ, your pastor wishes grace, mercy, and peace.

It gives me great joy to address you once more; and if I could only grave on your heart some of those words which make wise unto salvation, my time and labor would be amply repaid. The providences of every day convince me that I have followed not my own will, but God's, in leaving you for a time. If the Lord permit, I shall come to you again, and I trust more fully taught by the Spirit—a holier, happier, and a more useful minister. I did not know when I last preached to you that I was to be so long parted from you; and though I felt a solemn tenderness stealing over my soul which I could not well account for, and eternity seemed very near, and your souls seemed very precious, yet the Lord was "leading the blind by a way which we knew not." I have been searching God's Word to find examples of this, and I find them very many.

You remember *Abraham,* how he was living quietly in his father's house, in Ur of the Chaldees, when the Lord appeared to him, and said, "Get thee out of thy country, and from thy kindred, and from thy father's house, unto a land that I will show thee" (Gen. 12:1). And he went out, not knowing whither he went. You remember *Jacob:* his mother said unto him, "Arise, flee thou to Laban, my brother, to Haran, and tarry with him *a few days."* But the Lord meant it otherwise; and it was twenty years before Jacob came back again (Gen. 27:43, 44). You remember *Joseph:* his father sent him a message to his brethren: "Go, I pray thee, see whether it be well with thy brethren, and well with the flocks, and bring me word again" (Gen. 37:14). He expected to see him return in a few days; but God had another purpose with him. It was more than twenty years before he saw the face of Joseph again; till he said, "It is enough; Joseph my son is yet alive: and I will go and see him before I die."

You will find the same method of dealing in the New Testament. How little *Peter* knew that morning when he went up to the housetop to pray, that he was that very day to be sent away to open the door of faith to the Gentiles (Acts 10:9); and yet God said to him, "Arise, get thee down, and go with them, nothing doubting" (v. 20). Again, you remember *Barnabas* and *Saul,* how happily they were engaged with the brethren at Antioch, ministering to the Lord and fasting. Little did they think that the next day they would be sailing away to carry the gospel to other lands. As they ministered to the Lord and fasted, the Holy Ghost said, "Separate me Barnabas and Saul for the work whereunto I have called them. And when they

had fasted and prayed, and laid their hands on them, they sent
them away" (Acts 13:2, 13).

Once more, when Paul had preached the gospel in all the
cities of Asia, and was come to Troas, on the seacoast, how
little did he think that night when he laid his head upon his
pillow, that by the next morning the swift ship would be
carrying him across the seas, to bear the message of salvation
to another continent! "A vision appeared to Paul in the night:
there stood a man of Macedonia, and prayed him, saying,
Come over into Macedonia and help us. And after he had
seen the vision, immediately we endeavored to go into Macedonia, assuredly gathering that the Lord had called us for to
preach the gospel unto them" (Acts 16:9, 10).

Now, has not God dealt with us in a similar manner? Although we are nothing in ourselves but evil and hell-deserving
creatures, yet, when accepted in the Beloved, God cares for us.
Oh! we err, not knowing the Scriptures, nor the power of
God, when we think that God is indifferent to the least of all
that are in Christ. We are fastened on the Redeemer's shoulder. We are graven on His breastplate, and that is on the
Redeemer's heart. Surely He hath directed our steps. "O
the depth of the riches both of the wisdom and the knowledge
of God!" In other circumstances, I suppose, I would not have
listened to this proposal. I could not have torn myself away
had I been in strength and usefulness among you, and indeed
the expedition probably would never have been thought of.

But God, who chose *Israel* to be His peculiar treasure, can
easily open up ways when *His set time* is come. I parted from
you only for a *few days;* but God meant otherwise, and He
will make it His own fixed time. And now, behold, I know
that there are some of you among whom I have gone preaching the kingdom of God, who "shall see my face no more."
"He that keepeth Israel" may preserve your pastor under His
almighty feathers. I know you will pray for me, as you have

done in secret, and in your families, and in your meetings for prayer, "that the sun may not smite me by day, nor the moon by night"; but if I should come back again, will I find you all where I left you? Alas! I know it cannot be so. "For what is your life? It is even a vapor"; and God is still crying, "Return, return, ye children of men."

For some among you, I give thanks unto the Father that He hath made you meet to be partakers of the inheritance of the saints in light (Col. 1:12). There are some among you from whom I have learned more than I taught you, "who have been succorers of many, and of myself also" (Rom. 16:2), and who have often reminded me of corn, when it was fully ripe. Shall we be surprised if the Son of Man puts in the sickle? (Rev. 14:13, 16). Dear advanced believers, we may never meet again. I feel it almost wrong to pray that ye may be kept to comfort us on our return. It is wrong to grudge you "an entrance into perfect day," where you shall lay aside that body of death and sin which is your greatest grief; yet may the Lord spare you, and bless you, and make you a blessing, that ye may bear fruit in old age. Oh, fill up the little inch of time that remains to His glory; walk with God; live for God. Oh, that every thought, and word, and action might be in His favor, and to His praise! The Lord grant that we may meet again here, and with you be refreshed; but if not, may we meet where we shall walk with Christ in white. God, who knows my heart, knows it would be a hell to me to spend an eternity with unconverted, Christless souls; but to be with Christ and His people is heaven to me, wherever it is.

There are many young believers among you, whom I may never meet again. It is hard to think of parting with you; the mother feels it hard to part with the sucking child. It was my highest delight in this world to see you growing day by day— to see your sense of the plague in your own heart deepening —to see you cleaving to Christ with full purpose of heart—

to see your "peace widening like a river," and to see your
love burning higher and higher toward the throne of God.
You are in my heart to live and to die with me. Still *He* who
at any time fed you by *me,* can as easily feed you by another.
I commend you to the Lord, on whom you believe. Read
II Peter 3:17; meditate over it, pray over it; beware lest ye
also, being led away with the error of the wicked, fall from
your own steadfastness; but grow in grace.

The only way to be kept from *falling* is to *grow.* If you
stand still, you will fall. Read Proverbs 11:28, "The righteous shall flourish as a branch." Remember you are not a *tree,*
that can stand alone; you are only "a branch," and it is only
while you abide in *Him,* as a branch, that you will flourish.
Keep clear your sense of justification; remember *it is not* your
own natural goodness, nor your tears, nor your sanctification,
that will justify you before God. It is Christ's sufferings and
obedience *alone.* Seek to be made holier every day; pray, strive,
wrestle for the Spirit, to make you like God. Be as much as
you can with God. I declare to you that I had rather be one
hour with God, than a thousand with the sweetest society on
earth or in heaven. All other joys are but streams; God is the
fountain: "all my springs are in Thee."

Now may the blessings that are on the head of the just be
on your head. Be faithful unto death, and Christ will give you
a crown of life; and if I never meet you again in this world,
may I meet you as pillars in the house of my God, where
you "shall go no more out." Pray for me when you have access to the throne, when you have a heart for it. I will try to
pray for you, that ye may endure to the end. I have a word
more for those of you that are still unconverted, whom I may
never see again in the flesh. My heart bleeds to think of parting with you; but I must defer this to my next letter, for I
expect to write you again before I go. Farewell for the present,
and may the grace of the Lord Jesus Christ be with you.

Eighth Pastoral Letter

Warnings to the unsaved. Why so many among us are unsaved.

Edinburgh, March 20, 1839.

TO all of you my dear flock, who are dearly beloved and longed for, my joy and crown, your pastor wishes grace, mercy, and peace, from God our Father, and from our Lord Jesus Christ.

In my last letter I showed you that, in all human probability, there are many of you to whom I have preached the gospel of salvation, to whom I shall never preach it again face to face. I cannot be blind to the many dangers that accompany foreign travel—the diseases and accidents to which we shall be exposed; but if, through your prayers, I be given to you again, how many blanks shall I find in my flock! How many dear children of God gone to be "where the weary are at rest," where the imperfect "are made perfect!" How many of you that have stood out against all the invitations of Christ, and all the warnings of God, shall I find departed, to give in your account before the throne! It is to these last I wish now to speak.

For two years I have testified to you the gospel of the grace of God. I came to you in "weakness, and in fear, and in much trembling"; and if the case of the children of God and of backsliding souls has often lain heavy at my heart, I can truly say that your dreadful condition—"settled like wine upon her lees," when you are about to be "turned upside down, as a man turneth a dish and wipeth it"—has been a continued anxiety to me; and sometimes, when I have had glimpses of the reality of eternal things, it has been an unsupportable agony to my spirit. I know well that this is a jest to you, that you care not whether ministers go or stay; and if you get a short sermon on the Sabbath day that will soothe and not prick your conscience, that is all you care for. Still, it may be the Lord who opened Manasseh's heart will open yours, while I go over solemnly, in the sight of God, what appear to be the chief reasons that, after my two years' ministry among you, there are still so many unconverted, perishing souls.

One cause is to be sought in *your minister.* In Malachi 2:6 you will find a sweet description of a faithful and successful minister: "The law of truth was in his mouth, and iniquity was not found in his lips: he walked with me in peace and equity, and did turn many away from iniquity." This is what *we should* have done; but the furnace brings out the dross, and afflictions discover defects unknown before. Oh, that I could say with Paul: "That I have been with you at all seasons serving the Lord with all humility of mind, and with many tears!" Ye are witnesses, and God also, "how holily, and justly, and unblameably, we behaved ourselves among you that believe." I am indeed amazed that the ministry of such a worm as I am should ever have been blessed among you at all; and I do this day bewail before God every sin in my heart and life that has kept back the light from your poor dark souls. Oh, you that can pray, pray that I may come back a holy minister—a shepherd not to lead the flock by the voice only, but to *walk* before them in the way of life.

Looking back over my pulpit work, alas! I see innumerable deficiencies. I always prayed that I might "not keep back anything that was *profitable,*" that I might not shun to declare the whole counsel of God, "that I might decrease, and Christ increase." Still, alas! alas! how dimly I have seen and set before you "the truth as it is in Jesus!" How coldly have I pleaded with you to "save yourselves from this untoward generation!" How many things I have known among you "besides Christ and Him crucified!" How often have I preached myself, and not the Saviour! How little I have "expounded to you in all the scriptures the things concerning Jesus!"

One error more has been in my private labors among you. How much fruitless intercourse have I had with you! I have not been like a *shepherd* crying after the lost sheep, nor like a *physician* among dying men, nor like a servant bidding you to the marriage, nor like one plucking brands from the burning! How often have I gone to your houses to try and win your souls, and you have put me off with a little worldly talk, and the words of salvation have died upon my lips! I dared not tell you, you were perishing, I dared not to show you plainly of the Saviour. How often I have sat at some of your tables, and my heart yearned for your souls, yet a false shame kept me silent! How often I have gone home crying bitterly, "Free me from *blood-guiltiness,* O God, thou God of my salvation!"

I turn now to the causes in you, dear children of God. You also have hindered in great measure God's work in the parish. *First,* by your want of *holiness.* "Ye are the light of the world." I have often told you that a work of revival in any place almost always begins with the children of God. God pours water first on "him that is thirsty," and then on the dry ground. But how little has "the word of the Lord sounded out from you!" I do not mean that you should have been loud talkers about religious things. "In the multitude of words there wanteth not sin, and the talk of the lips leadeth to penury." But you should have been "living epistles, known and read of all men."

You know that a lighted lamp is a very small thing, and it burns calmly and without noise; yet "it giveth light to all that are within the house." So, if you had day by day the blood of Christ upon your conscience, walking a forgiven and adopted child of God, having a calm peace in your bosom and a heavenly hope in your eye, having the Holy Spirit filling you with a sweet, tender, chaste, compassionate, forgiving love to all the world—oh! had you shone thus for two years back, how many of your friends and neighbors that are going down to hell might have been saying this day, "Thy people shall be my people, and thy God my God!" Think, my beloved friends, that every act of unholiness, of conformity to the world, of selfishness, of whispering and backbiting, is hindering the work of God in the parish and ruining souls eternally.

And what shall I say to those of you who, instead of emitting the sweet winning light of holiness, have given out only rays of darkness? "I have this against thee, that thou hast left thy first love. Remember, therefore, from whence thou art fallen, and repent, and do thy first works, or else I will come unto thee quickly, and will remove thy candlestick out of his place, except thou repent."

Second, you have hindered God's work by your want of prayer. When God gives grace to souls, it is in answer to the prayers of His children. You will see this on the day of Pentecost (Acts 2); Ezekiel 37:9 shows, that in answer to the prayer of a single child of God, God will give grace to a whole valley full of dry and prayerless bones. Where God puts it into the heart of His children to pray, it is certain that He is going to pour down His Spirit in abundance. Now, where have been your prayers, O children of God? The salvation of those around you depends on your asking, and yet "hitherto ye have asked nothing in Christ's name." Ye that are the Lord's remembrancers, keep not silence, and give Him no rest. Alas! you have given God much rest—you have allowed His hand to remain unplucked out of His bosom.

It is said of John Welsh, minister of Ayr, that he used always to sleep with a plaid upon his bed, that he might wrap it around him when he arose in the night to pray. He used to spend whole nights in wrestling with God for Zion, and for the purity of the Church of Scotland; and he wondered how Christians could lie all night in bed without rising to pray. Oh! we have few Welshes now; therefore our church is so dim, and our land a barren wilderness. Dear Christians, I often think it strange that ever we should be in heaven, and so many

in hell through our soul-destroying carelessness. The good
Lord pardon the past, and stir you up for the future. I learn
that you are more stirred up to pray since I left, both in secret
and unitedly. God grant it be so. Continue in it, dear children.
Do not let it slip again. Plead and wrestle with God, showing
Him that *the cause is His own,* and that it is all for *His own
glory* to arise and have mercy upon Zion.

*Last of all, think of the causes in yourselves, O unconverted
souls!* Be sure of this, that you will only have yourselves to
blame if ye awake in hell. You will not be able to plead God's
secret decrees, nor the sins of your minister, nor the carelessness of your godly neighbors—you will be speechless. If you
die, it is because you *will* die; and if you *will* die, then you must
die.

Think, first, on your carelessness about ordinances. They are
the channels through which God pours His Spirit. The Bible,
prayer, the house of God—these are the golden pipes through
which the golden oil is poured. How many of you utterly neglect the Bible! You know not the blessedness of the man
spoken of in the First Psalm. How many of you restrain prayer
before God! How many of you have dead, useless prayers,
learned by rote! And oh, how you despise the house of God!
Alas, that church shall rise against you in judgment. It was a
door of the ark brought near to you. Two years and more,
its gates have been wide open to you, and yet how you have
slighted it! Already I seem to hear your loud wailing when
you mourn at the last, and say, "How have I hated instruction, and my heart despised reproof, and have not obeyed the
voice of my teachers!"

Think, second, how you have been mockers. It has been too
common for you to make a mock of eternal things and of godly
people. When there have been anxious souls seeking the way
to be saved, and they could not conceal their tears, you have
called them hypocrites! When some have got a new heart,

and have changed their way of life, you have spoken scoffingly of them, and tried to bring them into contempt. Alas! poor soul, look within. You have hardened your hearts into an adamant stone. Look at Proverbs 17:5: "He that mocketh the poor reproacheth his maker." And again, Isaiah 28:22: "Now, therefore, be ye not *mockers,* lest your bands be made strong."

To sum up all. The great cause that I leave you hardened is, that you "despise the Son of God." You see no beauty in Him that you should desire Him. You lightly esteem the Rock of your salvation. You have not had a soul-piercing look at a pierced Saviour. You have not seen the infinite load of sins that weighed down His blessed head. You have not seen how open His arms are to receive, how often He would have gathered you. You have not heard that sweet word whispered of the Spirit, "Behold me, behold me," which, when a man once hears, he leaves all and follows. You have trampled under foot the blood of the Son of God. Farewell, dear, dear souls. God knows that my whole heart prays that you may be saved.

Perhaps there are some of you that never would bend under my ministry, that will melt like wax before the fire under the word of the dear young minister who is to speak to you in my absence. May the Lord give him hundreds for my tens! I will often pray for you, and sometimes write to you, when I am far away. If I reach Immanuel's land, I will say, "The Lord bless you out of Zion." And if you will not turn, remember I take God for a record that I am pure from the bood of you all.

Dear children of God, I now cast you on Him who cast you on me when I was ordained over you. He said to me, "Feed my sheep . . . feed my lambs . . . feed my sheep." Now, when He sends me away, I would humbly return His own words to Him, saying, "O Shepherd of Israel, feed my sheep, feed my lambs, feed my sheep." Little children, love one another. Keep yourselves from idols. Bear me ever on your hearts. Pray that when I have preached to others, I may not be a castaway. Pray that I may save some.

"Now the God of peace, that brought again from the dead our Lord Jesus Christ, that great Shepherd of the sheep, through the blood of the everlasting covenant, make you perfect in every good work to do His will, working in you that which is well pleasing in His sight, through Jesus Christ; to whom be glory for ever and ever. Amen."

My next, if God will, may be from England.

NINTH PASTORAL LETTER

Incidents of the way as far as Leghorn. Exhortations.

Leghorn, May 2, 1839.

TO all of you, my beloved flock, who have received Christ, and walk in Him, your pastor wishes grace, and mercy, and peace, from God our Father, and from our Lord Jesus Christ.

My heart's desire and prayer for you every day is that you may be saved. I am now far from you in the flesh, yet am I with you in the spirit. I thank my God without ceasing, for as many of you as have been awakened to flee from the wrath to come, have rested your souls upon the good word of God concerning Jesus, and have tasted the love of God. In every prayer of mine for you all, I ask that ye may continue in the faith, grounded and settled—that ye may be like trees, rooted in Christ Jesus, or like a holy temple built up in Him who is the only foundation stone.

I expected to have written you from London, and again before leaving France; but we have traveled so rapidly, often day and night, and the fatigue was so great to my weak frame, that I was disappointed in this; but I did not forget you night or day, and I know well I am not forgotten by you. Since I wrote you last I have passed through many cities and countries, and seen many faces and things strange to me. Many lessons for my own soul, and for yours, I have learned. At present I must write you shortly.

We left London on April 11, and next morning crossed the British Channel from Dover to Boulogne, and found ourselves on the shores of France. The very first night we spent in France, we were visited by a most interesting Jew, evidently anxious about his soul. He spoke with us for many hours, accepted the New Testament in Hebrew, and bade goodby with much emotion. We thanked God for this token for good. Pray for us, that God may give us good success, that we may have the souls of Israel for our hire.

From Boulogne we traveled to Paris, by day and by night, and spent a Sabbath there. Alas! poor Paris knows no Sabbath; all the shops are open, and all the inhabitants are on the wing in search of pleasures—pleasures that perish in the using. I thought of Babylon and of Sodom as I passed through the crowd. I cannot tell how I longed for the peace of a Scottish Sabbath.

There is a place in Paris called the *Champs Elysées,* or Plains of Heaven, a beautiful public walk, with trees and gardens; we had to cross it on passing to the Protestant church. It is the chief scene of their Sabbath desecration, and an awful scene it is. Oh, thought I, if this is the heaven a Parisian loves, he will never enjoy the pure heaven that is above. Try yourselves by that text, Isaiah 58:13, 14. I remember of once preaching to you from it. Do you really delight in the Sabbath day? If not, you are no child of God. I remember with grief that there are many among you that despise the Sabbath, some who buy and sell on that holy day, some who spend its blessed hours in worldly pleasures, in folly and sin. Oh! you would make Dundee another Paris if you could. Dear believers, oppose these ungodly practices with all your might. The more others dishonor God's holy day, the more do you honor it, and show that you love it of all the seven the best. Even in Paris, as in Sardis, we found a little flock of believers. We heard a sweet sermon in English, and another in French. There are only two thousand Protestant hearers out of the half million that inhabit Paris, and there are fourteen faithful sermons preached every Sabbath.

We left the French capital on April 16, a lovely evening, with a deep blue sky above, and a lovely country before us, on the banks of the Seine. This would be a delightsome land, if it only had the light of God's countenance upon it. We traveled three days and three nights, by Troyes, Dijon, and Chalons, till we came to Lyons, upon the rapid river Rhone, in the south of France. The Lord stirred up kind friends to meet us. Lyons is famous as being the place where many Christians were martyred in the first ages, and where many were burned at the time of the Reformation because they loved and confessed the Lord Jesus. God loves the place still. There is a small body of three hundred believers, who live here under a faithful pastor, Mr. Cordées. He cheered our hearts much, and sent us away with affectionate prayers.

That day we sailed down the Rhone more than 100 miles, through a most wonderful country. We hoped to have spent the Sabbath at Marseilles; but just as we entered the Mediterranean Sea, a storm of wind arose, and drove the vessel on a barren island at the mouth of the Rhone. We all landed and spent our Sabbath quietly on the desert island. It was your communion Sabbath, and I thought that perhaps this providence was given me that I might have a quiet day to pray for you. There were about twelve fishermen's huts on the island, made of reeds, with a vine growing before the door, and a fig tree in their garden. We gave tracts and books in French to all our fellow passengers, and to the inhabitants, and tried to hallow the Sabbath.

My heart went up to God the whole day for you all, and

for my dear friends who would be ministering to you. I tried
to go over you one by one, as many as I could call to mind.
My longing desire for you was, that Jesus might reveal Himself to you in the breaking of bread, that you might have
heart-filling views of the lovely person of Immanuel, and
might draw from *Him* rivers of comfort, life, and holiness.
I trust your fellowship was with the Father, and with His
Son, Jesus Christ. Many I know are ignorant of Jesus. I
trembled when I thought of their taking the bread and wine.
You all know my mind upon this.

The next morning the storm abated, and we sailed over
the tideless sea, and reached the beautiful harbor of Marseilles
by eight o'clock. We had conference with a faithful young
minister, and with the rabbi of the Jews. We also attended
the synagogue the same evening. The Jews of France are
fast falling into infidelity, especially the younger Jews. They
do not love the law and the prophets as their fathers did.
They are, indeed, the dry bones in Ezekiel 37. Still God can
make them live. It is our part to speak to them the Word of
the Lord, and to pray for the quickening Spirit.

True Christians in France are increasing. There are four hundred Protestant ministers, and nearly one-half of these are faithful men, who know nothing among their flocks but Christ and
Him crucified. In some places Christians seem more bold and
devoted than in Scotland. It is very pleasant to hear them
singing the French psalms: they sing with all their heart,
and are much given to prayer. Oh, my dear Christians, be like
them in these things! May the same Holy Spirit, who has
often visited you in times gone by, fill your hearts more than
ever with praise and prayer!

Catholicism in France is waxing bolder. The first day we
landed on the shore, it was evident we were in a land of darkness. On the height above Boulogne, a tall white cross attracted our eyes. We found on it an image of our Saviour

nailed to the tree, larger than life; the spear, the hammer, the nails, the sponge, were all there. It was raised by some shipwrecked fishermen; and sailors' wives go there in a storm to pray for their absent husbands. The Catholic priests meet us in every street: they wear a three-cornered hat, black bands, a black mantle with a sash, and large buckles on their shoes; they have all a dark, suspicious look about them. At the entrance of every village there is a cross, and the churches are full of pictures and images. I went into one church in Paris, the finest in France, where the crosses were all of pure silver, and there was a large white image of the Virgin Mary, holding the infant Jesus in her arms. Many rich and poor were kneeling on the pavement before the image, silently praying. Gross darkness covers the people.

A priest traveled one whole night with us in the coach. We argued with him first in French and then in Latin, trying to convince him of his errors, showing him his need of peace with God, and a new heart. In Psalm 137 you will see that Babylon, or Catholicism, is "doomed to destruction"; and in Revelation 18 you will see that her destruction will be very sudden and very terrible. Oh, that it may come soon, for thousands are perishing under its soul-destroying errors! And yet remember what I used to read to you out of Martin Boos, and remember the saying of the Lord to Elijah, I Kings 19. There may be many hidden ones even in Babylon. The whole way through France we distributed French tracts. Many hundreds in this way received a message of life. In every village they came crowding around us to receive them. Pray that the dew of the Spirit may make the seed sown by the wayside spring up.

We were too late for the first vessel to Malta, and therefore resolved to sail into Italy. We left Marseilles on April twenty-third, and landed at Genoa on the twenty-fourth. Genoa is one of the most beautiful towns in the world: the most of the houses and churches are of pure white marble, and from the sea look like palaces. But Satan's seat is there: we dared not distribute a single tract or book in Genoa—we would have been imprisoned immediately. The Catholic priests, in their black, dismal cloaks, and the monks with their coarse, brown dress, tied with a cord, a crucifix and beads hanging round their neck, bare feet, and cowl, swarm in every street. I counted that we met twenty of them in a ten minutes' walk. Catholicism reigns here triumphant, yet the people "are sitting still, and at ease," living for this world only. Oh! it is an awful thing to be at ease when under the wrath of God. Every place I see in Italy makes me praise God that you have the gospel so freely preached unto you. Prize it highly; do not neglect the wells of salvation that flow so freely for you.

The next day we sailed for Leghorn, where we have been ever since. We are living in the house where the excellent Mr. Martin, once minister of St. George's, Edinburgh, died in 1834. We visited his grave. I prayed that, like him, we might be faithful unto the end.

There are from ten to twenty thousand Jews here. We went to the synagogue the night we arrived, and twice since; it is a beautiful building inside, capable of holding two thousand persons. The place where they keep the law, written on a parchment roll, is finely ornamented with marble; so is the desk kept where they read the prayers. Lamps are continually burning. One rabbi was chanting the prayers when we entered. Beside the ark there stood three rabbis, in the Eastern dress, with turbans and flowing robes, and long beards. They were much reverenced, and many came to kiss their hand and receive their blessing. One of them is from Jerusalem; we have had many interesting conversations with him. Every day we have met with several Jews; they are very friendly to us, and we try to convince them out of the Scriptures that Jesus is the Christ. There are about 250 Protestants here; and we have tried to stir them up also to care for their souls. Dr. Black preached to them in our hotel last Sabbath evening.

Hitherto the Lord hath helped us. Tomorrow we sail from Italy to Malta, then for Egypt, and then for the Holy Land. Dear believers, it is a sweet consolation to me that your prayers go with me wherever I go. Often, perhaps, they close the mouth of the adversary, often keep back the storms from our vessels, often open a way to the hearts of those we meet, often bring down a sweet stream of the Spirit to water my thirsty soul. May I be enabled to make a sweet exchange with you, praying my heavenly Father to render double unto each of your bosoms what you pray for me! May my dear brother, who, I trust, fills my place among you, be made a blessing to you all! May his own soul be watered while he waters yours! Join him with me in your supplications. May he win many souls among you that I could never win.

This is Thursday evening. I trust you are at this moment met together in the prayer meeting. Oh! do not forsake the assembling of yourselves together. My heart is with you all. May the Spirit fill the whole church and every heart with His presence and power. My body is still far from being strong. I am more and more convinced that I did right in leaving you. I trust to be restored to you again in the fullness of the blessing of the gospel of Christ. "The will of the Lord be done."

My dear brother who is with me, whom you know well, and who daily joins me in fervent prayers for you, sends his salutations. Remember me to all who are sick and afflicted. Alas! how many of you may be laboring and heavy laden, that I know not of; but Jesus knows your sorrows. I commend you to the good Physician.

My dear classes, I do not, and cannot forget. I pray Psalm 119:9 may be written in your hearts.

My dear children in the Sabbath schools I always think upon on the Sabbath evenings, *and on those* who patiently labor

among them. The Lord Himself give you encouragement, and
a full reward.

To all I say, keep close to Christ, dear friends. Do not be
enticed away from Him; He is all your righteousness, and
all mine; out of *Him* you have all your strength, and I mine.
It pleased the Father that in *Him* should all fullness dwell.

The grace of the Lord Jesus Christ be with your spirits.
Farewell.

TENTH PASTORAL LETTER

Incidents of the way in Palestine and other lands—Request.

Breslau, in Prussia, October 16, 1839.

TO my dear flock, whom I love in the Lord Jesus, grace,
mercy, and peace, be multiplied from God the Father,
and from His Son, Jesus Christ.

I fear that many of you will be thinking hardly of your
distant pastor, because of his long silence; and, indeed, I
cannot but think hardly of myself. I little thought, when
leaving Italy, that I would be in Europe again before writing
to you. I did not know how difficult it is to write at any
length when traveling in the East.

From the day we left Egypt till we came to Mount Lebanon,
for more than two months, we were constantly journeying
from place to place, living in tents, without the luxury of a
chair or a bed. In these circumstances, with my weak body,
and under a burning sun, you must not wonder at my silence.
At the foot of Mount Carmel I began one letter to you, and
again in sight of the Sea of Galilee I began another, but
neither did I get finished. Last of all, before leaving the
Holy Land, I set apart a day for writing to you; but God
had another lesson for me to learn. He laid me down under

a burning fever, bringing me to the very gates of death. Indeed, my dear people, I feel like Lazarus, whom the Lord Jesus raised from the tomb. I feel like one sent a second time with the message of salvation, to speak it more feelingly and more faithfully to your hearts, as one whose eye had looked into the eternal world.

In all our wanderings, you have been with me by night and by day. Every scene of Immanuel's land brought you to my remembrance, because every scene tells of Jesus Christ and Him crucified. In the wilderness, in Jerusalem, beside the Sea of Galilee, at Smyrna, on the Black Sea, on the Danube, you have all been with me. I have, day and night, unceasingly laid your case before God. It has been one of my chief comforts, that, though I could not preach to you, nor come to you, I could yet pray for you. Perhaps I may obtain more for you in this way, than I could have done by my personal services among you.

Another joy to me has been, that I know all of you who pray, pray for me. This has been a lamp to me in many a dark hour. God has wonderfully preserved us through your prayers. In the south of the Holy Land, we were daily exposed to the plague. Every night we heard the wail of the mourners going about the streets of Jerusalem; yet no plague came near our dwelling. Near the Sea of Galilee we were often in danger of being robbed and murdered by the wild Arabs; yet we passed unhurt through the midst of them. Sailing to Smyrna, your pastor was brought low indeed, insomuch that I never thought to see you again; yet He sent His word and healed me. In Poland, the Sabbath before last, I was actually in the hands of robbers; but through God's wonderful mercy, I escaped safe. In every step of our journey, I am persuaded we have been watched over by our all-loving Father, who is the hearer of prayer! And the Lord shall deliver us from every evil work, and will preserve us unto His heavenly kingdom. I speak of these things only that you may give Him the glory, and trust in Him to your dying day. Sing Psalm 116 in all your families.

Another joy to me has been, that God has given you the dear brother who watches over you so tenderly. You know not what joy it gave me to hear of you all through him. The letter reached me at Smyrna, when I was so weak that I could not walk alone. It was like health and marrow to my bones, to hear that the Lord's work is not yet done in the midst of you, and that so many of you stand fast in the Lord, having your conversation in heaven. I have no greater joy than to hear that my children walk in the truth. It is not like common joy. All joys of this world are short and fading, they reach not beyond the dark boundary of the grave; but to rejoice over those whom the Lord has given me out of a perishing world—this is joy which God Himself shares, and which reaches into the light of eternity. Ye are my joy and crown.

In like manner, there is no sorrow like the sorrow of the pastor, who has to weep over a backsliding people. I do tremble to return to you, for I know well I shall have deep sorrow from some of whom I expected joy. I fear lest I have to mourn over some branches that are without fruit, on the good vine tree; over some, who once gave their hand to the Saviour, but are now saying, "I will go after my lovers." Are there none of you who have left your first love, and broken the bands that bound you to follow Jesus? Shall I find none of whom I must needs say, "They went out from us, but they were not of us"? Oh, there is no sorrow like unto this sorrow. Had I been able, as I hoped, to have written you from all the chief places in our journeyings, I would have attempted to describe to you all I saw; but now there are so many countries to look back upon, that it would be vain to attempt it. I do hope, that if the Lord bring us together again, I may be able to tell you many things of our wanderings, and especially of Immanuel's land, which may both refresh and improve you. Nothing that I have heard I keep back from you, if only it be for your soul's good and God's glory.

Of the Holy Land, I can only say, like the Queen of Sheba, "that the half was not told me." It is far more wonderful than I could have believed. I shall always reckon it one of the greatest temporal blessings of my lot, that I have been led to wander over its mountains with the Bible in my hand, to sit by its wells, and to meditate among its ruined cities. Not a single day did we spend there without reading, in the land itself, the most wonderful traces of God's anger and of His love. Several times we went to the Mount of Olives, to the Garden of Gethsemane, to the Pool of Siloam, and to the village of Bethany, and every stone seemed to speak of the love of God to sinners. These places are probably very little altered from what they were in the days when Jesus tabernacled among men, and they all seemed to say, "Hereby perceive we the love of God, because He laid down His life for us."

We were four days in sight of the Sea of Galilee. I could not help thinking of you, my dear young people, for we used to go over the Sea of Galilee so often on the Monday evenings, and all the scenes of divine love it has been witness to. One day we rode through the plain of Gennesaret, and passed the moldering ruins of Capernaum, the Saviour's city, where His voice of mercy was so often heard, and where His hand was so often stretched out to heal. We asked in vain for Chorazin and Bethsaida. The woe which Jesus pronounced has fallen upon them.

Oh, my dear flock, "how shall you escape if you neglect so great salvation?" See how desolate they are left, that refuse Him that speaketh from heaven. The free offer of a divine Surety rings through your churches, now that God continues faithful teachers among you. Every Sabbath, and oftener, the fountain for sin is publicly opened for you, and souls, all defiled with sin, are invited to come and wash. But these mercies will not always last.

If you tread the glorious gospel of the grace of God under your feet, your souls will perish; and I fear Dundee will one day be a howling wilderness like Capernaum. I spent nearly the whole of August, during my illness in Bouja, a village near Smyrna, under the care of tenderest friends, whom the Lord wonderfully provided for me in a strange land. You remember Smyrna is one of the Seven Churches in Asia to which the Saviour sent those quickening messages in the Revelation of St. John. I thought again and again of the happy Thursday evenings which I once spent with you in meditating on these seven epistles to the churches. You know it is said of Samuel, even when he was a child, that God did not let one of his words fall to the ground; and the same is true to this hour of the very weakest of God's faithful ministers. What we have spoken to you is not like the passing wind, which hurries on and leaves no trace behind. It is like the rain and snow—it will not return to God without accomplishing some end in your hearts, either melting or hardening. Smyrna is the only one of these churches where a pure golden candlestick is now to be found with the light burning. There is a small company who believe in Jesus. It was pleasant indeed to hear the gospel preached there in all its purity and power. Be you also faithful to death, and you shall receive a crown of life.

Leaving Smyrna, we sailed past Troas and Bithynia, and visited Istanbul, the most beautiful city in the world, and yet the most miserable. Looking round from the deck of the vessel, I could count above ninety minarets, many of them pure marble, carved and gilded in the richest manner. These all form part of mosques, or temples of the false prophet Mohammed. This religion is a singular invention of Satan;

their Koran, or Bible, is a book filled with nonsense, and with much wickedness. All their belief is comprehended in the short saying, "Lo Ullah il Allah, a Mahomed Rasal Allah"— "There is no God but God, and Mohammed is His prophet." They expect to be saved chiefly by making pilgrimages to Mecca, by abstaining from wine and pork, and by praying five times a day. Every day, at sunrise or sunset, we saw them at prayer; wherever they are, in the open street, on the top of the house, or on the deck of a ship, they take off their shoes, wash hands, face, and feet, spread their garment before them, and turning their face towards Mecca, pray, bending and kissing the ground, often fifteen and twenty times. They are rather pleased if you look at them. They are very proud of their own faith, and will not listen for a moment to the gospel of Jesus. It would be instant banishment or death if any missionary were to attempt their conversion.

Ah! my dear flock, how differently you are situated! How freely salvation is offered to you—a faith that really saves you from your sins—that makes you love one another! For love is of God, and every one that loveth is born of God. If you are not growing humble and loving, be sure your faith is no better than a Mohammedan's. You are not of God, but of the world. The next countries we visited were Walachia and Moldavia. We sailed to them from Istanbul, across the raging waves of the Black Sea, and up the mighty river Danube. These are two singular countries, seldom visited by travelers; they are governed by two princes, and the established religion is of the Greek Church. I wish I could show you all that I have seen of the superstitions and wickedness practiced among them, that you might give more earnest heed to the pure gospel that flows as freely as air and water through our beloved land.

One day, in Bucharest, the capital city of Walachia, I was present at a festival on the prince's birthday. An immense

crowd was present in their finest church, and all the nobles
of the land. The service consisted of prayers and chanting by
a number of priests, dressed in the most splendid manner.
When all was over, I stayed behind to see a curious superstition. At one side of the altar lay an open coffin, highly ornamented; within I observed a dead body wrapped in cloth of
gold; a dead withered hand alone was left out. This is said
to be the body of St. Demetrius, lately found in a river, by
the water parting asunder miraculously. Such is the tale we
are told.

I stood beside it when the worshipers approached the coffin
in great numbers, men and women, rich and poor. First
they crossed themselves and kneeled, kissing the floor three
times. Then they approached reverently, and kissed the withered hand of the dead body, and a cross that lay beside it.
Then they gently dropped a small coin into a little plate at
the dead man's feet, and after receiving a blessing from the
priest, with three prostrations more to the ground, they retired.

This is one specimen of their abominable worship of dead
men. Do I tell you these things that you may be proud of your
superior light? Ah! no. I write these things, that those of you
who live no better lives than they do, may be convinced of
your danger. What can you expect of these poor idolaters, but
that they will live after the flesh, in rioting and drunkenness,
in chambering and wantonness, in strife and envying? But
are there none of you, my dear flock, for whom night and
day my prayers ascend—are there none of you who do
the same things, though you have the holy Bible, and a freely
preached gospel, and no superstition? Yet how many of you
live an unholy life! Ah! remember Sardis: "I know thy
works, that thou hast a name that thou livest, and art dead.
Be watchful, and strengthen the things which remain, that
are ready to die; for I have not found thy works perfect
before God."

The next kingdom we came through was Austrian Poland —the land of graven images. We came through its chief towns, Tarnopol, Brody, Lemburg, and from thence to Krakow, traveling many hundred miles. You would be amazed, as I have been, if you saw the abominable idolatry of this land. The Roman Catholic is the established faith; and the government is a bitter persecutor of any who change. At every village there are numbers of crosses, of immense size, with the image of the Saviour. There are also statues of the Virgin Mary, and of other saints as large as life, all along the roads. Often there are wooden boxes set up full of images; often in the middle of a square there is a small covered chamber full of these idols, of wood and stone, whom the poor people worship every day.

The Bible is an unlawful book in this country. All our Bibles were taken away from us, even our Hebrew ones, that we might not preach to the Jews the glad tidings of a Saviour. Blessed be God, they could not take them from our memories and hearts. Should not this make you all pray for the coming of the day when the towers of Catholicism shall fall—the day when God shall avenge us on her? For the Bible which she hates so much says, "Her plagues shall come in one day, death, and mourning, and famine; and she shall be utterly burned with fire; for strong is the Lord God who judgeth her." Pray for that day, for it will be the same day when God will bind up the breach of His people Israel, and shall heal the stroke of their wound. It will be the day when the Lamb's wife shall come forth in all her loveliness and when the Lord Jesus shall wear the crown of His espousals.

I began this letter to you in Krakow, the ancient capital of Poland, but now an independent state. We spent three days there inquiring after the poor despised Jews. We had much intercourse with a faithful, prayerful missionary, who labors among them there; and on the Sabbath we celebrated the

Lord's Supper. During the four years he has been in Krakow, the missionary had never once enjoyed the ordinance, for all around are sunk in Catholicism or infidelity. We were but five souls in all, and yet we felt it very pleasant, when surrounded with them that hated us, and far from our homes, with the door of the chamber shut, to remember Jesus.

My thoughts and desires were much toward you. I had greatly hoped to be present at your next Lord's Supper, but now I see it cannot be. My only comfort is, I have committed you to those who are beloved of the Lord, workmen that need not to be ashamed, whose names are in the Book of Life; and the Chief Shepherd, I feel persuaded, will not leave you orphans, but will come to you, and breathe upon you. May the Lord keep back from the table all who are not united to Christ; and may you, who are His own children, have communion with the Father, and with His Son, Jesus Christ.

Since yesterday morning we have traveled 180 miles nearer home. We are now in Breslau, and we breathe more freely, for this is the Protestant kingdom of Prussia. It makes my heart light to think that I am really on my way to you. It has been a sweet work indeed to me to carry, with poor stammering lips, the word of salvation to the scattered sheep of the house of Israel; still, I do long, if it be the Lord's will, to feed once more the flock that was given me in the dew of my youth. Whether I shall be permitted, and how long, to take up so great a work again, my Master only knows; but if you wish for it as fervently as I do, solemnly agree, in the presence of God, on the night on which this letter is read to you, to these two things:

First, strive together with me in your prayers to God for me, that it would please Him to forgive and forget our past sins and shortcomings—mine in carrying the message, yours in receiving it; and that He would really heal my body, and strengthen my soul, for again taking up the blessed work of the gospel ministry among you, and that He would grant us a prosperous journey to come unto you.

Second, solemnly agree, in the strength of the Lord Jesus, to break off your sins by righteousness, and your iniquities by showing mercy to the poor. The sin of one Achan troubled the whole camp of Israel. If any one of you who are God's children willfully continue in some old sin, then it may be God's will, for your sake, to trouble our camp, and continue His chastening. See that no fleshly lust, no covetousness which is idolatry, no hankering after the world and its unholy pleasures, no unlawful affection, be reigning in you. Clean out the old leaven from all your houses, so that we may meet again in peace, and be refreshed together by days of the Lord's presence and of the Spirit's power, such as we have never seen before. This is the hearty desire and prayer of your affectionate pastor.

————

To Rev. John Roxburgh, of St. John's, Dundee

The Holy Land.

Jerusalem, June 17, 1839.

I AM SURE you will be glad to hear from your brother in the ministry, in this land trodden by the feet of "God manifest in the flesh." My thoughts wander continually to the spot where God first counted me faithful, putting me into the ministry; where, for two years, He made me a happy minister of the gospel, and where I believe I have many praying friends who will not forget me so long as I live. In these sweet remembrances—whether in the vales of Italy, or on the mighty waters, or in the waste howling wilderness, or in this land of promise—you and your family have their constant place. I doubt not also that you often think and talk of me.

When some Church Extension expedition has turned out well,
you will say, "What would our traveling friend say to this?"
Or when the liberties of our church are infringed, and the
arm of unhallowed power is raised against her, you perhaps
think a moment, "How will our traveler bear this?" I am
thankful to Him who dwelt in the bush that we are all here
in safety, and I myself in moderate health, quite able to endure
the fatigues of traveling, although these have been very great.

You would hear of our swift journey through France, and
our pleasant stay in Italy. Malta was the next place of interest
we came to. It is a very lovely island, having customs from
almost every nation under heaven. It is highly important as
a center of missionary operations, having a printing press, and
some useful, excellent men employed. In riding round its rocky
shore, we looked on every creek with interest, remembering
Paul's shipwreck here, and his three months' stay in the island.
The atmosphere is truly pleasant, and the sky has a peculiarly
fine tinge of yellowish red.

We had a pleasant sail past Greece, and among the wonderful islands of the Aegean Sea. We landed on one called Syra,
and saw the mission actively engaged, six hundred Greek children reading God's Word in Greek. The same evening we
sailed between Naxos and Paros, where the beautiful marble
was found, and stretched our eyes to see Patmos, where the beloved John wrote the Revelation. We could only see the waves
that washed its shore.

We passed Crete, and read the Epistle to Titus with a
new interest; and the next day at four (May 13th) sailed
into the harbor of Alexandria. The costumes of the East are
very striking to the eye at first. The turban, the beard, the hyke
or immense plaid, the wide Arab trousers, the black visages
and legs of the men, quite arrest the attention. The close veil,
the forehead ornaments, the earrings, the anklets, the burden
carried on the head, the children carried on the shoulder, or

on the side—all these in the women are striking, especially at first. They will recall to you many of the words of the prophets. The plague having broken out at Alexandria the day we arrived, we were prevented from going up to Cairo; and after having visited the Jews in the synagogues, we determined on proceeding through the desert for the Holy Land, that we might escape quarantine. We left Alexandria on the fourteenth of May, and reached Jerusalem on the seventh of June. We were about twenty-two days living after the manner of Bedouins in the wilderness.

Mount Carmel, June 24th, 1839.—I thought to have got this letter finished in Jerusalem; but we were hurried away so unexpectedly in consequence of a considerable increase of the plague in the Holy City then, that I had to leave this and many others things undone. You will see by the heading that we are now beside that mountain where God did such wonders in the days of Elijah. We are encamped in our tents within a few yards of the sea. I am now writing upon a mat on the sand. The thermometer is somewhere about 80°, and I am writing with my desk on my knee. For the sake of distinctness, I will take up the thread of our story where I last left it off.

Our journey through the desert was a very trying one in many ways. I *now* understand the meaning of the text which says, "God led the Israelites through the wilderness to try them, and prove them, and make them know what was in their hearts." The loneliness is very great. The utter silence of all the world to you, the want of every necessary except what you carry along with you—all these try the soul in a way you can hardly imagine, whether we will cast all our care upon God or no. The first part of the desert journey we went upon asses; but the second and longest part upon camels—a mode of journeying of all others the most fatiguing.

I have thought a hundred times what a singular picture it would make, to draw our company riding through the desert,

exalted to the giddy height of the hunch of the camel. I
have often thought also, more seriously and properly, how
plainly God heard the prayers of all our dear friends in pre-
serving us from many dangers. It is quite a miracle that I
was enabled to bear the fatigue of being up before sunrise,
and sailing over that burning wilderness, often twelve hours
a day.

We came the nearest way from Egypt, alluded to in Exodus
13:17, and had opportunity of seeing Rosetta and Damietta,
two curious Egyptian towns. We sailed across a lake called
Menzaleh, and encamped one night beside the ruins of the
ancient Zoan. Amid these we could plainly trace the finger
of God in the fulfillment of the words in Ezekiel 30:14: "I
will set fire in Zoan." At El Arish, the last town of Egypt,
we clearly traced what we believed to be the river of Egypt,
so often spoken of as the boundary of Judah. Like all the
streams in the South, it is perfectly dry; but the watercourse
was very evident. By the way, this suggests the meaning of
a text which I never understood before, Psalm 126: "Turn our
captivity as the streams in the south." In the whole of the
south part of Canaan the streams dry up in the summer. I
think we only came upon *one* flowing stream between the Nile
and Jerusalem. In the winter God restores these streams, supplying them with abundance of water. Now this is the very
prayer of the Psalmist: "Do for our brethren in captivity
what thou doest for the streams in the south. Restore them
in all their life, and fullness, and beauty." So may it be in
all our parishes in all our beloved Scotland, never so lovely
or desirable as when we are far from it and from its pleasant
Sabbaths.

I must tell you now about Jerusalem. It is indeed the most
wonderful place I was ever in. We reached it about twelve
o'clock, under a burning sun. The bleak, rocky hills over
which we crossed were like a heated oven; but all was forgotten

when the city of the great King came in sight. "Your house
is left unto you desolate." That word was upon every tongue.
Almost every approach to Jerusalem gives you this desolate
feeling; but when you stay there, and wander down into its
deep valleys, or climb its terraced hills, or sit beside shady
Siloam, whose waters flow softly, or meditate on Mount Zion,
ploughed like a field, the whole current of your feelings is
made to flow, and Jerusalem presents the remains of departed
beauty such as you seek for in vain in any other land.

The scene which might seem of greatest interest in Jerusalem
is Calvary, where the Son of God died. But God has so
willed it that nothing but pain and disappointment follow the
inquirer after the spot where the blood flowed which cleanses
from all sin. You know there is a great church built over the
place. The hole made by the cross is enclosed in a star of
gold; and a marble slab covers what *they call* the sepulchre.
They tell you so many heinous falsehoods, that we were all
inclined to doubt the whole matter. The place in Jerusalem is
now within the walls, instead of "without the gate." There
is no mount, no garden—nothing to remind you of that day
of awful interest.

Gethsemane makes up in interest all that we want in Calvary.
The very place remains, and by its simplicity convinces the
mind that it was the spot that Jesus loved. Above you, on the
opposite side of Kedron, the high steep brow of Moriah rises;
then the wall of the city, and above it the Mosque of Omar,
which stands on the site of God's holy Temple. The road to
Bethany passes in front of the garden. The path up the Mount
of Olives forms another boundary. It is enclosed with old
stone walls like all the walls of Judea, of rude stones, without
any cement. Eight very old olives, of a thousand years at least,
stand as monuments in the place. It is a sweet and sacred spot;
and you will not wonder that we were often drawn to visit it,
and to pray on the spot where Jesus sweat drops of blood.

The Mount of Olives is a hill of which you never weary. As you ascend it from Gethsemane, every step gives you a new prospect. We turned round again and again to look upon Jerusalem. Jeremiah says, "From the daughter of Zion all beauty is departed." And I believe, if we had seen "the perfection of beauty" in the day of its glory, we would say the same. Still from the Mount of Olives it is most beautiful. You see "the mountains all standing round about Jerusalem." The whiteness of the buildings gives it a dazzling appearance. The deep valleys on every side are very remarkable. On the north, a rising tower marks Ramah, where Samuel was born; and on the south, the eye fixes on Herodion, a conical hill beside Bethlehem.

When you come to the top of Olivet, you look to the east, and the Dead Sea seems to be stretched at your feet. The mountains of Moab look quite near; and you try to find out Pisgah, where Moses enjoyed his view of the good land. Bethany appears upon the east side of a declivity near you—a pleasant village. Twice we wandered out as far as Bethany. It was pleasant indeed to sit under its spreading fig trees, and to read over John 11.

Returning by the Jericho road, we stopped at the spot where Jesus wept over the city. It is the place where you "come near and behold the city," at the descent of the Mount of Olives. After full consideration, I believe it to be the very spot. *Zion* is literally ploughed like a field. I have brought with me some barley that I found growing on its summit. Jerusalem is become heaps. The heaps of ruins within the city are amazing; in some parts they are higher than the walls. "The mountain of the house is like the high places of the forest." Mount Moriah has now two Turkish mosques upon it.

Aceldama is a peaceful spot, overhanging the pleasant valley of Hinnom, once the scene of hideous rites. The plague was very severe in the city during our stay there, which prevented us from having that close intercourse with the inhabitants, and especially with the Jews, which was so desirable. Mr. Nicolayson, the English missionary, acted towards us like a brother. He lodged us in one of the mission houses upon Mount Zion, and gave us opportunity of preaching and of receiving the Lord's Supper. It was truly pleasant to eat of that bread and drink of that cup in an upper room in Jerusalem.

There are about five thousand Jews in Jerusalem, very poor and very divided among themselves, looked down upon as dogs by the Moslems; still they bear in their faces and manners the proof that the land is their own. They are entirely supported by contributions from Europe. They devote themselves to the study of the Law and the Talmud. I had an interesting meeting with one Jew at the large stones, the only remains of God's Temple. He was sitting praying, and looking very sad. I asked him what he was reading. He showed me; it was Psalm 22 in Hebrew. I took it up and read it over to him. He said he understood it, and that it applied to David. I showed him that could *not* be, for David was never pierced in hands and feet. I shortly explained to him the gospel, and showed him the only way of forgiveness. He looked very sad sitting on the ground.

I must hurry on. We visited Hebron, and had an interesting meeting with the Jews there. It is a delightful place. We visited Bethlehem on our return. It is curious that almost all the inhabitants of Bethlehem are Christians, that is, Greeks and Catholics. We left Jerusalem on the eighteenth and proceeded north by Ramah, Gibeon, Bethel, Sychar and Samaria to Carmel. I cannot tell you the delightful and solemn feelings with which we traverse this Land of Promise. The fulfillment of prophecy is everywhere remarkable. At Sychar we tried to find out the well where Jesus sat wearied. Mr. Bonar found it, and let his Bible fall into it. He could not get it

again, "for the well is deep." Ebal on the north, is a frowning
rocky hill. Gerizzim is also precipitous, but smiles with verdant
gardens. Sychar is a beautiful place. We spent a most interesting morning among the Jews and Samaritans, saw both their
synagogues, and reasoned with them out of the Scriptures, prov-
ing that Jesus is the Christ. Oh, that the Saviour would do
as He did before in this place—say plainly, "I that speak unto
thee am *He!*"

When we meet, if that be the will of God, I shall have
many descriptions to give you of the scenes of this land. It
has far surpassed all my expectations. We arrived at Carmel
on Saturday, and are now in quarantine. We and all our
clothes were yesterday bathed in the sea. In consequence of
undergoing this process our quarantine is seven days shorter;
and on Monday next we hope to proceed to Tiberias and
Saphet, the only places of importance for Jews, except Tyre
and Sidon, which we shall visit on our way to Beirut. We are
sorry that so much of our time is taken up, but we have gone
as quickly as possible in the circumstances.

We are all in good health. I suffer occasionally from my
heart, but much less than I did. I do hope, if it be the will
of my Master, that I may yet again serve Him in the gospel
of His Son. This is a delicious climate. I have heard once
from home. I am thankful to hear of the peace and grace
given to my people on our communion day. Dear people, may
the Great Shepherd feed them! I was happy to hear of Dr.
Chalmers' success. Dismayed at the decision of the Lord
Chancellor; but "Jehovah nissi," the Lord is our banner. My
kindest regards to Mrs. R., and to the brethren that ask for
me. I often pray most humbly for *all*, even my enemies.

———

To Rev. R. Macdonald of Blairgowrie

The Holy Land.

Mount Carmel, June 26, 1839.

I WROTE to you from the land of Egypt, and now from the Land of Promise. I would have written from Jerusalem; but our departure was so hurried, owing to an increase of the awful disease of plague, that I could not accomplish it. Indeed, I thought it would be more for the pleasure and advantage of all my friends if I spent my time in fully seeing the wonders of the city of the great King. It is all deeply graven on my memory and my heart.

The first sight of Jerusalem made my heart sink within me, it was so desolate; the walls appeared so low, so dark, so poor. But better acquaintance with its deep valleys and singular hills, its trees and fountains, has made it appear one of the loveliest spots Jesus visited. There is a holy beauty about Jerusalem, for you cannot walk a step without remembering the scenes that have passed there, and without looking forward to a time when it will again become the joy of the whole earth.

You will be glad to know that I have stood all our great fatigues wonderfully, and even without being the worse of them, but rather the better. I may almost say I feel that God has been answering the continued prayer of those that love me; still I am not yet what I was, though I hope to be. All my companions had the privilege of preaching in Jerusalem. I felt that it was kept from me; but that it was overflowing goodness that gave us to receive the broken bread and poured-out wine in an upper chamber, where Jesus first instituted it. I wish I could recount to you all that we have seen with our eyes, so as to make you almost see it all over again. Joy is increased by spreading it to others. Thus Christ's joy and glory are increased by making us partakers of it.

Our life in the wilderness was a singular one. Since the day I wrote you we have never known the luxury of a bed. We spread our mats upon the sand, and God watches over us, when we are under the cover of our frail tent, as much as if we were within brazen gates and bars. We often hear the cry of the wolves at night, and there are many lynxes and hyenas in this very mountain; but God keeps us safely. The burning heat of the desert, the long fatiguing journeys—sometimes twelve hours or fourteen in the day upon a camel—the insatiable thirst and our weakness, were very trying to our faith and to our temper; it proved us and made us know what was in our heart. Ah! dear friend, wherever we journey, union to Jesus and holiness from His Spirit flowing into us, is our chief and only happiness. Never cease to show your people that to be holy is to be happy; and that to bring us to perfect holiness and likeness to God was the very end for which Christ died.

We entered the land of the Philistines the first of June. You know the prophets say that the seacoast there is to be "cottages for shepherds and folds for flocks" (Zeph. 2:6). It is really so. You cannot imagine a country more completely covered with flocks and herds—camels and asses, and oxen and sheep and goats. The inhabitants are Arabs, a poor and ignorant race of men. How often we have wished for the Arabian tongue, to preach to them the unsearchable riches of Christ! We passed like the spies through the valley of Eshcol. We came to a small Arab town, Bet-hanoon. In all Arab towns, every roof is flat, so that the people sit there, pray there, dry their corn and sift it there.

There are no vines in Eshcol now, but immense bunches of grapes are still produced in some places of the Holy Land. The trees around the village are figs, beautiful, dark green trees. We are now tasting the first ripe figs, which are, like Jeremiah's, very good. We crossed the brook Sorek—quite dry; indeed, I think we met with only one flowing stream between the desert and Jerusalem. The streams in the South are all dry in the summer (see Psaim 126). We slept that night beside a small town, which we take to be Eshtaol, near which Samson was born. We saw there the brown tents of some Bedouin Arabs, illustrating Song of Solomon 1—the brown tents of Kedar. This was in the tribe of Dan.

Next day we went due east, across the vast plain Sephela, where Asa fought his battle (II Chron. 14), till we entered among the lovely hills of Judah. A wonderful fulfillment of God's Word was pressed on our attention all that day. The quantities of weeds in the plains are quite remarkable, and all of them are of a briery, prickly nature. I counted eleven different kinds of thistle, some of them of gigantic size. In a field where barley had been sown, there were more of these thorns and briers than of the barley. Now turn to Isaiah 32:13: "Upon the land of my people shall come up thorns and briers"; and see how long (v. 15), "Until the Spirit be poured upon us from on high." Indeed, every mountain and valley of this land is a witness for God, speaking silently but mightily, declaring that God's Word abideth for ever.

We arrived at Jerusalem on June seventh, and lighted off our camels within the Jaffa gate. The first thing that struck me was the quantity of various heaps. (See Micah 3:12.) It was two or three days before we recovered from fatigue. The first time we went out was to the two pools of Gihon; the upper pool still contains water.

Again we went to Mount Olivet. Winding round the noble walls at Jerusalem, Mount Olivet appears with its softly rounded, triple point. It is a beautiful hill of very great extent. It is composed of a pure white limestone, which appears in many places, and gives the whole a whitish appearance. Fine old olives adorn it on every side; fig trees here and there, and pomegranates, with their beautiful deep red flowers. A monas tery and a mosque are on the top, and three or four small towers, on different points of it. Crops of barley may be discerned here and there. It is altogether a pleasant hill. Between you and it lies the deep valley of Jehosaphat. The bed of the Kedron, quite dry, forms the lowest part.

Going along by the east wall of Jerusalem till you are nearly opposite the place where the Temple stood (now the Mosque of Omar), you then descend the steep bank of Moriah to the Kedron. A small bridge now helps you to cross. Here David went flying from Absalom. Here Jesus used to cross going to Gethsemane or to Bethany. The path before you leads right up the steepest part of Mount Olivet. It is a pleasant path. Turning every now and then, you see Jerusalem in all its faded glory, minarets and cupolas lying beneath you.

Another path winds upwards round the hill to Bethany, the sweet village of Martha and Mary, two miles off. The little nook between these two paths forms all that remains of Gethsemane. It is a pleasant spot. No one that knows the Saviour can visit it and look upon its eight old olive trees without feeling drawn to it. We tried to pray there, where Jesus sweat blood for us. It was sweet to intercede for you and all we love in that sacred spot.

Another favorite spot was the fountain of Siloam, farther down the valley of Jehoshaphat. It flows so softly from under the Temple that you cannot hear the ripple of its waters. You descend a great many steps in the rock, and drink its delightful waters. I send you a small hymn on the other side, which will imprint it on your memory. The valley of Hinnom is a deep gorge or vale to the south of Jerusalem. Mount Zion is actually ploughed like a field. It descends steeply into Hinnom, which again has a rocky barrier on the opposite side. Aceldama is a fearful spot above.

We left Jerusalem on June eighteenth and arrived here on the twenty-first. Many a pleasant scene we saw between. It

is a delightsome land. One only I can mention—Sychar. It
was a sweet evening when we entered the valley made by Ebal,
a gloomy barren hill, and Gerizim, a rocky hill, but garnished
with gardens. The town lies beautiful between, keeping nearer
to Gerizim. The next morning we visited the synagogue.
Andrew Bonar was in time for the service at six o'clock. He
had very interesting discussions with several of the Jews, all
carried on in Hebrew. You may believe we are not very fluent
in the holy tongue, and yet it is wonderful how we get on.
We visited the Samaritans also, and, after taking off our
shoes, we were admitted into their synagogue to see the
manuscript of the Pentateuch, 3,600 years old. Andrew alone
found out the well where Jesus sat, and dropped his Bible in
by accident.

The Jews here are far kinder and pleasanter than in Europe.
They wear a beautiful dress. They are much fairer in color
than the Arabs, and every way a more noble people; and then,
when you look at your Bible, and see the promises that are
waiting to be fulfilled to them, how does the heart fill towards
them! God will yet gather them one by one. Pray still for
their inbringing. It is not easy to pray really for Israel; it
needs you to have much of the peculiar mind of God.

The same evening we visited Samaria, about six or eight
miles north of Sychar. It is now a poor Arab village, but the
finger of God is there. It is a hill surrounded by hills on all
sides. Micah 1:6 is the clearest description of it. It is like an
heap of the field. Just as you have seen the stones gathered
out of a field into heaps, such is Samaria. The vast ruins are
all thrown down, and form just heaps in the field. It is as the
plantings of a vineyard. There is but one vine on the whole
hill, but it is all terraced and cleared, just as if it were to be
planted with vines. "And I will pour down the stones thereof
into the valley, and I will discover the foundations thereof."
This is wonderfully fulfilled. It filled me with holy awe to

look at the heaps of stones—fragments of pillars all rolling down into the valley. The foundations are actually discovered. What a monument of the truth of God! I have only time to commend you to God, and to say, Brother, pray for us.

P.S.—Commend me to your true yokefellow, Mr. Smith, and to Mr. Gillies, and to Mr. Baxter. I cease not to mention all in my prayers, and hope that they do not forget me. "We are made partakers of Christ if we hold the beginning of our confidence firm unto the end."

———

To Rev. William C. Burns, Dundee

Inquiries about the revival on first coming home.

20 Hill Street, Edinburgh, November 15, 1839.

I ARRIVED last night once more in my beloved home, conducted through every danger by the unseen hand of our Father in heaven. I cannot lose a moment in writing you a few lines. It was not till we arrived in Hamburg that we heard anything of what has been doing in our beloved land for the last five months. There we heard only a rumor that God had visited His people in love, and those also that were Lo-Ammi. You may believe that it was with a thankful, joyful spirit that we read of these things.

I cannot rest till I hear from you what has been done among my own dear flock. I do not like to impose a task on you; but if you have an hour's leisure, it would be truly gratifying to me to hear from you, before I come over, a minute account of all that God seems to have wrought in Dundee during my absence. You remember it was the prayer of my heart when we parted, that you might be a thousandfold more blessed to the people than ever my ministry had been. How it will gladden my heart, if you can really tell me that it has been so! My poor, dear flock, hardhearted and stiff-necked as they were, if the Lord has really opened their hearts, and brought them to a saving knowledge of Christ, and if their hearts and lives are together changed, I will bless God while I have any being!

The work at Kilsyth seems to be owned by all God's true servants as not the work of man, but indeed divine. What a great joy to you and to your excellent father, to have your labor thus honored of God! The Lord preserve you both from all the personal danger to your own souls which such success exposes you to!

I must not write much, having agreed to preach on Sabbath. I would often have written you when away; but you know my weakness, and I was always uncertain as to your movements. Do write me if you have time. Tell me all the good and all the bad. I know well that when Christ is nearest, Satan also is busiest. What of my elders? of my dear, established Christians? What of those who were but lambs? And what of those whom I left in darkness and in the shadow of death?

The Lord send me good news.

I shall try to be over on Thursday evening next, if I am well, and trust to join you in praising God together for all His mercy and grace and faithfulness since we parted. Whether I shall be able to resume the full work of the ministry again or no, I cannot tell. My heart still beats too much. But I shall try; and if the Lord shows me that my work in that way is done, I shall pray for submission.

Do write me speedily, for I weary to hear.

With regard to temporal things, remember I shall expect you honestly to tell how far your small salary has gone to cover your expenses. And if it has not covered them, remember I insist on your demanding as much more as will. The workman is worthy of his hire.

And now the Lord keep you humble and prayerful in secret,

and may it not be needful that you be afflicted as I have been; and may your ministry be blessed still a thousand times more! With kindest love to all my people.

———

To Miss Collier, Dundee

Riches of Christ—resemblance to Him.

Edinburgh, February 26, 1840.

I AM sorry to leave town without seeing you, but I find myself obliged to do so. A long and interesting meeting of presbytery took up the greater part of my time. I am delighted to hear that you are still keeping a little better, and fondly hope the Lord may restore you to us once more, to help us by your prayers in these trying but glorious times. I would like to have seen you once again before going back; but I must just content myself with casting you on the Lord on whom you believe. Precious friend and unchangeable priest is Christ—sweeter to you than honey and the honeycomb. How great is the goodness He hath *laid up* for them that fear Him! Just as the miser lays up money that he may feast his eyes upon it, so Christ has laid up unsearchable riches that He may supply all our need out of them. Unfathomable oceans of grace are in Christ for you. Dive and dive again, you will never come to the bottom of these depths. How many millions of dazzling pearls and gems are at this moment hid in the deep recesses of the ocean caves! But there are unsearchable riches in Christ. Seek more of them. The Lord enrich you with them. I have always thought it a very pitiful show when great people ornament themselves with brilliants and diamonds; but it is truest wisdom to adorn the soul with Christ and His graces. "Can a maid forget her ornaments, or a bride her attire? yet my people have forgotten me, days without number."

You see my pen runs on, though I fear you will hardly be able to read what I write. The Lord Jesus give you out of His fullness, and grace for grace. In a mirror you will observe that every feature of the face is reflected—both the large and small features. Now our soul should be a mirror of Christ; we should reflect every feature; for every grace in Christ there should be a counterpart grace in us. The Lord give you this; then I can ask no more for you. Your times are in His hand—Psalm 31. May you have the blessing of Asher: "As thy days, so shall thy strength be."

Farewell till we meet. Kindest regards to Miss N. and Mrs. Coutts, and believe me ever yours in lasting bonds.

To Mr. J. T. Just

How to conduct prayer meetings.

March 27, 1840

I WAS GLAD to receive your letter, and am happy to answer you on the matter in which you apply to me. No person can be a child of God without living in secret prayer; and no community of Christians can be in a lively condition without unity in prayer. In Daniel's time you see how it was (Dan. 2:17, 18). You see what Jesus said to His disciples on it (Matt. 18:19), and what a sweet promise of His presence and a gracious answer He connects with meeting for prayer. You see how it will be in the latter day (Zech. 8:21), when meetings for prayer, or at least concerts for prayer, shall be held by different towns.

One great rule in holding them is, that they be really meetings of disciples. If four or five of you that know the Lord would meet together regularly, you will find that far more profitable than a meeting open to all. In an open meeting you are apt to become teachers, and to be proud. In a secret meeting you feel all on a level, poor and needy, seeking water. If a young man, acquainted with any of you, becomes concerned about his soul, or a lively Christian is visiting any of you, these may be admitted; but do not make your meeting more open.

The prayer meeting I like best is where there is only praise and prayer, and the reading of God's Word. There is then least room for frail human nature to pervert the meeting to an improper end. It is well to read regularly through a book of Scripture, or at least to fix the chapter the evening before, that it may be prayed over in secret, before coming to the meeting. If you *only read,* then two chapters may be read, and then two members pray at a meeting. Each member would take his turn. Let there be no presiding of one over another, for all are brethren. When a godly minister or elder or experienced Christian is visiting you, he should be invited to take the whole service.

Many meetings are not contented with merely reading God's Word; they fix upon some verse or two as matter of conversation, and each one gives his opinion round. Some take a question of the Shorter Catechism each evening, and speak on it in the same manner. Some propose cases of conscience, and how Christians ought to act in different cases. Now, I never forbid any of these where the members prefer this; still, I must confess I feel the danger to which they are exposed. You require more grace to be kept humble and meek and loving, if you engage in this service. You are exposed to the danger of differing from one another—disputing, seeking admiration and pre-eminence, to all which you know, dear John, your hearts are naturally most prone. If you choose any of these, the first appears the best, that of fixing on a verse or two of the chapter read. But do seek meekness in speaking together upon it.

Meet weekly, at a convenient hour. Be regular in attendance.

Let nothing keep you away from your meeting. Pray in secret before going. Let your prayers in the meeting be formed as much as possible upon what you have read in the Bible. You will thus learn variety of petition, and a Scripture style. Pray that you may pray to God, and not for the ears of man. Feel His presence more than man's. Pray for the outpouring of the Spirit on the Church of Christ and for the world; for the purity and unity of God's children; for the raising up of godly ministers, and the blessing of those that are so already. Pray for the conversion of your friends, of your neighbors, of the whole town. Pray for the sending of the gospel to the Jews, and to the Gentile nations.

Pride is Satan's wedge for splitting prayer meetings to pieces: watch and pray against it. If you have not the Spirit of God among you, you will have the spirit of the devil. Watch against seeking to be greater than one another; watch against lip-religion. Above all, abide in Christ, and He will abide in you. He is able to keep you from falling, and to make you happy, holy young men. There is no joy like that of holiness. May Enoch's Companion be yours.

Write me how you come on.

TO A PARISHIONER ON A SICKBED

How cares and troubles sanctify.

March 31, 1840

I MAY not see you for a little, as I am not strong; and therefore I send you a line in answer to your letter. I like to hear from you, and especially when God is revealing Himself to your soul. All His doings are wonderful. It is, indeed, amazing how He makes use of affliction to make us feel His love more. Your house is, I trust, in some measure like that house in Bethany of which it is said, "Now Jesus loved Martha, and her sister, and Lazarus." They had different degrees of grace. One had more faith, and another more love, still Jesus loved them all. Martha was more inclined to be worldly than Mary, yet Jesus loved them both. It is a happy house when Jesus loves all that dwell in it. Surely it is next door to heaven.

The message of Martha and Mary to Christ (John 11:3) teaches you to carry all your temporal as well as your spiritual troubles to His feet. Leave them there. Carry one another's case to Jesus. Is it not a wonderful grace in God to have given you *peace in Christ,* before laying you down on your long sickbed? It would have been a wearisome time if you had been an enemy to God, and then it would have been over in hell.

Do you feel Romans 5:3 to be true in your experience? You cannot love trouble for its own sake; bitter must always be bitter, and pain must always be pain. God knows you cannot love trouble. Yet for the blessings that it brings, He can make you pray for it. Does trouble work patience in you? Does it lead you to cling closer to the Lord Jesus—to hide deeper in the Rock? Does it make you be still and know that He is God? Does it make you lie passive in His hand, and know no will but His? Thus does patience work experience— an experimental acquaintance with Jesus. Does it bring you a fuller taste of His sweetness, so that you know whom you have believed?

And does this experience give you a further hope of glory— another anchor cast within the veil? And does this hope give you a heart that cannot be ashamed, because convinced that God has loved you, and will love you to the end? Ah! then you have got the improvement of trouble, if it has led you thus. Pray for me still, that I may get the good of all God's dealings with me. Lean all on Jesus. Pray for a time of the pouring-out of God's Spirit, that many more may be saved. I hope the Lord's work is not done in this place yet.

———

To a Soul Whom He Had Never Seen, But Whose Case
Was Laid Before Him by a Friend

Colossians 2:1, 2.

Looking unto Jesus.

March 20, 1840

I DO NOT EVEN KNOW YOUR NAME, but I think I
know something of the state of your soul. Your friend has
been with me, and told me a little of your mind; and I write a
few lines just to bid you to look to Jesus and live. Look at
Numbers 21:9, and you will see your disease and your remedy.
You have been bitten by the great serpent. The poison of sin
is through and through your whole heart, but Christ has been
lifted up on the cross that you may look and live. Now, do not
look so long and so harassingly at your own heart and feelings.
What will you find there but the bite of the serpent? You
were shapen in iniquity, and the whole of your natural life has
been spent in sin. The more God opens your eyes, the more
you will feel that you are *lost in yourself.* This is your disease.

Now for the remedy. Look to Christ; for the glorious Son
of God so loved lost souls, that He took on Him a body and
died for us—bore our curse, and obeyed the law in our place.
Look to Him and live. You need no preparation, you need no
endeavors, you need no duties, you need no strivings, you only
need to look and live. Look at John 17:3. The way to be
saved is to know God's heart and the heart of Jesus. *To be
awakened,* you need to know your own heart. Look in at your
own heart, if you wish to know your lost condition. See the
pollution that is there—forgetfulness of God, deadness, insensibility to His love. If you are judged as you are in yourself,
you will be lost. *To be saved,* you need to know the heart of
God and of Christ. The four Gospels are a narrative of the
heart of Christ. They show His compassion to sinners, and

His glorious work in their stead. If you only knew that heart
as it is, you would lay your weary head with John on His
bosom. Do not take up your time so much with studying your
own heart as with studying *Christ's heart.* "For one look at
yourself, take ten looks at Christ!"

Look at Romans 15:13. That is my prayer for you. You are
looking for peace in *striving,* or peace in *duties,* or peace in
reforming your mind; but ah! look at His Word. "The God of
hope fill you with all joy and *peace in believing."* All your
peace is to be found in believing *God's Word* about His Son. If
for a moment you forget your own case altogether, and meditate on the glorious way of salvation by *Christ for us,* does
your bosom never glow with a ray of peace? Keep that peace;
it is joy in believing. Look as straight to Christ as you sometimes do at the rising or setting sun. Look direct to Christ.

You fear that your convictions of sin have not been deep
enough. This is no reason for keeping away from Christ. You
will never get a truly broken heart till you are really *in Christ.*
(See Ezek. 36:25-31.) Observe the order: *First,* God sprinkles
clean water on the soul. This represents our being washed in
the blood of Christ. *Then* He gives "a new heart also."
Third, He gives a piercing remembrance of past sins. Now,
may the Lord give you all these! May you be brought as you
are to the blood of the Lamb! Washed and justified, may He
change your heart—give you a tender heart, and His Holy
Spirit within your heart; and thus may He give you a broken
heart for your past sins.

Look at Romans 5:19. By the sin of Adam, many were
made sinners. We had no hand in Adam's sin, and yet the
guilt of it comes upon us. We did not put out our hand to the
apple, and yet the sin and misery have been laid at our door.
In the same way, "by the obedience of Christ, many are made
righteous." Christ is the glorious One who stood for many.
His perfect garment is sufficient to cover you. You had no

hand in His obedience. You were not alive when He came into the world and lived and died; and yet, in the perfect obedience, you may stand before God righteous. This is all my covering in the sight of a holy God. I feel infinitely ungodly *in myself:* in God's eye, like a serpent or a toad; and yet, when I stand *in Christ alone,* I feel that God sees no sin in me, and loves me freely. The same righteousness is free to you. It will be as white and clean on your soul as on mine. Oh, do not sleep another night without it! Only consent to stand in Christ, not in your poor self.

I must not weary you. One word more. Look at Revelation 22:17. Sweet, sweet words! "Whosoever will, let him take of the water of life freely." The last invitation in the Bible, and the freest—Christ's parting word to a world of sinners! Anyone that pleases may take this glorious way of salvation. Can you refuse it? I am sure you cannot. Dear friend, be persuaded by a fellow worm not to put off another moment. Behold the Lamb of God that taketh away the sins of the world.

You are sitting, like Hagar, within reach of the well. May the Lord open your eyes, and show you all that is in Christ! I pray for you, that you may spiritually see Jesus and be glad— that you may go to Him and find rest.

REV. W. C. BURNS

A minister's afflictions to be improved.

June 10, 1840

I AM TRULY THANKFUL that you have been raised up again—renewed, I trust, both in the inner and outer man. "I will cause you to pass under the rod, and I will bring you into the bond of the covenant." Sweet rod that drives the soul into such a precious restingplace! "I will visit their iniquity with stripes; nevertheless, my loving-kindness I will not take from him." This has been the experience of the greater part of my life, at least of my spiritual life. Remember Edwards' magnificent resolution: "Resolved to improve afflictions to the uttermost." Spread the sail when the breeze of adversity blows, and let it drive your vessel onwards on its course.

When I was laid aside from the ministry, I felt it was to teach me the need of prayer for my people. I used often to say, Now God is teaching me the use of prayer. I thought I would never forget the lesson, yet I fear I am grown slack again when in the midst of my work.

All these remarks I have transferred to myself, that you may learn in me the same things. Exhort one another daily. My object in writing now is to say that I have engaged to be at Collessie next Wednesday, at Alloa on Thursday, and at Errol on Sabbath week. Now the people here were disappointed by your not appearing lately; and it would be very gratifying, if you are not better engaged, if the Lord would direct your steps towards us. If you would take both Thursday and the Sabbath, it would be pleasant to me. I have been weakened a little by the hard labors of the Assembly, but I trust to recruit shortly for our glorious warfare. I feel there are two things it is impossible to desire with sufficient ardor—personal holiness, and the honor of Christ in the salvation of souls.

The Lord give you both more than He has given me, and may He send you to us, if it be His will. Send me a line quickly, and believe me, ever yours in sweet bonds.

To Rev. Dan Edwards

Before his ordination as missionary to the Jews. What he must seek.

Dundee, June 15, 1840

THE GRAND MATTER of study, however, must still be divinity,—a knowledge of divine things, a spiritual discernment of the way of pardon for the chief of sinners. I feel that the best of ministers are but babes in this. Pray for more knowledge of your own heart—of the total depravity of it, of the awful depths of corruption that are there. Pray for glorious discoveries of Christ, His person, beauty, work, and peace. But I need not tell you these things; only I feel persuaded that God will put all natural and literary qualifications in the dust, if there be not the simple exhibition of Christ for us in the preaching of our missionaries.

To Rev. Dan Edwards

Holiness and success.

Dundee, October 2, 1840

I TRUST you will have a pleasant and profitable time in Germany. I know you will apply hard to German; but do not forget the culture of the inner man—I mean of the heart. How diligently the cavalry officer keeps his sabre clean and sharp; every stain he rubs off with the greatest care. Remember you are God's sword, His instrument—I trust a chosen vessel unto Him to bear His name. In great measure, according to the purity and perfections of the instrument, will be the success. It is not great talents God blesses so much as great likeness to Jesus. A holy minister is an awful weapon in the hand of God.

I am now almost well, but have not yet got my full strength.

We had a sweet night last night, though there was no external movement. Some waited after; one from St. Andrews, awakened deeply, she knows not how. God is still working here, and I look for far greater things. I am very anxious to know how I could do more good to many people and to the whole world; and not to know only, but to do it. It is our truest happiness to live entirely for the glory of Christ—to separate between "I" and "the glory of Christ." We are always saying, What have *I* done?—was it *my* preaching—*my* sermon—*my* influence? whereas we should be asking, What hath God wrought? Strange mixed beings we are! How sweet it will be to drop our old man, and be pure as Christ is pure! I hope you will come and see us again before your departure for your mission station. The Lord direct all your steps, comfort your heart, and stablish you in every good word and work to do His will.

To Mrs. Thain, Heath Park

When invited to rest a while.

Dundee, June 1840

YOU KNOW how glad I would be of some such retreat as Elijah had by the brook of Cherith, where I might learn more of my own heart, and of my Bible, and of my God, where I might while away the summer hours in quiet meditation, or talking of His righteousness all the day long. But it is only said of *the dead* in the Lord that they rest from their labors; and I fear I must not think of resting till then. Time is short, my time especially, and souls are precious; and I fear many are slumbering because I watch not with sufficient diligence, nor blow the trumpet with sufficient clearness.

I have to be away so much on business, that I feel I dare not be away on pleasure only—at least at present. I rather think I must be in Ireland next week, at the Synod of Ulster, which prevents me coming to Mr. Macdonald's communion.

There is some request as to another communion in St. Peter's also, which I shall be glad to see carried into effect, provided it be done with all the heart of the Lord's children. In these circumstances, you must not think me neglectful of your kindness, if I put off my visit to you a little longer.

I trust that you are keeping strong, and able to enjoy the open air, and that your souls all prosper, that you have often such times as Jacob had at Mahanaim, when the angels of God met him, or such times as that at Peniel, when God had to cry out, "Let me go, for the day breaketh." Alas, we do not weary God now with our wrestlings, but with our sins. The dark clouds gather, and the Church and we should all be entering into our chambers, and shutting our doors upon us. "In that day sing ye unto her, A vineyard of red wine." His song will be with us in the dark night. May you and yours be hid in the day of the Lord's anger! A smile of His can lighten up a thundercloud.

Read Psalm 29 and meditate on the last verse. Live near to God, and so all things will appear to you little in comparison with eternal realities.

To a Stranger

Intended to lead on one whose face was Zionward, but who was not fully decided.

Dundee, July, 1840

I DO NOT even know your name; but your cousin has been telling me about your case, and wishes me to write you a line inviting you to lay hold on Jesus Christ, the only refuge for a perishing soul. You seem to have been thinking seriously of your soul for some time. Do remember the words of Peter (II Pet. 1:10), "Give diligence to make your calling and elec-

tion sure." Never rest till you can say what John says (I John
5:19), *"We know* that we are of God." The world always
loves to believe that it is impossible to know that we are converted. If you ask them, they will say, "I am not sure—I cannot
tell"; but the whole Bible declares we may receive, and know
we have received, the forgiveness of sins. (See Ps. 32:1; I John
2:12.) Seek this blessedness—the joy of having forgiveness; it
is sweeter than honey and the honeycomb.

But where shall I seek it? In Jesus Christ. "God hath given
to us eternal life, and this life is in his Son." "He that hath the
Son hath life, and he that hath not the Son hath not life"
(I John 5:12). Get deeply acquainted with yourself, your sins
and misery. Most people are like the Laodiceans (Rev. 3:17).
Even those that are most deeply concerned about their souls do
not see the millionth part of the blackness of their hearts and
lives. Oh! if we could but put our sins where God puts them
(Ps. 90:8), how we would cry out, Unclean, unclean! Woe is
me, for I am undone! Have you ever discovered your lost condition? Many know that they are great sinners; but where God
is teaching, He will make you feel as an *undone* sinner. Have
you felt this? What things were gain to you, those do you
count loss for Christ? Do you know that no human righteousness can cover you? In His holy, pure sight, all our righteous-
nesses are as filthy rags (Isa. 64:6).

If you have been convinced of sin, have you been convinced
of righteousness (John 16:8)? Have you heard the voice of
Jesus knocking at the door of your heart? Have you opened
the door and let Him in? Awfully momentous question! Your
eternity depends upon the answer. "He that hath the Son hath
life, and he that hath not the Son hath not life." Oh, what a
simple thing the gospel is! How fearful to think it is hid from
so many (II Cor. 4:3, 4)!

Jesus stands at your door willing to be your shield (Ps. 84:9,
11); your righteousness (Jer. 33:6); your all in all. Now, then,

throw open the door and let Him in. Accept His white raiment, that you may be clothed. And oh! remember, if Christ justifies you, He will sanctify you. He will not save you and leave you in your sins. Why did He get the name Jesus? (Matt. 1:21). Here is a prayer for everyone that has been found of Christ: "Order my steps in thy word, and let not any inquity have dominion over me" (Ps. 119:133). If you are redeemed, you are not your own—not the world's—not Satan's. Think of this when you are tempted to sin.

Now, did I not say well that you should make your calling and election sure? Oh, beware of being a hypocrite, a mere professor, with an unholy heart and life. That your sister is on the road to Zion, I am glad, and pray that you may go hand in hand. Be diligent; the time is short. Try and persuade your friends to go with you. It is an awful thing to separate at the throne of Christ, for that will be for eternity. Pray much for the Holy Spirit to open your eyes, to soften your heart, to make Christ lovely and precious, to come and dwell in your hearts, and fit you for glory. Come to the Living Stone, and you will be built up as living stones (I Pet. 2:4, 5). Oh, how sweet to be made living stones in that glorious temple!

Pray much in secret. Pray for ministers that we may speak the Word boldly. Christ is doing great things in our day, which should make us wrestle at a throne of grace. Oh, that the Lord, that was pierced with many thorns, might soon be crowned with many crowns!

Praying that you and your sister may both be saved, I am, your friend in the gospel . . .

To Miss A. S. L.

The person and heart of Jesus. Consolation to believers.

August 16, 1840

I MAY NOT be able to see you for a little time, and therefore I am sending you a few lines to minister a little of the peace and grace of the Lord Jesus to you. I hear that you are worse in health than when I saw you; still I have no doubt you can say, "It is well . . . He doeth all things well." You remember Jacob said, when they wanted to take Benjamin away from him, "All these things are against me" (Gen. 42:36). But in a little while he saw that all these things were working together for good to him. In a little while all his lost children were restored to him, and he and his seed preserved from famine.

So will it be with you. If at any time unbelief steals over your heart, if you lose sight of Jesus, our Passover sacrificed for us, if you forget the hand of the all-tender gracious Father of Jesus and of your soul, you will be crying out, All these things are against me. But ah! how soon you will find that everything in your history, except *sin*, has been *for* you. Every wave of trouble has been wafting you to the sunny shores of a sinless eternity. Only believe. Give unlimited credit to our God.

Think on Jesus when your mind wanders in search of peace; think where He came from—from the bosom of His Father. He was *from the beginning*. He is the life—the life of all that truly live. He is that eternal life which was with the Father. Let the beams of the divinity of Jesus shine in upon your soul. Think how He was manifested—God manifest in the flesh—to be a Surety for sinners. Made sin for us, although He knew no sin, made a curse for us. Oh, if I could declare Him unto you, you might have fellowship with apostles, and with the Father, and with His Son, Jesus Christ. These things will we write unto you, that your joy may be full. Other joys do not fill the heart.

But to know the Lord Jesus as our Surety, satisfies the soul; it brings the soul unto rest under the eye of our pardoning God.

I met[1] the other day with a thought which has filled my heart often since. It is intended to explain that wonderful verse, John 14:18, "I will not leave you orphans: I will come to you." Jesus, at the right hand of the Father, is yet present with all His younger brethren and sisters in this vale of weeping. His *human nature* is at the right hand of God upon the throne—a Lamb as it had been slain. But His divine nature is unlimited, fills all worlds, and is present in every dwelling of every disciple in this world. His divine nature thus brings in continual information to His human heart of everything that is going on in the heart and history of His people; so that His human heart beats towards us just as if He were sitting by our side. Hence He cried to Saul, "Why persecutest thou me?"

Dear friend, do you feel that Jesus is your Surety and Elder Brother? Then remember that, by reason of His real divinity, He is now by your bedside, afflicted in all your afflictions, touched with a feeling of your infirmities, and able to save you to the uttermost. He is as really beside you as He was beside Mary when she sat at His feet. Tell Him all your sorrows, all your doubts and anxieties. He has a willing ear. Oh, what a friend is Jesus, the sinner's friend! What an open ear He has for all the wants, doubts, difficulties of His people! He has an especial care for His sick, weakly, and dying disciples. You know how it is with a kind mother, even though a worldly person. In a time of danger she clasps her children to her breast. In a time of health she may often let them wander out of her sight, but in hours of sickness she will *watch* beside their bed. *Much more* will Jesus watch over you.

I trust you feel real desire after complete holiness. This is the truest mark of being born again. It is a mark that He has made us meet for the inheritance of the saints in light. If a

---

[1] It was in a sermon by J. B. Patterson of Falkirk.

nobleman were to adopt a beggar boy, he would not only feed and clothe him, but educate him, and fit him to move in the sphere into which he was afterwards to be brought; and if you saw this boy filled with a noble spirit, you would say he is meet to be put among the children. So may you be made meet for glory. The farmer does not cut down his corn till it is ripe. So does the Lord Jesus: He first ripens the soul, then gathers it into His barn. It is far better to be with Christ than to be in Christ. For you to live is Christ, and to die is gain. Nevertheless, I trust God will keep you a little longer for our sake, that you may pray for us, and encourage us to work on in the service of Jesus till our change come.

I began this letter about two weeks ago, and now send it away to you. I was called very suddenly to Edinburgh, and then sent to the north, and am just returned again, so that I did not get it sent away. I will try to see you this week, if it be the will of God. However, you must not be disappointed if I am prevented. I pray for you, that according as your day, so your strength may be. Keep your eye upon Jesus and the unsearchable riches that are in Him; and may the gentle Comforter fill your soul, and give you a sweet foretaste of the glory that is to follow. May He leave His deep eternal impress upon your soul, not healing you and going away, but abiding within you, keeping the image of Christ in your heart, ever fresh and full— Christ in you the hope of glory. The Comforter is able to fill you with calmness in the stormiest hour. May He fill your whole soul and transform you into a child of light. Good-by till we meet, if it be the Lord's will. If not in this world, at least before the throne, casting our crowns at His feet.

———

To Rev. W. C. Burns

Awakenings. Personal holiness in ministers.

Dundee, September, 1840

I HAVE HAD a severe illness, or would have answered your kind note long before this. I fear you may have left Breadalbane before this can reach it; still I write in hope. You may be sure I ever follow you with my prayers and earnest longings of heart that God may humble, purify, and make use of you to carry glad tidings of great joy to the inmost hearts of poor, guilty, perishing sinners, wherever you go.

I have been much interested by all that I have heard of the good that has attended you in the north. I long to hear still more. The very name of Moulin stirs up the inmost depths of the heart, when I remember what great things the Lord Jesus did there of old. Do write to me when you have a moment, and stir me up. You know a word to a minister is worth a word to three or four thousand souls sometimes. Nothing stirs me up so much to be instant and faithful as hearing of the triumphs of the Lord Jesus in other places.

I am glad and thankful to say that we are not left quite desolate. There have been evident tokens of the presence of the Spirit of God among my dear people many nights, more, I think, upon the Thursday nights than on the Sabbaths. Some I have met with seemingly awakened without any very direct means. A good number of young mill-girls are still weeping after the Lord Jesus. I have been out of my pulpit only one Sabbath, and I hope to be back to it next Sabbath, if the Lord will.

What Mr. T. mentioned to you was true of some having followed after an enthusiastic kind of man, who in my absence came among them. Doubtless Satan wanted to carry off some of the sheep, and succeeded so far. Still I trust it will end in good. Some have been a good deal humbled in the dust on ac-

count of it, and I have been roused up to cry for more knowledge to guide them in the right way. I think, if strength
were restored to me, I will try, in the name of the Lord Jesus,
to catechize through my parish. I ask your advice and prayers
on this. If it could be conducted humbly and with patience and
aptness to teach, I am persuaded it would tend to ground them
more deeply in divine things. Hypocrites also might be de-
nounced and warned, and the unconverted pointedly dealt with.
I feel the immense difficulty of it in a town, and such a neglected, ignorant one as this. Still, if God were with me, who
can be against me?

Everything I meet with, and every day I study my Bible,
makes me pray more that God would begin and carry on a
deep, pure, widespread, and permanent work of God in Scotland. If it be not *deep and pure,* it will only end in confusion,
and grieving away the Holy Spirit of God by irregularities and
inconsistencies; Christ will not get glory, and the country generally will be hardened, and have their mouths filled with reproaches. If it be not *widespread,* our God will not get a large
crown out of this generation. If it be not *permanent,* that will
prove its impurity, and will turn all our hopes into shame. I
am much more afraid of Satan than I used to be. I learned a
good deal by being with Cumming in Strathbogie.

I am also deepened in my conviction, that if we are to be instruments in such a work, we must be purified from all filthiness of the flesh and spirit. Oh, cry for personal holiness, constant nearness to God by the blood of the Lamb! Bask in His
beams, lie back in the arms of love, be filled with His Spirit;
or all success in the ministry will only be to your own everlasting confusion.

You know how I have always insisted on this with you. It is
because I feel the need thereof myself. Take heed, dear friend;
do not think any sin trivial; remember it will have everlasting
consequences. Oh, to have Brainerd's heart for perfect holiness

—to be holy as God is holy, pure as Christ is pure, perfect as our Father in heaven is perfect! Oh, what a cursed body of sin we bear, that we should be obliged by it to break these sweet gospel rules! How much more useful might we be, if we were only more free from pride, self-conceit, personal vanity, or some secret sin that our heart knows! O hateful sins, that destroy our peace, and ruin souls!

But I must be done. I have not attained the full use of the pen. Go on, dear brother; but an inch of time remains, and then eternal ages roll on forever—but an inch on which we can stand and preach the way of salvation to a perishing world. May He count us faithful, keeping us in the ministry.

————

To Rev. Patrick L. Miller

Then laboring in Strathbogie, on his being elected minister of Wallacetown.

Dundee, September 18, 1840

I CANNOT TELL YOU how sincerely I thank God for the event of this evening. You are unanimously chosen minister of Wallacetown. I have already been on my knees to praise God for it, and to pray that you may be filled with the Holy Spirit for this glorious work. I hope you will see your way clear in leaving your attached people at Botriphnie. Make good use of your last days among them. Warn every man. Take each aside, and tell him you will be a witness against him at the last day if he do not turn and obey the gospel. The Lord give you a spiritual family in that place; and may you come to us in the fullness of the blessing of the gospel of Christ. I am persuaded the Spirit of God is still remarkably present in this town. You could not become a minister in a more blessed season, or in a more promising field. Oh, pray to be fitted for the arduous work! I was just praying this morning over Matthew

9:36-38, and little thinking that God was about to answer so
graciously.

I have had a severe illness of late, and been taught to look
more toward the Church above. But I am better, and my heart
warms again towards the Lord's work below. Now, farewell!
The Lord humble, empty, satisfy, and fill you—make you a
Boanerges and a Barnabas all in one. May the Lord arise, and
His enemies be scattered; and may poor parched Angus become
like the garden of the Lord.

————

To Mr. George Shaw, Belfast

Prophecies concerning Israel. Revival. Conduct of Studies.

Dundee, September 16, 1840

IT GIVES ME GREAT JOY to be able to answer your kind
letter, although I fear you have almost despaired of me.
In writing your esteemed pastor, I mentioned to him my intention of writing you very soon; but I have since then been laid
down upon a sickbed by a severe, feverish illness, from which I
am now only recovering. Like you, my dear friend, God has
seen it meet to train me often by the rod, and I have always
found that He doeth all things well. Indeed, who would have
his own health in his own guidance? Ah! how much better to
be in His all-wise, all-powerful hand, who has redeemed us,
and is making us vessels to hold His praise, now and in eternal
ages! I have been only twice in the open air, and cannot yet
manage the pen with facility; but I cannot delay writing to
you any longer.

You cannot tell how much real joy your letter gave me when
you tell me of the dear brethren who meet along with you on
Monday mornings, to read and pray concerning Israel. This is
indeed a delightful fruit of my short visit among you, for which
I give humble and hearty thanks to Him who has stirred up

your hearts in what I have felt, by experience, to be His own blessed cause. I feel deeply persuaded from prophecy, that it will always be difficult to stir up and maintain a warm and holy interest in outcast Israel. The lovers and pleaders of Zion's cause will, I believe, be always few. Do you not think this is hinted at in Jeremiah 30:13: "There is none to plead thy cause, that thou mayest be bound up"? And again, verse 14: "All thy lovers have forgotten thee; they seek thee not." And is not this one of the very reasons why God will at last take up their cause? See verse 17: "I will restore health unto thee . . . because they called thee an outcast, saying, This is Zion, whom no man seeketh after."

It is a sweet encouragement also to learn, that though the friends of Zion will probably be few, so that it may almost be said, no one seeketh after her, yet there always will be some who will keep watch over the dust of Jerusalem, and plead the cause of Israel with God and with man. See Isaiah 62:6, 7. If any of your company know the Hebrew, you will see at once the true rendering: "I have set watchmen *over* thy walls, O Jerusalem, which shall never hold their peace day nor night. *Ye that are the Lord's remembrancers,* keep not silence, and give Him no rest till He establish, and till He make Jerusalem a praise in the earth." Oh, my dear brethren, into whose hearts I trust God is pouring a scriptural love for Israel, what an honor is it for us, worms of the dust, to be made watchmen by God over the ruined walls of Jerusalem, and to be made the Lord's remembrancers, to call His own promises to His mind, that He would fulfill them, and make Jerusalem a blessing to the whole world! The first verse is supposed to be the language of our Lord Himself—our glorious Advocate with the Father. Oh, what an example does He set us of unwearied intercession! The second verse showeth the great effect which the conversion of Israel will have on the Gentile world. The third verse shows how converted Israel will be a glorious diadem in God's hand, held out to show forth His praise. The fourth verse shows that it is *literal Israel* that is spoken of, for there is a sweet promise to *their land*.

I think you must take these two verses, 6, 7, as the motto of your praying society, not in boasting, but in all humility of mind, and with much self-upbraiding for the neglect of the past. Indeed, you will find it a difficult matter to keep your heart in tune really to desire the salvation of Israel, and the widely extended glory of the Lord Jesus. You must keep in close union to Jesus, and much in the love of God, and be much filled with the infinite, almighty Spirit of God. He will help your infirmities. It is when you feel the sweetness of the kingdom of God within you, that you will truly fall down on your knees, and pray, "Thy kingdom come." The possession of grace fills us with very different feelings from the possession of anything else. A man who has much money is not very anxious that all the world should be rich; one who has much learning does not long that all the world were learned; but if you have tasted the grace of the gospel, the irresistible longing of your hearts will be, Oh, that all the world might taste its regenerating waters! And if it be true, as I think it is, that God's method of bringing in the kingdom is to be by the salvation of Israel, how can an enlightened, gracious soul but pray, "Do good in thy good pleasure unto Zion"?

As to the mode of studying prophecy, dear friend, I am far from being a capable adviser. My advice, however, is that you begin with the simple and more unquestioned parts, and then advance to the more difficult ground. Begin with fulfilled prophecy: you will thus gain an intimate acquaintance with the language and manner of the prophetic writings. Then advance to the marks of unfulfilled prophecy, and cautiously and prayerfully to those parts that are obviously unfulfilled. This would be a most interesting course, and, if humbly followed out, cannot but give you great light and interest in the cause of Israel, and the world's conversion. For fulfilled prophecy, you might follow the guidance of Keith on *Fulfilled Prophecy*, or Bishop Newton, or both.

I am delighted to hear of the thankoffering you mention. It is sweet when thankfulness does not end in mere words, but in gifts to God and devotedness of our all to Him. I am happy to say that the Lord's cause seems still to advance in Scotland. On the very day I arrived from Ireland we had very sweet tokens of the presence of the Spirit of God in the congregation, and many Thursday evenings since.

I have been in Strathbogie also, and seen some of the Lord's wonders there. He that hath the key of David has opened a door there, for the salvation of many souls. I am still as anxious as ever that God's work should be pure, and unmixed with error and satanic delusions; and, therefore, when I pray for the revival of God's work, I always add that it may be pure and permanent. I have seen two awakened since I came home, with the use of hardly any means. If they shall turn out real conversions, I think I shall never despair of any.

I trust that your own studies get on well, dear friend. Learn much of your own heart; and when you have learned all you can, remember you have seen but a few yards into a pit that is unfathomable. "The heart is deceitful above all things, and desperately wicked: who can know it?" (Jer. 17:9). Learn much of the Lord Jesus. For every look at yourself, take ten looks at Christ. He is altogether lovely. Such infinite majesty, and yet such meekness and grace, and all for sinners, even the chief! Live much in the smiles of God. Bask in His beams. Feel His all-seeing eye settled on you in love, and repose in His almighty arms.

Cry after divine knowledge, and lift up your voice for understanding. Seek her as silver, and search for her as for hid treasure, according to the word in Proverbs 2:4. See that verse 10 be fulfilled in you. Let wisdom *enter into your hearts,* and knowledge *be pleasant to thy soul;* so you will be delivered from the snares mentioned in the following verses. Let your soul be filled with a heart-ravishing sense of the sweetness and excellency of Christ and all that is in Him. Let the Holy Spirit fill every chamber of your heart; and so there will be no room for folly, or the world, or Satan, or the flesh. I must now commend you all to God and the word of His grace. My dear people are just assembled for worship. Alas! I cannot preach to them tonight. I can only carry them and you on my heart to the throne of grace. Write me soon.

———

TO HIS SABBATH SCHOOL TEACHERS, DURING A WEEK
OF ABSENCE FROM THEM

(Accompanied by notes on the Scripture lesson that was to be taught in the
classes that week.)

Kelso, February 24, 1841

I SEND YOU a few notes on the parable for next Sabbath evening. May you find them profitable. You cannot tell what a sweet comfort it is to me, when I am so far distant from my flock, to know that you are in the midst of the lambs, speaking to God for them, and speaking to them for God. I thank my God without ceasing for your work of faith, and labor of love, and patience of hope. Be not weary in welldoing, dear friends, for in due season we shall reap, if we faint not. Do not be impatient—wait on the Lord. The blessing will come. Use a few spare half-hours in seeking after the lambs on the weekdays. This will prove to the parents that you are in earnest. To bring one child to the bosom of Christ would be reward in eternity for all our pains. Oh, with what glowing hearts we shall meet in heaven those whom God has used us as humble instruments in saving! Meditate on Philippians 1:8. And may the Lord meet with you and the lambs on Sabbath day, and bless you, and do you good.

Farewell, dear fellow laborers. Ever your affectionate friend and pastor, absent in body, not in spirit.

To a Society in Blairgowrie for Diffusing the Knowledge of the Truth

Advices.

Dundee, March 27, 1841

I WAS HAPPY indeed to receive your letter, and the rules of your Society, which interested me very much. I would have answered you sooner, but have been laid down by my heavenly Father on a bed of sickness, from which I am just recovering by His grace. Spared fig trees should bear much fruit; pray that it may be so with me. Luther used to say that *temptations, afflictions,* and *prayer,* made a minister. I do trust that your Society may be greatly blessed, *first,* in the comforting, enlivening, and sanctifying of your own souls, and *then* in bringing others to know the same fountain where you have found peace and purity. Let Jesus come into your meetings and sit at the head of the table. It is a fragrant room when the bundle of myrrh is the chief thing there.

Let there be no *strife* among you, but *who* to be lowest at His feet, *who* to lean his head most fully on His breast. Let all your conversation, meditation, and readings lead you to the Lamb of God. Satan would divert your minds away to questions and old wives' fables, which gender strifes. But the Holy Spirit *glorifies* Jesus—*draws* to Jesus—*makes you cleave* to the Lord Jesus with full purpose of heart. Seek advance of personal holiness. It is for this the grace of God has appeared to you. (See Titus 2:11, 12.) For this Jesus died; for this He chose you; for this He converted you, to make you holy men—living epistles of Christ—monuments of what God can do in a sinner's heart. You know what true holiness is. It is *Christ in you, the hope of glory.* Let Him dwell in you, and so all His features will shine in your hearts and faces. Oh, to be like Jesus! This is heaven, wherever it be. I think I could be happy among devils, if only the old man were slain in me, and I was made altogether like Jesus! But, blessed be God, we shall not be called to such a trial, for we shall not only be like Jesus, but be with Him to behold His glory.

Pray to be taught to pray. Do not be content with old forms that flow from the lips only. Most Christians have need to cast their formal prayers away, to be taught to cry, Abba. Arrange beforehand what you have to pray for. Do not forget *confession of sin,* nor *thanksgiving.* Pray to get your closed lips opened in intercession; embrace the whole world, and carry it within the veil. I think you might with advantage keep a small book in which you might mark down objects to be prayed for. I pray God to make you very useful in the parish and in the world. Do all things without murmurings and disputings. (See Phil. 2:14, 16.)

Live for eternity. A few days more, and our journey is done. Oh! fight hard against sin and the devil: the devil never sleeps. Be you also active for good. The Lord bless you and your dear minister. Pray for us. Pray for the dead parishes around you.

———

LETTERS TO A SOUL SEEKING JESUS—No. I

Seek to know your corruption.

Dundee, 1841

A CCORDING to promise, I sit down to talk with you a little concerning the great things of an eternal world. How kind it is in God that He has given us such an easy way of

communicating our thoughts, even at a distance! My only reason for writing to you is, that I may direct your soul to Jesus,
the sinner's friend. "This man receiveth sinners." I would wish
much to know that you were truly united to Christ, and then,
come life, come death, you will be truly and eternally happy.

Do you think you have been *convinced of sin?* This is the
Holy Spirit's work, and His first work upon the soul. (John
16:8; Acts 2:37.) If you did not know your body was dan-
gerously ill, you would never have sent for your physician; and
so you will never go to Christ, the heavenly Physician, unless
you feel that your soul is sick even unto death. Oh! pray for
deep discoveries of your real state by nature and by practice.
The world will say you are an innocent and harmless girl; do
not believe them. The world is a liar. Pray to see yourself ex-
actly as God sees you; pray to know the worth of your soul.
Have you seen yourself *vile,* as Job saw himself (Job
42:5, 6)? undone, as Isaiah saw himself (Isa. 6:1, 5)? Have
you experienced anything like Psalm 51? I do not wish you to
feign humility before God, nor to use expressions of self-
abhorrence which you do not feel; but pray that the Holy
Spirit may let you see the very reality of your natural condition
before God!

I seldom get more than a glance at the true state of my soul
in its naked self. But when I do, then I see that I am wretched,
and miserable, and poor, and blind, and naked (Rev. 3:17). I
believe every member of our body has been a servant of sin
(Rom. 3:13, 18)—throat, tongue, lips, mouth, feet, eyes. Every faculty of our mind is polluted (Gen. 6:5). Besides, you
have long neglected the great salvation; you have been gainsaying and disobedient. Oh, that you were brought to pass sentence on yourself, *guilty of all!* Hear what a dear believer
writes of himself: "My wickedness, as I am in myself, has long
appeared to me perfectly ineffable, and swallowing up all
thought and imagination, like an infinite deluge, or mountains

over my head. I know not how to express better what my sins appear to me to be, than by heaping infinite upon infinite, and multiplying infinite by infinite. When I look into my heart and take a view of my wickedness, it looks like an abyss infinitely deep, and yet it seems to me that my conviction of sin is exceeding small and faint."

Perhaps you will ask, Why do you wish me to have such a discovery of my lost condition? I answer, that you may be broken off from all schemes of self-righteousness; that you may never look into your poor guilty soul to recommend you to God; and that you may joyfully accept of the Lord Jesus Christ, who obeyed and died for sinners. Oh, that your heart may cleave to Christ! May you forsake all, and follow Jesus Christ. Count everything loss for the excellency of the knowledge of Christ. You never will stand righteous before God in yourself. You are welcome this day to stand righteous before God in Jesus. Pray over Philippians 3:7, 9. I will try to pray for you. Grace be with you.

————

To a Soul Seeking Jesus—No. II

Seek the righteousness of Christ.

I WAS GLAD to hear of your safe arrival, and that your health had not suffered by the voyage. I trust the Lord is dealing gently with your frail body, so that your mind may get leave freely to fix itself on Jesus Christ and Him crucified. Above all, I pray that the Holy Spirit may sweetly and silently open your heart, to relish the way of salvation through the blood and obedience of Immanuel. Through this Man is preached unto you the forgiveness of sins, and by Him all that believe are justified from all things (Acts 13:38, 39).

You would be deeply concerned to hear that your roommate, ——, has been so suddenly and awfully called away. Should it not be a solemn warning to you? Oh, that you may be even now clothed in the righteousness of Jesus, so that, if you were called away, you may meet God in peace, and hear Jesus say, "Enter thou into the joy of thy Lord." In yourself you never will stand righteous before Jehovah. Psalm 143:2 answers your case. "Enter not into judgment with me," must be your cry. In your nature, in your past life, in your breaking of the holy law, in your contempt and neglect of Jesus, in your indwelling sin, God can see nothing but what He must condemn. Oh, that you would be of the same mind with God about your own soul! Do not be afraid to look upon its loathsomeness; for God offers to clothe you in Jesus Christ. "By the obedience of *one* shall many be made righteous" (Rom. 5:19). There is only *One* in all the world on whose face God can look and say, "He is altogether lovely." Jesus is that One.

Now God is willing that you and I should *hide in Jesus*. I feel at this moment that He is my righteousness. "This is his name whereby he shall be called, The Lord our Righteousness" (Jer. 23:6). I feel that the love of God shines upon my guilty soul through Jesus. This is all my peace. Your tears will not blot out sin. They do nothing but weep in hell; but that does not justify them. Your right views of the gospel will not justify you; you must be covered with a spotless righteousness. Your change of heart and of life will not justify you; it cannot cover *past sins*—neither is it perfect. Your amended life is still fearfully sinful in Jehovah's sight, and yet nothing but perfect righteousness can stand before Him.

Jesus offers you this perfect righteousness; in Him you may stand and hear God say, "Thou art all fair, my love." There is no spot in me. Do you thus look to Jesus? Do you believe the record that God has given concerning Him? Do you receive Christ with open arms? Do you cry, "My Lord and my God—my Surety, my all?" Dear friend, do not tarry. Eternity may be near. *Now* is your best time, perhaps your only time, of closing with Christ. How many worlds would a lost soul in hell give for such an opportunity of cleaving to Christ as you have now! "He that hath the Son hath life." This is all my prayer and desire for your precious, precious soul.

To a Soul Seeking Jesus—No. III

Joy in believing.

I SEND YOU another line to tell you Jesus is *the way*. I would like much to hear how your weak body prospers, and whether your soul is resting under the apple tree (S.S. 2:3); but till some opportunity occurs, I must just content myself with committing your soul and body into the hand of Jesus, your faithful Creator (I Pet. 4:19). We are now looking forward to another communion season, and I am busy instructing young persons for that holy and blessed ordinance. I think you said you were a good deal impressed at our last communion, and wished that you had been one of those seated at the Table: perhaps you may never be permitted to sit at the Table on earth; perhaps your first communion may be in glory.

There is a text in Romans 15:13, which expresses all my desire for you: "Now the God of hope fill you with all joy and peace in believing, that you may abound in hope, through the power of the Holy Ghost." You see here who is the author of conversion—"the God of hope." He must open your heart to attend to the things that are spoken. The truths that are presented to you will not convert your heart; the God of hope must breathe on your heart and water it oft.

Then see how He gives you joy and peace—"in believing." When Jesus revealed himself to Thomas (John 20:28), Thomas cried out with joy, "My Lord and my God!" If Jesus reveals Himself to you in all the glory of His person, the

completeness of His work, and the freeness of His love, you
too will be filled with appropriating, joyful faith, and will
cry, "My Lord and my God!" It is a difficult thing to explain what it is to believe—I suppose it is impossible. But
when Jesus unveils His matchless beauty, and gives you a
sweet glimpse of His matchless face that was buffeted and
spit upon, then the soul joyfully clings to Him. This is
believing, and this is joy and peace in believing.

The truest, purest joy flows from a discovery of Jesus Christ.
He is the hidden treasure that gives such joy to the finder
(Matt. 13:44). Do you think you have found that treasure?
Touching question! for if not, you are poor indeed. But
how much joy may you have in Christ? "The God of hope
fill you with all joy." You need not be afraid to take the
full joy that Jesus gives. If you really come unto Christ, you
come unto the love of Jehovah, and that is a filling love. The
love of the creature does not fill the heart; but God's love
coming full upon the soul gives fullness of joy (I John 1:4).
It is holy love, sovereign love. I have been interrupted several
times in writing this little note. I will not be long in writing
you again. Do decide the question of your eternity. One
thing is needful: have you closed with the great Mediator?
Have you a saving knowledge of Jesus? Then only will death
lose its power, and the grave become the bed of peaceful rest.

> There is a land of pure delight,
> Where saints immortal reign;
> Infinite day excludes the night,
> And pleasures banish pain.

Lean all your care for time and eternity on Jesus; that is the
softest of all pillows—the bosom of our guardian Immanuel.

To a Soul Seeking Jesus—No. IV

Taste that Christ is precious.

December, 1841

IT IS WRITTEN, *"Unto you who believe He is precious";*
and if you are a child of God, you will know and feel
what the words mean (I Pet. 2:7). At one time Christ was
"like a tender plant" to you, and like "a root out of a dry
ground." You saw "no form nor comeliness in him, no
beauty that you should desire him." At that time you were
at ease in Zion—you had no concern for your soul Do you
remember that time? Is it otherwise with you now? Have
you been pricked in your heart by the Holy Spirit? Have you
been made to see how impossible it is for man to be just with
God? And has the Spirit drawn away the veil from the fair
face of Immanuel, and given you an unfeigned glance at
the brow that was crowned with the thorns, and the cheek from
which they plucked off the hair?

Has the Spirit opened a window into the heart of Jesus,
and let you see the fountainhead of that love that "passeth
knowledge"? Then you will be able to say, "To me *He is
precious."* If you see plainly that all your standing before
God is in Him, that He is your foundation-stone, your fountain, your wedding garment, then you will feel Him to be
precious. Most people refuse to come to Christ. Read Luke
14:16-24. They all with one consent began to make excuse.
Why is this? Just because they do not see and feel that He
is precious. But oh! if you, my dear friend, feel that He is
your only righteousness, your only fountain of living water,
your High Priest, your Shepherd, your Advocate, then you
will say, *"He is precious!"* You will never say, "Have me
excused." I carry to you the sweet invitation, "Come, for all
things are now ready." Jesus is ready to wash and clothe
you in His own blood and righteousness. The Holy Spirit

is ready to come into your heart and make it new. The Father is ready to put His arms around your neck and kiss you (Luke 15:20). The angels are ready to give thanks for you, and to love you as a sister for eternity.

Now, will you come, for *all things are ready?* Are you now saying in your heart, "I cannot but believe I am the chief of sinners, and Jesus offers to be my refuge, my Mediator, my all in all; I feel He is precious"? Oh! dear friend, I trust you do. This only will make you happy in living, and blessed in dying. This is a poor, dying world. Man that is born of a woman is of few days and full of trouble. There is no part here that death cannot take from us. But if you have Christ, you have the only imperishable portion! Oh, may the Holy Spirit give you a firm hold of Jesus! Then we shall meet in that sweet place, where there shall be no more death, neither sorrow nor crying, neither shall there be any more pain. The Lord deal kindly and gently with you, both soul and body. Farewell, dear friend.

To a Soul Seeking Jesus—No. V

Be found in Christ.

December 8, 1841

I SEND YOU another line to tell you of Him who is altogether lovely. I have a very dear boy in my parish, who is dying just now. He said to me the other day, "I have just been feeding for some days upon the words you gave me, 'His legs are like pillars of marble set upon sockets of fine gold' (S.S. 5:15); for (said he) I am sure He is able to carry me and all my sins." You may say the same, if your eyes have been opened to see the beauty, fullness, freeness, and compassion of the Lord Jesus. Nothing but the hand of God can open your eyes to see your lost condition as it truly is.

Flesh and blood cannot reveal Him unto you, but my Father. Oh! call upon Him to do this for you. A spiritual discovery of yourself and of Jesus is better than a million of worlds to you, and to me also.

Remember, you cannot be fair in yourself before God. Song of Solomon 1:6 must be all your prayer: *"Look not upon me."* Take yourself at your best moments, you are but a vile worm in Jehovah's sight, and so am I. Remember, you may be "perfect in Christ Jesus." Allow yourself to be found in Christ. Oh! what will come of you if you are found in yourself? Where will you appear? You will shrink back, and call on rocks and mountains to fall upon you and cover you. But if you are hiding in Jesus—if your eye and heart are fixed upon His wounds made by our sins—if you are willing to be righteous in His righteousness, to lie down under the stream of His blood, and to be clothed upon with the snowy fleece of the Lamb of God—then God will love you with His whole soul exceedingly. The pure, full love of God streams through the blood and obedience of Jesus to every soul that is lying under them, however vile and wretched in themselves.

Have you tried—have you tasted the holy love of a holy God? Thy love is better than wine. It is better than all creature love or creature enjoyments. Oh! do not live—oh! do not die, out of this sweet, sweet, sin-pardoning, soul-comforting love of God! Remember, Jesus is quite willing to gather you under His wings (Matt. 23:37). Put that beyond all doubt. Remember also, the present is your only time to be saved (Eccles. 9:10). There is no believing, no repenting, no conversion in the grave—no minister will speak to you there. This is the time of conversion. We must either gain you now, or lose you forever. Oh, that you would use this little time! Every moment of it is worth a world. Your soul is very dear to me—dearer far to Jesus. Look to Him and you will be saved.

To a Soul Seeking Jesus—No. VI

Go up, leaning on Jesus.

I HAVE HEARD OF YOU from ——, and have been praying for you, that your eye may rest on Jesus, and that
your soul may lie in perfect peace under His blood shed
for the sins of many. I have been thanking my Father, too,
for dealing so bountifully with you. "He is the Father of
mercies, and the God of all comforts." I will give you a sweet
verse to meditate upon: "Who is this that cometh up from
the wilderness, leaning upon the beloved?" (S.S. 8:5). Do
you think this is your position?

Truly this world is a wilderness if you have seen it rightly.
It is a place of guilt and shame. Every natural heart is a
wilderness—a dead place without a drop of living water; and
then all natural hearts put together make up a wilderness
world. The whole world lieth in wickedness. There are few
that know and love Jesus, and these few are panting to get
more of the living water. But if you have truly fled to
Jesus, you are coming up from the wilderness. Now is our
salvation nearer than when we believed. "The night is far
spent, the day is at hand."

Have you found Jesus truly? Do you feel willing to be
all vile, all hell-deserving in yourself, and to let God's dear
Son be all your shield and righteousness? Oh! make sure of
this. Never mind what *man* thinks of you. I would not give
a straw for the opinions of men, as to whether I was safe or
no. It is not what man thinks of us that will cover us on
the judgment day. Oh no! You must be in Jesus, sitting at
His feet, allowing Him to wash your stains away, allowing
Him to enwrap your guilty soul in divine righteousness.

If you were lying at the bottom of the sea, no eye could
see your deformities: so when the infinite ocean of Immanuel's
righteousness flows over the soul, you are swallowed up as

it were in Christ. Your blackness is never seen, only His
fairness; and thus a God of truth can say, "Behold thou
art fair; behold thou art fair, my love. Thou art all fair, my
love; there is no spot in thee" (S.S. 4:1-7). Keep this always
in memory; and when guilt comes on the conscience, as it
will, lie down again beneath the righteousness of Jesus. Never
lose sight of this.

Jesus must be seen by the Father instead of our guilty soul.
It is no change in our black soul that is to be our covering.
You must leave self, and stand in your Elder Brother. Hide
behind Him. Let the Father's eye fall on Him, not on you.
This is what Jesus wants. He died to be a shelter for such
as you. This is what the Father wants; for He is not willing
that any should perish. If you are seen by the Father a naked,
guilty sinner, you must die; there is no help for it.

But if Jesus appear for you—if you hide in His wounds
like the dove in the clefts of the rock, and under His snowy
raiment—then the Father Himself loveth you, and now you
are coming up from the wilderness. Every hour that strikes,
that is an hour less between you and glory. Oh! do not grieve
to part with the world if you are in Christ: an hour with
Christ will make up for all your griefs and pains. Half an
hour in the presence of our God will make us forget a lifetime of agony. "Leaning on her beloved!"

Is this the position of your soul? Do you feel empty, weak,
and helpless; and do you see Him mighty to save, able to
save to the uttermost? "His legs are like pillars of marble."
This is Christ's glory, that He justifies sinners who have no
righteousness, and sanctifies souls that have no inborn holiness. Let Jesus bear your whole weight. Remember, He
loves to be the only support of the soul. He is a jealous Saviour. He wants to be entirely trusted.

There is nothing that you can possibly need but you will
find it in Him. *"All my springs are in thee."* Do you want

righteousness? He has the spirit of a weaned child to give you
(Ps. 131). Do you want love? He is the fountain of love: all
the promises of God in Him are yea and in Him amen. I
am sure, if you get a glimpse of Him, you would lay your
head in His breast and die there. May the Spirit anoint your
eyes to see Him more and more, and soften your heart to lean
on Him. Those that have leaned on Him through the wilderness shall sit with Him on the throne (Rev. 3:21). Farewell,
dear soul! the Lord feed you sweetly, as He feeds the flowers,
by silent drops of dew.   _____

To the Members of a Prayer Meeting

Parable of the sower.

I T HAS BEEN a matter of great joy to me to hear that
you meet together from time to time to read the Word of
God and pray—to pray for a blessing on yourselves and
families, that you may be brought to the saving knowledge of
the Lord Jesus Christ, and to pray for ministers, that they
may be filled with the Holy Spirit, and made insatiably greedy
for the salvation of souls, and that the Word of God preached
on the Sabbath may rise and be glorified till the whole world
bow the knee at the name of Jesus.

Oh, you that have had your eyes opened to see your lost
condition by nature and by wicked works, you that have been
drawn by the Father to believe in Jesus, to wash in the blood
of the Lamb, and to put on the righteousness of God—oh!
pray with all your heart that your dear friends may be brought
to take the peace you feel, that your enemies may be brought
to the same Saviour, and that all the world may be brought
to know Him, whom to know is life eternal.

If you look at Matthew 13:3-9, you will see how much of
our preaching is in vain, and what need there is to pray that
God would open the hearts we speak to.

Many among you, I fear, are like the hard wayside, so that, when the seed falls, it cannot get into your hearts, and the devil plucks it all away (v. 3, 4). Is it not true that some of your hearts are like the footpath, trodden all the week by wicked thoughts? *"Free passage this way"* is written over your hearts—common worldly thoughts—busy, covetous desires of money—malicious thoughts—impure, abominable thoughts. Oh, who can tell what a constant thoroughfare of wicked imaginations is passing night and day through every unconverted mind! Oh, look at Genesis 6:5, and weep over the Bible description of your own hard hearts.

Now, when you come to the church on Sabbath, your heart is like a footpath; the seed cannot fall in, it lies upon the surface. You do not understand the minister. Perhaps he preaches of the desperate wickedness of the heart, and the danger you are in of going to hell if you be not born again. You feel it to be a dry subject, and turn your head away. Perhaps he is preaching of the love of Jesus, in tasting death for every man; and that He will in no wise cast the vilest sinner out. Still you feel no interest, and perhaps you fall asleep during the sermon. Oh, you are the wayside hearers, the devil plucks all the seed away.

When you turn your back on the church, you turn your back on divine things; and before you have got halfway home, the devil has carried off every word of the sermon. Yea, often, I fear, before you have got a sight of your own cottage, or the trees before the door, the devil has filled your hearts with abominable, worldly thoughts, and your tongue with evil talk, unworthy of the Sabbath. O Satan, Satan! what a cunning fiend thou art! Even when the hard hearts will not receive the Word, thou wilt not suffer it to remain; lest it should come back in a time of sickness or danger, thou carriest all away.

Dear believers, pray that it be not so with you, nor with

your friends; pray for a soft heart and a retentive memory; and often speak together of the sermons you hear, and get them harrowed into your hearts, that Satan may be cheated, and your soul saved.

Many, I fear, among you, are receiving the seed into stony places (Matt. 13:6)—receiving the Word for a while, but soon withering away in time of persecution. I fear there may be some among you who are charmed with something about the gospel, instead of cleaving in heart to Christ. I can imagine that some of the wounded Israelites, that were bitten by the serpent, were much taken with Moses, as he held up the brazen serpent, instead of looking at the serpent itself. Many are fond of ministers, who are not fond of Christ. Read over Ezekiel 33:30-32, and pray that this be not your case.

Now, I will give you two marks, by which you may know whether you are one of these unfruitful hearers. *First*, The *rocky heart* will remain the same. If you find that your liking to the gospel is from the surface, from curiosity, or fancy, or love to a minister—if you find that your rocky heart has never been broken by conviction of sin, has never melted to flow towards Jesus—then you are an empty professor; you have a name to live, while you are spiritually dead.

Second, You will endure for a while. A really converted soul is like a branch. "I am the vine, ye are the *branches.*" It will cleave to it summer and winter. But if you have only a mock conversion, you will wither away when persecution comes. God knows how soon days of trial may come in Scotland. Be ye therefore ready. He that endureth to the end shall be saved. I fear, dear friends, that many of you receive the seed among thorns (Matt. 13:7). Look into your heart and see, when you read your Bible in the morning, how many cares and anxieties are dancing before your eyes, so that you can hardly see the page you are reading. How often you come to the house of God, and you see the minister preaching of eternal things with all his might; but your heart is stuffed full of cares, and plans, and pleasures. Alas, alas! the world has got the first hold of your heart, and so you can think of nothing else. What will it profit you if you gain the whole world and lose your own soul?

One thing is plain, that thorns and wheat cannot grow on the same spot of ground; so that, if you will keep to your thorns, you must burn with them. Oh, dear souls, if you got but a glimpse of the beauty of Jesus, you would leave all and follow Him! If you got but a taste of the sweetness of forgiveness, you would count everything else but loss for the excellence of the knowledge of Christ. See how Matthew did (Matt. 9:9). He was once as worldly as yourselves, and as greedy of money as any one of you; and yet a word from the sweet mouth of Christ made him leave all. Read that sweet command of Christ (Matt. 10:37, 38). Oh! pray to be made willing to leave all for Christ. He is kinder than father or mother—more precious than son or daughter. Take up your cross, then, and follow Him.

Last of all, I trust there are some among you like the good ground (Matt. 13:8), who receive the Word into a heart broken up by the Spirit of God, watered by prayer, and who bear fruit unto *life eternal*. Have you had your hearts broken, dear friends? Has God ploughed up your hard, unbelieving hearts? Have you had real concern for your perishing soul? Have you been driven to your knees? Have you ever wept in secret for your sins? Have you been made to tremble under your load of guilt? Do you come thus to the house of God, *your heart like an open furrow, waiting for the seed?* Inquire earnestly whether the fallow ground of your heart has ever been broken up (Jer. 4:3). *A broken heart alone can receive a crucified Christ.*

Have you understood the gospel? Have you believed the

record that God has given concerning His Son? Do you feel that it is true that God is love? that Christ has died, the just for the unjust? that He is beckoning you to come to Him? Do you believe on the Son of God? He that believeth shall be saved; he that believeth not shall be damned (Mark 16:16).

Do you bear fruit? Without holy fruit all evidences are vain. How vain would it be to prove to a farmer that his fields were good and productive, if they produced no corn! You might say to him, "Neighbor, your land is good; the soil is dry and well trenched." "Oh! but," he would say, "where is the yellow grain—where are the full ears falling before the sickle of the reaper?" Dear friends, you have awakenings, enlightenings, experiences, a full heart in prayer, and many due signs; but if you want holiness, you will never see the Lord. If you are a drinker, a swearer, a liar, a lascivious talker, a wanton, a slanderer, you are in the broad way that leads to destruction.

Read Matthew 7:21-23, and pray that you may not be deceiving your own souls. Dear believers, pray that you may bear fruit an hundredfold. Do not be content with bearing thirtyfold or sixtyfold; pray to be *sanctified wholly* (I Thess. 5:23). Pray that the whole lump may be leavened (Matt. 13:33). Pray that, day or night, in company or alone, Sabbath and weekday, you may adorn the doctrine of God our Saviour in all things. I often pray for you all, and desire that in secret, and in your families, you will not forget me.

To E. R.

A sight of corruption drives to Christ.

Dundee, 1842

I SEND YOU A HURRIED LINE, and may the Spirit accompany it with His divine power to your heart! It is a good thing to be shown much of the deceitfulness and desperate wickedness of your heart, provided it lead you to the Lord Jesus, that He may pardon and subdue it. Slightness and carnal ease are much more to be dreaded than discoveries of our leprosy.

The groans and triumphal song of a believer are not far separated, as you may see in Paul, Romans 7:24, 25: "O wretched man," and "I thank God," all in one breath! David felt the same (Ps. 73). At one verse he feels himself a fool and a beast in the sight of a holy God, and in the very next verses he is cleaving to Christ with a song of unspeakable joy (vv. 22-24). Ah! there is a sweet mystery here—bitter herbs along with our passover Lamb. It is sweet to see ourselves infinitely vile, that we may look to Jehovah our Righteousness, as all our way to the Father.

The sweet psalmist of Israel felt this on his dying bed: "Although my house be *not so* with God; yet hath He made with me an everlasting covenant" (II Sam. 23:5). His house had been the scene of many a black sin; and now, when dying, he could not but confess that it was not right with God. Not a day he had lived appeared clean—not a moment. So may you say in the house where you live, and looking at the pollutions of your own heart: "Although my house be not so with God"—although my heart and life be not so, yet hath He made with me an everlasting covenant, ordered in all things and sure.

God makes that covenant with you, when He brings you to

lay hold on Jesus as your Surety—your curse-bearing, law-fulfilling Surety. Then you are brought into the bond of the everlasting covenant, and all its blessings are yours—pardon, righteousness, consolation, grace upon grace, life, love, the spirit of supplications—all are yours, and you are Christ's, and Christ is God's.

Pray to be made like Caleb, who had another spirit, and followed the Lord fully. Follow Christ all the day. He is the continual burnt offering in whom you may have peace. He is the Rock that follows you, from whom you may have constant and infinite supplies. Give yourself wholly away to Him. You are safe in no other keeping but in the everlasting arms of Jehovah Jesus.

Keep yourself from other men's sins. Do not go *to the end of the string,* that is, going as far as you can in dallying with temptation without committing open sin. Remember that it is our happiness to be under grace, and every sin will be bitterness in the end, and will take something out of your eternal portion of glory.

Grace be with your dear and much honored minister, and with all that love Christ in sincerity. Never cease to pray for the parish, and for all parishes, that God would pour down His life-giving Spirit, to the conversion of perishing sinners and the glory of His own great name. I will remember you on the twelfth of June.—May the Lord remember us.

To J. T.

To a young boy anxious about his soul.

Collace, January 27, 1842

I WAS VERY GLAD to receive your kind note, and am glad to send you a short line in return, although my time is much taken up. You are very dear to me, because your soul is precious; and if you are ever brought to Jesus, washed and justified, you will praise Him more sweetly than an angel of light. I was riding in the snow today where no foot had trodden, and it was pure, pure white; and I thought again and again of that verse: *"Wash me, and I shall be whiter than snow."* That is a sweet prayer—make it your own. Often go alone and look up to Jesus, who died to wash us from our sins, and say, *"Wash me."*

Amelia Geddie was one day dressed in a new white frock, with red ribbons in her bonnet, and someone said to her, "No doubt you will think yourself very trim and clean?" "Ah! no," she said, *"I will never think that until I have the fine white robe of my Redeemer's righteousness put upon me."* I am glad, my dear boy, you think that God is afflicting you to bring you to Himself. It is really for this that He smites you. His heart, His hand, and His rod, are all inscribed with love. But then, see that He does bring you to *Himself.* Do not delay. The lake of fire and brimstone stretches beneath every soul that lives in sin. "There is no peace, saith my God, to the wicked." If the Lord Jesus would but draw the curtain and let you see His own fair face, and His wounded side, and how there is room for the guiltiest sinner in Him, you would be drawn to Jesus with the cords of love.

I was preaching in Perth last Sabbath. When I came out, a little girl came up to me, I think about three or four years old. She wanted to hear of the way to be saved. Her mother said she had been crying the whole night before about her soul, and would take no comfort till she should find Jesus. Oh! pray that the same Spirit may waken you. Remember, Johnnie, you once wept for your soul too, and prayed and sought Jesus. Have you found Him? or have you looked back, like Lot's wife, and become a hard, cold pillar of salt? Awake again, and call upon the name of the Lord. Your time may be short, God only knows. The longest lifetime is short enough. It is

all that is given you to be converted in. They are the happiest
who are brought soonest to the bosom of Jesus.

Write me again. At present I must draw to a close. Give
my kindest remembrances to your mamma, and to A. when
you write. Tell him to write me. May you all meet at the
table of Jesus above; and may I be there too, a sinner saved
by grace.   ———

To A. T.

On the death of his brother, the little boy to whom the preceding letter
was written.

St. Peter's, March 1, 1842

I DID NOT THINK I was to have answered your kind
letter in the time of bitter grief. But so it pleases Jehovah,
whose will must be our will, if we would be happy. It is good
for you to bear the yoke in your youth. This is the way God
trains His saints, and especially His ministers. I saw your dear
little brother twice on his dying bed, and indeed I could not
believe he was dying, except that his calm eye was directed to
the hills of Immortality, and he seemed already to breathe
some of the atmosphere of the world of sinless joy. I do
trust and believe that he was a saved boy. You know I am
rather slow of coming to this conviction, and not fond of
speaking when I have not good evidence; but here, I think,
God has not left us in doubt.

At Blairgowrie he used several times to speak to me about
divine things, and the tear would gather in his eye when he
said that he feared he had never been brought to Jesus. Once,
when he had a sore throat, he told me he was not ready to die.
But now he was quite different. The veil seemed to be lifted
away from his heart, and he saw divine things simply and fully.

Over and over he told me that he was not afraid to die, for
Christ had died. "How kind it was in God to send Jesus to

die for sinners." He seemed tranquil and happy, even when
the pain came on in his head and made him knit his brows.
You have reason to mingle praise with your tears. Do not
sorrow as one who has no hope. Only seek a right improvement of this bereavement. He is not lost, but gone before,
and we shall soon put off this clay cottage also. And soon we
and he, made new, body and soul, shall meet the Lord in the
air, and so be forever with the Lord. I was at your house on
Sabbath night, and saw them all—sorrowful, yet rejoicing.
Your dear little brother lies like a marble statue in the peaceful sleep of death, till Jesus' voice shall waken him. Happy
boy! he shall hunger no more, neither thirst any more, neither
shall the sun light on him, nor any heat. The days of his
mourning are ended, and his eternity of love and holy joy is
begun.

Improve this sharp wind, dear A., for you will soon lose the
benefit, if not carefully sought after. Search out the Achan in
your heart at such an hour. Let affliction strike heavy blows at
your corruptions, your idolatries, and self-pleasing and *worldly
schemes*. Learn much of Christ at such an hour. Study Him at
the grave of Lazarus (John 11); and at the gate of Nain (Luke
7); and also within the veil (Rev. 1:18). Do not be
ashamed to grieve deeply; but let your sadness find relief in
the bosom that was pierced with the spear.

"Is any afflicted? let him pray." Strange, Satan often tempts
us to restrain prayer at such a time. Be very gentle towards
the souls of your kindred now.

Remember D. and H. at the throne of grace. If God had
taken them, where would they have been? Learn also that
ministers must care for lambs. "Preach the gospel to every
creature."

Pray for me, also, that I may do so, that I may be made a
better man and a more faithful pastor of old and young.

To Rev. H. Bonar, Kelso

Ministerial arrangements. Breathings after holiness.

August 18, 1842

I LAID ASIDE YOUR NOTE, and cannot find it again. I think you asked me for the second Sabbath of November, on my way back from London. I fear I must not do it, but abide by my former arrangement. Mr. Hamilton presses me hard to stay two Sabbaths, and I would have agreed, but am to elect elders on the second Sabbath of November. According to the new law of the church, the signed lists are read in a meeting of session on the third Sabbath after the intimation is given, so that I will need to be back, even though I should need to be in Edinburgh the week after. If spared then, I shall hold to our former arrangement.

We have had a very sweet season here during the concert, which was also our communion week. Andrew, Candlish, Cormick, Cumming, Milne, and Graham from Ireland, all assisted me. We had meetings every morning.

Your scheme was very helpful; I enclose mine. About seven hundred people attended each morning; and on the fast-day, and Sabbaths too. Several souls have been deeply awakened.

I have great desire for personal growth in faith and holiness. I love the Word of God, and find it sweetest nourishment to my soul. Can you help me to study it more successfully? The righteousness of God is all my way to the Father, for I am the chief of sinners; and were it not for the promise of the Comforter, my soul would sink in the hour of temptation.

Did you observe that the Charlinch Revival took place in the week of the concert for prayer last year?

The trials of the church are near. May we be kept in the shadow of the Rock. Farewell! May Jesus shine on you.

To Rev. R. Macdonald, Blairgowrie

Inward life. Words of counsel.

Dundee, 1842

THIS IS Friday evening, and I do not know what to preach on Sabbath next, else I would have written you at greater length; but as I am to see you so soon face to face, there is the less need of communing with ink and pen.

I hope your health keeps good, and your labors abundant; that you have a continued interest in the blood which speaketh peace, a sense of forgiveness and acceptance in the Beloved; that you feel "his right hand under your head," and the power of His indwelling Spirit dwelling in you and walking in you. These sweet experiences alone make the minister's life calm and serene, like this autumnal evening. Ah! how easy it is to speak or write about them! What a different thing to feel them! It is my constant desire, and yet I am constantly disappointed. I think I never was brought to feel the wickedness of my heart as I do now. Yet I do not feel it as many sweet Christians do, while they are high above it, and seem to look down into a depth of iniquity, deep, deep in their bosoms. Now, it appears to me as if my feet were actually in the miry clay, and I only wonder that I am kept from open sin. My only refuge is in the word, "I will put my Spirit within you." It is only by being made a partaker of the *divine nature* that I can escape the corruption that is in the world through lust.

All things go on here much as they did. I cannot say that my sermons are much shorter, though I have tried to shorten them. My meeting is still an hour and a half, nor do I see how I can shorten it. It is very well attended. A stranger started up and prayed one evening. I did not interrupt him, or take notice of it, but have thought it best to forbid it. None but ordained servants should speak in churches.

I hope you have got all your preparations well forward. Deal faithfully by all that speak to you for the communion, especially the young. If you would have a clear conscience, none but those who are seeking really to close with Jesus Christ should be allowed to take the bread and wine, if a word of yours can help it.

Be decided in keeping back the scandalous. Stir up your elders to this. They are very apt to be remiss. May you have much grace given you at this time, and peace—droppings of the Spirit, and refreshings of peace in the heart. I invite all who have any wish to speak to their minister before communicating, to do so. May you have much fruit at this time that shall appear many days hence! I have been surprised to find even a poor table service blessed. Expect much, and much will be given. Pray for me, for I am all but desolate.

To One of His Flock, Who Had Been Appointed to the Charge of a Girls' School in the Country

Do what you can.

Collace, July 25, 1842

I HAVE BEEN LAID ASIDE for a short time, and did not receive your letter till it was too late to send the communicant's line, which you desired. I have no doubt Mr. B. would give you a token, however, even without a line. I am truly glad to hear that you are so fully employed, and earnestly trust that your labors may be owned by God. Souls are perishing every day, and our own entrance into eternity cannot be far distant. Let us, like Mary, "do what we can," and no doubt God will bless it, and reward us openly. Sit under a living ministry if you can. Seek much personal holiness and likeness to Christ in all the features of His blessed character.

Seek to be lamblike, without which all your efforts to do good to others will be as sounding brass or a tinkling cymbal.

Pray for dear St. Peter's, that the dew may never cease to fall there; continue in prayer, and watch in the same with thanksgiving.

To One Awakened

Call upon a soul to choose Jesus.

Dundee, September, 1842

I WAS GLAD INDEED to see, by the line you sent me, that though your mind is dark and troubled, you have not gone back to the world. Ah, it is a false, deceiving world! It smiles only to betray. Fain would I lead you to taste the peace that passeth understanding, and that is only to be found in Jesus. You are quite wrong in thinking that I do not understand your misery. I know it well. It is true Jesus does give me peace. He washes me from all sin in His own blood. I often feel Him standing by my side and looking down upon me, saying, "Thou art mine."

Yet still I have known more misery than you. I have sinned more deeply than you. I have sinned against more light and more love, and yet I have found mercy; why may not you? Remember what James Covey said: "Tell poor sailors that none of them need to despair, since poor blaspheming Covey found mercy."

I was interrupted just while writing this, by a very little girl coming to ask, "What must I do to be saved?" Poor thing, she has been weeping till I though her heart would break. She lives several miles off; but a companion was awakened and told her, and ever since she has been seeking Christ with all her heart. I was telling her that sweet verse:

"Christ Jesus came into the world to save sinners, of whom I am the chief" (I Tim. 1:15). It will answer you also, dear friend.

Christ Jesus was God's dear Son. He made all things—sun, moon, and stars, men and angels. He was from all eternity in the bosom of the Father, and yet He came into the world. He did not say, "I will keep my throne and my happiness, and leave sinners to die and perish in their sins." No; "He came into the world." He became a babe, and was laid in a manger, for there was not room in the inn. The inn was like your heart; it was filled with other lodgers, and had no room for Jesus. He became "a man of sorrows, and acquainted with grief." He bore our sins in His own body on the tree. While we were sinners, "Christ died for us." Why did He do all this? Ah! it was to save sinners. Not to save good people, not to save angels, but sinners.

Perhaps you will say, "But I am too bad a sinner"; but Paul says, "of whom I am the chief." Paul was the chief of sinners, and yet he was saved by Christ. So Christ is willing and able to save you, though you were the chief sinner on the face of the earth. If Christ came into this world and died to save such as you, will it not be a fearful thing if you die without being saved by Him? Surely you have lived long enough without Christ. You have despised Jesus long enough.

What has the world done for you, that you love it so much? Did the world die for you? Will the world blot out your sins or change your heart? Will the world carry you to heaven? No, no! You may go back to the world if you please, but it can only destroy your poor soul. "She that liveth in pleasure is dead while she liveth" (I Tim. 5:6). Read these words in your Bible, and mark them; and if you go back, that mark will be a witness against you before the great white throne, when the books are opened. Have you not lived long enough in pleasure?

Come and try the pleasures of Christ—forgiveness and a new heart. I have not been at a dance or any worldly amusement for many years, and yet I believe I have had more pleasure in a single day than you have had all your life. You will ask, In what? In feeling that God loves me, that Christ has washed me, and in feeling that I shall be in heaven when the wicked are cast into hell. "A day in thy courts is better than a thousand" (Ps. 84:10).

I do not know what is to be the result of your anxieties. I do not know whether you will be drawn to Christ, or driven back into the whirlpool of a perishing world; but I know that all will soon be settled for eternity. I was in a very wicked family today, where a child had died. I opened my Bible, and explained this verse to them over the coffin of their little one: "It is appointed unto men once to die, but after this the judgment" (Heb. 9:27). Solemn words! we have only once to die, and the day is fixed. If you die wrong the first time, you cannot come back to die better a second time. If you die without Christ, you cannot come back to be converted and die a believer—you have but once to die. Oh! pray that you may find Christ before death finds you. "After this the judgment." Not, after this, purgatory. No further opportunity to be saved: "after this the judgment." As death leaves you, so judgment finds you. If you die unsaved, you will be so in *the judgment*. May I never see you at the left hand! If I do, you will remember how I warned you, and prayed for you, and besought you to come to the Lord Jesus.

Come to Jesus, He will in no wise cast you out.

To a Soul Inquiring After Jesus

The wise men. Guilt in us, righteousness in Jesus.

St. Peter's, Monday, September 18, 1842

I DO NOT and cannot forget you; and though it is very late, I have to write you a few lines to say, Follow on to know Jesus. I do not know if you can read my crooked writing, but I will make it as plain as I can. I was reading this morning, Luke 2:29, what old Simeon said when he got the child Jesus into his arms: "Now lettest thou thy servant depart in peace, according to thy word: for mine eyes have seen thy salvation." If you get a firm hold of the Lord Jesus, you will be able to say the same.

If you had died in your ignorance and sin, dear soul, where would you have been this night? Ah! how shall we sufficiently praise God if He really has brought you to the blood of the Lord Jesus Christ! If you all are really brought to Christ, it will be something like the case of the wise men of the East (Matt. 2). When they were in their own country, God attracted their attention by means of a star. They followed it, and came to Jerusalem, saying, "Where is he that is born King of the Jews? . . . for we are come to worship him." Herod and Jerusalem were troubled at the saying. No one was seeking Christ but the wise men. The world thought they were mad; but soon they saw the star again, and it led them to the house where the infant Saviour lay, His robe of state a swaddling band, His cradle the manger. Yet they kneeled down and called Him, "my Lord and my God," they got their own souls saved, and gave Him gifts, the best they had, and then departed into their own country with great joy in their hearts, and heaven in their eyes.

So it may be with you. The most around you care not for Jesus. But you are asking, "Where is He? We are come to be saved by Him." None around you can tell. They think you are going out of your mind. But God is leading you to the very spot where the Redeemer is—a lowly, despised, spit-upon, crucified Saviour. Can this be the Saviour of the world? Yes, dear soul; kneel down and call Him your Redeemer. He died for such as you and me. And now you may go away into your own country again, but not as you came. You will carry with you joy unspeakable and full of glory.

A young woman called upon me on Wednesday last, whom I had never seen before. She said she was a stranger from another part of Scotland; she came to this town about a year ago, and attended St. Peter's, and there for the first time learned that she was a sinner and needed Christ. About four weeks ago she found rest and joy at the Saviour's feet. I said to her, "Then you will bless God that He brought you from your own country to this place." She said, "I often do that." Another woman came the same evening, whom I had never seen. She said she had been married eight years to a wicked husband. One of her neighbors had brought her to our church, and now she feels that Christ has saved her soul.

Thus the work goes on: "The Lord added to the church daily such as should be saved. A young woman was with me tonight in great distress. She said, "I have a wicked heart within me that would sink a world." I said, "I am thankful to hear you complain of your wicked heart, dear friend, it is unsearchably wicked. There is not a sin committed on earth or in hell but has its spring and fountain in your breast and mine. You are all sin, your nature is sin, your heart is sin, your past life is sin, your prayers are all sin." Oh, that you would despair of being righteous in yourself! Then take the Lord Jesus for your righteousness. In Him is no sin. And He stood for us, and offers to be your shield, your way to the Father.

You may be righteous in Christ with a perfect righteousness, broad as the law, and pure as the light of heaven. If you had an angel's righteousness, you might well lay it down and put on Jesus. The robe of a blood-washed sinner is far whiter than that of an angel. Do not fear the frown of the world. When a blind man comes against you in the street, you are not angry at him; you say he is blind, poor man, or he would not have hurt me.

So you may say of the poor world, when they speak evil of Christians, they are blind. If they knew their sin and misery, and the love of Jesus, they would cleave to Him also. Fear not them which kill the body, and after that have no more that they can do. Keep close to the Lord Jesus. He is greater than all that can be against you; He is the Shepherd of His sheep; He will defend you from wolves. Pray for the Holy Spirit, dear friend. Ask Him to come into your heart, and abide there. It is a mean dwelling for such a guest. Still He will make it clean and holy by dwelling in it. Ask Him to teach you to pray (Rom. 8:26, 27). He will give you "groanings that cannot be uttered." Ask Him to change your heart and make it like that of Jesus. Ask Him to write the law upon your heart, and to keep you in every time of need. I fear you are weary of my long sermons. Remember, if you are not saved, I will be a witness against you in the judgment day.

> Come, ye weary, heavy laden,
>   Lost and ruined by the Fall;
> If ye tarry till you're better,
>   You will never come at all.
> Not the righteous—sinners Jesus came to call.

Farewell! Write me soon all your heart.

To a Soul Inquiring After Jesus

Trials from a blind world. How the death of Christ is an atonement.

London, November 5, 1842

I PRAY FOR YOU that your faith may not fail. Hold fast by Jesus for a little while, and then we shall be forever with the Lord, where the unbelieving will never be. I got safely up to town without stopping. The young man in the coach with us was Lord P. He and I were alone all night in the railway carriage, and I would fain have told him the way to be saved, but when morning dawned I lost him. I preached twice on Thursday, and once last night, and now I am preparing for tomorrow. I feel, like John the Baptist, the voice of one crying in the wilderness. The mad world presses on like a bird hasting to the snare. They do not know that the dead are there, and her guests are in the depths of hell.

I thank God without ceasing when I remember you all—how God opened your eyes and hearts, and made you flee from the wrath to come, and believe the record which God hath given concerning His Son. "Fear none of those things which thou shalt suffer. . . Be thou faithful unto death, and I will give thee a crown of life" (Rev. 2:10). Do not be surprised if worldly people mock you, and say all manner of evil against you falsely. Jesus told you it would be so. "If you were of the world, the world would love its own." You have been long enough of the world. Did the world ever hate you then? So now, when you have come out from among them, and are cleaving to Jesus, do you think they will love you? Remember Jesus loves you. God is for you, and who can be against you? Remember, all who have gone to heaven before you suffered the same things: "These are they that came out of great tribulation" (Rev. 7:14).

You wish to understand more about Christ's death being an

atonement. I shall try to explain. The curse which Adam by his sins brought upon us all was this, "Thou shalt surely die" (Gen. 2:17). This included the death of the body, the death of the soul, and the eternal destruction of both in hell. This is the curse that hangs over every unpardoned sinner. And our sins have only added certainty and weight to the awful curse, for the "wages of sin is death." Now, when the Son of God said He would become our Surety and Saviour, the Father said, "Thou must die for them" (see John 10:17, 18): "I lay down my life. . . This commandment have I received from my Father."

It is true, Christ did not suffer eternal destruction in hell; but He was a person so glorious and excellent—God's own Son—that His short sufferings were equal in value to our eternal agonies. So that, in the eye of law, and in God's account, Jesus has suffered all that you and I were condemned to suffer. Hence that sweet, sweet passage, "Comfort ye, comfort ye . . . for she hath received (in Christ) of the Lord's hand double for all her sins" (Isa. 40:1, 2). Christ's dying for us is as much in God's account as if we had twice over borne the eternal agonies of hell. Hence that sweet song which God enabled you and G. to sing: "I will praise thee; though thou wast angry with me, thine anger is turned away, and thou comfortedst me" (Isa. 12:1). Hence also that triumphant question, "Who is he that condemneth? It is Christ that died" (Rom. 8:34).

Keep looking, then, to Jesus, dear soul, and you will have the peace that passeth all understanding. Whenever Satan accuses you, send him to the stripes of the Lord Jesus. Deal gently and tenderly with your unconverted friends. Remember you were once as blind as they. "He was despised, and we esteemed Him not" (Isa. 53). Honor your mother in the Lord. Give her all reverence and obedience in things not sinful. Ask —— to read and pray over Matthew 18:3-6.

I would love much to visit the cottage on my return, but I fear I shall be kept in town till Friday, so that I must travel night and day on the way home. The Lord bless you, and keep you cleaving to Christ the true vine. You have found the pearl of great price. Go and sin no more. "If any man draw back, my soul shall have no pleasure in him." God is able to keep you from falling. In His dear arms I leave you.

To a Soul That Had Begun to See Christ

What you want in yourself is to be found in double measure in Christ.

Dundee, November, 1842

WHY did you not write me a few lines? It would be occupation for you, and your soul might find rest, even when pouring itself out to another. I do trust you are seeking hard after Him whom your soul loveth. He is not far from any one of us. He is a powerful and precious Saviour, and happy are they who put their trust in Him. He is the Rose of Sharon, lovely to look upon, having all divine and human excellences meeting in Himself; and yet He is the Lily of the Valley, meek and lowly in heart, willing to save the vilest. He answers the need of your soul. You are all guilt; He is a fountain to wash you. You are all naked; He has a wedding garment to cover you. You are dead; He is life. You are all wounds and bruises; He is the Balm of Gilead. His righteousness is broader than your sin, and then He is so free. Remember the word we read at the well: "Whosoever will, let him take the water of life freely."

Look at Isaiah 40:1, 2: "Comfort ye, comfort ye my people." If you receive Christ as your Surety, you have realized double punishment for all your sins. The sufferings of Christ for us were as honoring to God as if we had suffered eternal punishment thrice over. If you will only open your arms to receive Christ as your Surety, then your iniquity is pardoned. You will taste immediate forgiveness. Your warfare with the law and an accusing conscience will be immediately accomplished. If you will only lay hold on Christ now, you will feel the force of that sweet command, "Comfort ye, comfort ye"; double comfort, double peace, for in Jesus you have suffered double wrath.

Pray over that verse; and may He who first made the light to shine out of darkness shine into your heart, to let you see the way of salvation clearly. Soon may you sing: "Thou wast angry with me; but thine anger is turned away, and thou comfortedst me." Oh, to grace how great a debtor! You are always in my prayers, that God would reveal Himself unto you. Oh, the joy of being able to say, "My beloved is mine, and I am his!"   _____

To Rev. P. L. Miller, Wallacetown

A word in season to the weary.

September 14, 1842

WHEN I last saw Horatius, I agreed not to ask him at all at the autumn communion, but only in the spring. I know not well where to look, as A. is to undertake the Edinburgh communion.

Don't be cast down, except for sin. Lie low in self, and set both feet on the Rock of Ages. The sun, by one blink, can give a smile to nature; so can the Lord's face give life to our dark souls. Numbers do not prove life always. Remember the well of Sychar. Get much of the hidden life in your own soul; soon it will make life spread around.

Try prayer, when preaching fails. He can turn the water into wine. Farewell!

To Rev. J. Milne, Perth

Another word in season to a brother.

September 24, 1842

I LONG AFTER YOU in the bowels of Jesus Christ. If I make you sorry, who is he that maketh me glad, but the same who is made sorry by me? I often try to carry you to Jesus, as the four friends did the palsied man, and I have been longing to hear you say that His word to you was, "Be of good cheer, thy sins be forgiven thee"; and then, "Arise and walk." I wonder often God does not hide His face from me and lay me low, yet He restores my soul after many falls. He holds me by my right hand, and I believe will bring me to glory, though the weakest and most inconstant of all His saved ones. We shall praise more loudly than other men, and love more ardently, and gaze upon His wounds more wistfully, and say, He gave Himself for us. Cheer up, brother, and tell poor sinners what Jesus can do; for if He could not save the vilest of them all, we had never preached the good news.

If I could be with you, how gladly would I, but I do not see my way. I have promised to be in London the first Sabbath of November, which will take me soon away, and for a long time, from this poor flock.

Will you come to me on Monday the seventeenth, the last day of the concert for prayer? I think of printing a similar tract to last year's, or perhaps the same, with improvements. Suggest something.

This is Saturday, and I am empty. Oh, for fullness out of Him! Why do we not take all out of Jesus?

———

To Rev. J. Milne, Perth

Breathings of heart.

December 13, 1842

WE ARE TO HAVE the communion, if God permit, on January 1, 1843. A. B. is to be with me. Could you come down on the Thursday or Friday previous, and give us a good and comfortable word in the evening—either, or both if you prefer?

I preach at Newtyle tonight, and tomorrow evening at Lintrathen in a barn, and on Thursday at Kirriemuir. Pray for me, for I am a poor worm, all guilt and all helplessness, but still able to say, In the Lord have I righteousness and strength. When shall the day break and the shadows flee away? When that which is perfect is come, then that which is in part shall be done away. I long for love without any coldness, light without dimness, and purity without spot or wrinkle. I long to be at Jesus' feet, and tell Him I am all His, and ever will be.

To One Who Had Lately Taken Up the Cross

Kept by God—meeting with God.

St. Peter's, January 31, 1843

I WAS GLAD INDEED to hear that you are prospering, and that you do not repent having made Moses' choice (Heb. 11:24, 25), of which I used to tell you so often. Happy is that people whose God is the Lord. You remember what Ruth said when she cleaved to Naomi—"Thy people shall be my people, and thy God my God." I have not got your note by me, and it is late, but I will answer it tomorrow. I only write a line tonight to strengthen your faith, "that I may be comforted together with you, by the mutual faith both of you and me"

(Rom. 1:12). I have been remaining quiet since I wrote you last, that I may gather strength for the North. I expect hard service, but I hope Jesus will be with me. You remember the sweet promise Jacob got at Bethel while he slept at the foot of that wondrous ladder: "Behold, I am with thee, and will keep thee in all places whither thou goest; for I will not leave thee until I have done that which I have spoken to thee of." That promise is to you and me as truly as to Jacob. Therefore do not fear though you may be taken among those who are strangers to Jesus and His love.

There is a sweet promise (Ezek. 11:16). I have felt its preciousness in foreign lands. Jesus Himself will be our sanctuary not made with hands. I was preaching on Thursday last on Revelation 19:12: "On his head were many crowns," trying to teach them the kingly office of the Lord Jesus. It was a very solemn night. On Sabbath I lectured on Hebrews 9: 9, 10, and preached in the evening on Isaiah 49:5: "Though Israel be not gathered"; showing that however many will be lost by unbelief, still Christ would not lose one beam of His glory. If all the world were blind, and said the sun was dark, that would not take away one bright ray from it. It was a very awful subject, and my heart yearned over poor lost sinners. Four little girls have come since, asking, "What must I do to be saved?" Three of them were awakened before, and one very lately. A widow came last night whom I never saw before, to tell me that she had found the Lord Jesus. Tonight we have been at a large meeting about the tracts which are distributed monthly to every house in town—a very sweet society.

It is now late, and I am talking a little while with you as we used to do before retiring. Did you read Genesis 32 today? What a solemn chapter! Do you ever come to a spot you can call Mahanaim, where the angels of God meet you? I trust you are one of the heirs of salvation, and that the angels are sent forth to minister to you. Unconverted souls have no such privilege. You see Jacob was going on God's errand, at God's command (see 31:3), when the angels of God met him. Oh, it is sweet to go on God's errands! How long we went Satan's, and the world's, and our own, "serving divers lusts and pleasures!"

Do you not feel your heart lighter now as you walk on the narrow way? Is not a Christian's darkest hour calmer than the world's brightest? Is not Jacob's prayer in his distress an interesting one? He puts God in remembrance of His promise. This is what we should do: "The Lord which said unto me." And "Thou saidst, I will surely do thee good" (Gen. 32:9-12). God commands us to do this: "Put me in remembrance" (Isa. 43:26). It is a blessed way of praying, to pray upon a promise, and to plead, "Do as thou hast said." You remember *Faith's Plea*, a little book Miss C. gave you. Who do you think the man was that wrestled with Jacob? Was it not Jesus, the sinner's Friend? At the daybreak Jacob began to see His blessed features, and when his thigh was out of joint he could do nothing but hang upon Him. This is what you and I should do. Say, "I will not let thee go except thou bless me." Are there not some spots that you can call Peniel, where you have met Jehovah-Jesus face to face? When you do get into His presence, oh, do not weary of it; do not soon let go your hold. I am sure we lose much by our slight hold on Jesus.

I was telling an interesting story tonight. Thirty thousand Spaniards lately came over the Pyrenees into France, to escape the civil wars. Some Geneva youths determined to take the opportunity of providing them with Spanish Testaments. The London Society granted them ten thousand copies. With these they set off and distributed freely. But the Spanish priests had come over, and would not allow the Spaniards to receive or keep them. Many were burned or torn; they called them "The Plague." One Spanish youth bought a Testament—kept it, read it, believed on Jesus; and when his countrymen returned to Spain, he stayed behind to hear more of these wonders of redeeming love. Was not this one precious soul worth all the expense and trouble a thousand times over? "Be not weary in well-doing, for in due season we shall reap if we faint not."

Be active for God; you have lost much time already. Do nothing rashly, nothing unfeminine: give no just cause for reproach, but do not fear ridicule or proud men's sneers. If they knew what you know, they would rather inquire, "Oh, that I knew where I might find Him!" Meanwhile, good night. May He who never slumbers nor sleeps watch over you all, and keep you till your dying day! May Jesus be near you, and make you His own!

I fear I must not visit Kelso this season. I leave for the North on Monday, and do not expect to be home till the twenty-fifth. I fear this cuts off all hope of my visiting R—— the time you mention. I do hope to be in England early in the summer, but before that I do not see my way. But I shall gladly leave myself in Jehovah's hand. Present duty is ours; neither must we consult our mere wishes. If I hear from you before I leave, I shall try and send you another line. I am glad you teach in the classes, and I think I see you telling all you know. Remember Paul; when his heart was changed, for thirty years he did nothing else than serve Jesus. He labored away in the service of Him who died for him, and plucked him from the burning. It is interesting to notice also, how often Paul told them of his own conversion. He told it to the Jews (Acts 22); then to Agrippa (Acts 26); then to the Galatians (Gal. 1:13-16); then to the Philippians (Phil. 3:4). I think this is an example for us to do the same, cautiously and wisely. John Newton once preached in Newgate to the prisoners. He chose I Timothy 1:15 for his text, and told them his own history, so that they wept and he wept.

Pray for me still, that my way may be made plain. This is one of the blessings of having spiritual children, that you will surely pray for me. Do not cease to pray for——, that her eyes may be opened to see her true condition, and that she may call upon Jesus before it be too late. I must now leave you and write a little to others. I preach at Wallacetown tonight. May the Master be there! Oh, He is a sweet Master! One smile from Jesus sustains my soul amid all the storms and frowns of this passing world. Pray to know Jesus better. Have no other righteousness, no other strength, but only Jesus. Soon we shall see Him coming in the clouds of heaven. May you be kept faithful to death.

————

To M.B.,

To one of his flock who had felt deserted in soul.

Peterhead, February 7, 1843

I WAS VERY HAPPY to hear from you. I grieve to hear of your sorrow; but Job's sorrow was deeper, and David's also (Ps. 42). If you cannot say, "I found him whom my soul loveth," is it not sweet that you can say, "I am sick of love"— He is my Beloved still, though He has withdrawn Himself and is gone for a time?

Seek into the cause of your declension. See that it be not some Achan in your bosom, some idol set up in the corner of your heart. See that it be not some allowed sin, an unlawful attachment that is drawing you away from the bleeding side of Jesus, and bringing a cloud between you and the bright Sun of Righteousness. When you find out the cause, confess it and bewail it in the ear of a listening God. Tell Him all; keep nothing back. If you cannot find out the cause, ask Him to tell it you. Get it washed in the blood of Jesus; then get it subdued (Micah 7:19). None but the Lord Jesus can either pardon or subdue. Remember not to rest in a state of desertion.

"I will rise now and go about the city." And yet do not think that you have some great thing to do before regaining peace with God. The work on which peace is given has all been done by Jesus for us. "The word is nigh thee." Christ is the end of the law for righteousness to every one that believeth.

The sunshine is always sweeter after we have been in the shade; so will you find Jesus in returning to Him. True, it is better never to wander; but when you have wandered, the sooner you return the happier you will be. "I will go and return to my first husband; for then it was better with me than now" (Hos. 2:7).

Do not delay, but humble yourself under His mighty hand, and He will exalt you in due season. I have been speaking tonight in this place to a large and attentive audience on Zechariah 9:9. May you be enabled to apply it. Remember me to Mrs. K——, and also to all your fellow servants whom I know and love in the truth. Tell N—— C—— to make sure that she is in Christ, and not to take man's word for it. Tell E—— L—— to abide in Jesus; and tell her brother to take care lest he be a rotten branch of the true vine. Tell W—— J—— to be faithful unto death.

I have no greater joy than to know that my children walk in the truth.

———

To the Rev. Alex. Gatherer, Dundee

During his visit to the North.

Ellon, February 20, 1843

I WAS GLAD to hear from you in this far-off land. I am deeply grieved to hear that fever still prevails. God is pleading hard with my poor flock. I am glad to hear of your preaching on such precious texts, and hope they were blessed to many. Never forget that the end of a sermon is the salvation of the people. I feel more and more that it is God's cause in which we are embarked. King Jesus is a good master. I have had some sweet seasons of communion with an unseen God, which I would not give for thousands of gold and silver. May you have much of His presence with you!

———

To One Who Had Met with a Bereavement

March 8, 1843

I KNOW you will be wearying to hear from me; but it has scarcely been in my power till now, I have had so many things to do since my return. I trust Jesus is making known to you His power to calm the soul in the deepest trials. "Where is your faith?" He said to the disciples; and He says to you, "All things are possible to him that believeth."

I was much afflicted for your sakes to read the solemn letter you sent me. Do you remember the words, "He must needs go through Samaria"? We are getting new light upon their meaning.

I was reading today about godly sorrow, and the sorrow of the world. Do you know the difference between these two?

Had this blow come upon you in your unconverted state, it would have wrought, perhaps, only the sorrow of the world— carnal sorrow that drives us away from God and makes us murmur and complain of His dealings, like Pharaoh who turned harder every blow that God struck—even the loss of his first-born only hardened him. But godly sorrow, or more literally, "sorrow towards God," grief that brings us to the feet of God, worketh repentance unto salvation, not to be repented of. It is used as an instrument to bring the humbled soul to cleave to Jesus. Oh, may it be so with you!

Humble yourselves under the mighty hand of God, and He

shall exalt you in due season. Improve the season while it lasts. The farmer improves the seedtime, to cast in the seed into the furrows. Now, when God has made long the furrow by the plough of affliction in your heart, oh see that you let the sower sow the good seed deep in your heart. I trust H. B. may be made a great blessing and comfort to you next Sabbath. May you all be enabled to meet with Jesus at His own table, and to tell Him all your sorrows there, and ask grace to keep you in the evil day.

I would like well to be with you; but in body this may not be. In heart I am often with you, because I can say what I was reading today: "Ye are in my heart to live and to die with you" (II Cor. 7:3).

I preached twenty-seven times when I was away, in twenty-four different places. I was very, very tired, and my heart has beat too much ever since, but I am wonderfully well. I have "fightings without and fears within" just now. Do pray earnestly for me—as indeed I know you do. I wish you had been with me last night. When I was away, the people agreed to meet twice a week in the lower schoolroom to pray for me; and now that I have come back, we have continued the meetings. The school is quite crammed. Such sweet, loud singing of praise I never heard, and many tears.

I stood by a poor socialist in the agonies of death today. He was quite well yesterday. He anxiously wished me to come and pray. Oh, to be ready when the Bridegroom comes!

Farewell. Peace from above fill your soul.

ANOTHER TO ONE BEREAVED

Betake yourself to Him that is ever the same.

March 9, 1843

I DID NOT THINK I would have been so long in answering you in your time of sorrow, but I have been more than occupied. I earnestly trust that this sad bereavement may be greatly blessed by God to you. Pray that you may not lose this precious opportunity of giving your hand and heart forever away to the Lord Jesus. May Hosea 2:14 be fulfilled in you all: "Behold, I will allure her, and *bring her into the wilderness, and speak comfortably unto her*"; and that clear promise: "I will cause you to pass under the rod, and I will bring you into the bond of the covenant" (Ezek. 20:37). This solemn event shows you what I always used to tell you, *how short* your life is, what a vapor, how soon the joys that depend on the creatures may be dried up; that "one thing is needful," and that Mary was wise in choosing *the good part that cannot be taken away from her.*

You remember the first night you were in St. Peter's I showed you this preaching from Psalm 16:6: "The lines have fallen to me in pleasant places, and I have a goodly heritage." I am indeed more than ever anxious about you, that you receive not the grace of God in vain. It is the furnace that tries the metal, and it is affliction that tries the soul whether it be Christ's or not. I am jealous over you with a godly jealousy, lest the furnace should show you to be reprobate silver. Do let me hear how your soul truly is, whether you can see the hand of a Father in this bereavement, and whether you are more than ever determined, through grace, to be the Lord's. How sweet that *Jesus ever liveth!* He is the same yesterday, and today, and forever.

You will never find Jesus so precious as when the world is one vast howling wilderness. Then He is like a rose blooming

in the midst of the desolation, a rock rising above the storm.
The Bible, too, is more full of meaning. Have you ever prayed
over that verse: *"He doth not afflict willingly?"* (Lam. 3:33).
O precious book, that conveys such a message to the mourn-
er's dwelling! And does not trial bring more meaning out of
that verse: "We know that *all* things work together for the
good of them that love God, to them who are the called according to his purpose" (Rom. 8:28)? The Bible is like the
leaves of the lemon tree—the more you bruise and wring them,
the sweeter the fragrance they throw around. "Is any afflicted?
let him pray." Do you not find that prayer is sweeter now?
The soul finds vent for its feelings toward God. *"Call upon
me in the day of trouble:* I will deliver thee, and thou shalt
glorify me." When I had my fever abroad, Mr. Bonar whispered that verse into my ear. I had nearly lost all my faculties
—I could remember nothing except that I was far from home;
but that verse kept sounding in my ears when I was nearly in-
sensible: "I called, and he delivered me."

Are you preparing to go to the Lord's Table next Lord's day?
May you indeed have the wedding garment—righteousness
without works—and see the King in His beauty, and give yourself away to Him, saying, "I am my beloved's, and my beloved
is mine!" It should be a solemn sacrament to you. I can add no
more. Write me soon, dear G——, and tell me all that is in
your heart, and whether the voice of the Comforter does not
say, Be still! when death has left so deep a silence in your
family.

To One Complaining of the Plagues of the Heart

Passing on to glory.

St. Peter's, March 8, 1843

I SEND A FEW LINES to you in answer to yours. You complain of the plague of your own heart, and so you will till you die. You know little yet of its chambers of imagery. All that is ours is sin. Our wicked heart taints all we say and do; hence the need of continual atonement in the blood of Jesus. It is not one pardoning that will serve the need of our souls. We must have daily, hourly pardons. I believe you are in the furnace, but for a short time. Soon the Bridegroom will come, and we shall be with Him, and like Him, and God shall wipe away all tears from our eyes. I burst through all the cobwebs of present things, and, His Spirit anointing my eyes, look at Jesus as one beside me. Blessed Elder Brother, with two natures—God and man—ever-living, never-dying, never-changing!

I was preaching last Sabbath on Hebrews 9:13, 14: "He through the eternal Spirit offered himself." It was very sweet to me. In the afternoon I preached on Revelation 2:4, 5: "I have this against thee, that thou has left thy first love." I fear many of my people have done so; therefore it was very suitable. Several I see have felt it very deeply. In the evening I preached on Psalm 78:41: "They turned back, and tempted God, and limited the Holy One of Israel"—on the sinfulness of limiting God. It was a very sweet and solemn day.

Meantime, stay your soul on God. "Thou wilt keep him in perfect peace whose mind is stayed on thee, because he trusteth in thee." A few more trials, a few more tears, a few more days of darkness, and we shall be forever with the Lord! "In this tabernacle we groan, being burdened." All dark things shall yet be cleared up, all sufferings healed, all blanks supplied, and we shall find fullness of joy (not one drop wanting)

in the smile and presence of our God. It is one of the laws of
Christ's kingdom, "We must through much tribulation enter
into the kingdom of God." We must not reckon upon a smooth
road to glory, but it will be a short one. How glad I am that
you have "received the word in much affliction, with joy of the
Holy Ghost"! Cleave closely to Jesus, that you may not have
to say in a little, "Oh that I had affliction back again to quicken
me in prayer, and make me lie at His feet!"

> Trials make the promise sweet,
> Trials give new life to prayer;
> Trials bring me to His feet,
> Lay me low, and keep me there.

This land will soon be strangely convulsed, if God prevent
not. The plans now preparing for carrying the gospel into
every corner of the land are sweet indeed. If I be spared and
strengthened, I go to London toward the end of April. My
stay must be very short. It is also intended to send me to the
General Assembly in May. My poor flock, how I yearn over
them! So many of them careless, and judgment at the door!
Mr. Burns comes to me tomorrow.

I must add no more, as I have work before me. May you experience more and more, that "when he giveth quietness, none
can make trouble"—even as you once experienced the other,
"When he hideth his face, who then can behold him?" Soon
we shall see Him as He is; then our trials shall be done. We
shall reign with Him, and be entirely like Him. The angels
will know us by our very faces to be brothers and sisters of
Jesus.

Remember Jesus *for us* is all our righteousness before a holy
God, and Jesus *in us* is all our strength in an ungodly world.
Persevere even to death; eternal life will make up for all.
Remember Barnabas' advice, "Cleave to the Lord"—not to
man, but to the Lord. May He perfect all that concerneth you.
Do not fear the face of man. Remember how small their
anger will appear in eternity.

BIBLE MESSAGES

Those who had an opportunity of hearing Mr. McCheyne at those times when his soul was most enlarged, and his lips fresh touched with the live coal, will be ready to remark that some of his most impressive Sermons (*e.g.*, "The Great White Throne") are not here. This is true; and the reason is, that they were not found in his manuscripts. I might indeed have given full notes from the records of hearers; but it was far better to adhere to what was found in his own handwriting, that so the reader may be sure that, if he has not before him the discourses as they were delivered, he has at least what passed through the author's soul.

BIBLE MESSAGES

MESSAGE I

"Jesus saith unto him, I am the way, the truth, and the life; no man cometh
unto the Father but by me."—John 14:6.

IT IS THE SAYING of an old divine, that God often orders
it that when He is in hand with the greatest mercies for us,
then we are most of all sinning against Him; which He doth to
magnify His love the more.

In the words I have read, we find an example of this. At no
time did the heart of Jesus overflow with a tenderer and more
sovereign love to His disciples, than when He said, "Let not
your heart be troubled." They were troubled by many things.
He had told them that He was going to leave them; He had
told them that one should betray Him, that another should
deny Him, that they should all be offended because of Him
that very night; and perhaps they thought He was going from
them in anger. But whatever the cause of their trouble was,
Jesus' bosom was like a vessel full to overflowing, and these
words were the overflowing drops of love: "Let not your heart
be troubled: ye believe in God, believe also in me."

Surely such words of confiding tenderness were never whispered in this cold world before; and oh then, think how cold,
how dark, how dull is the question with which Thomas breaks
in upon the heavenly discourse: "Thomas saith unto him, Lord,
we know not whither thou goest; and how can we know the
way?" And yet how condescendingly does Jesus bear with their

cold-hearted dullness! How lovingly does He begin the very alphabet of salvation with them, and not only answers, but overanswers Thomas—gives him more than he could ask or think. He asked about the way and the place; but Christ answers, "I am the way, the truth, and the life: no man cometh unto the Father but by me." Regarding this, then, as a complete description of the gospel salvation, let us go over the different parts of it.

I. *Christ is the Way.*—"I am the way; no man cometh," and so forth. The whole Bible bears witness that by nature we have no way to the Father. We are by nature full of sin, and God is by nature infinitely holy, that is, He shrinks away from sin. Just as the sensitive plant, by its very nature, shrinks away from the touch of a human hand, so God, by His very nature, shrinks away from the touch of sin. He is everlastingly separate from sinners; He is of purer eyes than to behold iniquity.

1. This was impressively taught to Adam and the patriarchs. As long as Adam walked holily, God dwelt in him, and walked in him, and communed with him; but when Adam fell, "God drove the man out of paradise; and he placed at the east of the garden of Eden, cherubim and a flaming sword, which turned every way to keep the way of the tree of life." This flaming sword between the cherubim was a magnificent emblem of God —the just and sin-hating God. In the bush, He appeared to Moses as a consuming fire; in the temple, He appeared between the cherubim in the milder glory of the Shekinah; but here He appeared between the cherubim as a sword, a just and sin-hating God.

And I beseech you to remark, that this flaming sword turned *every way* to keep the way of the tree of life. If it had not turned *every way*—if it had left some footpath unglared across —then Adam might have stolen in by that footpath, and made his own way to the tree of life. But no: whatever avenue he tried, however secret, however narrow, however steep and difficult, however silently he crept along, still this flaming meteor met him, and it seemed to say, "How can men be just with God? by the deeds of the law there shall be no flesh living be justified." Well might Adam sit down, wearied with the vain search for a pathway into life; for man by nature has no way to the Father.

But Christ says, "I am the way." As He says in Psalm 16, "Thou wilt show me the path of life." No man could find out this path of life; but Jesus says, "Thou wilt show it me: in thy presence is fullness of joy; at thy right hand are pleasures for evermore." *Jesus pitied* the poor sons of Adam vainly struggling to find out a way into the paradise of God, and He left the bosom of the Father, just that He might open up a way for us into the bosom of the Father. And how did He do it? Was it by escaping the vigilance of the flaming sword? No; for it turned every way. Was it by exerting His divine authority, and commanding the glittering blade to withdraw? No; for that would have been to dishonor His Father's law instead of magnifying it. He therefore became a man in our stead—yea, became sin. God caused to meet on Him the iniquities of us all. He advanced in our stead to meet that fiery meteor, He fell beneath its piercing blade; for He remembered the word of the prophet, which is written: "Awake, O sword! against my shepherd, and against the man that is my fellow, saith the Lord of hosts."

And now, since the glittering blade is bathed in the side of the Redeemer, the guiltiest of sinners—whoever you be, whatever you be—may enter in over His bleeding body, may find access to the paradise of God, to eat of the tree of life, and live forever. Come quickly—doubt not; for He says, *I am the way.*

2. The same fact—that man has by nature no way to the Father—was impressively taught to Moses and the people of Israel.

When God condescended to dwell among the children of Israel, He dwelt peculiarly in the Holiest of all—the innermost apartment of the Jewish Temple. There the visible token of His presence rested between the cherubim, at one time described to us as a light inaccessible and full of glory, at another time as a cloud that filled the Temple. But this innermost apartment, or Holiest of all (or secret place, as it is called in the Psalms), was separated from the holy place by a curtain or veil; and through that veil no man was allowed to pass, lest he should die, except the high priest, who entered in once in the year, not without blood. Now, no picture could express more plainly that the way into the Holiest was not made manifest, that no sinful man has any way of coming into the presence of God.

But Jesus says, "I am the way." Jesus was grieved that we were shut out from the Holiest of all—from the presence of God; for He knew by experience that in that presence there is fullness of joy. But how did He open the way? Did He pull aside the veil, that we might steal in secretly and easily into the presence of the Father? No; but He offered Himself an offering to satisfy divine justice and reconcile us to God. "He said, It is finished, and bowed his head and gave up the ghost. And, behold, the veil of the temple was rent in twain, from the top to the bottom." It is finished: the punishment of the law is borne, the demands of the law are answered, the way is finished, the veil is rent from the top to the bottom! Not a shred of the dreadful curtain now remains to intercept us. The guiltiest, the vilest sinner of you all, has now liberty to enter in through the rent veil, under the light of Jehovah's countenance, to dwell in the secret of His Tabernacle, to behold His beauty, and to inquire in His Temple.

And now, my friends, is this your way of coming to the Father? Christ says, "I am the way; no man cometh unto the Father but by me." If, then, you will still keep to your own way, whatever it be—whether it be the way of tears, or penances, or vows of amendment, or hopes that God will not deal strictly—if you will not be warned, you will find in the judgment day that the cherubic sword turned every way, and that you are left a prey to the consuming fire.

But oh! if there be one soul that can find no peace in any self-righteous way, if there be one of you who find that you are lost in yourself, behold, Christ says to you, "I am *the* way," as He says in another place, "I am *the* door." It is a full, free, and open way, and it is a way for sinners. Why wait a moment longer? There was once a partition wall between you and God; but Christ hath cast it down. God was once angry; but His anger is turned away from this blessed path. In Christ He is ever well pleased.

II. *Christ is the Truth.*—The whole Bible and the whole of experience bear witness that by nature we are ignorant of *the truth.* No doubt there are many truths which an unconverted man does know. He may know the truths of mathematics and arithmetic—he may know many of the common everyday truths; but still it cannot be said that an unconverted man knows *the truth,* for Christ is the truth. Christ may be called the keystone of the arch of truth. Take away the keystone of an arch, and the whole becomes a heap of rubbish. The very same stones may be there; but they are all fallen, smothered, and confused, without order, without end. Just so take Christ away, and the whole arch of truth becomes a heap of rubbish. The very same truths may be there; but they are all fallen, without coherence, without order, without end.

Christ may be called the sun of the system of truth. Take away the sun out of our system, and every planet would rush into confusion. The very same planets would be there; but their conflicting forces would draw them hither and thither, orb dashing against orb in endless perplexity. Just so take Christ away, and the whole system of truth rushes into confusion. The same truths may be in the mind, but all conflicting and jarring in inextricable mazes; for "the path of the wicked is as darkness; they know not at what they stumble." But let Christ be revealed to an unconverted soul—let it not be merely a man speaking about Christ unto him, but let the Spirit of God reveal Him—and there is revealed, not a truth, but *the truth*. You put the keystone into the arch of truth; you restore the sun to the center of the system. All truth becomes orderly and serviceable in that mind.

Now he knows the truth with regard to himself. Did the Son of God really leave the bosom of the Father to bear wrath in our stead? Then I must be under wrath. Did the Lord Jesus become a servant, that He might obey the will of God instead of sinners? Then I must be without any righteousness, a child of disobedience.

Again, knowing Christ, he knows the truth with regard to God. Did God freely give up His Son to the death for us all? Then, if I believe in Jesus, there is no condemnation to me. God is my Father, and God is love.

My friends, have you seen Christ, who is the truth? Has He been revealed to you, not by flesh and blood, but by the Spirit of our God? Then you know how true it is that in Him "are hid all the treasures of wisdom and knowledge," that He is the "Alpha and Omega," the beginning and the ending of all knowledge. But if you have not seen Christ, then you know nothing yet as you ought to know; all your knowledge is like a bridge without a keystone, like a system without a sun. What good will it do you in hell that you knew all the sciences in the world, all the events of history, and all the busy politics of your little day? Do you not know that your very knowledge will be turned into an instrument of torture in hell? Oh, how will you wish in that day that you had read your newspaper less and your Bible more, that with all your getting, you had got understanding, that with all your knowledge, you had known the Saviour, whom to know is life everlasting!

III. *Christ is the Life.*—The whole Bible bears witness that by nature we are dead in trespasses and sins, that we are as unable to walk holily in the world, as a dead man is unable to rise and walk.

Both Scripture and experience alike testify that we are by nature dead in trespasses and sins; and yet it is not a death in which we are wholly inactive, for in it we are said to walk according to the course of this world, according to the prince of the power of the air.

This truth is taught us impressively in that vision of the prophet Ezekiel, where he was carried out by the Spirit, and set down in the midst of an open valley full of dry bones; and as he passed by them round about, behold, there were very many in the open valley, and lo! they were very dry.

Just such is the view which every child of God gets of the world. The dry bones are very many, and they are very dry; and he asks the same question which God asked of Ezekiel: "Can these bones live?" Oh yes, my friends; and does not experience teach you the same thing? True, the dead cannot know that they are dead; and yet, if the Lord touch your heart, you will find it out. We prophesy to dry bones; for this is the Lord's way; while we prophesy, the breath enters in. *Look back over your life, then.* See how you have walked according to the course of this world. You have always been like a man swimming with the stream, never like a man swimming against the current. *Look into your heart,* and see how it has turned against all the commandments: you feel the Sabbath to be a weariness, instead of calling it a delight and honorable.

If ever you tried to keep the commandments of God, if ever you tried to keep your eyes from unlawful desires, your tongue from words of anger or gossiping or bitterness, your heart from malice and envy and covetousness, if ever you have tried this— and I fancy most unconverted men have tried it—if ever you have tried this, did you not find it impossible? It was like

raising the dead. Did you not find a struggle against yourself?
Oh how plain that you are dead—not born again! Marvel not
that we say unto you, Ye must be born again. You must be
joined to Christ, for Christ *is the life*.

Suppose it were possible for a dead limb to be joined into a
living body so completely that all the veins should receive the
purple tide of living blood, suppose bone to join to bone, and
sinew to sinew, and nerve to nerve, do you not see that that
limb, however dead before, would become a living limb? Before, it was cold and stiff and motionless, and full of corruption; now it is warm and pliable, and full of life and motion.

It is a living limb, because joined on to that which is life.
Or, suppose it possible for a withered branch to be grafted into
a living vine so completely that all the channels should receive
the flow of the generous sap, do you not see that that branch,
however dead before, becomes a living branch? Before, it was
dry and fruitless and withered; now, it is full of sap, of life,
and vigor. It is a living branch, for it is joined to the vine,
which is its life. Well, then, just in the same way, Christ is the
life of every soul that cleaves to Him. He that is joined to the
Lord is one spirit. Is your soul like a dead limb—cold, stiff, motionless, and full of corruption? Cleave you to Christ, be joined
to Him by faith, and you shall be one spirit, you shall be made
warm and vigorous and full of activity in God's service.

Is your soul like a withered branch—dry, fruitless, and withered, wanting both leaves and fruit? Cleave you to Christ; be
joined to Him, and you shall be one spirit. You will find it
true that Christ is the life; your life will be hid with Christ in
God. You will say, "I live; yet not I, but Christ liveth in me;
and the life which I now live in the flesh, I live by the faith of
the Son of God, who loved me, and gave himself for me."

Remember then, my unbelieving friends, the only way for
you to become holy is to become united to Christ. And remember you, my believing friends, that if ever you are relaxing

in holiness, the reason is, you are relaxing your hold on Christ. "Abide in me, and I in you; so shall ye bear much fruit. Severed from me, ye can do nothing."

DUNDEE, 1836.

MESSAGE II

"Consider the Apostle and High Priest of our profession, Christ Jesus."—
Hebrews 3:1.

WHEN A TRAVELER passes very rapidly through a country, the eye has no time to rest upon the different objects in it, so that, when he comes to the end of his journey, no distinct impressions have been made upon his mind; he has only a confused notion of the country through which he has traveled.

This explains how it is that death, judgment, eternity, make so little impression upon most men's minds. Most people never stop to think, but hurry on through life, and find themselves in eternity before they have once put the question, "What must I do to be saved?" More souls are lost through want of consideration than in any other way.

The reason men are not awakened and made anxious for their souls is that the devil never gives them time to consider. Therefore God cries, Stop, poor sinner, stop and think. Consider your ways. "Oh that you were wise, that you understood this, that you considered your latter end!" And, again He cries, "Israel doth not know, my people doth not consider."

In the same way does the devil try to make the children of God doubt if there be a Providence. He hurries them away to the shop and market. Lose no time, he says, but make money. Therefore God cries, Stop, poor sinner, stop and think; and Jesus says, "Consider the lilies of the field, how they grow . . . consider the ravens, which have neither storehouse nor barn."

In the same way does the devil try to make the children of

God live uncomfortable and unholy lives. He beguiles them away from simply looking to Jesus: he hurries them away to look at a thousand other things, as he led Peter, walking on the sea, to look round at the waves. But God says, Look here, consider the Apostle and High Priest of your profession; look unto Me and be ye saved; run your race, looking unto Jesus; consider Christ, the same yesterday, today, and forever.

I. *Believers should live in daily consideration of the greatness and glory of Christ.*

1. There was once a time when time was not—when there was no earth, neither sun, nor moon, nor star; a time when you might have wandered through all space, and never found a resting-place to the sole of your foot, when you would have found no creatures anywhere, but God everywhere; when there were no angels with golden harps hymning celestial praises, but God alone was all in all.

Question—Where was Jesus then?

Answer—He was with God. "In the beginning was the *Word,* and *the Word was with God."* He was near to God, and in perfect happiness there. "The Lord possessed me in the beginning of his way, before his works of old. Then I was by him as one brought up with him; and I was daily his delight, rejoicing always before him." He was in the bosom of God: "The only begotten Son which is in the bosom of the Father." He was in perfect glory there: "O Father, glorify thou me with thyself, with the glory which I had with thee before the world was!"

Question—What was Jesus then?

Answer—He was God. The Word was with God, and "was God." He was equal with the Father. "He thought it not robbery to be equal with God." He was rich. He was the brightness of His Father's glory, and the express image of His person.

Now, brethren, could I lift you away to that time when God

was alone from all eternity; could I have shown you the glory of
Jesus then—how He dwelt in the bosom of the Father, and
was daily His delight; and could I have told you, "That is
the glorious Being who is to undertake the cause of poor lost
sinners; that is He who is going to put Himself in their room
and stead, to suffer all they should suffer, and obey all they
should obey; consider Jesus, look long and earnestly, weigh
every consideration in the balance of the soundest judgment;
consider His rank, His nearness, His dearness to God the Father; consider His power, His glory, His equality to God the
Father in everything; consider, and say do you think you would
entrust your case to Him? do you think He would be a sufficient Saviour?" Oh, brethren, would not every soul cry out,
He is enough—I want no other Saviour?

2. Again, there was a time when this world sprang into
being—when the sun began to shine, and earth and seas began
to smile. There was a time when myriads of happy angels
springing into being, first spread their wings, doing His commandments—when the morning stars sang together, and all the
sons of God shouted for joy.

Question—What was Jesus doing then?

Answer—"Without him was not anything made that was
made. . . By him were all things created that are in heaven, and
that are in earth, visible and invisible, whether they be thrones,
or dominions, or principalities, or powers: all things were created by him and for him." Oh, brethren, could I lift you away
back to that wonderful day, and show you Jesus calling all the
angels into being, hanging the earth upon nothing; could you
have heard the voice of Jesus saying, "Let there be light, and
there was light"; and could I have told you, "That is He who
is yet to undertake for sinners; consider Him, and see if you
think He will be a sufficient Saviour; look long and earnestly";
good news, good news for sinners, if this mighty Being under-
takes for us! I can as little doubt the sureness and completeness

of my salvation as I can doubt the sureness of the solid earth beneath my feet.

3. But the work of creation is long since passed. Jesus has been upon our earth. And now He is not here—He is risen. Eighteen hundred years and more have passed since Christ was upon the earth.

Question—Where is Jesus now?

Answer—"He is set down at the right hand of the Majesty on high." He is upon the throne with God in His glorified body, and His throne is forever. A scepter is put into His hand —a scepter of righteousness, and the oil of gladness is poured over Him. All power is given to Him in heaven and on earth.

Oh, brethren, could you and I pass this day through these heavens, and see what is now going on in the sanctuary above; could you see what the child of God now sees who died last night; could you see the Lamb with the scars of His five deep wounds in the very midst of the throne, surrounded by all the redeemed, everyone having harps and golden vials full of odors, could you see the many angels round about the throne, whose number is ten thousand times ten thousand, and thousands of thousands, all singing, "Worthy is the Lamb that was slain"; and were one of these angels to tell you, "This is He that undertook the cause of lost sinners; He undertook to bear their curse and to do their obedience; He undertook to be the second Adam—the man in their stead. And lo! there He is upon the throne of heaven; consider Him; look long and earnestly upon His wounds—upon His glory—and tell me, do you think it would be safe to trust Him? do you think His sufferings and obedience will have been enough?" Yes, yes, every soul exclaims, Lord, it is enough! Lord, stay Thy hand! Show me no more, for I can bear no more. Oh, rather let me ever stand and gaze upon the almighty, all-worthy, all-divine Saviour, till my soul drinks in complete assurance that His work undertaken for sinners is a finished work! Yes, though the sins of all the world were on my one wicked head, still I could not doubt that His work is complete, and that I am quite safe when I believe in Him.

I would now plead with believers. Some of you have really been brought by God to believe in Jesus. Yet you have no abiding peace, and very little growing in holiness. Why is this? It is because your eye is fixed anywhere but on Christ. You are so busy looking at books, or looking at men, or looking at the world, that you have no time, no heart, for looking at Christ.

No wonder you have little peace and joy in believing. No wonder you live so inconsistent and unholy a life. Change your plan. Consider the greatness and glory of Christ, who has undertaken all in the stead of sinners, and you would find it quite impossible to walk in darkness, or to walk in sin. Oh, what mean, despicable thoughts you have of the glorious Immanuel! Lift your eyes from your own bosom, downcast believer—look upon Jesus. It is good to consider your ways, but it is far better to consider Christ.

I would now invite anxious souls. Anxious soul! have you understood all the glory of Christ? Have you understood that He undertook for guilty sinners? And do you doubt if He be a sufficient Saviour? Oh, what mean views you have of Christ if you dare not risk your soul upon Him!

Objection—I do not doubt that Christ has suffered and done quite enough, but I fear it was for others, and not for me. If I were sure it was for me, I would be quite happy.

Answer—It is nowhere said in the Bible that Christ died for this sinner or that sinner. If you are waiting till you find your own name in the Bible, you will wait forever. But it is said a few verses before that, "He tasted death for every man"; and again, "He is the propitiation for the sins of the whole world." Not that all men are saved by Him. Ah! no; the most never come to Jesus, and are lost; but this shows that any sinner may

come, even the chief of sinners, and take Christ as his own
Saviour. Come you then, anxious soul; say you, He is my refuge and my fortress; and then, be anxious, if you can.

II. *Consider Christ as the Apostle or Messenger of God.*

The word apostle means messenger, one ordained and sent
on a particular embassy. Now Christ is an Apostle, for God
ordained and sent Him into the world.

In the Old Testament, the name He is most often called is
the Angel of the Lord, or the Messenger of the Covenant. He
is called God's Elect, chosen for the work; He is called God's
Servant; He is called the Messiah, or the Christ, or the
Anointed, because God anointed Him and sent Him to the
work. In the New Testament, over and over again Christ calls
Himself the Sent of God. "As thou hast sent me into the world,
so have I sent them into the world, that the world may know
that thou hast sent me. . . And these have known that thou
hast sent me." All this shows plainly that it is not the Son alone
who is interested in the saving of poor sinners, but the Father
also. "The Father sent his Son to be the Saviour of the
world."

Objection—True, Christ is a great and glorious Saviour,
and able to accomplish anything to save poor sinners; but perhaps God the Father may not agree to pour out His wrath
upon His Son, or to accept of His Son as a surety in our stead.

Answer—Look here, Christ is the Apostle of God. It is as
much God the Father's work, as it is Christ's work. It occupied as much of the heart of God as ever it did of the heart
of Christ. God loved the world as much and truly as ever
Christ loved the world. God gave His Son, as much as Christ
gave Himself for us. So God the Holy Spirit is as much interested in it as the Father and Son. God gave His Son; the
Spirit anointed Him and dwelt in Him without measure. At
His baptism God acknowledged Him for His beloved Son—
the Holy Spirit came on Him like a dove.

Oh! brethren, could I lift you away to the eternity that is past—could I bring you into the council of the Eternal Three; and as it was once said, "Let us *make* man," could I let you hear the word, "Let us *save* man"; could I show you how God from all eternity designed His Son to undertake for poor sinners; how it was the very plan and the bottommost desire of the heart of the Father that Jesus should come into the world, and do and die in the stead of sinners; how the Holy Spirit breathed sweetest incense, and dropped like holiest oil upon the head of the descending Saviour; could I show you the intense interest with which the eye of God followed Jesus through His whole course of sorrow and suffering and death; could I show you the anxious haste with which God rolled away the stone from the sepulchre while it was yet dark, for He would not leave His soul in hell, neither suffer His Holy One to see corruption; could I show you the ecstasies of love and joy that beat in the bosom of the infinite God when Jesus ascended to His Father and our Father; how He welcomed Him with a fullness of kindness and grace which God alone could give, and God alone could receive, saying, "Thou art my Son, this day have I begotten Thee; Thou art indeed worthy to be called my Son; never till this day wert Thou so worthy to be called mine; thy throne, O God, is for ever and ever; sit Thou on my right hand until I make thine enemies thy footstool."

O sinner, will you ever doubt any more whether God the Father be seeking thy salvation—whether the heart of Christ and of His Father be the same in this one grand controversy? O believer, consider this Apostle of God; meditate on these things; look and look again, until your peace be like a river, and your righteousness like the waves of the sea—till the breathing of your soul be, Abba, Father!

III. *Consider Christ as the High Priest of our profession.*

The duty of the high priest was twofold: *First,* to make atonement; *second,* to make intercession.

When the high priest slew the goat at the altar of burnt-
offerings, he did it in presence of all the people, to make
atonement for them. They all stood around, gazing and considering their high priest; and when he gathered the blood into
the golden basin, and put on the white garments, and passed
away from their sight within the veil, their eye followed him,
till the mysterious curtain hid him from their sight. But even
then the heart of the believing Jew followed him still. Now
he is drawing near to God for us; now he is sprinkling the
blood seven times before the mercy seat, saying, Let this blood
be instead of our blood; now he is praying for us.

Brethren, let us also consider our great High Priest.

1. *Consider Him making atonement.* You cannot look at
Him on the cross as the disciples did; you cannot see the blood
streaming from His five deep wounds; you cannot see Him
shedding His blood that the blood of sinners might not be shed.
Yet still, if God spare us, you may see bread broken and wine
poured out, a living picture of the dying Saviour. Now, brethren, the atonement has been made, Christ has died, His sufferings are all past. And how is it that you do not enjoy peace?
It is because you do not consider. "Israel doth not know,
my people doth not consider." Consider—has Jesus died in
the stead of guilty sinners, and do you heartily consent to
take Jesus to be the man in your stead? Then, you do not need
to die. Oh, happy believer, rejoice evermore! Live within
sight of Calvary, and you will live within sight of glory; and,
oh, rejoice in the happy ordinance that sets a broken Saviour
so plainly before you!

2. *Consider Christ as making intercession.* When Christ
ascended from the Mount of Olives, and passed through these
heavens, carrying His bloody wounds into the presence of God,
and when His disciples had gazed after Him, till a cloud received Him out of their sight, we are told that *they returned
to Jerusalem with great joy.* What! are they joyful at parting

with their blessed Master? When He told them He was to leave them, sorrow filled their hearts, and He had to argue with them and comfort them, saying, "Let not your heart be troubled . . . it is expedient for you that I go away." How, then, are they changed? Jesus has left them, and they are filled with joy. Oh! here is the secret: they knew that Christ was now going into the presence of God for them, that their great High Priest was now entering within the veil to make intercession for them.

Now, believer, would you share in the great joy of the disciples? Consider the Apostle and High Priest of our profession, Christ Jesus. He is above yon clouds, and above yon sky. Oh that you would stand gazing up into heaven, not with the bodily eye, but with the eye of faith! Oh, what a wonderful thing the eye of faith is! It sees beyond the stars, it pierces to the throne of God, and there it looks on the face of Jesus making intercession for us, whom having not seen we love; in whom, though now we see Him not, yet believing, we rejoice with joy unspeakable and full of glory.

Oh! if you would live thus, what sweet peace would fill your bosom! And how many droppings of the Spirit would come down on you in answer to the Saviour's prayer! Oh! how your face would shine like Stephen's; and the poor, blind world would see that there is a joy which the world cannot give, and the world cannot take away—a heaven upon earth!

DUNDEE, 1836.

MESSAGE III

"As the lily among thorns, so is my love among the daughters. As the apple tree among the trees of the wood, so is my beloved among the sons. I sat down under his shadow with great delight, and his fruit was sweet unto my taste."—Song of Solomon 2:2, 3.

IF AN UNCONVERTED MAN were taken away into heaven, where Christ sits in glory, and if he overheard Christ's words of admiring love towards the believer, he could not understand them; he could not comprehend how Christ should see a loveliness in poor religious people whom *he* in the bottom of his heart despised. Or again, if an unconverted man were to overhear a Christian at his devotions when he is really within the veil, and were to listen to his words of admiring, adoring love towards Christ, he could not possibly understand them; he could not comprehend how the believer should have such a burning affection toward One unseen, in whom he himself saw no form nor comeliness. So true it is that the natural man knoweth not the things of the Spirit of God, for they are foolishness unto him.

There may be some now hearing me who have a rooted dislike to religious people—they are so stiff, so precise, so gloomy, you cannot endure their company! Well, then, see here what Christ thinks of them: "As the lily among thorns, so is my love among the daughters." How different you are from Christ! There may be some hearing me who have no desires after Jesus Christ, who never think of Him with pleasure; you see no form nor comeliness in Him, no beauty that you should desire Him; you do not love the melody of His name; you do not pray to Him continually. Well, then, see here what the believer thinks of Him—how different from you—"As the apple tree among the trees of the wood, so is my beloved among the sons. I sat down under his shadow with great delight, and his fruit was sweet to my taste." Oh, that you would be awakened by this very thing—that you are so different from Christ, and so different from the believer —to think that you must be in a natural condition, you must be under wrath!

Doctrine.—The believer is unspeakably precious in the eyes of Christ, and Christ is unspeakably precious in the eyes of the believer.

I. *Inquire what Christ thinks of the believer.*—"As the lily among the thorns, so is my love among the daughters."

Christ sees nothing so fair in all this world as the believer. All the rest of the world is like thorns, but the believer is like a beautiful lily in His eyes. When you are walking in a wilderness all overgrown with briars and thorns, if your eye falls upon some lonely flower, tall and white, and pure and graceful, growing in the midst of the thorns, it looks peculiarly beautiful. If it were in the midst of some rich garden among many other flowers, then it would not be so remarkable; but when it is encompassed with thorns on every side, then it engages the eye. Such is the believer in the eyes of Christ. "As the lily among thorns, so is my love among the daughters."

1. See what Christ thinks of the unconverted world. It is like a field full of briars and thorns in His eyes. *First,* Because fruitless. "Do men gather grapes of thorns, or figs of thistles?" So Christ gets no fruit from the unconverted world. It is all one wide, thorny waste.

Second, Because, when the Word is preached among them, it is like sowing among thorns. "Break up your fallow ground and sow not among thorns." When the sower sowed, some fell among thorns, and the thorns sprang up and choked them; so is preaching to the unconverted.

Third, Because their end will be like that of thorns—they are dry, and fit only for the burning. "As thorns cut up shall they be burned in the fire." "For the earth, which is often rained upon and only bears thorns and briars, is rejected, and nigh unto cursing, whose end is to be burned."

My friends, if you are in a Christless state, see what you are in the eyes of Christ—*thorns.* You think that you have many admirable qualities, that you are valuable members of society, and you have a hope that it shall be well with you in eternity. See what Christ says, You are thorns and briars, useless in this world, and fit only for the burning.

2. See what Christ thinks of the believer: "As the lily among thorns, so is my love among the daughters." The be-

liever is like a lovely flower in the eyes of Christ. *First,* Because justified in the eyes of Christ, washed in His blood,
as pure and white as a lily. Christ can see no spot in His
own righteousness, and therefore He sees no spot on the
believer. Thou art all fair, my love, as a lily among thorns, so
is my love.

Second, A believer's nature is changed. Once he was like
the barren, prickly thorn, fit only for burning; now Christ
has put a new spirit in him; the dew has been given to him,
and he grows up like the lily. Christ loves the new creature.
"All my delight is in them." "As the lily among thorns, so
is my love among the daughters." Are you a Christian? then
never mind though the world despise you, though they call
you names; remember Christ loves you; He calls you "my
love." Abide in Him, and you shall abide in His love. "If ye
continue in my word, then are ye my disciples indeed."

Third, Because so lonely in the world. Observe, there is
only one lily, but many thorns. There is a great wilderness all
full of thorns, and only one lonely flower. So there is a world
lying in wickedness, and a little flock that believe in Jesus.
Some believers are cast down because they feel solitary and
alone. If I be in the right way, surely I would not be so lonely.
Surely the wise, and the amiable, and the kind people I see
round about me—surely, if there were any truth in religion,
they would know it. Be not cast down. It is one of the marks
of Christ's people that they are alone in the world, and yet
they are not alone. It is one of the very beauties which Christ
sees in His people, that they are solitary among a world of
thorns. "As a lily among thorns, so is my love among the
daughters."

Do not be discouraged. This world is the world of loneliness. When you are transplanted to yon garden of God, then
you shall be no more lonely, then you shall be away from all
the thorns. As flowers in a rich garden blend together their

thousand odors to enrich the passing breeze, so, in the paradise above, you shall join the thousands of the redeemed, blending with theirs the odor of your praise; you shall join with the redeemed to form a garland for the Redeemer's brow.

II. *Inquire what the believer thinks of Christ.*—"As the apple tree among the trees of the wood, so is my beloved among the sons. I sat down under his shadow with great delight, and his fruit was sweet to my taste."

1. Christ is more precious than all other saviours in the eye of the believer. As a traveler prefers an apple tree to every other tree of the wood, because he finds both shelter and nourishing food under it, so the believer prefers Christ to all other saviours. When a man is traveling in eastern countries, he is often about to drop down under the burning rays of the sun. It is a great relief when he comes to a wood. When the Israelites were traveling in the wilderness, they came to Elim, where were twelve wells of water and seventy palm trees, and they encamped there by the water. They were glad of the shelter of the trees. So Micah says that God's people "dwell solitarily in the wood"; and Ezekiel promises, "they shall sleep in the woods."

But if the traveler be hungry and faint for lack of food, then he will not be content with any tree of the wood, but he will choose out a fruit tree, under which he may sit down and find nourishment as well as shade. He sees a fair apple tree; he chooses it out of all the trees of the wood, because he can both sit under its shadow and eat its pleasant fruits. So is it with the soul awakened by God. He feels under the heat of God's anger; he is in a weary land; he is brought into the wilderness; he is about to perish; he comes to a wood; many trees offer their shade; where shall he sit down? Under the fir tree? Alas! what fruit has it to give? he may die there. Under the cedar tree, with its mighty branches? Alas! he may perish there, for it has no fruit to give. The soul that

is taught of God seeks for a complete Saviour. The apple
tree is revealed to the soul. The hungry soul chooses that
evermore. He needs to be saved from hell and nourished for
heaven. "As the apple tree among the trees of the wood, so
is my beloved among the sons."

Awakened souls, remember you must not sit down under
every tree that offers itself. "Take heed that no one deceive
you; for many shall come in Christ's name, saying, I am
Christ, and deceive many." There are many ways of saying,
Peace, peace, when there is no peace. You will be tempted
to find peace in the world, in self-repentance, in self-reformation. Remember, choose you a tree that will yield fruit as
well as shade. "As the apple tree among the trees of the
wood, so is my beloved among the sons." Pray for a choosing faith. Pray for an eye to discern the apple tree. Oh! there
is no rest for the soul except under that Branch which God
has made strong. My heart's desire and prayer for you is, that
you may all find rest there.

2. Why has the believer so high an esteem of Christ?

First, Because he has made trial of Christ. "I sat down
under his shadow with great delight." All true believers have
sat down under the shadow of Christ. Some people think that
they shall be saved because they have a head-knowledge of
Christ. They read of Christ in the Bible, they hear of Christ
in the house of God, and they think that is to be a Christian.
Alas! my friends, what good would you get from an apple
tree, if I were only to describe it to you—tell you how beautiful it was, how heavily laden with delicious apples? Or, if I
were only to show you a picture of the tree, or if I were to
show you the tree itself at a distance, what the better would
you be? You would not get the good of its shade or its pleasant
fruit.

Just so, dear brethren, what good would you get from Christ,
if you only hear of Him in books and sermons, or if you see

Him pictured forth in the sacrament, or if you were to see Him with your bodily eye? What good would all this do, if you do not sit down under His shadow? Oh, my friends, there must be a personal sitting down under the shadow of Christ if you would be saved! Christ is the bush that has been burned, yet not consumed. Oh! it is a safe place for a hell-deserving sinner to rest.

Some may be hearing me who can say, "I sat down under His shadow." And yet you have forsaken Him. Ah! have you gone after your lovers, and away from Christ? Well, then, may God hedge up your way with thorns. Return, return, O Shulamite! There is no other refuge for your soul. Come and sit down again under the shadow of the Saviour.

Second, Because he sat down with great delight.

Some people think there is no joy in religion, that it is a gloomy thing. When a young person becomes a Christian, they would say, Alas! he must bid farewell to pleasure, farewell to the joys of youth, farewell to a merry heart. He must exchange these pleasures for reading of the Bible and dry sermon books, for a life of gravity and preciseness. This is what the world says.

What does the Bible say? "I sat down under his shadow with great delight." Ah! let God be true, and every man a liar. Yet no one can believe this except those who have tried it. Ah! be not deceived, my young friends; the world has many sensual and many sinful delights, the delights of eating and drinking, and wearing gay clothes, the delights of revelry and the dance. No man of wisdom will deny that these things are delightful to the natural heart; but oh! they perish in the using, and they end in an eternal hell. But to sit down under the shadow of Christ, wearied with God's burning anger, wearied with seeking after vain saviours, at last to find rest under the shadow of Christ, ah! this is great delight. Lord, evermore may I sit under this shadow!

Some people are afraid of anything like joy in religion. They have none themselves, and they do not love to see it in others. Their religion is something like the stars, very high, and very clear, but very cold. When they see tears of anxiety, or tears of joy, they cry out, Enthusiasm, enthusiasm! Well, then, to the law, and to the testimony. "I sat down under his shadow *with great delight."* Is this enthusiasm? O Lord, evermore give us this enthusiasm! May the God of hope fill you with all joy and peace in believing! If it be really in sitting under the shadow of Christ, let there be no bounds to your joy. Oh, if God would but open your eyes, and give you simple, child-like faith, to look to Jesus, to sit under His shadow, then would songs of joy rise from all our dwellings. Rejoice in the Lord always, and again I say, Rejoice!

Third, Because the fruit of Christ is sweet to the taste. All true believers not only sit under the shadow, but partake of His pleasant fruits. Just as when you sit under an apple tree, the fruit hangs above you and around you, and invites you to put out the hand and taste; so when you come to submit to the righteousness of God, bow your head, and sit down under Christ's shadow, all other things are added unto you. Temporal mercies are sweet to the taste. None but those of you who are Christians know this, when you sit under the shadow of Christ's temporal mercies, because covenant mercies. "Bread shall be given you; your water shall be sure." These are sweet apples from the tree Christ. O Christian! tell me, is not bread sweeter when eaten thus? Is not water richer than wine, and Daniel's pulse better than the dainties of the king's table?

Afflictions are sweet to the taste. Every good apple has some sourness in it. So is it with the apples of the tree of Christ. He gives afflictions as well as mercies; He sets the teeth on edge; but even these are blessings in disguise, they are covenant gifts. Oh! affliction is a dismal thing when you are not under His shadow. But are you Christians? look on your sorrows as apples from that blessed tree. If you knew how wholesome they are, you would not wish to want them. Several of you know it is no contradiction to say, These apples, though sour, are sweet to my taste.

The gifts of the Spirit are sweet to the taste. Ah! here is the best fruit that grows on the tree; here are the ripest apples from the topmost branch. You who are Christians know how often your soul is fainting. Well, here is nourishment to your fainting soul. Everything you need is in Christ. "My grace is sufficient for thee." Dear Christian, sit much under that tree, feed much upon that fruit. "Stay me with flagons, comfort me with apples, for I am sick of love."

Promises of glory are sweet to the taste. Some of the apples have a taste of heaven in them. Feed upon these, dear Christians. Some of Christ's apples give you a relish for the fruit of Canaan—for the clusters of Eshcol. Lord, evermore give me these apples; for they are sweet to my taste.

St. Peter's, 1837.

MESSAGE IV

"A sword, a sword is sharpened, and also furbished: it is sharpened to make a sore slaughter; it is furbished that it may glitter: should we then make mirth? it contemneth the rod of my son, as every tree."—Ezekiel 21:9, 10.

FROM THE SECOND VERSE of this chapter we learn that this prophecy was directed against Jerusalem: "Son of man, set thy face toward Jerusalem, and drop thy word toward the holy places, and prophesy against the land of Israel."

We have already told you that Ezekiel, while yet a youth, was carried captive by Nebuchadnezzar, and placed, with a number of his countrymen, by the river of Chebar. It was there that he delivered his prophecies during a space of twenty-two years. The prophecy I have read was delivered in the seventh year of his captivity, and just three years before Jerusalem was

destroyed and the Temple burned. From verse 2, we learn that
these words were directed against Jerusalem; for though God
had taken Ezekiel away to minister to the captives by the river
of Chebar, yet He made him send many a message of warning
and of mercy to his beloved Jerusalem. "Son of man, set thy
face toward Jerusalem, and drop thy word toward the holy
places, and prophesy against the land of Israel."

God had already fulfilled many of the words of His prophets
against Jerusalem. He had fulfilled the word of Jeremiah
against one of their kings (Jehoiakim). "He shall be buried
with the burial of an ass: drawn and cast forth beyond the
walls of Jerusalem." He had fulfilled the word of the same
prophet in carrying another king (Jehoiachin) to Babylon with
all the goodly vessels of the house of the Lord. But still neither
prophecies nor judgments would awaken Jerusalem; so that
we are told (II Chron. 36:12) that Zedekiah, the next king,
"did that which was evil in the sight of the Lord his God, and
humbled not himself before Jeremiah the prophet, speaking
from the mouth of the Lord." Verses 14-16: "Moreover, all
the chief of the priests and the people transgressed very
much, after all the abominations of the heathen; and polluted
the house of the Lord, which he had hallowed in Jerusalem.
And the Lord God of their fathers sent to them by his messengers, rising up betimes, and sending; because He had compassion on his people, and on his dwelling place: but they
mocked the messengers of God, and despised his works, and
misused his prophets, until the wrath of the Lord arose against
his people, till there was no remedy."

It was in a time of great hardness and impenitence in Jerusalem that the prophecy before me was delivered, and just
three years before the wrath of God was poured on them to
the uttermost. *First,* All was mirth and sensuality in Jerusalem.
Second, The false prophets prophesied peace, and the people
loved to have it so. *Third,* There was no noise but that of

revelry within the devoted city. But in the midst of that din and revelry, the lone prophet by the river of Chebar heard the muttering of the distant thunder. The faithful servant of God saw God arming Himself as a mighty man for the war, and the glittering sword of vengeance in His hand, and he calls aloud to his countrymen, all at ease, with awakening thunders, "A sword, a sword is sharpened, and also furbished: it is sharpened to make a sore slaughter; it is furbished that it may glitter: should we then make mirth?"

My friends, those of you who are unconverted are in the very same situation as Jerusalem was. In the years that are now fled like the mists of the morning, how many messages have you had from God! How many times has He sent His messengers to you, rising up early and sending them! His Bible has been in your houses, a silent but most mighty pleader for God; His providence has been in your families, in sickness and death, in plenty or poverty—all, all beseeching you to flee from the wrath to come—all, all beseeching you to cleave to the Lord Jesus, the only, the all-sufficient Saviour.

All these messages have come to you, and you are yet unconverted—still dead, dry bones, without Christ and without God in the world; and you are saying, Soul, take thine ease, eat and drink and be merry. But do, my friends, hearken once more, for God does not wish any to perish. I have a word from God unto thee: "A sword, a sword is sharpened, and also furbished: it is sharpened to make a sore slaughter; it is furbished that it may glitter: should we then make mirth?"

Doctrine.—It is very unreasonable in unconverted persons to make mirth.

1. It is unreasonable, *because they are under condemnation.* —The sword is sharpened, and also furbished. It is sharpened to make a sore slaughter; it is furbished that it may glitter. Should we then make mirth? There is a common idea that men are under probation, as Adam was, and that Christless

persons will not be condemned till the judgment; but this is
not the case. The Bible says, "He that believeth not is condemned already." "He that hath not the Son shall not see
life, but the wrath of God abideth on him." "Cursed *is* every
one [not, *shall be*] who continueth not in all things written
in the book of the law to do them." Christless souls are at
present in the horrible pit, every mouth is stopped, and they
are guilty before God. They are in prison, ready to be brought
out to execution. Therefore, when God sends us to preach to
Christless persons, He calls it "preaching to the spirits in
prison," that is, who are under condemnation. The sword is
not only unsheathed, it is sharpened and furbished. It is held
over their heads.

Should they then make mirth? It is unreasonable in a condemned malefactor to make mirth. Would it not greatly
shock every feeling mind to see a company of men condemned
to die, meeting and making merry, talking lightly and jest-
ingly, as if the sword were not over them? Yet this is the
case of those of you who are unconverted and yet live lives
of mirth. You have been tried in the balance and found
wanting. You have been condemned by the righteous Judge.
Your sentence is past. You are now in prison; neither can
you break out of this prison: the sword is whetted and drawn
over you. And oh! is it not most unreasonable to make mirth?
Is it not most unreasonable to be happy and contented with
yourself and merry with your friends? Is it not madness to
sing the song of the drunkard? "Eat, drink, and be merry,
for tomorrow we die."

2. *Because God's instruments of destruction are all ready.*—
Not only are Christless persons condemned already, but the
instruments of their destruction are prepared and quite ready.
The sword of vengeance is sharpened, and also furbished.
When swords are kept in the armory, they are kept blunt, that
the rust may not hurt their edge; but when work is to be done,

and they are taken out for the slaughter, then they are furbished and sharpened, made sharp and glittering. So it is with the sword of the executioner: when not in use, it is kept blunt; but when work is to be done, it is sharpened and made ready. It is sharpened and furbished just before the blow is struck, that it may cut clean. So is it with God's sword of vengeance. It is not sheathed and blunt, it is sharpened and furbished; it is quite ready to do its work; it is quite ready for a sore slaughter. The disease by which every unconverted man is to die is quite ready; it is perhaps in his veins at this very moment. The accident by which he is to drop into eternity is quite ready, all the parts and means of it are arranged. The arrow that is to strike him is on the string—perhaps it has left the string, and is even now flying towards him.

The place in hell is quite ready for every unconverted soul. When Judas died, the Scripture says, "he went to his own place." It was his own place before he went there, being quite prepared and ready for him. As when a man retires at night to his sleeping room, it is said he has gone to his own room, so a place in hell is quite ready for every Christless person. It is his own place. When the rich man died and was buried, he was immediately in his own place. He found everything ready. He lifted up his eyes in hell, being in torments. So hell is quite ready for every Christless person. It was prepared, long ago, for the devil and his angels. The fires are all quite ready, and fully lighted and burning.

Ah! should Christless souls then make mirth? A malefactor might perhaps say that he would be merry as long as the scaffold was not erected on which he was to die. But if he were told that the scaffold was quite ready, that the sword was sharpened, and the executioner standing ready—oh! would it not be madness to make mirth? Alas! this is your madness, poor Christless soul. You are not only condemned, but the sword is sharpened and ready that is to smite your soul; and yet you can be happy, and dream away your days and nights in pleasures that perish in the using. The disease is ready, the accident is ready, the arrow is on the string, the grave is ready, yea, hell itself is ready, your own place is made ready; and yet you can make mirth! You can play games and enjoy company! How truly is your laughter like the crackling of thorns under a pot: a flashy blaze, and then the blackness of darkness forever!

3. *The sword may come down at any moment.*—Not only are Christless persons condemned already, and not only is the sword of vengeance quite ready, but the sword may come down at any moment. It is not so with malefactors; their day is fixed and told them, so that they can count their time. If they have many days, they make merry today at least, and begin to be serious tomorrow. But not so Christless persons; their day is fixed, but it is not told them. It may be this very moment. Ah! should they then make mirth?

Some malefactors have been found very stouthearted to the very last. Many have received their sentence quite unmoved, and with a determined countenance. Some have even gone to the scaffold quite unmoved; some even with a light, careless spirit. But when the head is laid down upon the block, when the eyes are covered, and the neck laid bare, when the glittering sword is lifted high in the air, and may come down any moment—that is a dreadful time of suspense. It would be very horrible to see a man in a light careless spirit at that time. Oh! it would be madness to be merry then.

Alas! this is your madness, poor Christless soul. You are not only condemned, and not only is the sword ready, but it may fall on you at any moment. Your head is, as it were, on the block. Your neck is bared before God, and the whetted sword is held over you; and yet can you make mirth? Can you take up your mind with business and worldly things, and getting rich, building and planting, and this night your soul may be required of you? Can you fill up your time with games and amusements, and foolish books and entertaining companions? Can you fill up your hours after work with loose talk and wanton behavior, adding sin to sin, treasuring up wrath against the day of wrath, when you know not what hour the wrath of God may come upon you to the uttermost? Can you go prayerless to your bed at night, your mind filled with dark and horrid imaginations not fit to be named, and yet you may be in hell before the morning? A sword, a sword; it is furbished!

4. *Because God has made no promise to Christless souls to stay His hand one moment.*—All the promises of God are yea and amen, that is, they are true. He always fulfills His promises. But the same scripture says they are "yea and amen *in Christ Jesus.*" All God's promises are made to Christ, and to sinners that cleave to Christ. I believe that it is impossible, in the nature of things, that God would make a promise to an unconverted man. Accordingly, all God's promises are made to Christ, and to every sinner that cleaves to Christ. But unconverted persons are those who have never come to Christ; therefore there are no promises made to them. God nowhere promises to make them anxious. He nowhere promises to bring them to Christ. He nowhere promises to keep them one moment out of hell. "Should they then make mirth?"

Let me speak to Christless persons who are at ease. Many of you hearing me may know that you are in a Christless state; and yet you know that you are at ease and happy. Why is this? It is because you hope to be brought to Christ before you die. You say, Another day will do as well, and I will hear thee again of this matter; and therefore you take your ease now. But this is very unreasonable. It is not worthy of a rational being to act in this way. God has nowhere promised to bring you to Christ before you die. God has laid Himself under no manner of obligation to you. He has no-

where promised that you shall see tomorrow, or that you shall
hear another sermon. There is a day near at hand when
you shall not see a tomorrow. If this be not the last, there
is a sermon yet to be preached which will be the last you
will ever hear.

Let me speak to Christless persons who are anxious about
their souls. Some hearing me know that they are in a Christless condition, and this made them anxious; and yet it is
to be feared some are losing that anxiety, and now going
back to the mirth of the world. Why is this? This is most
unreasonable. If you are still out of Christ, however anxious
you have been, remember God has made no promises to save
you. The sword is still over you, furbished and sharpened.
Ah! do not then make mirth. Strive to enter in at the strait
gate. Take the kingdom of heaven by violence. Press into it.
Never rest till you are in the bonds of the covenant. Then
be as happy as the day is long.

5. *It is a sore slaughter: "A sword! a sword!"*

Sore, because it will be on all who are Christless.—The
dreadfulness of the slaughter in Jerusalem was, that all were
slain, both old and young. The command which the prophet
heard was (9:5, 6), "Go ye through the city, and smite. Let
not your eye spare, neither have ye pity. Slay utterly old and
young, both maids and little children and women; but come
not near any man upon whom is the mark." Such is the sore
slaughter waiting on unconverted souls. All Christless persons will perish, young and old. God will not spare, neither
will His eye pity.

Think of this, *old grey-headed persons,* that have lived in
sin, and never come to Christ; if you die thus, you will certainly
perish in the sore slaughter.

Think of this, *middle-aged persons,* hard-working merchants
and laborers, who make money, but do not sell all for the
pearl of great price. Think of this, ye *Marthas,* who are care-

ful and troubled about many things, but who forget the one thing that is needful, you also will fall in the sore slaughter.

Think of this, *young persons,* who live without prayer, yet in mirth and jollity; you that meet to jest and be happy on Sabbath evenings; you that walk in the sight of your own eyes—you, too, will fall in that sore slaughter.

Think of this, *little children,* you that are the pride of your mother's heart, but who have gone astray, from the womb, speaking lies. Little children who are fond of your plays, but are not fond of coming to Jesus Christ, who is the Saviour of little children, the sword will come on you also. Oh! it is a sore slaughter that will not spare the young, nor the lovely, nor the kind—the gentle mother and affectionate child, the widow and her only son. Should you then make mirth? Unconverted families, when you meet in the evening to jest and sport with one another, ask this one question, Should we make mirth? Is your mirth reasonable? Is it worthy of rational beings? Unconverted companions, who meet so often for mirth and amusement, should you make mirth together when you are in such a case? Ah! how dismal will the contrast be when God says, Bind them in bundles to burn them!

Sore slaughter because the sword is the sword of God.—If it were only the sword of man that is furbished and sharpened for the slaughter, it would not be very terrible. But it is the sword of Almighty God, and therefore it is very terrible. "Fear not them that kill the body, but after that have no more that they can do. But I will forewarn you whom ye shall fear: Fear him, who after he hath killed the body, is able to cast body and soul into hell; yea, I say unto you, fear him." If it were the sword of man, it could reach only to the body; but, ah! it is the sword of God, and the iron will enter into the soul. It is the same sword that appeared in the garden of Eden, "a flaming sword, that turned every way to keep the way of the tree of life." It is the same sword which pierced the

side of Jesus Christ in His agony. "Awake, O sword, against
my Shepherd, and against the man that is my fellow, saith the
Lord of Hosts: I will smite the Shepherd, and the sheep shall
be scattered." It is that sword of which Christ speaks, when
He says, "It shall cut him asunder, and appoint him his portion with hypocrites: there shall be wailing and gnashing of
teeth."

Dear brethren, it is not a few flesh wounds that that
sword will make. It will cut asunder; it will be a deathblow
—eternal death. It is a death which body and soul will be
always dying, yet never dead.

1. *Let me speak to the old.*—There may be some hearing
me in whom these three things meet, namely, that they are old,
and Christless, and full of mirth. Oh! if there be such hearing me, consider your ways, consider if your mirth be worthy
of a rational being. I have shown you plainly out of the
Scriptures what your case is: *First,* that you are condemned
already; *second,* that God's sword is ready; *third,* that it may
come down any moment; *fourth,* that God has made you no
promise to stay His hand; and, *fifth,* that it will be a sore
slaughter. Consider, then, if it be reasonable to believe a lie,
to deceive your own soul, and say, Peace, peace, when there is
no peace. In the ordinary course of things, you must soon go
the way of all living; you must be gathered to your fathers,
and then all that I have said will be fulfilled. Should you then
make mirth? Are you tottering on the brink of hell, and
yet living prayerless and Christless, and playing with straws,
telling over the oft-repeated tale of youth, and laugh-
ing over the oft-repeated jest? Alas! what a depth of meaning
was there in the word of Solomon! "I said of laughter, It is
mad; and of mirth, What doeth it? Even in laughter the heart
is sorrowful, and the end of that mirth is heaviness."

2. *Let me speak to the young.*—There may be many hearing me in whom these three things meet: They are young in

years, far from Christ, and yet full of mirth. Now, my dear friends, I entreat you to consider whether your mirth is reasonable. The sword is sharpened for a sore slaughter. Should you then make mirth?

Objection 1.—Youth is the time for mirth.

Answer.—I know well youth is the time for mirth. The young lamb is a happy creature as it springs about on the green pasture. The young kid leaps from rock to rock with liveliest glee. The young horse casts its heels high in the air, full of life and activity. But then they have no sin, and you have; they have no hell, and you have. If you will come to Jesus Christ now, and be freed from wrath, ah! then you will find that youth is the time for mirth, youth is the time for enjoying sweet peace in the bosom, and liveliest intercourse with God, and brightest hopes of glory.

Objection 2.—You would have us to be gloomy and sad.

Answer.—God forbid. All that I maintain is, that until you are come to Christ, your mirth is mad and unreasonable. If you will come to Christ, then be as happy as you will; there are no bounds to your joy there, for you will joy in God. And when you die, you will come to fullness of joy in His presence, and pleasures at His right hand for evermore.

Objection 3.—If I be Christless, it will not bring me into Christ to be sad, and therefore I may as well be merry.

Answer.—True, to be sad will not bring you into Christ; and yet, if you were really awakened to cry to God, peradventure He would hear your cry. If you were striving to enter in, you might find entrance. If you were pressing into the kingdom, you might take it by violence. Seek meekness, seek righteousness. It may be ye shall be hid in the day of the Lord's anger. If you stay. where you are, you are sure to be lost. If you live on in carnal security, in mirth and jollity, while you are out of Christ, you are sure to perish.

"Rejoice, O young man, in thy youth, and let thy heart cheer thee in the days of thy youth, and walk in the ways of thine heart, and in the sight of thine eyes; but know thou that for all these things God will bring thee into judgment."

Dundee, 1837.

___

MESSAGE V

"Unto you, O men, I call; and my voice is to the sons of men."—Proverbs 8:4.

THESE are the words of wisdom; and wisdom in the book of Proverbs is none other than our Lord and Saviour Jesus Christ. This is evident from chapter 1, verse 23, where He says, "Behold, I will pour out my Spirit unto you"; but it is Christ alone who has the gift of the Holy Spirit. And again, from 8:22, where He says, "The Lord possessed me in the beginning of his way"; and verse 30: "Then I was by him as one brought up with him; and I was daily his delight, rejoicing always before him." These words are true of none but of Jesus Christ, the Word that was with God, and was God, by whom all things were made.

Observe the places He goes to with the invitation.—*First,* He goes to the country. He climbs every eminence, and cries there; then He descends to the highway where many roads meet.

Second, He goes to the city. He begins at the gates, where the people are assembled to make bargains and hear causes; then He proceeds along the principal avenue into the city, and cries in at every door as He passes. He first goes out into the highways and hedges, then goes into the streets and lanes of the city, carrying the blessed message.

Observe the manner in which He invites.—He cries aloud, He puts forth the voice, He stands and cries, He calls and lifts up His voice, He seems like some merchant offering his wares, first in the market, and then from door to door. Never did busy crier offer to sell his goods with such anxiety as Jesus

offers His salvation; verse 10: "Receive my instruction, and
not silver; and knowledge rather than choice gold."

Observe to whom the invitation is addressed.—Verse 4:
"Unto you, O men, I call; and my voice is to the sons of
men." Merchants only offer their goods to certain classes of
the people that will buy; but Jesus offers His to all men.
Wherever there is a son of Adam, wherever there is one born
of woman, the word is addressed to him: he that hath ears
to hear, let him hear.

Doctrine.—Christ offers Himself as a Saviour to all of the
human race.

I. *The most awakening truth in all the Bible.*—It is commonly thought that preaching the holy law is the most awakening truth in the Bible, that by it the mouth is stopped, and
all the world becomes guilty before God; and, indeed, I
believe this is the most ordinary means which God makes use
of. And yet to me there is something far more awakening
in the sight of a Divine Saviour freely offering Himself to
every one of the human race. There is something that might
pierce the heart that is like a stone in that cry: "Unto you,
O men, I call; and my voice is to the sons of men."

1. Had you lived in the days when Noah built the ark, had
you seen that mighty vessel standing open and ready, inviting all the world to come into its roomy cavities, would it not
have been the most awakening of all sights? Could you have
looked upon it without thinking of the coming flood that
was to sweep the ungodly world away?

2. Had you lived in the times when Jesus was on the earth,
had you seen Him riding down the Mount Olivet, and stopping when He came in sight of Jerusalem, lying peaceful and
slumbering at His feet, had you seen the Son of God weep
over the city, and say, "If thou hadst known, even thou, at
least in this thy day, the things which belong to thy peace!
but now they are hid from thine eyes," would you not have

felt that some awful destruction was awaiting the slumbering city? Would He shed these tears for nothing? Surely He sees some day of woe coming which none knows but Himself.

3. Just so, dear friends, when you see Jesus here running from place to place, from the high places to the highways, from the highways to the city gates, from the gates to the doors; when you hear His anxious cry, "Unto you, O men, I call," does it not show that all men are lost, that a dreadful hell is before them? Would the Saviour call so loud and so long if there were no hell?

Apply this to slumbering souls.

Mark who it is that calls you—it is Wisdom! It is Jesus Christ, in whom are hid all the treasures of wisdom and knowledge. "Unto you, O men, I call." Often, when ministers prick your hearts in their sermons, you go home and say, "Oh! it was only the word of a minister—shall I tremble at the words of a man?" But here is the word of no minister, but of Christ. Here is the word of one who knows your true condition, who knows your heart and your history, who knows your sins done in the light, and done in the dark, and done in the recesses of your heart, who knows the wrath that is over you, and the hell that is before you. "Unto you, O men, I call."

Mark in how many places He calls you.—In the high places and the highways, in the gates, in the entries, at the coming in of the doors. Has it not been so with you? Have you not been called in the Bible, in the family, in the house of prayer? You have gone from place to place, but the Saviour has gone after you. You have gone to places of diversion, you have gone to places of sin, but Christ has followed you. You have lain down on a bed of sickness, and Christ has followed you. Must not the sheep be in great danger, when the Shepherd follows so far in search of it?

How loud He cries.—He calls and lifts up the voice. Has it not been so with you? Has He not knocked loudly at your

door, in warnings, in providences, in deaths? Has He not
cried loudly in the preached Word? Sometimes, when reading
the Bible alone, has not the voice of Christ been louder than
thunder?

He cries to all.—Had He cried to the old, then the young
would have said, "We are safe, we do not need a Saviour."
Had He cried to the young, the old men among you would
have said, "He is not for us." Had he called to the good or
to the bad, still some would have felt themselves excused.
But He cries to you all. There is not one person hearing, but
Jesus cries to you. Then all are lost—old and young, rich
and poor. Whatever you think of yourselves, Jesus knows
you to be in a lost condition; therefore this piercing cry, "Unto
you, O men, I call."

II. *The most comforting truth in the Bible.*—When awakened persons are first told of Jesus Christ, it generally adds
to their grief. They see plainly that He is a very great and
glorious Saviour; but then they feel that they have rejected
Him, and they fear that He never can become their Saviour.
Very often awakened persons sit and listen to a lively description of Christ, of His work of substitution in the stead of
sinners; but their question still is, "Is Christ a Saviour to me?"
Now, to this question I answer, Christ is freely offered to all
the human race. "Unto you, O men, I call." If there were
no other text in the whole Bible to encourage sinners to come
freely to Christ, this one alone might persuade them. There
is no subject more misunderstood by unconverted souls than
the unconditional freeness of Christ. So little idea have we
naturally of free grace, that we cannot believe that God can
offer a Saviour to us, while we are in a wicked, hell-deserving
condition. Oh, it is sad to think how men argue against their
own happiness, and will not believe the very word of God!

All the types show the Saviour to be free to all.

1. The brazen serpent was lifted up in sight of all Israel,

that anyone might look and be healed; and Christ Himself explains this: "So must the Son of man be lifted up, that whatsoever believeth on him should not perish, but have everlasting life."

2. The Refuge City set on a hill, with its gates open night and day, showed this. Whosoever will, may flee for refuge to the hope set before us.

3. The angels over Bethlehem repeated the same thing: "Behold, I bring you glad tidings of great joy, which shall be to all people." And the last invitation of the Bible is the freest of all: "Whosoever will, let him take the water of life freely." Mark, also, in the text before us: "Unto you, O men, I call." This shows that He is not free to devils; but to all *men*, to every one that has human form and human name the Saviour is now free. It is not for any goodness in men, not for any change in them that Christ offers Himself, but just in their lost condition as men. He freely puts Himself within their reach. There are many stratagems by which the devil contrives to keep men away from Christ.

Some say there is no hope for them. "There is no hope, no; for I have loved strangers, and after them I will go. I have committed such great sins, I have sunk so deep in the mire of sin, I have served my lusts so long, that there is no use of me thinking of turning. There is no hope, no." To you I answer, There is hope; your sins may be forgiven for Christ's sake; there is forgiveness with God. Ah, why should Satan so beguile you? True, you have waded deep into the mire of sin, you have destroyed yourself; and yet in Christ there is help. He came for such as you. Christ speaks in these words to you: you are of the human race, and Christ is free to all of the human race—"Unto you, O men, I call."

"I have not the least care about my soul. Up to this moment I never listened to a sermon, nor attended to a word in the Bible. I have no wish to hear of Christ, or God, or eternal things." To you I answer, Still Christ is quite free to you. Though you have no care for your soul, yet Christ has, and wishes to save it. Though you do not care for Christ, yet He cares for you, and stretches out His hands to you. Christ did not come to the earth because people were caring about their souls, but because we were lost. You are only the more lost. Christ is all the more seeking you. This day you may find a Saviour. "Unto you, O men, I call."

"If I knew I were one of the elect, I would come; but I fear I am not." To you I answer, Nobody ever came to Christ because they knew themselves to be of the elect. It is quite true that God has of His mere good pleasure elected some to everlasting life, but they never knew it till they came to Christ. Christ nowhere invites the elect to come to Him. The question for you is not, Am I one of the elect? but, Am I of the human race?

Some of you may be saying, "If I could see my name in the Bible, then I would believe that Christ wants me to be saved. When Christ called Zaccheus, He said, 'Zaccheus, come down.' He called him by name, and he came down immediately. Now, if Christ would call me by name, I would run to Him immediately." Now, to you I say, Christ does call you by your name, for He says, "To you, O men, I call." Suppose that Christ had written down the names of all the men and women in the world, your name would have been there. Now, instead of writing down every name, He puts them all together in one word, which includes every man, and woman, and child: "Unto you, O *men*, I call; and my words are to the *sons of men*." So your name is in the Bible. "Go and preach the gospel to every creature."

"If I could repent and believe, then Christ would be free to me; but I cannot repent and believe." To you I say, Are you not a man, before you repent and believe? then Christ is offered to you before you repent. And, believer, Christ is

not offered to you because you repent, but because you are a
vile, lost sinner. "Unto you, O men, I call."

"I fear the market is over. Had I come in the morning of
life—I believe Christ was offered me then, in youth, at my
first sacrament—but now I fear the market day is done." Are
you not still a man, one of the human race? True, you have
refused the Saviour for years, yet still He offers Himself to
you. It was not for any goodnes that He offered Himself to
you at first, but because you were vile and lost. You are vile
and lost yet, so He offers Himself to you still. "Unto you, O
men, I call."

I would here, then, take occasion to make offer of Christ
with all His benefits to every soul in this assembly. To every
man and woman and child I do now, in the name of my Master, make full, free offer of a crucified Saviour, to be your
surety and righteousness, your refuge and strength. I would
let down the gospel cord so low, that sinners, who are low of
stature, like Zaccheus, may lay hold of it. Oh! is there none
will lay hold on Christ, the only Saviour?

III. *The most condemning truth in the Bible.*

If Christ be freely offered to all men, then it is plain that
all who live and die without accepting Christ shall meet with
the doom of those who refuse the Son of God. "He that sin-
neth against me wrongeth his own soul: all they that hate me
love death." Ah! it is a sad thing that the very truth, which is
life to every believing soul, is death to all others. This is the
condemnation. We are a sweet savor of Christ unto God.
When the ignorant heathen stand at the bar of God, Hindus,
and Africans, and Chinese who have never had the offer of
Christ made to them, they will not be condemned as those
will that have lived and died unsaved under a preached gospel.
Tyre and Sidon will not meet the same doom as Chorazin and
Bethsaida, and unbelieving Capernaum.

Oh, brethren, you are without excuse in the sight of God, if you go home unsaved this day! The gospel cord has been let down very low to every one of you this day. If you go away without laying hold, your condemnation will be heavier at the last day. If Christ had not come to you, you had not had sin, but now you have no cloak for your sin.

Objection.—But my heart is so hard that I cannot believe; my heart is so set upon worldly things that I cannot turn to Christ. I was born this way.

Answer.—This does but aggravate your guilt. It is true you were born thus, and that your heart is like the nether millstone. But that is the very reason God will most justly condemn you; because from your infancy you have been hardhearted and unbelieving. If a thief, when tried before the judge on earth, were to plead guilty, but to say that he had always been a thief, that even in infancy his heart loved stealing, would not this just aggravate his guilt, that he was by habit and repute a thief? So with you.

Oh, brethren, if you could die and say that Christ had never been offered to you, you would have an easier hell than you are likely to have! You must go away either rejoicing in or rejecting Christ this day; either won, or more lost than ever. There is not one of you but will yet feel the guilt of this Sabbath day. This sermon will meet you yet. See that ye refuse not him that speaketh: "How shall we escape if we neglect so great salvation?"

St Peter's, 1838.

MESSAGE VI

"That which was from the beginning, which we have heard, which we have
seen with our eyes which we have looked upon, and our hands have handled,
of the Word of life (for the life was manifested, and we have seen it, and
bear witness, and show unto you that eternal life which was with the Father,
and was manifested unto us); that which we have seen and heard declare we
unto you, that ye also may have fellowship with us: and truly our fellowship is with the Father, and with his Son Jesus Christ. And these things
write we unto you, that your joy may be full."—I John 1:1-4.

IT WAS JESUS CHRIST and Him crucified that John
preached. "That which we have seen and heard, declare
we unto you." This was the preaching of *John the Baptist:*
"Behold the Lamb of God, which taketh away the sins of
the world." He pointed to Jesus. This was the preaching of
Philip—Acts 8:5: "Philip went down to Samaria, and preached
Christ unto them." And when he came to the Ethiopian
eunuch, "he preached unto him Jesus." This was the preaching of *Paul:* "I determined to know nothing among you, but
Jesus Christ and him crucified." This was the beginning, and
middle, and end of the preaching of Paul. This was the
preaching of *John:* To declare all that he had seen with his
eyes, heard with his ears, handled with his hands, of Immanuel
—this was the object of his life, this was the Alpha and Omega
of his preaching. He knew that Jesus was like the *alabaster
box,* full of spikenard, very costly; and his whole labor was to
break the box and pour forth the good ointment before the
eyes of fainting sinners, that they might be attracted by the
sweet savor. He knew that Jesus was *a bundle of myrrh,* and
his whole life was spent in opening it out to sinners, that they
might be overcome by the refreshing odors. He carried about
the savor of Christ with him wherever he went. He knew
that Jesus was the Balm of Gilead, and his labor was to
open out this bruised balm before the eyes of sick souls,
that they might be healed.

   I. *The things John preached concerning Christ.*

1. *His eternity.*—"That which was from the beginning."
John had often heard Jesus speak of His eternity. "In the
beginning was the Word." "Before Abraham was, I am."
He remembered how Jesus said in prayer in the garden,
"Glorify me with the glory which I had with thee before the
world was." "Thou lovedst me before the foundation of the
world." John thus knew that He was the Eternal One, that He
was before all visible things, for He made them all. By Him
God made the world. Even at the time John was leaning on
His bosom, he felt that it was the bosom of the Uncreated
One. John always declared this; he loved to make Him known.
O beloved! if you have come to lean on the bosom of Jesus,
you have come to the Uncreated One—the Eternal One.

2. *His eternal pre-existence with the Father.*—John
knew, from Proverbs 8:30, that Jesus had been with the
Father: "Then I was by him, as one brought up with him,
and I was daily his delight, rejoicing always before him." He
had heard Jesus tell many of the secrets of His Father's bosom,
from which he knew that He had been with the Father: "All
things that I have heard of my Father I have made known
unto you." He had heard Jesus plainly say, "I came forth
from the Father, and am come into the world." "Again I
leave the world, and go to the Father." John felt, even when
Jesus was washing his feet, that this was the man that was
God's fellow. Even when he saw Jesus on the cross, with
His pale lips and bleeding hands and feet, like a tortured
worm, and "no man," he knew that this was the man that
was God's fellow. He lived to declare this. Do you thus look
to Jesus? Have you beheld the glory, as of the only begotten
of the Father, full of grace and truth? O tempest-tossed soul,
this is He that comes to save thee!

3. *His eternal life.*—John knew that Jesus was the Author of
all *natural life*, that not a man breathes, no beast of the forest
roars, no bird stoops on the wing, but they all receive the

stream of life from the hand of Immanuel. He had seen
Jesus raise the ruler's daughter from the dead, and call Lazarus
from the tomb. He knew that Jesus was the Author of all
life in the soul. He had heard Jesus say, "As the Father
raiseth up the dead, and quickeneth whom he will, even so the
Son quickeneth whom he will." "My sheep know my voice,
and I give unto them eternal life." He had heard Him say,
"I am the way, the truth, and the life."

Above all, he had *felt in his own soul* that Christ was the
Eternal Life. In that morning, when he sat with his father
Zebedee in the boat, mending their nets, Jesus said, "Follow
me!" and the life entered into his soul, and he found it a never-
failing spring of life. Christ was his life; therefore did he make
Him known as the Eternal Life. Even when he saw Him give
up the ghost; when he saw His pale, lifeless body, the stiff
hands and feet, the glazed eye, the body cold as the rocky
tomb where they laid Him; still he felt that this was the
Eternal Life. O beloved! do you believe that He is the life of
the world? Some of you feel your soul to be dead—lifeless in
prayer—lifeless in praise. Oh look on Him whom John declares to you! All is death without Him. Bring your dead
soul into union with Him, and He will give you eternal life.

4. *His Being Manifested.*—O beloved, if Jesus had not been
manifested, you had never been saved! It would have been
quite righteous in God to have kept His Son in His own bosom,
to have kept that jewel in His own place upon the throne of
heaven. God would have been the same lovely God; but we
would have lain down in a burning hell. If that Eternal Life
which was with the Father had remained in His glory as the
Living One, then you and I would have borne our own curse.
But He was manifested: "God was manifest in the flesh, justified in the Spirit, seen of angels, believed on in the world, received up into glory."

John saw Him: he saw His lovely countenance; he beheld

His glory, as the glory of the only begotten of the Father, full of grace and truth. He saw that better Sun veiled with flesh that could not keep the beams of His Godhead from shining through. He saw Him on the Mount, when His face shone like the sun. He saw Him in the garden, when He lay upon the ground. He saw Him on the cross, when He hung between earth and heaven. He looked upon Him—many a time he looked upon His heavenly countenance—his eye met His eye.

He heard Him, heard the voice that said, "Let there be light!" He heard the voice like the sound of many waters. He heard all His gracious words—His words concerning God and the way of peace. He heard Him say to a sinner, "Be of good cheer, thy sins are forgiven thee."

He handled Him, he put his hands in His hands, his arms around His arms, and his head upon His bosom. Perhaps he handled His body when it was taken from the cross, touched the cold clay of Immanuel. O beloved, it is a manifested Christ we declare unto you. It is not the Son in the bosom of the Father; that would never have saved you. It is Jesus manifested in flesh. The Son of God living and dying as man in the stead of sinners; Him we declare unto you.

Learn the true way of coming to peace.—It is by looking to a manifested Jesus. Some of you think you will come to peace *by looking in* to your own heart. Your eye is riveted there. You watch every change there. If you could only see a glimpse of light there, oh, what joy it would give you! If you could only see a melting of your stony heart, if you could only see your heart turning to God, if you could only see a glimpse of the image of Jesus in your heart, you would be at peace; but you cannot, all is dark within. Oh, dear souls, it is not there you will find peace! You must *avert the eye* from your bosom altogether. *You must look to a declared Christ.* Spread out the record of God concerning His Son. The Gospels are the narrative of the heart of Jesus, of the work of Jesus, of the grace of

Jesus. Spread them out before the eye of your mind, till they fill your eye. Cry for the Spirit to breathe over the page, to make a manifested Christ stand out plainly before you; and the moment that you are willing to believe all that is there spoken concerning Jesus, that moment you will wipe away your tears, and change your sighs for a new song of praise.

II. *The object John had in view by preaching Christ.*

1. *That ye may have fellowship with us.*—To have fellowship with another is to have things in common with him. Thus, in Acts 4:32, the first Christians were "of one heart and of one soul; neither said any that aught of the things which he possessed was his own, but *they had all things in common."* They had all their goods in common; they shared what they had with one another. This is what John desired in spiritual things —that we should share with him in his spiritual things, share and share alike.

In Forgiveness.—Some people think it impossible to have the same forgiveness that the apostles had, that it would be very bold to think of tasting the same. But is it not far bolder to say that John is a liar, and that the Holy Spirit is a liar? For he here says plainly, that all his preaching, and all his desire was, that you should have fellowship with Him. Yes, sinner, forgiveness is as open to you as it was to John. The blood that washed him is ready to wash you as white as snow. John had the same need of Christ that the vilest of you have. Only look to a declared Immanuel; clear your eye from unbelief, and look at a freely-revealed Jesus, and you will find the same forgiveness is as free to you as it was to John.

In the same love of Jesus.—John was the disciple whom Jesus loved. Just as Daniel was the prophet whom He greatly loved, "a man greatly beloved," so John was the disciple whom Jesus loved. At the Last Supper which Jesus had in this world, John leaned upon His bosom. He had the nearest place to the heart of Christ of any in all the world. Perhaps you think it is impossible you can ever come to that. Some of you are trembling afar off; but you, too, if you will only look where John points you, if you will only believe the full record of God about Jesus, will share the love of Jesus with John, you will be one of His peculiarly beloved ones. Those that believe most, get most love; they come nearest to Jesus—they do, as it were, lay their head on His breast; and no doubt you will one day really share that bosom with John. If you believe little, you will keep far off from Jesus.

In the same fatherly dealings as John.—John experienced many wonderful dealings of God. He experienced many of *the prunings* of the Father. He was a fruitful branch, and the Father pruned him that he might bring forth more fruit. When he was very old, he was banished to Patmos, an island in the Ægean Sea, and, it is supposed, made a slave in the mines there. He was a companion in tribulation; but he had many sweet shinings of the Father's love to his soul. He had sweet revelations of Christ in the time of his affliction; and he was joyfully delivered out of all his troubles. He experienced peculiarly the fatherly dealings of God. And so may you do, believer. Look where John looked, believe as John believed; and, like him, you will find that you have a Father in heaven, who will care for you, who will correct you in measure, who will stay His rough wind in the day of His east wind, who will preserve you unto His heavenly kingdom.

2. *That ye may have fellowship with the Father.*—O beloved, this is so wonderful, that I could not have believed it, if I had not seen it! Shall a hell-deserving worm come to share with the holy God? Oh the depth and the length of the love of God, it passeth knowledge!

In His holiness.—A natural man has not a spark of God's holiness in him. There is a kind of goodness about you. You may be kind, pleasant, agreeable, good-natured, amiable people; there may be a kind of integrity about you, so that you are above stealing or lying; but as long as you are in a natural state, there is not a grain of God's holiness in you. You have not a grain of that absolute hatred against all sin which God has; you have none of that flaming love for what is lovely, pure, holy, which dwells in the heart of God. But the moment you believe on a manifested Christ, that moment you receive the Spirit, the same Spirit which dwells in the infinite bosom of the Father dwelleth in you; so you become partakers of God's holiness, you become partakers of the divine nature. You will not be as holy as God; but the same stream that flows through the heart of God will be given you. Ah! does not your heart break to be holier? Look then to Jesus, and abide in Him, and you will share the same spirit with God Himself.

In His joy.—No joy is like the divine joy. It is infinite, full, eternal, pure unmingled joy. It is light, without any cloud to darken it; it is calm, without any breath to ruffle it. Clouds and darkness are round about Him, storms and fire go before Him; but within all is peace ineffable, unchangeable. Believers in some measure share in this joy. We might mention some of the elements of God's joy. *First,* All things happen according to the good pleasure of His will. He has foreordained whatsoever comes to pass. Nothing comes unprepared upon God. Many things are hateful in His sight, yet, looking on the whole, He can delight in all. If you have come to Christ, you will have some drops of His joy. You can look upon all events with a calm, holy joy, knowing that your Father's will and purposes alone shall stand. *Second,* The conversion of souls. There is joy in the presence of the angels of God over one sinner repenting, more than over ninety-nine who need no repentance. I have no doubt that this is one of the great elements of His joy —seeing souls brought into His favour. He loves to save; He delighteth in mercy; He delights when He can be a just God and a Saviour. If you are come to Christ, you will have the same joy.

3. *That ye may have fellowship with the Son.*

We share with the Son in His justification.—Once Jesus was unjustified; once there were sins laid to His charge—the sins of many. It was this that occasioned His agony *in the garden, on the cross.* His only comfort was, "He is near that justifieth me." He knew the time would be short. But now the wrath of God has all fallen upon Him. The thunderclouds of God's anger have spent all their lightnings on His head. The vials of God's wrath have poured out their last drops upon Him. He is now justified from all the sins that were laid upon Him. He has left them with the graveclothes. His fellow men and devils laid all sins to His charge; He was silent. Do you believe this record concerning the Son? Do you cleave to Jesus as yours? Then you have fellowship with Him in His justification. You are as much justified as Christ is. There is as little guilt lying upon you as there is upon Christ. The vials of wrath have not another drop for Christ, nor another drop for you. You are justified from all things.

In His adoption.—When Jesus went up to heaven, He said, "I go to my Father." When He entered heaven, the word of God was "Thou art my Son; sit thou on my right hand until I make thine enemies thy footstool." Oh, it was a blessed exchange, when He left the frowns and curses of this world for the embrace of His Father's arms; when He left the thorny crown for a crown of glory; when He came from under the wrath of God into the fatherly love of God! Such is your change, you that believe in Jesus. You have fellowship with the Son, you share in His adoption. He says, "I ascend to my Father and your Father." God is as much your Father as He is Christ's Father, your God as Christ's God. Oh, what a change! for an heir of hell to become an heir of God, and joint-heir with Christ; to inherit God; to have a son's interest in God! Eternity alone will teach you what is in that word, "heir of God."

4. *That your joy may be full.*—Other joys are not filling.

Creature joys only fill a small part of the soul. Money, houses, lands, music, entertainments, friends, these are not filling joys; they are just drops of joys. But Christ revealed makes the cup run over. "Thou anointest my head with oil, my cup runneth over." Believing in a manifested Christ fills the heart full of joy. "In thy presence is fullness of joy." Christ brings the soul into God's presence. One smile of God fills the heart more than ten thousand smiles of the world.

You that have nothing but creature joy, hunting after butter-flies, feeding upon carrion, why do you spend money for that which is not bread? You that are afflicted, tempest-tossed, and not comforted, look to a manifested Jesus. According to your faith so be it unto you. Believe none, and you will have no joy. Believe little, and you will have little joy. Believe much, and you will have much joy. Believe all, and you will have all joy, and your joy will be full. It will be like a bowl running over, good measure, pressed down, and running over. Amen.

St. Peter's, 1839.

Message VII.

"A garden enclosed is my sister, my spouse; a spring shut up, a fountain sealed."
—Song of Solomon 4:12.

THE NAME here given to believers is "my sister, my spouse," or rather, "my sister-spouse." There are many sweet names from the lips of Christ addressed to believers: "O thou fairest among women" (1:8); "My love" (2:2); "My love, my fair one" (2:10); "O my dove" (2:14); "My sister, my love, my dove, my undefiled" (5:2); "O prince's daughter" (7:1). But here is one more tender than all, "*My sister, my spouse*" (4:9); and again, verse 10, and here, verse 12. To be spoken well of by the world is little to be desired; but to hear Christ speak such words to us, is enough to fill our hearts with heavenly joy. The meaning you will see by what Paul says,

I Corinthians 9:5: "Have we not power to lead about a sister, a wife, as well as other apostles?" He means power to marry one who is likeminded—a sister in the Lord; one who will be both a wife and a sister in Christ Jesus—a *wife* by covenant, a *sister* by being born of the same Father in heaven. So Christ here says of believers, "My sister, my spouse," that they are not only united to Him by choice and covenant, but are likeminded also.

I. *These two things are inseparable.*—Some would like to be *the spouse* of the Saviour, without being the sister. Some would like to be saved by Christ, but not to be made like Christ. When Christ chooses a sinner, and sets His love on the soul, and when He woos the soul and draws it into covenant with Himself, it is only that He may make the soul a sister, that He may impart His features, His same heart, His all, to the soul. Now, many rest in the mere forgiveness of sins. Many have felt Christ wooing their soul, and offering Himself freely to them, and they have accepted Him. They have consented to the match. Sinful and worthless and hell-deserving, they find that Christ desires it; that He will not be dishonored by it; that He will find glory in it; and their heart is filled with joy in being taken into covenant with so glorious a bridegroom. But why has He done it? To make you partaker of His holiness, to change your nature, to make you sister to Himself, of His own mind and spirit. He has sprinkled you with clean water, only that He may give you a new heart also. He brings you to Himself and gives you rest only that He may make you learn of Him His meekness and lowliness in heart.

1. You cannot be the spouse of Christ without becoming sister also. Christ offers to be the bridegroom of sin-covered souls. He came from heaven for this; took flesh and blood for this. He tries to woo sinners, standing and stretching out His hands. He tells them of all His power, and glory, and riches, and that all shall be theirs. He is a blood-sprinkled bridegroom; but

that is His chief loveliness. The soul believes His Word, melts under His love, consents to be His. "My beloved is mine, and I am his." Then He washes the soul in His own blood; clothes it in His own righteousness; takes it in with Him to the presence of His Father. From that day the soul begins to reflect His image. Christ begins to live in the soul. The same heart, the same spirit, are in both. The soul becomes sister as well as spouse—Christ's not only by choice and covenant, but by likeness also. Some of you Christ has chosen; you have become His justified ones. Do you rest there? No; remember you must be made like Him, reflect His image; you cannot separate the two.

2. *The order of the two.*—You must be first the spouse before you can be the sister of Christ, His by covenant before His by likeness. Some think to be like Christ first, that they will copy His features till they recommend themselves to Christ. No, this will not do. He chooses only those that have no comeliness—polluted in their own blood, that He may have the honor of washing them. "When thou wast in thy blood," Ezekiel 16:6. Are there any trying to recommend themselves to Christ by their change of life? Oh, how little you know Him! He comes to seek those who are black in themselves. Are there some of you poor, defiled, unclean? You are just the soul Christ woos. Proud, scornful? Christ woos you. He offers you His all, and then He will change you.

II. *To what Christ compares believers:*

1. *"A garden enclosed."*—The gardens in the East are always enclosed; sometimes by a fence of reeds, such are the gardens of cucumbers in the wilderness; sometimes by a stone wall, as the garden of Gethsemane; sometimes by a hedge of prickly pear. But what is still more interesting is, they are often enclosed out of a wilderness. All around is often barren sand; and this one enclosed spot is like the garden of the Lord. Such is the believer.

Enclosed by election.—In the eye of God, the world was one great wilderness, all barren, all dead, all fruitless. No part was fit to bear anything but briers. It was nigh unto cursing. One part was no better than another in His sight. The hearts of men were all hard as rock, dry and barren as the sand. Out of the mere good pleasure of His will, He marked out a garden of delights where He might show His power and grace, that it might be to His praise. Some of you know your election of God by the fruits of it, by your faith, love, and holiness. Be humbled by the thought that it was solely because He chose you. Why me, Lord, why me?

Enclosed by the Spirit's work.—Election is the planning of the garden. The Spirit's work is the carrying it into effect. "He fenced it" (Isa. 5:2). When the Spirit begins His work, it is separating work. When a man is convinced of sin, he is no more one with the careless, godless world. He avoids his companions—goes alone. When a soul comes to Christ, it is still more separated. It then comes into a new world. He is no more under the curse—no more under wrath. He is in the smile and favor of God. Like Gideon's fleece, he now receives the dew when all around is dry.

Enclosed by the arms of God.—God is a wall of fire. Angels are around the soul. Elisha's hill was full of horses of fire. God is round about the soul, as the mountains stand round about Jerusalem. The soul is hid in the secret of God's presence. No robber can ever come over the fence. "A vineyard of red wine: I the Lord do keep it; I will water it every moment: lest any hurt it, I will keep it night and day" (Isa. 27: 2, 3). This is sung over thee.

An Eastern garden was watered in three ways: by a hidden well—it is the custom in the East to roll a stone over the mouth of a well, to preserve the water from sand; by a fountain of living water—a well always bubbling up; by streams from Lebanon.

2. *"A spring shut up."*—This describes the Spirit in the heart, in His most secret manner of working. In some gardens there is only this secret well. A stone is over the mouth. If you wish to water the garden, you must roll away the stone, and let down the bucket. Such is the life of God in many souls. Some of you feel that there is a stone over the mouth of the well in you. Your own rocky heart is the stone. Stir up the gift of God which is in thee.

3. *A well of living water.*—This is the same as John 4—a well that is ever full and running over. Grace new every moment; fresh upspringings from God. Thus only will you advance.

4. *Streams from Lebanon.*—These are very plentiful. On all sides they fall in pleasant cascades, in the bottom unite into broad full streams, and on their way water the richest gardens. The garden of Ibrahim Pacha, near Acre, is watered with streams from Lebanon. So believers are sometimes favored with streams from the Lebanon that is above. We receive out of Christ's fullness—drink of the wine of His pleasures. Oh, for more of these streams of Lebanon! Even in the dry season they are full. The hotter the summer, the streams from Lebanon become the fuller, because the heat only melts the mountain snows.

III. *The fruit.*—The very use of a garden is to bear fruit and flowers. For this purpose it is enclosed, hedged, planted, watered. If it bear no fruit nor flowers, all the labor is lost labor. The ground is nigh to cursing. So is it with the Christian. Three remarkable things are here:

1. *No weeds are mentioned.*—Pleasant fruit trees, and all the chief spices; but no weeds. Had it been a man that was describing his garden, he would have begun with the weeds— the unbelief, corruption, evil tempers, etc. Not so Christ. He covers all the sins. The weeds are lost sight of. He sees no perversity. As in John 17: "They have kept thy word; they

are not of the world." As in Revelation 2:2: "I know thy works."

2. *The fruit was the very best—the pomegranate.* All were pleasant fruits, and all His own. "From me is thy fruit found"; "His pleasant fruits" (v. 16). The graces that Christ puts into the heart and brings out of the life are the very best, the richest, most pleasant, most excellent that a creature can produce. Love to Christ, love to the brethren, love to the Sabbath, forgiveness of enemies, all the best fruits that can grow in the human heart. Unreasonable world! to condemn true conversion, when it produces the very fruits of paradise, acceptable to God, if not to you. Should not this make you stand and consider?

3. *There were spices in this garden.*—These spices do not naturally grow in gardens. Even in the East there never was such a display as this. So the fragrant graces of the Spirit are not natural to the heart. They are brought from a far country. They must be carefully watched. They need the stream, and the gentle zephyr. Oh, I fear most of you should hang your heads when Christ begins to speak of fragrant spices in your heart! Where are they? Are there not talkative, forward Christians? Are there not self-seeking, praise-seeking, man-pleasing Christians? Are there not proud-praying Christians? Are there not ill-tempered Christians? Are there not rash, inconsiderate ones? Are there not idle, lazy, bad-working Christians? Lord, where are the spices? Verily, Christ is a bundle of myrrh. Oh to be like Him! Oh that every flower and fruit would grow! They must come from above. Many there are of whom one is forced to say, "Well, they may be Christians; but I would not like to be next them in heaven!" Cry for the wind: "Awake, O north wind; and come, thou south; blow upon my garden, that the spices thereof may flow out."

———

MESSAGE VIII.

"Who is this that cometh up from the wilderness leaning upon her beloved? I
raised thee up under the apple tree: there thy mother brought thee forth,
there she brought thee forth that bare thee. Set me as a seal upon thine
heart, as a seal upon thine arm: for love is strong as death; jealousy is cruel
as the grave: the coals thereof are coals of fire, which hath a most vehement
flame. Many waters cannot quench love, neither can the floods drown it: if
a man would give all the substance of his house for love, it would utterly
be contemned."—Song of Solomon 8:5-7.

W E ARE INTRODUCED to the great Redeemer and a
believing soul, and are made to overhear their converse.

I. *The posture of the church.*

1. *From the wilderness.*—To a child of God this world is a
wilderness. *First, Because everything is fading here.* Here is
nothing abiding; money takes wings and flees away; friends die.
All are like grass; and if some are more beautiful or more engaging than others, still they are only like the flower of the
grass—a little more ornamented, but withering often sooner.
Sometimes a worldly comfort is like Jonah's gourd; it came up
over his head to be a shadow to deliver him from his grief. So
Jonah was exceeding glad of the gourd. But God prepared a
worm, when the sun rose the next day, and it smote the
gourd that it withered. So our worldly comfort sometimes
grows up over our head like a shadow, and we are exceeding
glad of our gourd; but God prepares a worm, we faint, and are
ready to die. Here we have no continuing city; but we seek
one to come. This is a wilderness: "Arise, depart, this is not
thy rest, for it is polluted." An experienced Christian looks
upon everything here as not abiding; for the things that are
seen are temporal, but the things that are not seen are eternal.

Second, Because everything is stained with sin here. Even
the natural scenery of this world is stained with sin. The
thorns and thistles tell of a cursed earth. Above all, when you
look at the floods of ungodly men.

"We are of God, and the whole world lieth in wickedness."

The world does not know a Christian, and does not love him. Though you love them, and would lay down your body that they might pass over to glory, yet they will not hear. Above all, the sin in our own heart makes us bend down under our burden, and feel this to be a valley of weeping. Ah! wretched man, if we had no body of sin, what a sweet glory would appear in everything; we would sing like the birds in spring.

2. *Coming out of it.*—Unconverted souls are going down into the wilderness to perish there. All Christians are coming up out of it. Sabbath days are like milestones, marking our way; or rather they are like the wells we used to come to at evening. Every real Christian is making progress. If the sheep is on the shoulder of the shepherd, it is always getting nearer the fold. With some the shepherd takes long steps. Dear Christians, you should be advancing, getting higher, nearer to Canaan, riper for glory. In the south of Russia, the country is of vast plains, rising by steppes. Dear friends, you should get on to a higher place; up another step every Sabbath day.

In traveling, you never think of making a house in the wilderness. So, dear friends, do not take up your rest here; we are journeying. Let all your endeavors be to get on in your journey.

3. *Leaning upon her beloved.*—It is very observable that there is none here but the bride and her Beloved in a vast wilderness. She is not leaning on Him with one arm, and upon somebody else with the other; but she is leaning on Him alone. So is it with the soul taught of God; it feels alone with Christ in this world; it leans as entirely upon Christ as if there were no other being in the universe. She leans all her weight upon her Husband. When a person has been saved from drowning, he leans all his weight on his deliverer. When the lost sheep was found, He took it upon His shoulder. You must be content then to lean all your weight on Christ. *Cast the burden of temporal things on Him. Cast the care of your soul on Him. If*

God be for us, who can be against us? They that wait upon
the Lord shall renew their strength. The eagle soars so directly
upward, that poets have fancied it was aiming at the sun. So
does the soul that waits on Christ.

II. *Christ's word to the leaning soul.*

1. *"I raised thee up."*—He reminds the believer of his natural state. Every soul now in Christ was once like an exposed
infant (Ezek. 16), cast out into the open field. "Behold, I was
shapen in iniquity." Do not forget what you were. If ever you
come to forget what you were, then you may be sure you are
not right with God. Observe when the contrition comes. When
you are leaning on Christ, then He tells you of your sin and
misery (Ezek. 36:31).

2. He reminds you of His love: "I raised thee up." *He
Himself* is the apple tree, open on all sides, affording shadow
and fruit. *I raised thee.* Christ not only shelters, but draws into
the shelter. *"To Him be glory."* Are there not some who feel
like an infant—cast out? Turn your eye to Christ, He only can
raise up your soul under the apple tree.

III. *The leaning soul cries for continued grace.*

Set me as a seal.—It is a sure mark of grace to desire more.
The high priest had a beautiful breastplate over his breast,
adorned with jewels—make me one of these. He had also a
jewel on each shoulder—make me one of these. These were
bound with chains of gold, but the believer with chains of love.
This is a true mark of grace. If you be contented to remain
where you are, without any more nearness to God, or any more
holiness, this is a clear mark you have none. Hide me deeper,
bind me closer, and carry me more completely.

1. *The love of Christ is strong as death.*—Death is awfully
strong. When he comes upon a stout young man, he brings
him down. So is the love of Christ.

2. *Cruel, or stubborn, as the grave.*—The grave will not give
up its dead, nor will Christ give up His own. Oh! pray that

this love may embrace you. Vehement as hell—unquenchable fire. You have your choice, dear friends, of two eternal fires. "Who shall separate us from the love of Christ?" (Rom. 8). Floods cannot drown it, afflictions cannot.

3. *It cannot be bought.*—"If a man would give all the substance," etc. You must accept it free or not at all.

DUNDEE, 1840.

MESSAGE IX.

"After this I beheld, and, lo, a great multitude, which no man could number, of all nations, and kindreds, and people, and tongues, stood before the throne, and before the Lamb, clothed with white robes, and palms in their hands; and cried with a loud voice, saying, Salvation to our God which sitteth upon the throne, and unto the Lamb. And all the angels stood round about the throne, and about the elders and the four beasts, and fell before the throne on their faces and worshiped God, saying, Amen: Blessing, and glory, and wisdom, and thanksgiving, and honor, and power, and might, be unto our God for ever and ever. Amen. And one of the elders answered, saying unto me, What are these which are arrayed in white robes? and whence came they? And I said unto him, Sir, thou knowest. And he said unto me, These are they which came out of great tribulation, and have washed their robes, and made them white in the blood of the Lamb. Therefore are they before the throne of God, and serve him day and night in his temple: and he that sitteth on the throne shall dwell among them. They shall hunger no more, neither thirst any more; neither shall the sun light on them, nor any heat. For the Lamb, which is in the midst of the throne, shall feed them, and shall lead them unto living fountains of waters: and God shall wipe away all tears from their eyes."—Revelation 7:9-17.

IT IS ONE THING to read these words with a poet's eye, and another thing to read them with the eye of a Christian. Oh pray, dear friends, that the Spirit may tear away the veil from our hearts, and show us the grand realities that are here! It is sweet and profitable—

1. *For the awakening of the ungodly,* that you may see what are the exercises of the heavenly world, and how unfit you would be for them. I suppose many of you feel that you have not washed your robes, and that you could not sing their song. Then you must be on the road to hell.

2. *For the instruction of believers.*—It shows you what are

the chief employments of that happy world, where we shall so soon be; it gives you the keynote of the heavenly song; it teaches you to spend much of your time in the same exercises in which you shall spend eternity.

3. *For comfort to afflicted believers.*—It shows you how short your trials will be. These light afflictions are but for a moment; you need not murmur nor grieve. A little while, and we shall be with Christ, and God shall wipe away all your tears. For this end it was given to John.

I. *What John saw and heard.*

1. *A great multitude of all nations.*—When John was on earth he saw but few believers: "We are of God, and the whole world lieth in wickedness." The church was like a lily in a field of thorns, lambs in the midst of wolves; but now quite different—thorns are plucked away, the lilies innumerable. *"Out of all nations."* Perhaps he could discern his fellow apostles, his own brother James, and holy Paul, and angel-faced Stephen; the dark Egyptian, the swarthy Ethiopian, the wooly-headed Negro, the far distant Chinese, the Burman, the Hindu, the blue-eyed German, the dark-eyed Italian, and multitudes perhaps from a distant island of the sea. Every country had its representatives there, some saved out of every land. All were like Christ, and yet all retained their different peculiarities.

Learn that Christ will have a glorious crown.—He shall see of the travail of His soul, and be satisfied. Often, when I look at a large town like Dundee, and see so few converted to Christ, my heart sickens within me; I often feel as if we were laboring for nought and in vain. Although there has been so much blessing, yet such masses of ungodly families! But oh, cheer up, Christ shall have His full crown! Though there should not be another saved out of this place, Christ will have His full reward. We shall be quite satisfied when we see the whole. He hath mercy on whom He will have mercy. Learn the power of His blood. It blots out the sins of all that multitude, sins of every name and dye. Why not yours? Oh! when such a glorious company are saved, why should you be lost? When so many are going out of this place, why should you keep back?

2. *Their position.*—They stood before the throne—yea, nearer than the angels, for they stood round about. The redeemed stood next the throne, the angels round them. This marks their complete righteousness. But the ungodly cannot stand in the judgment. If God were only to bring an ungodly man into His presence, he would die. You greatly mistake if you think God needs to put out great strength to destroy you. As a cloud is dried up by being in the light of the sun, so you would perish at the presence of God as a moth in a candle. But this great company stand next the throne, God's eye full upon them. In Christ they stand, not in themselves. Nearer than angels: the angels have only creature-righteousness; these have on Creator-righteousness. The righteousness of Christ is a million times more lovely than that of the highest angel, therefore they stand nearer. The righteousness of God is upon them all—who shall condemn? If you are ever to be near God, you may come freely to Him now. Why keep so far away?

3. *Their dress; white robes and palms.*—They have all the same dress, there is no difference. It is the garment of Christ. One was a far greater believer than another—made far greater advances in holiness—yet the same dress. *Whiter than the angels,* verse 13. The angels also are represented as dressed in white; yet it would appear that their robes were far outshone by the bright shining raiment of the redeemed. The angels have on creature-righteousness, the redeemed the righteousness of God. This is what is now offered to you, sinners. Awakened persons are sometimes led to cry, "Oh that I had never sinned!" but here is something better than if you had never sinned. *Palms* are signs of victory. The Jews used to take branches of palms at the feast of tabernacles, or ingathering, which was a

type of heaven. The angels have no palms, for they have fought no fight, they have gained no victory. Everyone that has a white robe has a palm. Everyone that is in Christ shall overcome. Be not afraid of your enemies.

4. *Their song. The substance of it—salvation.*—They give God all the glory. On earth, there are many that cannot believe in an *electing* God—that God chose them for no good in them; but in heaven they all feel it, and give Him all the praise. On earth, many speak of making themselves willing; but in heaven they sing "Salvation to God." On earth, many go about to establish their own righteousness; in heaven, "glory to the Lamb." On earth, many take Christ as part of their righteousness, and their duties as part; in heaven, all give glory to the Lamb. What say you to this song? Does it find an echo in your heart? Remember you must begin it now, if you are to sing it afterwards.

The effect of it—it stirs up the hearts of the angels (vv. 11, 12). Often on earth, when one believer begins to praise God for what He has done for his soul, it stirs up the hearts of others. So in heaven, when the angels hear the voice of redeemed sinners—brands plucked out of the fire—standing near the throne, they will obtain a ravishing view of the glory of God, His mercy and grace, and they will fall down and worship God. They will not envy the redeemed their place; but, on the contrary, be filled with intense praise by hearing of what God has done for their souls. How do you feel when you hear of others being saved and brought nearer to God than you? Do you envy and hate them, or do you fall down and praise God for it?

II. *Their past history* (vv. 13, 14).

Two particulars are given. Each had a different history; still in these two they were alike:

1. *They had washed their robes.*—This leads us back to their conversion. Once every one of that company had filthy

garments. They were like Joshua, their garment was spotted by the flesh. It was like a garment with the leprosy in it. Some stained with blood, spots of blood upon their garments; some with adultery; some with disobedience to parents; some with pride, falsehood, evil speaking—all, all were stained. Everyone was convinced that he could not make himself clean; he could not wash his garments nor throw them off; he was brought to see himself lost and helpless. Jesus was revealed to him, and His precious blood shed for sinners, even the chief, saying to the heavy-laden, "Come to me." Of all that company, there is not one stands there in any other way. All are washed in blood. It is their only way of standing. Have you been washed in blood? You will find not one in heaven who went there in any other way. You think to go to heaven by your own decency, innocency, attention to duties. Well, you would be the only such one there: all are washed in blood. Come and let us reason together.

2. *They came out of great tribulation.*—Every one that gets to the throne must put his foot upon the thorn. The way to the crown is by the cross. We must taste the gall if we are to taste the glory. When justified by faith, God led them into tribulations also. When God brought Israel through the Red Sea, He led them into the wilderness; so, when God saves a soul, He tries it. He never gives faith without trying it. The way to Zion is through the Valley of Baca. You must go through the wilderness of Jordan if you are to come to the Land of Promise. Some believers are much surprised when they are called to suffer. They thought they would do some great thing for God; but all that God permits them to do is to *suffer.* Go round everyone in glory; everyone has a different story, yet every one has a tale of suffering. One was persecuted in his family, by his friends and companions; another was visited by sore pains and humbling disease, neglected by the world; another was bereaved of children; another had all these afflictions.

Mark, all are *brought out of them*. It was a dark cloud, but it passed away; the water was deep, but they have reached the other side. Not one of them blames God for the road He led them: "Salvation" is their only cry. Are there any of you, dear children, murmuring at your lot? Do not sin against God. This is the way God leads all His redeemed ones. You must have a palm as well as a white robe. No pain, no palm; no cross, no crown; no thorn, no throne; no gall, no glory. Learn to glory in tribulations also. "I reckon that the sufferings of this present time are not worthy to be compared with the glory that shall be revealed in us."

III. *Future history.*

1. *Immediate service of God.*—Here, we are allowed to spend much of our time in our worldly callings. It is lawful for a man to win his bread, to plough, sow, reap, to spin and weave. Then, all our strength will be put forth in the immediate service of God. We shall stand before Him, and He shall dwell among us. It will be a perpetual Sabbath. We shall spend eternity in loving God, in adoring, admiring, and praising God. We should spend much of our present time in this. Some people imagine that they are not serving God unless they are visiting the sick, or engaged in some outward service; whereas the highest of all service is the love of adoration in the soul. Perhaps God gets more glory by a single adoring look of some poor believer on a sickbed, than from the outward labors of a whole day.

2. *Not in the wilderness any more.*—At present we are like a flock in the wilderness, our soul often hungry, and thirsty, and sorely tried. Often we feel as if we could go no farther, but must lie down and die. Often we feel temptations too much for us, or persecutions too strong for us to bear. When we are with Christ we shall hunger no more, all our pains shall be ended. Learn to glorify Him in the fires, to sing in the wilderness. This is the only world where you can give God that glory.

3. *Father, Son, and Spirit will bless us.*—The Lamb shall feed us: He that died for us. We shall always see our security before us in our Surety; no trembling shall ever come over our soul. He shall be one like us—a *Lamb*—like the least of us; we shall learn of God from Him. The *Spirit* will be like "living fountains of waters." Here, we never have enough; there, without measure. The *Father* will be a father to us. He will wipe away tears—the tears we shed in dying, wilderness tears, the tears over lost friends and a perishing world. "What manner of persons ought we to be!"

DUNDEE, 1840.

MESSAGE X.

"For verily he took not on him the nature of angels; but he took on him the seed of Abraham. Wherefore in all things it behooved him to be made like unto his brethren, that he might be a merciful and faithful high priest in things pertaining to God, to make reconciliation for the sins of the people. For in that he himself hath suffered being tempted, he is able to succor them that are tempted."—Hebrews 2:16-18.

CHRIST IS a merciful High Priest. "For verily he took not on him the nature of angels; but he took on him the seed of Abraham."

I. *The sovereign mercy of Christ in becoming man.*

We read of two great rebellions in the history of the universe —the rebellion of the angels, and the rebellion of man. For infinitely wise and gracious purposes God planned and permitted both of these, that out of evil He might bring forth good. The *first* took place in heaven itself. Pride was the sin by which the angels fell, and therefore it is called "the condemnation of the devil." "They kept not their first estate, but left their own habitation." "God spared them not, but cast them down to hell, and delivered them into chains of darkness, to be reserved unto judgment."

The *next* fall took place on earth. Satan tempted, and man fell—believed the devil rather than God, and so came under the curse: "Thou shalt surely die." Both of these families came under the same frown—under the same condemnation; both were condemned to the same "everlasting fire." But the glorious Son of God resolved, from all eternity, to die for sinners. Now, for which of the two shall He die? Perhaps the angels in heaven would long that He should die for their once brother angels. The angelic nature was higher than that of man. Men had fallen deeper into sin than the rebel angels. Will He not die for angels? Now, here is the answer: "Verily he took not on him the nature of angels; but he took on him the seed of Abraham." Here is sovereign mercy passing by one family and coming to another. Let us wonder and adore the sovereign mercy of Jesus.

1. Do not be surprised if Jesus passes many by. The Lord Jesus has been riding through our country in a remarkable manner, seated on His white horse, and wearing many crowns. He has sent out many arrows and pierced many hearts in this place, and brought many to His feet; but has He not passed many by? Are there not many given up to their own hearts' lust, and walking in their own counsel? Be not surprised. This is the very way He did when He came to this earth; He passed the gate of hell. Although His bosom was full of love and grace, although "God is love," He felt it not inconsistent to pass fallen angels by, and to come and die for men. And so, though Jesus is love still, yet He can save some, and leave others to be hardened. "Many widows were in Israel in the time of Elijah the prophet; but unto none of them was Elijah sent, save unto Sarepta, a city of Sidon, unto a woman that was a widow." And many lepers were in Israel at the time of Elisha the prophet, and none of them was cleansed, saving Naaman the Syrian.

2. If Christ has visited your soul, give Him all the glory. "Not unto us, Lord, not unto us, but unto thy name give glory." The only reason why you are saved is the sovereign compassion

of Jesus. It is not that you are better than others, that you were
less wicked, of better dispositions, more attentive to your Bible.
Many who have been left have been much more upright in their
life. It is not that you have sat under a peculiar ministry. God
has made the same ministry a means of hardening multitudes.
It is the free grace of God. Love God forever and ever, because
He chose you of His own free will. Adore Jesus, that He passed
by millions, and died for you. Adore the Holy Ghost, that He
came out of free sovereign mercy and awakened you. It will be
matter of praise through eternity.

3. If Christ is now visiting your soul, do not trifle with
Him. Some persons, when Christ begins to knock at the door
of their heart, put Him off from time to time. They trifle
with their convictions. They say, I am too young yet, let me
taste a little more pleasure of the world: youth is the time for
mirth; another time I will open the door. Some say, I am
too busy; I have to provide for my family; when I have a
more convenient season I will call for Thee. Some say, I
am strong and healthy; I hope I have many years to live; when
sickness comes, then I will open the door. Consider that
Christ may not come again. He is knocking now: let Him in.
Another day He may pass by your door. You cannot command
convictions of sin to come when you like. Christ is entirely
sovereign in saving souls. No doubt, many of you have had
your last knock from Christ. Many of you that were once concerned are not so now; and you cannot bring it back again.
There is no doubt a time in every man's life, when, if he
opens the door, he will be saved; if he does not, he will
perish. Probably this may be that time to many of you.
Christ may be given last knocks to some today.

II. *Christ made like us in all things.*—Christ not only
became man, but it behooved Him to be made like us in *all*
things. He suffered, being tempted.

In my last lecture, I showed you the only two points in

which He was different from us. *First,* In being God as well
as man. In the manger at Bethlehem there lay a perfect infant,
but there also was Jehovah. That mysterious Being who rode
on an ass's colt, and wept over Jerusalem, was as much a man
as you are, and as much God as the Father is. The tears He
shed were human tears, yet the love of Jehovah swelled below
His mantle. That pale Being that hung quivering on the
cross was indeed man; it was human blood that flowed from
His wounds; but He was as truly God.

Second, In being without sin. He was the only one in human
form of whom it can be said, He was holy, harmless, undefiled,
and separate from sinners; the only one on whom God could
look down from heaven, and say, "This is my beloved Son, in
whom I am well pleased." Every member of our body and
faculty of our mind we have used as the servants of sin.
Every member of His body and faculty of His mind were
used only as servants of holiness. *His mouth* was the only
human mouth from which none but gracious words ever proceeded. *His eye* was the only human eye that never shot forth
flames of pride, or envy, or lust. *His hand* was the only human
hand that never was stretched forth but in doing good. *His
heart* was the only human heart that was not deceitful above
all things and desperately wicked. When Satan came to Him,
he found nothing in Him. Now, in these two things it behooved Him to be unlike His brethren, or He could not have
been a Saviour at all. In all other things it behooved Him to
be made like us. There was no part of our condition that He
did not humble himself unto.

1. He passed through all the terms of our life from
childhood to manhood. *First,* He was an infant of days,
exposed to all the pains and dangers of infancy. "Ye shall
find the babe, wrapped in swaddling clothes, lying in a
manger."

Second, He bore the trials and pains of boyhood. Many a

one, no doubt, would wonder at the holy boy in the carpenter's shop at Nazareth. He grew in wisdom, and in stature, and in favor with God and with man. *Third,* He bore the afflictions and anxieties of manhood, when He began to be about thirty years of age.

2. He tasted the difficulties of many situations in life. The first thirty years, it is probable, He shared the humble occupation of Joseph the carpenter; He tasted the trials of working for His daily bread. Then He subsisted on the kindness of others. Certain women, which followed Him, ministered unto Him of their substance. He had not where to lay His head. Many a night He spent on the Mount of Olives, or on the hills of Galilee. Then He bore the trials of a gospel minister. He preached from morning till night, and yet with how small success! so that He could say, "I have labored in vain, I have spent my strength for nought and in vain." How often He was *grieved by their unbelief!* He marveled at their unbelief. "Oh faithless generation! how long shall I be with you, how long shall I suffer you!" How often He *offended many* by His preaching! "Many said, This is a hard saying; who can hear it?" "From that time many of his disciples went back, and walked no more with Jesus" (John 6:66). How often *they hated* Him for His love! "For my love they are my adversaries: but I gave myself unto prayer" (Ps. 109:4). How His own disciples grieved Him by their want of faith! "O ye of little faith, have I been so long time with you!" The unbelief of Thomas; their sleeping in the garden; forsaking Him and fleeing; Peter denying, Judas betraying Him!

3. What trials He had from His own family! Even His own brothers did not believe on Him, but mocked. The people of His town tried to throw Him over the rocks. What pain He suffered from His mother, when He saw the sword piercing her fond heart! how He said to John, "Behold thy mother!" and to his mother, "Behold thy son!" even in His dying agonies.

4. What trials from Satan! Believers complain of Satan, but they never felt his power as Christ did. What an awful conflict was that during forty days in the wilderness! How fearfully did Satan urge on Pharisees, and Herod, and Judas, to torment Him! What an awful hour was that when He said, This is your hour, and the power of darkness! What an awful cry was that, "Save me from the lion's mouth!" (Ps. 22:21), when He felt His soul in the very jaws of Satan!

5. What trials from God! Believers often groan under the hidings of God's countenance; but ah! they seldom taste even a drop of what Christ drank. What dreadful agony was that in Gethsemane, when the blood gushed through the pores! How dreadful was that frown of God on the cross, when He cried, "My God, my God!" In all these things, and a thousand more, He was made like unto His brethren. He came into our place. Through eternity we shall study these sufferings.

Learn the amazing love of Christ, that He should leave glory for such a condition.

Learn to bear sufferings cheerfully. You have not yet suffered as He did.

III. *The end—That He might be a merciful and faithful High Priest.*—The work of Christ as an high priest is here laid down as twofold: *First,* to make an atonement for our sins; *second,* to succor His people under temptations.

1. *To make atonement.*—This is the great work of Christ as our High Priest. For this it was needful that He should become man and die. Had He remained God alone in the bosom of His Father, He might have pitied us, but He could not have died for us, nor taken our sins away. We must have perished. Every priest in the Old Testament was a type of Jesus in this; every lamb that was slain typified Jesus offering up His own body a sacrifice for our sins.

Let your eye rest there if you would be happy. Those few

dark hours on Calvary, when the great High Priest was offering up, the amazing sacrifice, give light for eternity to the believing soul. This only will cheer you in dying. Not your graces, not your love to Christ, not anything in you, but only this—Christ hath died. He loved me, and gave Himself for me. Christ hath appeared to put away sin by the sacrifice of himself.

2. *To succor the tempted.*—All believers are a tempted people. Every day they have their trials; every time is to them a time of need. The unconverted are little tempted; they are not in trouble as others, neither are they plagued like other men. They do not feel temptations rising in their hearts; nor do they know the power of Satan. Before conversion, a man believes as little in the devil as he believes in Christ. But when a man comes to Christ, then he becomes a tempted· soul, "poor and needy, seeking water and there is none."

He is tempted by God.—God did tempt Abraham; not to sin, for God cannot be tempted with evil, neither tempteth He any man. Still, God always tries His children. He never gives faith but He brings His child into a situation where he will be tried. Sometimes He exalts him, to try if he will turn proud and forget God; sometimes He brings him low, to see if he will murmur against God. Blessed is the man that endureth temptations. Sometimes He brings them into a strait, where the trial is, whether they will believe in Him alone, or trust to flesh and blood.

The world tempts a child of God.—They watch for their halting. They love nothing better than to see a child of God fall into sin. It soothes their conscience to think that all are equally bad. They frown; they smile.

Their own heart is a fountain of temptation.—Sometimes it says, What harm is there in that—it is a little sin; or, I will just sin this once, and never again; or, I will repent after and be saved.

Satan hurls his fiery darts.—He terrifies them away from
Christ, disturbs them at prayer, fills their mind with blasphemies, hounds on the world against them.

Ah! believers, you are a tempted people. You are always
poor and needy. And God intends it should be so, to give
you constant errands to go to Jesus. Some may say, it is not
good to be a believer; but ah! see to whom we can go.

We have a merciful and faithful High Priest. He suffered,
being tempted, just that He might succor them that are tempted.
The high priest of old not only offered sacrifice at the altar,
his work was not done when the lamb was consumed; he
was to be a father to Israel. He carried all their names graven
over his heart; he went in and prayed for them within the veil.
He came out and blessed the people, saying, "The Lord bless
thee and keep thee. The Lord make his face shine upon thee"
(Num. 6:24-26).

So it is with the Lord Jesus. His work was not all done on
Calvary. He that died for our sins lives to pray for us, to help
in every time of need. He is still Man on the right hand of
God. He is still God, and therefore, by reason of His divinity,
is present here this day as much as any of us. He knows your
every sorrow, trial, difficulty; every half-breathed sigh He
hears, and brings in notice thereof to His human heart at the
right hand of God. His human heart is the same yesterday,
today, and for ever; it pleads for you, thinks on you, plans
deliverance for you.

Dear tempted brethren! Go boldly to the throne of grace,
to obtain mercy and find grace to help you in your time of need.

Are you bereaved of one you loved? Go and tell Jesus;
spread out your sorrows at His feet. He knows them all;
feels for you in them all. He is a merciful High Priest. He
is faithful too, never wanting in the hour of need. He is able
to succor you by His Word, by His Spirit, by His providence.
He gave you all the comfort you had by your friends. He

can give it you without them. He has taken away the stream that you may go to the fountain.

Are you suffering in body? Go to this High Priest. He is intimately acquainted with all your diseases; He has felt that very pain. Remember how, when they brought to Him one that was deaf and had an impediment in his speech, He looked up to heaven and sighed, and said, "*Ephphatha!*" He sighed over his misery. So He sighs over you. He is able to give you deliverance, or patience to bear it, or improvement by it.

Are you sore tempted in soul—put into trying circumstances, so that you know not what to do? Look up; He is able to succor you. If He had been on earth, would you not have gone to Him—would you not have kneeled and said, Lord, help me? Does it make any difference that He is at the right hand of God? He is the same yesterday, today, and for ever.

Message XI

ORDINATION SERMON

(At the Ordination of the Rev. P. L. Miller, Wallacetown, Dundee, 1840.)

"I charge *thee* therefore before God, and the Lord Jesus Christ, who shall judge the quick and the dead at his appearing and his kingdom, preach the word; be instant in season, out of season; reprove, rebuke, exhort, with all long-suffering and doctrine."—II Timothy 4: 1, 2.

THERE IS NOT a more awfully affecting situation in the whole world than that in which a faithful minister stands.

I. *Where faithful ministers stand—"Before God and the Lord Jesus Christ."*

1. *Before God.*—This is true in two ways:

As a sinner saved by grace.—He was once far off, but is now brought nigh by the blood of Jesus. Having "boldness to enter into the holiest by the blood of Jesus, by a new and living way which he hath consecrated for us through the

veil, that is to say, his flesh," he draws near. He stands
within the veil—in the Holiest of all—in the love of God. He
is justified before God. A faithful minister is *an example to
his flock of a sinner saved.* God says to him as He did to
Abraham, "Walk before me, and be thou perfect." He can
say with Paul, "I was a blasphemer, and a persecutor, and
injurious, but I obtained mercy." A faithful minister is like
Aaron's rod, that was laid up beside the ark of God and
budded there.

As a servant.—In the East, servants always stand in the
presence of their master, watching his hand. The Queen of
Sheba said to Solomon, "Happy are these thy servants, which
stand continually before thee and hear thy wisdom." So it
is said of the angels, that "they do always behold the face of
my Father which is in heaven." Even when most engaged in
the service of the saints, they feel under His all-seeing, holy,
living eye. So *ought* faithful ministers to feel. They should
feel constantly in His presence, under His soul-piercing, gently
guiding, holy, living eye. "I will guide thee with mine eye."
"The eyes of the Lord are over the righteous." Ah! how often
we feel we are before *man.* Then all power withers, and
we become weak as other men; but oh! how sweet to feel in
the presence of God, as if there were no eye on us but God's.
In prayer, how sweet to feel before Him; to kneel at His
footstool, and to put our hand upon the mercy-seat—no curtain,
no veil, no cloud between the soul and God! *In preaching,*
how sweet to say, like Elijah, when he stood before Ahab,
"I stand before the Lord God of Israel!" To stand at His feet,
in His family, in His pavilion, oh believers, it is then we get
above the billows! The applause of men, the rage and contempt
of men, then pass by us like the idle wind which we regard
not. Thus is a minister like a rock in the ocean; the mountain-
billows dash upon its brow, and yet it stands unshaken.

2. *Before Jesus Christ.*—This also is true in two ways:

First, The faithful minister has a present sight of Christ as his Righteousness. He is like John the Baptist. "Seeing Jesus coming unto him, he saith, Behold the Lamb of God!" Or like Isaiah, he saw "his glory, and spake of him." His own soul is ever watching at Gethsemane and at Golgotha. Oh brethren, it is thus only we can ever speak with feeling, or with power, or with truth, of the unsearchable riches of Christ! We must have the taste of the manna in our mouth, "milk and honey under our tongue," else we cannot tell of its sweetness. We must be drinking the living water from the smitten Rock, or we cannot speak of its refreshing power. We must be hiding our guilty souls in the wounds of Jesus, or we cannot with joy speak of the peace and rest to be found there.

This is the reason unfaithful ministers are cold and barren in their labors. They speak, like Balaam, of a Saviour whose grace they do not feel. They speak, like Caiaphas, of the blood of Christ, without having felt its power to speak peace to the troubled heart. This is the reason many good men have a barren ministry. They speak from clear head-knowledge, or from past experience, but not from a present grasp of the truth—not from a present sight of the Lamb of God. Hence their words fall like a shower of snow, fair and beautiful, but cold and freezing. The Lord give us to stand in the presence of the Lord Jesus.

Second, The faithful minister should feel the presence of a living Saviour. A minister should be like the bride in the Song of Solomon: "Leaning upon her beloved." This was Jeremiah's strength (1:8): "Be not afraid of their faces, for I am with thee to deliver thee, saith the Lord." So it was with Paul (Acts 18:9, 10): "Be not afraid, but speak, and hold not thy peace: for I am with thee, and no man shall set on thee to hurt thee; for I have much people in this city." So Jesus told all the disciples: "Yet a little while and the world seeth me not; but ye see me: because I live, ye shall live also."

And again He says expressly: "Lo, I am with you alway, even to the end of the world." Yes, brethren, Christ is as truly walking in the midst of the seven golden candlesticks, as truly in this place today, as if you saw Him with your bodily eyes. His humanity is at the right hand of God, appearing in the presence of God for us. His Godhead fills all in all.

Thus He is with us, standing at our right hand, so that we cannot be moved. It is sweet to know and feel this. Thus only can we be sustained amid all the trials of the ministry. Are we weary? We can lean, like John, upon His bosom. Are we burdened with a sense of sin? We can hide in the clefts of that Rock of Ages. Are we empty? We can look up to Him for immediate supply. Are we hated of all men? We can hide under His wings. Stand before the Lord Jesus Christ, and then you may smile at Satan's rage, and face a frowning world. Learn here also the guilt of refusing a gospel ministry: "He that refuseth you, refuseth Me; and he that refuseth Me, refuseth him that sent Me."

3. *Within sight of judgment*—"*Who shall judge the quick and dead.*"—Ministers and their flocks shall meet together before the throne of the Lord Jesus. That will be a solemn day. They have many solemn meetings on earth. An ordination day is a solemn day. Their meetings from Sabbath to Sabbath are solemn meetings; and sacrament days are very solemn days. But their meeting at the judgment-seat will be by far the most solemn of all. Then,

First, The minister will give his account, either with joy or with grief. He will no more meet to plead with the people, or to pray with them, but to bear witness how they received the Word. Of some he will give account with a joyful countenance—that they received the Word with all readiness of mind, that they were converted and became like little children: these will be his joy and crown. Of most with grief—that he carried the message to them, but they would not come; they made light of it; or perhaps they listened for a while, but drew back into perdition. He will be a swift witness against them in that day. "Depart, ye cursed."

Second, Then the people will give their account of the minister. If he was faithful; if he made it his meat and drink to do the will of God; if he preached the whole truth with seriousness, urgency, love; if he was holy in his life; if he preached publicly, and from house to house; then that minister shall shine like the stars. If he was unfaithful; if he fed himself, but not the flock; if he did not seek the conversion of souls, did not travail in birth; if he sought his own ease, his own wealth, his own praise, and not their souls; then shall the loud curses of ruined souls fall on that wretched man, and God shall say, Take the unfaithful servant, and bind him hand and foot, and cast him into outer darkness. Oh! believers, it is the duty of ministers to preach with this solemn day in their eye. We should stand, like Abraham, looking down on the smoke of Sodom; like John, listening to the new song and golden harps of the new Jerusalem. Would not this take away the fear of man? Would not this make us urgent in our preaching? You must either get these souls into Christ, or you will yet see them lying down in everlasting burnings. Oh! brethren, did I not say truly that the place where a minister stands is the most solemn spot in all this world?

II. *The grand business of the faithful minister.*—Described in two ways: *first,* generally—preach the Word; *second,* more in detail—reprove, rebuke, exhort.

1. *Preach the Word.*—The grand work of the minister, in which he is to lay out his strength of body and mind, is preaching. Weak and foolish as it may appear, this is the grand instrument which God has put into our hands, by which sinners are to be saved, and saints fitted for glory. It pleased God, by the foolishness of preaching, to save them

that believe. It was to this *our blessed Lord* devoted the years
of His own ministry. Oh, what an honor has He put upon this
work, by preaching in the synagogues, in the Temple, and by
the blue waves of Galilee, under the canopy of heaven! Has
He not consecrated this world as preaching ground? This
was the grand work of Paul and all the apostles; for this
was our Lord's command: "Go ye into all the world, and
preach the gospel." Oh! brethren, this is our great work. It
is well to visit the sick, and well to educate children and
clothe the naked. It is well to attend presbyteries. It is well
to write books or read them. But here is the main thing—
preach the Word. The pulpit is, as George Herbert says, "our
joy and throne." This is our watchtower. Here we must
warn the people. The silver trumpet is put into our hand.
Woe be unto us if we preach not the gospel.

The Matter—The Word.—It is in vain we preach, if we
preach not the Word, the truth as it is in Jesus.

First, Not other matters—"Ye are my witnesses." "The
same came to *bear witness* of that light." We are to speak
of nothing but what we have seen and heard from God.
It is not the work of the minister to open up schemes of
human wisdom or learning, not to bring his own fancies, but
to tell the facts and glories of the gospel. We must speak of
what is within the Word of God.

Second, Preach the Word—the most essential parts especially. If you were with a dying man, and knew he had but
half an hour to live, what would you tell him? Would you
open up some of the curiosities of the Word, or enforce some
of the moral commands of the Word? Would you not tell
him his undone condition by nature and by wicked works?
Would you not tell him of the love and dying of the Lord
Jesus? Would you not tell him of the power of the Holy
Spirit? These are the essential things which a man must
receive or perish. These are the great subject matters of

preaching. Should we not preach as Jesus did when He went to Emmaus, when He began at Moses and all the prophets, and expounded to them the things concerning Himself? "Let there be much of Christ in your ministry," says the excellent Eliot. Rowland Hill used to say, "See there be no sermon without *three R's* in it: Ruin by the fall, Righteousness by Christ, and Regeneration by the Spirit." Preach Christ for awakening, Christ for comforting, Christ for sanctifying. "God forbid that I should glory, save in the cross of our Lord Jesus Christ."

Third, Preach as the Word—I would humbly suggest for the consideration of all ministers, whether we should not preach more in the manner of God's Word. Is not the Word the sword of the Spirit? Should not our great work be to take it from its scabbard, to cleanse it from all rust, and then to apply its sharp edge to the consciences of man? It is certain the fathers used to preach in this manner. Brown of Haddington used to preach as if he had read no other book than the Bible. It is the truth of God in its naked simplicity that the Spirit will most honor and bless. "Sanctify them through thy truth: thy word is truth."

2. *Reprove, rebuke, exhort.*—The first work of the Spirit on the natural heart is to *reprove the world of sin.* Although He is the Spirit of love, although a dove is His emblem, although He be compared to the soft wind and gentle dew, still His first work is to convince of sin. If ministers are filled with the same Spirit, they will begin in the same way. It is God's usual method to awaken them, and bring them to despair of salvation by their own righteousness, before He reveals Christ to them. So it was with the jailor. So it was with Paul; he was blind three days. A faithful minister must lay himself out for this. Plough up the fallow ground, and sow not among thorns. Men must be brought down by law work to see their guilt and misery, or all our preaching is

beating the air. Oh! brethren, is this our ministry? Let us do
this plainly. The most, I fear, in all our congregations, are
sailing easily down the stream into an undone eternity, unconverted and unawakened. Brethren, they will not thank
us in eternity for speaking smooth things, for sewing pillows
to their arm-holes, and crying, Peace, peace, when there is no
peace. No, they may praise us now, but they will curse our
flattery in eternity. Oh, for the bowels of Jesus Christ in every
minister, that we might long after them all!

Exhort.—The original word means to comfort, to speak as
the Comforter does. This is the second part of the Spirit's
work, to lead to Christ, to speak good news to the soul. This
is the most difficult part of the Christian ministry. Thus did
John: "Behold the Lamb of God." Thus did Isaiah: "Comfort ye, comfort ye." Thus did our Lord command: "Go,
preach the gospel to every creature." It is true this makes the
feet of the gospel messenger beautiful on the mountains. He
has to tell of a full, free, Divine Saviour.

And here I would observe what appears to me *a fault in
the preaching of our beloved Scotland.* Most ministers are
accustomed to set Christ before the people. They lay down
the gospel clearly and beautifully, but they do not urge men
to enter in. Now God says, Exhort—beseech men—persuade
men; not only point to the open door, but compel them to
come in. Oh, to be more merciful to souls, that we would
lay hands on men and draw them in to the Lord Jesus!

III. *The manner.*

1. *With long-suffering.*—There is no grace more needed in
the Christian ministry than this. This is the heart of God the
Father towards sinners: "He is long-suffering to usward, not
willing that any should perish." This is the heart of the Lord
Jesus. How tenderly does He cry, "Oh! Jerusalem, Jerusalem,
how often would I have gathered thy children together . . .
and ye would not." This is the mind of the Holy Spirit in

striving with men. He will not always strive, but oh, how long He does strive with men! Dear believers, had He not striven long with us, we would this day have been like Lot's wife, monuments of grace resisted. Now, such ought ministers to be. Above all men we need "love that suffers long and is kind." Sometimes, when sinners are obstinate and hard-hearted, we are tempted to give up in despair, or to lose temper and scold them, like the disciples calling down fire from heaven. But, brethren, we must be of another spirit. The wrath of man worketh not the righteousness of God. Only be filled with the Spirit of Christ, and it will make us patient toward all. It will make us cry, "How often would I . . . . ."

2. *With doctrine.*—Some good men cry, Flee, flee, without showing the sinner what he is to flee from; and again, they cry, Come, come, without showing plainly the way of pardon and peace. These men act as one would do who should run through the streets crying, Fire, fire, without telling where. In the preaching of the apostles you will observe the clear and simple statement of the truth preceding the warm and pathetic exhortation. This has always been followed by the most judicious and successful divines.

It behooves ministers to unite the cherub and the seraph in their ministry—the angel of knowledge and the angel of burning zeal. If we would win souls, we must point clearly the way to heaven, while we cry, Flee from the wrath to come. I believe we cannot lay down the guilt of man, his total depravity, and the glorious gospel of Christ too clearly; that we cannot too warmly urge men to embrace and flee. Oh, for a pastor who unites the deep knowledge of Edwards, the vast statements of Owen, and the vehement appeals of Richard Baxter!

3. *With urgency.*—If a neighbor's house were on fire, would we not cry aloud and use every exertion? If a friend

were drowning, would we be ashamed to strain every nerve
to save him? But alas! the souls of our neighbors are even
now on their way to everlasting burnings, they are ready to
be drowned in the depths of perdition. Oh! shall we be less
earnest to save their never-dying souls, than we would be to
save their bodies? How anxious was the Lord Jesus in this!
When He came near and beheld the city, He wept over it.
How earnest was Paul! "Remember that by the space of three
years I ceased not to warn everyone night and day with tears."
Such was George Whitefield; that great man scarcely ever
preached without being melted into tears. Brethren, there is
need of the same urgency now. Hell is as deep and as burning as ever. Unconverted souls are as surely rushing to it.
Christ is as free—pardon as sweet as ever! Ah! how we
shall be amazed at our coldness when we do get to heaven!

4. *At all times.*—Our Lord went about continually doing
good; He made it His meat and drink. "Daily in the temple."
So should we. *Satan is busy* at all times; he does not stand
upon ceremony; he does not keep himself to Sabbath days,
or canonical hours. *Death is busy.* Men are dying while we
are sleeping. About fifty die every minute; nearly one every
second entering into an unchangeable world! *The Spirit of
God is busy.* Blessed be God, He hath cast our lot in times
when there is the moving of the great Spirit among the dry
bones. Shall ministers then be idle, or stand upon ceremony?
Oh, that God would baptize us this day with the Holy Ghost
and with fire, that we might be all changed as into a flame
of fire, preaching and building up Christ's Church till our
latest, our dying hour!

CHARGE TO THE MINISTER

My dear brother, it is not many years ago since you and
I played together as children, and now, by the wonderful
providence of God, I have been appointed to preside at your

ordination to the office of the holy ministry. Truly His way is in the sea, and His path in the deep waters. Do not think, then, that I mean to assume an authority which I have not. I cannot speak to you as a father, but as a brother beloved in the Lord let me address a few words of counsel to you.

1. *Thank God for putting you into the ministry*—"I thank Christ Jesus my Lord for that he counted me faithful, putting me into the ministry." "To me, who am less than the least of all saints." Oh brother, thank God for saving your soul; for sending His Spirit into your heart, and drawing you to Christ! But this day you have a new cause of thankfulness in being put into the ministry. It is the greatest honor in this world. "Had I a thousand lives, I would willingly spend them in it; and had I a thousand sons, I would gladly devote them to it." True, it is an awfully responsible office: the eternity of thousands depends on your faithfulness; but ah! the grace is so full, and the reward so glorious. "If," said the dying Payson, "If ministers only saw the preciousness of Christ, they would not be able to refrain from clapping their hands with joy, and exclaiming, I am a minister of Christ! I am a minister of Christ!"

Do not forget, then, dear brother, amid the broken accents of confession from a broken heart, to pour out a song of thankfulness. Thanks be to God, for my own part, during the few years I have been a minister; I can truly say that I desire no other honor upon earth than to be allowed to preach the everlasting gospel. Thanks be to God for His unspeakable gift.

2. *Seek the anointing of the Holy Spirit.*—The more anointing of the Holy Spirit you have, the more will you be a happy, holy, and successful minister. You remember *the two olive trees* that stood close by the golden candlestick, and emptied the golden oil out of themselves. These represent successful ministers, anointed ones that stand by the Lord

of the whole earth. The Lord make you like one of them. Remember John the Baptist: "He shall be filled with the Holy Ghost, and many of the children of Israel shall he turn to the Lord their God." The Lord fill you in like manner, and then you will be a converting minister. Remember the apostles. Before the day of Pentecost they were dry, sapless trees, they had little fruit; but when the Spirit came on them like a mighty rushing wind, then three thousand were pricked to the heart.

Oh, brother, plead with God to fill you with the Spirit, that you may stand in His counsel, and cause the people to hear His words, and turn many from the evil of their ways. You know that a heated iron, though blunt, can pierce its way even where a much sharper instrument, if cold, could not enter. Pray that you may be filled with the fire of the Spirit, that you may pierce into the hard hearts of unconverted sinners.

3. *Do not rest without success in your ministry.*—Success is the rule under a living ministry; want of success is the exception. *"The want of ministerial success,"* says Robinson, *"is a tremendous circumstance, never to be contemplated without horror."* Your people will be of two kinds:

First, The Lord's people, those who are already in Christ. Seek for success among them. He gave some pastors and teachers for the perfecting of the saints. Never forget Christ's words: "Feed my sheep, feed my lambs." Be like Barnabas, a son of consolation. Exhort them to cleave to the Lord. Do not say, "They are safe, and I will let them alone." This is a great mistake. See how Paul laid out his strength in confirming the disciples. Be a helper of their joy. Do not rest till you get them to live under the pure, holy rules of the gospel.

Second, The great mass you will find to be unconverted. Go, brother, leaving the ninety-nine, go after the one sheep that was lost. Leave your home, your comforts, your bed, your ease, your all, to feed lost souls. The Lord of Glory left heaven for this; it is enough for the disciple to be as his Master. It is said of Alleine, that "he was infinitely and insatiably greedy of the conversion of souls." Rutherford wrote to his dear people, "My Witness is above, that your heaven would be two heavens to me, and the salvation of you all as two salvations to me." The Lord give you this heavenly compassion for this people. Do not be satisfied without conversion. You will often find that there is a shaking among the dry bones, a coming together bone to his bone, skin and flesh come upon them, but no breath in them. Oh, brother, cry for the breath of heaven. Remember a moral sinner will lie down in the same hell with the vilest.

4. *Lead a holy life.*—I believe, brother, that you are born from above, and therefore I have confidence in God touching you, that you will be kept from the evil. But oh, study universal holiness of life. Your whole usefulness depends on this. Your sermon on Sabbath lasts but an hour or two, your life preaches all the week. Remember, ministers are standard-bearers. Satan aims his fiery darts at them. If he can only make you a covetous minister, or a lover of pleasure, or a lover of praise, or a lover of good eating, then he has ruined your ministry forever. Ah, let him preach on fifty years, he will never do me any harm. Dear brother, cast yourself at the feet of Christ, implore His Spirit to make you a holy man. Take heed to thyself and to thy doctrine.

5. *Last of all, be a man of prayer.*—Give yourself to prayer, and to the ministry of the Word. If you do not pray, God will probably lay you aside from your ministry, as He did me, to teach you to pray. Get your texts from God, your thoughts, your words, from God. Carry the names of the little flock upon your breast, like the High Priest; wrestle for the unconverted. Luther spent his three best hours in prayer.

John Welsh prayed seven or eight hours a day. He used to
keep a plaid on his bed, that he might wrap himself in it
when he rose during night. Sometimes his wife found him
lying on the ground, weeping. When she complained, he
would say, "Oh woman! I have the souls of three thousand
to answer for, and I know not how it is with many of them."
Oh, that God would pour down this spirit of prayer on you
and me, and all the ministers of our beloved church, and
then we shall see better days in Scotland. I commend you to
God.

CHARGE TO THE PEOPLE

DEAR BRETHREN, I trust that this is to be the beginning
of many happy days to you in this place. Gifts in answer to
prayer are always the sweetest. I believe your dear pastor
has been given you in answer to prayer, for I do not think
your wonderful unanimity can be accounted for in any other
way.

1. *Love your pastor.*—So far as I know him, he is worthy
of your love. I believe he is one to whom the Lord has been
very merciful, that God has already owned his labors, and
I trust will a thousand times more. Esteem him very highly
in love for his work's sake. You will know the anxieties,
temptations, pains, and wrestlings, he will be called to bear
for you. Few people know the deep wells of anxiety in the
bosom of a faithful pastor. Love and reverence him much.
Do not make an idol of him; that will destroy his usefulness.
It was said of the Erskines, that men could not see Christ
over their heads. Remember, look beyond him and above him.
Those that would have worshiped Paul were the people who
stoned him. Do not stumble at his infirmities. There are
spots upon the sun, and infirmities in the best of men. Cover
them—do not stumble at them. Would you refuse gold because it was brought you in a ragged purse? Would you re-

fuse pure water because it came in a chipped bowl? The treasure is in an earthen vessel.

2. *Make use of your pastor.*—He has come with good news from a far country. Come and hear.

First, Wait patiently on his ministry. He does not come in his own name. The Lord is with him. If you refuse him, you will refuse Christ; for he is the messenger of the Lord of Hosts.

Second, Welcome him into your houses. He is coming, like his Master, to seek that which was lost, and to bind up that which is broken; to strengthen that which was sick, and to bring again that which was driven away. You have all need of him, whether converted or not. Remember there is an awful curse against those who receive not gospel messages. He will shake the dust off his feet against you, and that dust will rise against you in judgment.

Third, Do not trouble him about worldy matters. His grand concern is to get your soul saved. He is not a man of business, but a man of prayer. He has given himself to prayer, and to the ministry of the Word.

Fourth, Go freely to him about your souls. "The minister's house was more thronged than ever the tavern had wont to be." These were happy days. There is no trade I would like to see broken in this place but that of the taverners. It is a soul-destroying trade. I would like to see the taverns emptied, and the minister's house thronged. Do not hesitate to go to him. It is your duty and your privilege. It is your duty. It will encourage him, and show him how to preach to your souls. It is your privilege. I have known many get more light from a short conversation than from many sermons.

Fifth, Be brief. Tell your case. Hear his word and be gone. Remember his body is weak, and his time precious. You are stealing his time from others or from God. I cannot tell you what a blessing it will be if you will make very short calls.

3. *God's children, pray for him.*—Pray for his body, that he may be kept strong, and spared for many years. Pray for his soul, that he may be kept humble and holy, a burning and a shining light, that he may grow. Pray for his ministry, that it may be abundantly blessed, that he may be anointed to preach good tidings. Let there be no secret prayer without naming him before your God, no family prayer without carrying your pastor in your hearts to God. Hold up his hands, so Israel will prevail against Amalek.

4. *Unconverted souls, prize this opportunity.*—I look on this ordination as a smile of Heaven upon you. God might have taken away ministers from this town instead of giving us more. I believe the Lord Jesus is saying, "I have much people in this city." The door is begun to be opened this day. The Spirit is beginning to shine. Oh, that you would know the day of your visitation! This is the market-day of grace beginning in this end of the town, and you should all come to buy. Oh, that you knew the day of your visitation! Some, I fear, will be the worse of this ministry, and not the better. The election will be saved, and the rest be blinded. Some will yet wish they had died before this church was opened. Be sure, dear souls, that you will either be saved, or more lost, by this ministry. Your pastor comes with the silver trumpet of mercy. Why will ye turn it into the trumpet of judgment? He comes with glad tidings of great joy. Why should you turn them into sad tidings of endless woe? He comes to preach the acceptable day of the Lord. Why will ye turn it into the day of vengeance of our God?

Dec. 16, 1840.

MESSAGE XII

"There is no fear in love; but perfect love casteth out fear: because fear hath torment. He that feareth is not made perfect in love. We love him, because he first loved us. If a man say, I love God, and hateth his brother, he is a liar; for he that loveth not his brother whom he hath seen, how can he love God whom he hath not seen? And this commandment have we from him, That he who loveth God love his brother also."—I JOHN 4:18-21.

PERFECT LOVE casteth out fear."

I. *The state of an awakened soul.*—*"Fear hath torment."*

There are two kinds of fear mentioned in the Bible, very opposite from one another. The one is the very atmosphere of heaven, the other is the very atmosphere of hell.

1. *There is the fear of love.*—This is the very temper of a little child: the fear of the Lord is the beginning of wisdom. This was the mind of Job. "He feared God and hated evil." Nay, it is the very spirit of the Lord Jesus. On Him rested "the spirit of the fear of the Lord, and made Him of quick understanding in the fear of the Lord."

2. *There is the fear of terror.*—This is the very temper of devils: the devils believe and tremble. This is what was in Adam and Eve after the Fall; they fled from the voice of God, and tried to hide themselves in one of the trees of the garden. This was the state of the jailor when he trembled, and sprang in and brought them out, and fell at their feet, saying, "Sirs, what must I do to be saved?" This is the fear here spoken of—tormenting fear. "Fear hath torment." Some of you have felt this fear that hath torment. Many more might feel it this day; you are within reach of it. Let me explain its rise in the soul.

First, A natural man casteth off fear, and restrains prayer before God. "They have been at ease from their youth, and settled down upon their lees; they have not been emptied from vessel to vessel, therefore their taste remains in them, and their scent is not changed." They are like fallow ground that has never been broken up by the plough, but is overrun

with briers and thorns. Are there not some among you that
never trembled for your soul? You think you are as good
as your neighbors. Ah! well, your dream will be broken up
one day soon.

Second, When the Spirit of God opens the eyes, He makes
the stoutest sinner tremble. He shows him *the number of his
sins,* or rather that they cannot be numbered. Before, he
had a memory that easily forgot his sins; oaths slipped over
his tongue, and he knew it not; every day added new sins
to his page on God's book, yet he remembered not. But now
the Spirit of God sets all his sins straight before him. All
unpardoned, long-forgotten enormities, rise up behind him.
Then he begins to tremble. "Innumerable evils have com-
passed me about."

Third, The Spirit makes him feel the greatness of sin, the
exceeding sinfulness of it. Before, it seemed nothing; but
now, it rises like a flood over the soul. The wrath of God
he feels abiding on him; a terrible sound is in his ears. He
knows not what to do; his fear hath torment. Sin is seen
now as done against a holy God; done against a God of
love; done against Jesus Christ and His love.

Fourth, A third thing which awfully torments the soul is
corruption working in the heart. Often persons under conviction are made to feel the awful workings of corruption in
their heart. Often temptation and conviction of sin meet
together and awfully torment the soul, rending it in pieces.
Conviction of sin is piercing his heart, driving him to flee
from the wrath to come; and yet at the same moment some
raging lust, or envy, or horrid malice, is boiling in his
heart, driving him towards hell. Then a man feels a hell
within him. In hell there will be this awful mixture: there
will be an overwhelming dread of the wrath of God, and
yet corruption, boiling up within, will drive the soul more
and more into the flames. This is often felt on earth. Some

of you may be feeling it. This is the fear that hath torment.

Fifth, Another thing the Spirit convinces the soul of is his inability to help himself. When a man is first awakened, he says, I shall soon get myself out of this sad condition. He falls upon many contrivances to justify himself. He changes his life; he tries to repent, to pray. He is soon taught that "his righteousness are filthy rags"—that he is trying to cover rags with filthy rags; he is brought to feel that all he can do signifies just nothing, and that he never can bring a clean thing out of an unclean. This sinks the soul in gloom. This fear hath torment.

Sixth, He fears he shall never be in Christ. Some of you perhaps know that this fear hath torment. The free offer of Christ is the very thing that pierces you to the heart. You hear that He is altogether lovely—that He invites sinners to come to Him—that He never casts out those that do come. But you fear you will never be one of these. You fear you have sinned too long or too much—you have sinned away your day of grace. Ah, this fear hath torment.

Some will say, "It is not good to be awakened, then."

Answer. 1. It is the way to peace that passeth understanding. It is God's chosen method, to bring you to feel your need of Christ before you come to Christ. At present your peace is like a dream; when you awake you will find it so. Ask awakened souls if they would go back again to their slumber. Ah, no; if I die, let me die at the foot of the cross; let me not perish unawakened.

Answer. 2. You must be awakened one day. If not now, you will afterwards, in hell. After death, fear will come on your secure souls. There is not *one* unawakened soul in hell; all are trembling there. The devils tremble; the damned spirits tremble. Would it not be better to tremble now, and flee to Jesus Christ for refuge? *Now,* He is waiting to be gracious to you. *Then,* He will mock when your fear cometh. You will know to all eternity that "fear hath torment."

II. *The change on believing.*—"There is no fear in love." "Perfect love casteth out fear."

1. The love here spoken of is not our love to God, but *His love to us;* for it is called *perfect* love. All that is ours is imperfect. When we have done all, we must say, "We are unprofitable servants." Sin mingles with all we think and do. It were no comfort to tell us, that if we would love God perfectly, it would cast out fear; for how can we work that love into our souls? It is the Father's love to us that casteth out fear. He is *the Perfect One.* All His works are perfect. He can do nothing but what is perfect. His knowledge is perfect knowledge; His wrath is perfect wrath; His love is *perfect love.* It is this perfect love which casteth out fear. Just as the sunbeams cast out darkness wherever they fall, so does this love cast out fear.

2. But where does this love fall? On Jesus Christ. Twice God spake from heaven, and said, "This is my beloved Son, in whom I am well pleased." God perfectly loves His own Son. He sees infinite beauty in His person. God sees Himself manifested. He is infinitely pleased with His finished work. The infinite heart of the infinite God flows out in love towards our Lord Jesus Christ. And there is no fear in the bosom of Christ. All His fears are past. Once He said, "While I suffer thy terrors I am distressed"; but now He is in perfect love, and perfect love casteth out fear. *Hearken, trembling souls!* Here you may find rest to your souls. You do not need to live another hour under your tormenting fears. Jesus Christ has borne the wrath of which you are afraid. He now stands a refuge for the oppressed—a refuge in the time of trouble. Look to Christ, and your fear will be cast out. Come to the feet of Christ, and you will find rest. Call upon the name of the Lord, and you will be delivered.

You say you cannot look, nor come, nor cry, for you are helpless. Hear, then, and your soul shall live. Jesus is a Saviour to the helpless. Christ is not only a Saviour to those who are naked and empty, and have no goodness to recommend themselves, but He is a Saviour to those who are unable to give themselves to Him. You cannot be in too desperate a condition for Christ. As long as you remain unbelieving, you are under His perfect wrath—wrath without any mixture. The wrath of God will be as amazing as His love. It comes out of the same bosom. But the moment you look to Christ, you will come under His perfect love—love without any coldness, light without any shade, love without any cloud or mountain between. God's love will cast out all your fears.

III. *His love gives boldness in the day of judgment* (v. 17). —There is a great day coming, often spoken of in the Bible— the day of judgment—the day when God shall judge the secrets of men's hearts by Christ Jesus. The Christless will not be able to stand in that day. The ungodly shall not stand in the judgment. At present, sinners have much boldness; their neck is an iron sinew, and their brow brass. Many of them cannot blush when they are caught in sin. Among ourselves, is it not amazing how bold sinners are in forsaking ordinances? With what a brazen face will some men swear! How bold some ungodly men are in coming to the Lord's Table! But it will not be so in a little while. When Christ shall appear—the holy Jesus, in all His glory—then brazenfaced sinners will begin to blush. Those that never prayed will begin to wail. Sinners, whose limbs carried them stoutly to sin and to the Lord's Table last Sabbath, will find their knees knocking against one another.

Who shall abide the day of His coming, and who shall stand when He appears? When the books are opened—the one, the book of God's remembrance, the other the Bible—then the dead will be judged out of those things written in the books. Then the heart of the ungodly will die within them;

then will begin "their shame and everlasting contempt." Many
wicked persons comfort themselves with this, that their sin
is not known—that no eye sees them; but in that day the most
secret sins will be all brought out to the light. "Every idle
word that men shall speak, they shall give an account thereof
in the day of judgment." How would you tremble and blush,
O wicked man, if I were now to go over before this congregation the secret sins you have committed during the past week,
all your secret fraud and cheating, your secret uncleanness, your
secret malice and envy—how you would blush and be confounded! How much more in that day, when the secrets of
your whole life shall be made manifest before an assembled
world! What eternal confusion will sink down your soul in
that day! You will be quite chap-fallen; all your pride and
blustering will be gone.

All in Christ will have boldness

1. *Because Christ shall be Judge.*—What abundant peace
will it give you in that day, believer, when you see Christ is
Judge—He that shed His blood for you—He that is your Surety,
your Shepherd, your all. It will take away all fear. You will
be able to say, Who shall condemn? for Christ hath died. In
the very hand that opens the books you will see the marks of
the wounds made by your sins. Christ will be the same to you
in the judgment that He is now.

2. *Because the Father Himself loveth you.*—Christ and the
Father are one. The Father sees no sin in you; because, as
Christ is, so are you in this world. You are judged by God
according to what the Surety is; so that God's love will be
with you in that day. You will feel the smile of the Father,
and you will hear the voice of Jesus saying, "Come, ye blessed
of my Father."

Learn to fear nothing between this and judgment. Fear not;
wait on the Lord and be of good courage.

IV. *The consequences of being in the love of God.*

1. *"We love him, because he first loved us"* (v. 19).—
When a poor sinner cleaves to Jesus, and finds the forgiving
love of God, he cannot but love God back again. When the
prodigal returned home, and felt his father's arms around his
neck, then did he feel the gushings of affection toward his
father. When the summer sun shines full down upon the sea,
it draws the vapors upward to the sky. So when the sunbeams of the Sun of Righteousness fall upon the soul, they
draw forth the constant risings of love to Him in return.

Some of you are longing to be able to love God. Come into
His love, then. Consent to be loved by Him, though worthless
in yourself. It is better to be loved by Him than to love, and
it is the only way to learn to love Him. When the light of the
sun falls upon the moon, it finds the moon dark and unlovely;
but the moon reflects the light, and casts it back again. So
let the love of God shine into your breast, and you will cast
it back again. The love of Christ constraineth us. "We love
him, because he first loved us." The only cure for a cold heart
is to look at the heart of Jesus.

Some of you have no love to God because you love an idol.
You may be sure you have never come into His love, that
curse rests upon you: "If any man love not the Lord Jesus
Christ, let him be Anathema Maranatha."

2. *We love our brother also.*—If you love an absent person,
you will will love his picture. What is that the sailor's wife
keeps so closely wrapped in a napkin, laid up in her best drawer
among sweet-smelling flowers? She takes it out morning and
evening, and gazes at it through her tears. It is the picture of
her absent husband. She loves it because it is like him. It
has many imperfections, but still it is like him. Believers are
the pictures of God in this world. The Spirit of Christ dwells in
them. They walk as He walked. True, they are full of imperfections; still they are true copies. If you love Him, you
will love them; you will make them your bosom friends.

Are there none of you that dislike real Christians? You do not like their look, their ways, their speech, their prayers. You call them hypocrites, and keep away from them. Do you know the reason? You hate the copy, because you hate the original; you hate Christ, and are none of His.

ST. PETER'S, 1840.

MESSAGE XIII

ACTION SERMON.—*October 25, 1840.*

"But God forbid that I should glory, save in the cross of our Lord Jesus Christ, by whom the world is crucified unto me, and I unto the world."—GALA-TIANS 6:14.

THIS WORD is used in three different senses in the Bible. It is important to distinguish them.

I. *The subject here spoken of by Paul—The Cross of Christ.*

1. It is used to signify *the wooden cross*—the tree upon which the Lord Jesus was crucified. The punishment of the cross was a Roman invention. It was made use of only in the case of slaves, or very notorious malefactors. The cross was made of two beams of wood crossing each other. It was laid on the ground, and the criminal stretched upon it. A nail was driven through each hand, and one nail through both the feet. It was then lifted upright, and let fall into a hole, where it was wedged in. The crucified man was then left to die, hanging by his hands and feet. This was the death to which Jesus stooped. "He endured *the cross,* despising the shame." "He became obedient unto death, even the death of *the cross.*" (Matt. 27:40, 42; Mark 15:30, 32; Luke 23:26; John 19: 17, 19, 25, 31; Eph. 2:16.)

2. It is used to signify *the way of salvation by Jesus Christ crucified.* So I Corinthians 1:18, "The preaching of the cross

is to them that perish foolishness, but unto us who are saved it is the power of God"; compared with verse 23, "We preach Christ crucified." Here it is plain that the preaching of the cross and the preaching of Christ crucified are the same thing. This is the meaning in the passage before us, "God forbid that I should glory." It is the name given to the whole plan of salvation by a crucified Redeemer. That little word implies the whole glorious work of Christ for us. It implies the love of God in giving His Son (John 3:16); the love of Christ in giving Himself (Eph. 5:2); the incarnation of the Son of God; His substitution—one for many; His atoning sufferings and death. The whole work of Christ is included in that little word, *the cross of Christ.* And the reason is plain; His dying on the cross was the lowest point of His humiliation. It was there He cried, "It is finished! The work of My obedience is finished, My sufferings are finished, the work of redemption is complete, the wrath of My people is finished"; and He bowed the head and gave up the ghost. Hence His whole finished work is called *the cross of Christ.*

3. It is used to signify *the sufferings borne in following Christ.* "If any man will come after me, let him deny himself, and take up his cross and follow me" (Matt. 16:24). When a man determines to follow Christ, he must give up his sinful pleasures, his sinful companions; he meets with scorn, ridicule, contempt, hatred, the persecution of worldly friends; his name is cast out as evil. "He that will live godly in Christ Jesus must suffer persecution." Now, to meet all these is to "take up the cross." "He that taketh not up his cross and followeth after me, is not worthy of me."

In the passage before us the words are used in the second meaning, the plan of salvation by a crucified Saviour.

Dear friends, it is this that is set before you in the broken bread and poured out wine, the whole work of Christ for the salvation of sinners. The love and grace of the Lord Jesus are all gathered into a focus there. The love of the Father; the covenant with the Son; the love of Jesus; His incarnation, obedience, death; all are set before you in that broken bread and wine. It is a sweet, silent sermon. Many a sermon contains not Christ from beginning to end. Many show Him doubtfully and imperfectly. But here is nothing else but Christ, and Him crucified. Most rich and speaking ordinance! Pray that the very sight of that broken bread may break your hearts, and make them flow to the Lamb of God. Pray for conversions from the sight of the broken bread and poured out wine. Look attentively, dear souls and little children, when the bread is broken and the wine poured out. It is a heart-affecting sight. May the Holy Spirit bless it.

Dear believers, look you attentively, to get deeper, fuller views of the way of pardon and holiness. A look from the eye of Christ to Peter broke and melted his proud heart, and he went out and wept bitterly. Pray that a single look of that broken bread may do the same for you. When the Roman centurion, that watched beside the cross of Jesus, saw Him die, and the rocks rend, he cried out, "Truly this was the Son of God!" Look at this broken bread, and you will see the same thing, and may your heart be made to cry after the Lord Jesus. When the dying thief looked on the pale face of Immanuel, and saw the holy majesty that beamed from His dying eye, he cried, "Lord, remember me!" This broken bread reveals the same thing. May the same grace be given you, and may you breathe the cry, Lord, remember me.

Oh, get ripening views of Christ, dear believers! The corn in harvest sometimes ripens more in one day than in weeks before. So some Christians gain more grace in one day than for months before. Pray that this may be a ripening harvest day in your souls.

II. *Paul's feelings towards the cross of Christ*—"*God forbid that I should glory . . .*"

1. *It is implied that he had utterly forsaken the way of righteousness by deeds of the law.* Every natural man seeks salvation by making himself better in the sight of God. He tries to mend his life; he puts a bridle on his tongue; he tries to command his feelings and thoughts, all to make himself better in the sight of God. Or he goes further: tries to cover his past sins by religious observances; he becomes a religious man, prays, weeps, reads, attends sacraments, is deeply occupied in religion, and tries to get it into his heart; all to make himself appear good in the eye of God, that he may lay God under debt to pardon and love him.

Paul tried this plan for long. He was a Pharisee, touching the righteousness in the law blameless; he lived an outwardly blameless life, and was highly thought of as a most religious man. "But what things were gain to me, those I counted loss for Christ." When it pleased God to open his eyes, he gave up this way of self-righteousness forever and ever; he had no more any peace from looking in—"we have no confidence in the flesh"; he bade farewell for ever to that way of seeking peace. Nay, he trampled it under his feet. "I do count them but dung that I may win Christ." Oh, it is a glorious thing when a man is brought to trample under feet his own righteousness; it is the hardest thing in the world.

2. *He betook himself to the Lord Jesus Christ.*—Paul got such a view of the glory, brightness, and excellency of the way of salvation by Jesus, that it filled his whole heart. All other things sank into littleness. Every mountain and hill was brought low, the crooked was made straight, the rough places smooth, and the glory of the Lord was revealed. As the rising sun makes all the stars disappear, so the rising of Christ upon his soul made everything else disappear. Jesus, suffering for us, filled his eye, filled his heart. He saw, believed, and was happy. Christ for us, answered all his need. From the cross of Christ a ray of heavenly light flamed to his soul, filling him

with light and joy unspeakable. He felt that God was glorified, and he was saved; he cleaved to the Lord with full purpose of heart. Like Edwards, "I was unspeakably pleased."

3. *He gloried in the cross.*—He confessed Christ before men; he was not ashamed of Christ before that adulterous generation; he gloried that this was his way of pardon, peace, and holiness. Ah, what a change! Once he blasphemed the name of Jesus, and persecuted to the death those that called on His name; now it is all his boast. "Straightway he preached Christ in the synagogues, that he is the Son of God." Once he gloried in his blameless life when he was among Pharisees; now he glories in this, that he is the chief of sinners, but that Christ died for such as he. Once he· gloried in his learning, when he sat at the feet of Gamaliel; now he glories in being reckoned a fool for Christ's sake, in being a little child, led by the hand of Jesus. At the Lord's Table, among his friends, in heathen cities, at Athens, at Rome, among the wise or unwise, before kings and princes, he glories in it as the only thing worthy of being known—the way of salvation by Jesus Christ and Him crucified.

Dear friends, have you been brought to glory only in the cross of Christ?

Have you given over the old way of salvation by the deeds of the law? Your natural heart is set upon that way. You are always for making yourself better and better, till you can lay God under obligation to pardon you. You are always for looking *in* for righteousness. You are looking in at your convictions and sorrow for past sins, your tears and anxious prayers; or you are looking in at your amendment, the forsaking of wicked courses and struggles after a new life; or you are looking at your own religious exercises, your fervency and enlarged heart in prayer, or in the house of God; or you are looking at the work of the Holy Spirit in you, the graces of the Spirit. Alas! alas! The bed is shorter than that you can stretch yourself on it, the covering is narrower than that you can wrap yourself in it. Despair of pardon in that way. Give it up forever. Your heart is desperately wicked. Every righteousness in which your heart has anything to do is vile and polluted, and cannot appear in His sight. Count it all loss, filthy rags, dung, that you may win Christ.

Betake yourself to the Lord Jesus Christ. Believe the love of the Lord Jesus Christ. He delighteth in mercy; He is ready to forgive; in Him compassions flow; He justifies the ungodly. Have you seen the glory of the cross of Jesus? Has it attracted your heart? Do you feel unspeakably pleased with that way of salvation? Do you see that God is glorified when you are saved? that God is a God of majesty, truth, unsullied holiness, and inflexible justice, and yet you are justified? Does the cross of Christ fill your heart? Does it make a great calm in your soul, a heavenly rest? Do you love that word: "the righteousness of God," the righteousness which is by faith, the righteousness without works? Do you sit within sight of the cross? Does your soul rest there?

Glory only in the cross of Christ. Observe, there cannot be a secret Christian. Grace is like ointment hid in the hand, it betrayeth itself. A lively Christian cannot keep silence. If you truly feel the sweetness of the cross of Christ, you will be constrained to confess Christ before men. "It is like the best wine, that goeth down sweetly, causing lips to speak." Do you confess Him in your family? Do you make it known there that you are Christ's? Remember, you must be decided in your own house. It is the mark of a hypocrite to be a Christian everywhere except at home. Among your companions, do you own Him a friend whom you have found? In the shop and in the market, are you willing to be known as a man washed in the blood of the Lamb? Do you long that all your dealings be under the sweet rules of the gospel? Come, then, to the Lord's Table, and confess Him that has saved your soul. Oh, grant that

it may be a true, free, and full confession. This is my sweet
food, my lamb, my righteousness, my Lord and my God, my
all in all. "God forbid that I should glory, save in the cross."
Once you gloried in riches, friends, fame, sin; now in a crucified Jesus.

III. *The effects.*—"The world is crucified to me, and I unto
the world."—"If any man be in Christ Jesus, he is a new creature." When the blind beggar of Jericho got his eyes opened
by the Lord, this world was all changed to him, and he to the
world. So it was with Paul. No sooner did he rise from his
knees, with the peace of Jesus in his heart, than the world got
its deathblow in his eyes. As he hurried over the smooth stones
of the streets of Damascus, or looked down from the flat roof
of his house upon the lovely gardens on the banks of the
Abana, the world and all its dazzling show seemed to his eye
a poor, shriveled, crucified thing. Once it was his all. Once its
soft and slippery flatteries were pleasant as music to his ear.
Riches, beauty, pleasure, all that the natural eye admires, his
heart was once set upon; but the moment he believed on Jesus,
all these began to die. True, they were not dead, but they were
nailed to a cross. They no more had that living attraction for
him they once had; and now every day they began to lose
their power. As a dying man on the cross grows weaker and
weaker every moment, while his heart's blood trickles from the
deep gashes in his hands and feet, so the world, that was once
his all, began to lose every moment its attractive power. He
tasted so much sweetness in Christ, in pardon, access to God,
the smile of God, the indwelling Spirit, that the world became
every day a more tasteless world to him.

Another effect was, *"I to the world."*—As Paul laid his hand
upon his own bosom, he felt that it also was changed. Once it
was as a mettled race horse that paces the ground and cannot
be bridled in; once it was like the foxhounds on the scent, impatient of the leash. His heart thus rushed after fame, honor,

worldly praise; but now it was nailed to the cross, a broken, contrite heart. True, it was not dead. Many a fitful start his old nature gave, that drove him to his knees and made him cry for grace to help; but still, the more he looked to the cross of Jesus, the more his old heart began to die. Every day he felt less desire for sin, more desire for Christ, and God, and perfect holiness.

Some may discover that they have never come to Christ. Has the world been crucified to you? Once it was your all—its praise, its riches, its songs, and merrymakings. Has it been nailed to the cross in your sight? Oh! put your hand on your heart. Has it lost its burning desire after earthly things? They that are Christ's have crucified the flesh, with its affections and lusts. Do you feel that Jesus has put the nails through your lusts? Do you wish they were dead? What answer can you make, sons and daughters of pleasure, to whom the dance, and song, and the glass, and witty repartee, are the sum of happiness? Ye are none of Christ's.

What answer can you make, lovers of money, sordid money-makers, who had rather have a few more sovereigns than the grace of God in your heart? What answer can you make, flesh-pleasers, night-walkers, lovers of darkness? Ye are not Christ's. Ye have not come to Christ. The world is all alive to you, and you are living to the world. You cannot glory in the cross, and love the world. Ah! poor deluded souls, you have never seen the glory of the way of pardon by Jesus. Go on; love the world; grasp every pleasure; gather heaps of money; feed and fatten on your lusts; take your fill. What will it profit you when you lose your own soul?

Some are saying, Oh, that the world were crucified to me, and I to the world! Oh, that my heart were as dead as a stone to the world, and alive to Jesus! Do you truly wish it? Look, then, to the cross. Behold the amazing gift of love. Salvation is promised to a look. Sit down like Mary, and gaze upon a crucified Jesus. So will the world become a dim and dying thing. When you gaze upon the sun, it makes everything else dark; when you taste honey, it makes everything else tasteless: so when your soul feeds on Jesus, it takes away the sweetness of all earthly things; praise, pleasure, fleshly lusts, all lose their sweetness. Keep a continued gaze. Run, looking unto Jesus. Look, till the way of salvation by Jesus fills up the whole horizon, so glorious and peace-speaking. So will the world be crucified to you, and you unto the world.

MESSAGE XIV

"Wherewith shall I come before the Lord, and bow myself before the high God? Shall I come before him with burnt-offerings, with calves of a year old? Will the Lord be pleased with thousands of rams, or with ten thousands of rivers of oil? Shall I give my firstborn for my transgression, the fruit of my body for the sin of my soul? He hath showed thee, O man, what is good: and what doth the Lord require of thee, but to do justly, and to love mercy, and to walk humbly with thy God?"—MICAH 6:6-8.

THE QUESTION of an awakened soul is, "Wherewith shall I come before the Lord?" An unawakened man never puts that question. A natural man has no desire to come before God, or to bow himself before the High God. He does not like to think of God. He would rather think of any other subject. He easily forgets what he is told about God. A natural man has no memory for divine things, because he has no heart for them. He has no desire to come before God in prayer. There is nothing a natural man hates more than prayer. He would far rather spend half an hour every morning in bodily exercise or in hard labor, than in the presence of God. He has no desire to come before God when he dies. He knows that he must appear before God, but it gives him no joy. He had rather sink into nothing; he had rather never see the face of God. Ah, my friends, is this your condition? How surely you may know that you have "the carnal mind which is enmity against God"! You are like Pharaoh: "Who is the Lord, that I should obey Him?" You say to God, "Depart from me, for I desire not the knowledge of thy ways." What an awful state it is to be in, to have no desire after Him who is the fountain of living waters!

I. *Here is the piercing question of every awakened soul.*

1. An awakened soul feels that his chief happiness is in coming before God. This was *unfallen Adam's* happiness. He felt like a child under a loving Father's eye. It was his chief joy to come before God, to be loved by Him, to be like a mote in the sunbeam, to be continually basked in the sunshine of His love, no cloud or veil coming between. This is *the joy of holy angels,* to come before the Lord, and bow before the High God. In His presence is fullness of joy. "The angels do always behold the face of my Father." On whatever errand of love they fly, they still feel that His eye of love is on them—this is their daily, hourly joy. This is the true happiness of a believer. Hear David (Psalm 42), "As the hart panteth after the water-brooks, so panteth my soul after thee, O God. My soul thirsteth for God, for the living God: when shall I come and appear before God?" He panteth not after the gifts of God, not His favors or comforts, but after Himself. A believer longs after God, to come into His presence, to feel His love, to feel near to Him in secret, to feel in the crowd that He is nearer than all the creatures. Ah, dear brethren, have you ever tasted this blessedness? There is greater rest and solace to be found in the presence of God for one hour, than in an eternity of the presence of man. To be in His presence—under His love, under His eye—is heaven, wherever it be. God can make you happy in any circumstances. Without Him, nothing can.

2. An awakened soul feels difficulties in the way.—"Where-with . . ." There are two great difficulties:

The nature of the sinner.—"Wherewith shall I . . ." When God really awakens a soul, He shows the vileness and hate-

fulness in it. He directs the eye within. He shows him that
every imagination of his heart has been only evil continually;
that every member of his body he has used in the service of sin;
that he has treated Christ in a shameful manner; that he has
sinned both against law and love; that he has kept the door of
his heart barred against the Lord Jesus, till his head was filled
with dew, and his locks with the drops of the night. Oh,
brethren, if God has ever discovered yourself to you, you
would wonder that such a lump of hell and sin should have
been permitted to live and breathe so long, that God should
have had patience with you till this day! Your cry will be,
"Wherewith shall I come before the Lord?" Though all the
world should come before Him, how can I?

   The nature of God.—"The high God." When God really
awakens a soul, He generally reveals to him something of His
own holiness and majesty. Thus He dealt with Isaiah (6):
"I saw the Lord sitting upon a throne high and lifted up, and
his train filled the temple. Above it stood the seraphim; one
cried to another, Holy, holy, holy, is the Lord of hosts, the
whole earth is filled with his glory. Then said I, Woe is me,
for I am undone." When Isaiah saw that God was so great a
God, and so holy, he felt himself undone. He felt that he
could not stand in the presence of so great a God. Oh, brethren,
have you ever had a discovery of the highness and holiness of
God, so as to lay you low at His feet? Pray for such a discovery
of God as Job had: "I have heard of thee by the hearing of the
ear, but now mine eye seeth thee: wherefore I abhor myself,
and repent in dust and ashes." Alas! I fear that most of you
will never know that God with whom you have to do, till you
stand guilty and speechless before His great white throne. Oh
that you would pray for a discovery of Him now, that you may
cry, "Wherewith shall I come before the Lord, and bow myself
before the high God!"

   3. The anxiety of the awakened soul leads to the question—

"Wherewith?" Ah! it is a piercing question. It is the question of one who has been made to feel that "one thing is needful." Anything he has he would give up to get peace with God. If he had a thousand rams, or ten thousand rivers of oil, he would gladly give them. If the life of his children, the dearest objects on this earth, would attain it, he would give them up. If he had a thousand worlds, he would give all for an interest in Christ. Woe to you that are at ease in Zion. Woe to those of you that never asked this question, Wherewith shall I come before the Lord? Ah! foolish triflers with eternal things! Poor butterflies, that flutter on from flower to flower, and consider not the dark eternity that is before you! Prepare to meet thy God, O Israel! Ye are hastening on to death and judgment, yet never ask, What garment shall cover me, when I stand before the great white throne? If you were going to appear before an earthly monarch, you would ask beforehand, Wherewith shall I be attired? If you were to be tried at an earthly bar, you would make sure of an advocate. How is it you press on so swiftly to the bar of God, and never ask the question, Wherewith shall I appear? "If the righteous scarcely are saved, where shall the ungodly and the sinner appear?"

II. *The answer of peace to the awakened soul.*—"He hath showed thee, O man, what is good." Nothing that man can bring with him will justify him before God. The natural heart is always striving to bring something to be a robe of righteousness before God. There is nothing a man would not do, nothing he would not suffer, if he might only cover himself before God. Tears, prayers, duties, reformations, devotions; the heart will do anything to be righteous before God. But all this righteousness is filthy rags. For,

1. The heart remains an awful depth of corruption. Everything in which that heart has any share is polluted and vile. Their very tears and prayers would need to be washed.

2. Supposing this righteousness perfect, it cannot cover the

past. It answers only for the time in which it was done. Old
sins, and the sins of youth, still remain uncovered.

Oh, dear brethren, if Jesus is to justify you, He must do as
He did to Joshua, "Take away the filthy garments from him";
and "I will clothe thee with change of raiment," Zechariah
3:4. The hand of Jesus alone can take off your filthy garments.
The hand of Jesus alone can clothe you with change of raiment.

Christ is the good way.—"He hath showed thee." "Stand
ye in the ways, and see, and ask for the old paths where is the
good way, and walk therein, and ye shall find rest for your
souls." Christ is the good way to the Father. *First,* Because
He is so suitable. He just answers the case of the sinner: for
every sin of the sinner He has a wound, for every nakedness
He has a covering, for every emptiness He has a supply. There
is no fear but He will receive the sinner, for He came into the
world on purpose to save sinners. There is no fear but the
Father will be well pleased with us in Him, for the Father
sent Him, laid our iniquity upon Him, raised Him from the
dead, and points you to Him. "He hath showed thee, O man,
what is good."

Second, He is so free. "As by one man's disobedience many
were made sinners, so by the obedience of one shall many be
made righteous." As far as the curse by Adam extends, so far
does the offer of pardon by Jesus extend. Here is good news
to the vilest of men. You may be covered just as completely
and as freely as those that have never sinned as you have done.
"He hath showed thee, O man, what is good."

Third, He is so God-glorifying. All other ways of salvation
are man-glorifying, but this way is God-glorifying; therefore
it is good. That way is good and best which gives the glory to
the Lamb. The way of righteousness by Jesus is good, on this
account, that Jesus gets all the praise. To Him be glory. It is
of faith, that it might be by grace. If a man could justify him-

self, or if he could believe of himself and draw the righteousness of Christ over his soul, that man would glory. But when
a man lies dead at the feet of Jesus, and Jesus spreads His
white robe over him, out of free sovereign mercy, then Jesus
gets all the praise.

Have you chosen the good way of being justified? This is
the way which God has been showing from the foundation of
the world. He showed it in Abel's lamb, and in all the sacrifices, and by all the prophets. He shows it by His Spirit to the
heart. Has this good way been revealed to you? If it has, you
will count all things but loss for the excellency of the knowledge of it. Oh, sweet, divine way of justifying a sinner! Oh,
that all the world but knew it! Oh, that we saw more of it!
Oh, that you could make use of it! "Walk therein, and ye
shall find rest unto your souls."

III. *God's requirement of the justified.*—When Jesus healed
the impotent man at the pool of Bethesda, He said to him,
"Behold, thou art made whole: sin no more, lest a worse thing
happen unto thee." And again, when He covered the sin of
the adulteress, He said, "Neither do I condemn thee: go, and
sin no more" (John 8). So here, when He shows the good
way of righteousness, He adds, "And what doth the Lord require of thee?"

1. *God requires His redeemed ones to be holy.*—If you are
His brethren, He will have you righteous, holy men.

First, He requires you to do justly—to be just in your dealings between man and man. This is one of His own glorious
features. He is a just God. "Shall not the Judge of all the
earth do right?" "He is my rock, and there is no unrighteous-
ness in him." Are you come to Him by Jesus? He requires
you to reflect His image. Are you His child? You must be
like Him. Oh, brethren, be exact in your dealings! Be like
your God. Take care of dishonesty; take care of trickery in
business. Take care of crying up your goods when selling

them, and crying them down when buying them. "It is naught, it is naught, saith the buyer; but when he is gone his way, then he boasteth." It shall not be so among you. God requires you to do justly.

Second, He requires you to love mercy. This is the brightest feature in the character of Christ. If you are in Christ, drink deep of His spirit; God requires you to be merciful. The world is selfish, unmerciful. An unconverted mother has no mercy on the soul of her own child. She can see it dropping into hell without mercy. Oh, the hellish cruelty of unconverted men! It shall not be so with you. Be merciful, as your Father in heaven is merciful.

Third, He requires you to walk humbly with your God.— Christ says, "Learn of me, for I am meek and lowly of heart." If God has covered all your black sins, rebellions, backslidings, outbreakings, then never open your mouth except in humble praise. God requires this at your hand. Walk with God, and walk humbly.

2. *Remember this is God's end in justifying you.*—He loved the Church, and gave Himself for it, that He might sanctify and cleanse it. This was His great end, to raise up a peculiar people to serve Him, and bear His likeness, in this world and in eternity. For this He left heaven, for this He groaned, bled, died, to make you holy. If you are not made holy, Christ died in vain for you.

3. *Whatever He requires, He gives grace to perform.*— Christ is not only good as our way to the Father, but He is our fountain of living waters. Be strong in the grace that is in Christ Jesus. There is enough in Christ to supply the need of all His people. An old minister says, A child can carry little water from the sea in its two hands, and so it is little we get out of Christ. There are unsearchable riches in Him.

Be strong in the grace that is in Him. Live out of yourself, and live upon Him; go and tell Him, that since He requires all this of you, He must give you grace according to your need. My God shall supply all your need, according to His riches in glory by Jesus Christ. He hath showed you One that is good, even the fair Immanuel: now lean upon Him; get life from Him that shall never die; get living water from Him that shall never dry up. Let His hand hold you up amid the billows of this tempestuous sea. Let His shoulder carry you over the thorns of this wilderness. Look as much to Him for sanctification as for justification.

> So will your walk be close with God,
> Calm and serene your frame;
> So purer light shall mark the road
> That leads you to the Lamb.

MESSAGE XV

"For I delight in the law of God after the inward man: but I see another law in my members warring against the law of my mind, and bringing me into captivity to the law of sin, which is in my members. O wretched man that I am! who shall deliver me from the body of this death? I thank God, through Jesus Christ our Lord. So then with the mind I myself serve the law of God, but with the flesh the law of sin."—ROMANS 7:22-25.

A BELIEVER is to be known not only by his peace and joy, but by his warfare and distress. His peace is peculiar: it flows from Christ; it is heavenly, it is holy peace. His warfare is as peculiar: it is deep-seated, agonizing, and ceases not till death. If the Lord will, many of us have the prospect of sitting down next Sabbath at the Lord's Table. The great question to be answered before sitting down there is, Have I fled to Christ or no?

> 'Tis a point I long to know,
> Oft it causes anxious thought,
> Do I love the Lord or no?
> Am I His, or am I not?

To help you to settle this question, I have chosen the subject of the Christian's warfare, that you may know thereby whether you are a soldier of Christ, whether you are really fighting the good fight of faith.

I. *A believer delights in the law of God.*—"I delight in the law of God after the inward man" (v. 22).

1. Before a man comes to Christ, he hates the law of God— his whole soul rises up against it. "The carnal mind is enmity" (8:7). *First,* Unconverted men hate the law of God on account of *its purity.* "Thy word is very pure, therefore thy servant loveth it." For the same reason worldly men hate it. The law is the breathing of God's pure and holy mind. It is infinitely opposed to all impurity and sin. Every line of the law is against sin. But natural men love sin, and therefore they hate the law, because it opposes them in all they love. As bats hate the light, and fly against it, so unconverted men hate the pure light of God's law, and fly against it. *Second,* They hate it for *its breadth.* "Thy commandment is exceeding broad." It extends to all their outward actions, seen and unseen; it extends to every idle word that men shall speak; it extends to the looks of their eye; it dives into the deepest caves of their heart; it condemns the most secret springs of sin and lust that nestle there. Unconverted men quarrel with the law of God because of its strictness. If it extended only to my outward actions, then I could bear with it; but it condemns my most secret thoughts and desires, which I cannot prevent. Therefore ungodly men rise against the law. *Third,* They hate it for *its unchangeableness.* Heaven and earth shall pass away, but one jot or one tittle of the law shall in no wise pass away. If the law would change, or let down its requirements, or die, then ungodly men would be well pleased. But it is unchangeable as God: it is written on the heart of God, with whom is no variableness nor shadow of turning. It cannot change unless God change; it cannot die unless God die. Even in an eternal hell its demands and its curses will be the same. It is an unchangeable law, for He is an unchangeable God. Therefore ungodly men have an unchangeable hatred to that holy law.

2. When a man comes to Christ, this is all changed. He

can say, "I delight in the law of God after the inward man." He can say with David, "Oh how I love thy law! it is my meditation all the day." He can say with Jesus, in the Fortieth Psalm, "I delight to do thy will, O my God; yea, thy law is within my heart."

There are two reasons for this:

The law is no longer an enemy.—If any of you who are trembling under a sense of your infinite sins, and the curses of the law which you have broken, flee to Christ, you will find rest. You will find that He has fully answered the demands of the law as a surety for sinners; that He has fully borne all its curses. You will be able to say, "Christ hath redeemed me from the curse of the law, being made a curse for me, as it is written, Cursed is everyone that hangeth on a tree." You have no more to fear, then, from that awfully holy law: you are not under the law, but under grace. You have no more to fear from the law than you will have after the judgment day. Imagine a saved soul after the judgment day. When that awful scene is past; when the dead, small and great, have stood before that great white throne; when the sentence of eternal woe has fallen upon all the unconverted, and they have sunk into the lake whose fires can never be quenched; would not that redeemed soul say, I have nothing to fear from that holy law; I have seen its vials poured out, but not a drop has fallen on me? So may you say now, O believer in Jesus! When you look upon the soul of Christ, scarred with God's thunderbolts; when you look upon His body, pierced for sin, you can say, He was made a curse for me; why should I fear that holy law?

The Spirit of God writes the law on the heart.—This is the promise: "After those days, saith the Lord, I will put my law in their inward parts, and write it in their hearts; and will be their God, and they shall be my people" (Jer. 31:33). Coming to Christ takes away your fear of the law; but it is the Holy Spirit coming into your heart that makes you love the law. The

Holy Spirit is no more frightened away from that heart; He comes and softens it; He takes out the stony heart and puts in a heart of flesh; and there He writes the holy, holy, holy law of God.

Then the law of God is sweet to that soul; he has an inward delight in it. "The law is holy, and the commandment holy, and just, and good." *Now* he unfeignedly desires every thought, word, and action to be according to that law. "Oh that my ways were directed to keep thy statutes: great peace have they that love thy law, and nothing shall offend them." The One Hundred Nineteenth Psalm becomes the breathing of that new heart. Now also he would fain see all the world submitting to that pure and holy law. "Rivers of waters run down mine eyes because they keep not thy law." Oh that all the world but knew that holiness and happiness are one! Oh that all the world were one holy family, joyfully coming under the pure rules of the gospel! Try yourselves by this. Can you say, "I delight in the law of God"? Do you remember when you hated it? Do you love it now? Do you long for the time when you shall live fully under it—holy as God is holy, pure as Christ is pure?

Oh, come, sinners, and give up your hearts to Christ, that He may write on it His holy law! You have long enough had the devil's law graven on your hearts: come you to Jesus, and He will both shelter you from the curses of the law, and He will give you the Spirit to write all that law in your heart; He will make you love it with your inmost soul. Plead the promise with Him. Surely you have tried the pleasures of sin long enough. Come, now, and try the pleasures of holiness out of a new heart.

If you die with your heart as it is, it will be stamped a wicked heart to all eternity. "He that is unjust, let him be unjust still; and he that is filthy, let him be filthy still" (Rev. 22:11). Oh, come and get the new heart before you die; for except you be born again, you cannot see the kingdom of God!

II. *A true believer feels an opposing law in his members.*—
"I see another law" (v. 23). When a sinner comes first to
Christ, he often thinks he will now bid an eternal farewell to
sin: now I shall never sin any more. He feels already at the
gate of heaven. A little breath of temptation soon discovers
his heart, and he cries out, *"I see another law."*

1. Observe what he calls it—*"another law"*; quite a different
law from the law of God; a law clean contrary to it. He calls
it a *"law of sin"* (v. 25); a law that commands him to commit
sin, that urges him on by rewards and threatenings—*"a law of
sin and death"* (8:2); a law which not only leads to sin, but
leads to death, eternal death: "the wages of sin is death." It is
the same law which, in Galatians, is called *"the flesh":* "The
flesh lusteth against the Spirit" (Gal. 5:17). It is the same
which, in Ephesians 4:22, is called *"the old man,"* which is
wrought according to the deceitful lusts; the same law which
in Colossians 3 is called *"your members"*—"Mortify, therefore,
your members"; the same which is called *"a body of death"*
(Rom. 7:24). The truth then is, that in the heart of the believer there remains the whole members and body of an old
man, or old nature: there remains the fountain of every sin
that has ever polluted the world.

2. Observe again what this law is doing—*"warring."* This
law in the members is not resting quiet, but warring—always
fighting. There never can be peace in the bosom of a believer.
There is peace with God, but constant war with sin. This law
in the members has got an army of lusts under him, and he
wages constant war against the law of God. Sometimes, indeed, an army is lying in ambush, and they lie quiet till a
favourable moment comes. So in the heart the lusts often lie
quiet till the hour of temptation, and then they war against
the soul. The heart is like a volcano: sometimes it slumbers
and sends up nothing but a little smoke; but the fire is slum-

bering all the while below, and will soon break out again. There are two great combatants in the believer's soul. There is Satan on the one side, with the flesh and all its lusts at his command; then on the other side there is the Holy Spirit, with the new creature all at His command. And so "the flesh lusteth against the Spirit, and the Spirit against the flesh: and these two are contrary the one to the other; so that ye cannot do the things that ye would."

Is Satan ever successful? In the deep wisdom of God the law in the members does sometimes bring the soul into captivity. Noah was a perfect man, and Noah walked with God, and yet he was led captive. "Noah drank of the wine, and was drunken." Abraham was the "friend of God," and yet he told a lie, saying of Sarah his wife, "She is my sister." Job was a perfect man, one that feared God and hated evil, and yet he was provoked to curse the day wherein he was born. And so with Moses, and David, and Solomon, and Hezekiah, and Peter, and the apostles.

3. Have you experienced this warfare? It is a clear mark of God's children. Most of you, I fear, have never felt it. Do not mistake me. All of you have felt a warfare at times between your natural conscience and the law of God. But that is not the contest in the believer's bosom. It is a warfare between the Spirit of God in the heart, and the old man with his deeds.

4. If any of you are groaning under this warfare, learn to be humbled by it, but not discouraged.

Be humbled under it.—It is intended to make you lie in the dust, and feel that you are but a worm. Oh! what a vile wretch you must be, that even after you are forgiven, and have received the Holy Spirit, your heart should still be a fountain of every wickedness! How vile, that in your most solemn approaches to God, in the house of God, in awfully affecting situations, such as kneeling beside the deathbed, you should still have in your bosom all the members of your old nature!

Let this teach you your need of Jesus.—You need the blood
of Jesus as much as at the first. You never can stand before
God in yourself. You must go again and again to be washed;
even on your dying bed you must hide under Jehovah our
Righteousness. You must also lean upon Jesus. He alone can
overcome in you. Keep nearer and nearer every day.

Be not discouraged.—Jesus is willing to be a Saviour to such
as you. He is able to save you to the uttermost. Do you think
your case is too bad for Christ to save? Every one whom Christ
saves had just such a heart as you. Fight the good fight of
faith; lay hold on eternal life. Take up the resolution of Edwards: "Never to give over, nor in the least to slacken my
fight with my corruptions, however unsuccessful I may be."
"Him that overcometh will I make a pillar in the temple of
my God" (Rev. 3:12).

III. *The feelings of a believer during this warfare.*

1. *He feels wretched.*—"O wretched man that I am!"
(v. 24). There is nobody in this world so happy as a believer.
He has come to Jesus, and found rest. He has the pardon of
all his sins in Christ. He has near approach to God as a child.
He has the Holy Spirit dwelling in him. He has the hope of
glory. In the most awful times he can be calm, for he feels
that God is with him. Still there are times when he cries, O
wretched man! When he feels the plague of his own heart;
when he feels the thorn in the flesh; when his wicked heart is
discovered in all its fearful malignity; ah, then he lies down,
crying, O wretched man that I am! One reason of this wretch-
edness is, that sin, discovered in the heart, takes away the
sense of forgiveness. Guilt comes upon the conscience, and a
dark cloud covers the soul. How can I ever go back to Christ?
he cries. Alas! I have sinned away my Saviour. Another reason
is, the loathsomeness of sin. It is felt like a viper in the heart.
A natural man is often miserable from his sin, but he never
feels its loathsomeness; but to the new creature it is vile indeed.

Ah! brethren, do you know anything of a believer's wretched-
ness? If you do not, you will never know his joy. If you
know not a believer's tears and groans, you will never know
his song of victory.

2. *He seeks deliverance.*—"Who shall deliver me?" In
ancient times, some of the tyrants used to chain their prisoners
to a dead body; so that, wherever the prisoner wandered, he
had to drag a putrid carcase after him. It is believed that Paul
here alludes to this inhuman practice. His old man he felt a
noisome putrid carcass, which he was continually dragging
about with him. His piercing desire is to be freed from it. Who
shall deliver us? You remember once, when God allowed a
thorn in the flesh to torment His servant, a messenger of Satan
to buffet him, Paul was driven to his knees. "I besought the
Lord thrice, that it might depart from me." Oh, this is the
true mark of God's children! The world has an old nature;
they are all old men together. But it does not drive them to
their knees. How is it with you, dear souls? Does corruption
felt within drive you to the throne of grace? Does it make you
call on the name of the Lord? Does it make you like the im-
portunate widow: "Avenge me of mine adversary"? Does it
make you like the man coming at midnight for three loaves?
Does it make you like the Canaanitish woman, crying after
Jesus? Ah, remember, if lust can work in your heart, and you
lie down contented with it, you are none of Christ's!

3. *He gives thanks for victory.*—Truly we are more than
conquerors through Him that loved us; for we can give thanks
before the fight is done. Yes, even in the thickest of the battle
we can look up to Jesus, and cry, Thanks to God. The moment a soul groaning under corruption rests the eye on Jesus,
that moment his groans are changed into songs of praise. In
Jesus you discover a fountain to wash away the guilt of all
your sin. In Jesus you discover grace sufficient for you, grace
to hold you up to the end, and a sure promise that sin shall

soon be rooted out altogether. "Fear not, I have redeemed thee. I have called thee by my name; thou are mine." Ah, this turns our groans into songs of praise! How often a psalm begins with groans and ends with praises! This is the daily experience of all the Lord's people. Is it yours? Try yourselves by this. Oh, if you know not the believer's song of praise, you will never cast your crowns with them at the feet of Jesus! Dear believers, be content to glory in your infirmities, that the power of Christ may rest upon you. Glory, glory, glory to the Lamb!

MESSAGE XVI

THE BROKEN HEART

"The sacrifices of God are a broken spirit: a broken and a contrite heart, O God, thou wilt not despise."—PSALM 51:17.

NO PSALM expresses more fully the experience of a penitent believing soul: his humbling confession of sin (vv. 3, 4, 5); his intense desire for pardon through the blood of Christ (v. 7); his longing after a clean heart (v. 10); his desire to render something to God for all His benefits.

He says he will teach transgressors God's ways; that his lips shall show forth God's praise; that he will give a broken heart (vv. 16, 17). Just as, long ago they used to offer slain lambs in token of thanksgiving, so he says he will offer up to God a slain and broken heart. Every one of you, who has found the same forgiveness, should come to the same resolution—offer up to God this day a broken heart.

I. *The natural heart is sound and unbroken.*

The law, the gospel, mercies, afflictions, death, do not break the natural heart. It is harder than stone; there is nothing in the universe so hard. "Ye stout-hearted, that ire far from righteousness" (Isa. 46:12). "We have walked

to and fro through the earth, and behold all the earth
sitteth still and is at rest" (Zech. 1:11). "I will search Jerusalem with candles, and punish the men that are settled on
their lees" (Zeph. 1:12). "They have made their faces
harder than a rock" (Jer. 5:3). "Careless women" (Isa.
32:10). "Women that are at ease" (v. 11).

Why?—*First,* The veil is on their hearts. They do not
believe the Bible, the strictness of the law, the wrath to
come; the face of a covering is over their eyes.

Second, Satan has possession. Satan carries the seed away.

Third, They are dead in trespasses and sins. The dead
hear not, feel not; they are *past feeling.*

Fourth, They build a wall of untempered mortar. They
hope for safety in some refuge of lies—that they pray, or
give alms.

Pray God to keep away from you the curse of a dead, unbroken heart. *First,* Because it will not last long; you are
standing on slippery places; the waves are below your feet.

Second, Because Christ will laugh at your calamity. If you
were now concerned, there is hope. Ministers and Christians
are ready; Christ is ready; but afterwards He will laugh.

II. *The awakened heart is wounded, not broken.*

1. *The law makes the first wound.*—When God is going to
save a soul, He brings the soul to reflect on his sins: "Cursed
is every one . . ." "Whatsoever things the law saith . . ." "I
was alive without the law once . . ." *Life* and *heart* appear
in awful colors.

2. *The majesty of God makes the next wound.*—The sinner is made sensible of the great and holy Being against
whom he has sinned. *"Against Thee"* (Ps. 51:4).

3. *The third wound is from his own helplessness to make
himself better.*—Still the heart is not broken; the heart rises
against God. *First,* Because of the strictness of the law. *Second,* Because faith is the only way of salvation, and is the

gift of God. *Third,* Because God is sovereign, and may save or not as He will. This shows the unbroken heart. There is no more miserable state than this.

Learn—It is one thing to be awakened, and another thing to be saved. Do not rest in convictions.

III. *The believing heart is a broken heart two ways.*

It is broken from its own righteousness.—When the Holy Spirit leads a man to the cross, his heart there breaks from seeking salvation by his own righteousness. All his burden of performance and contrivances drops. *First,* The work of Christ appears so perfect—the wisdom of God and the power of God—divine righteousness. "I wonder that I should ever think of any other way of salvation. If I could have been saved by my own duties, my whole soul would now have refused it. I wonder that all the world did not see and comply with this way of salvation by the righteousness of Christ."—(*Brainerd,* p. 319.)

Second, The grace of Christ appears so wonderful. That all this righteousness should be free to such a sinner! That I so long neglected, despised, hated it, put mountains between, and yet that He has come over the mountains! "That thou mayest remember and be confounded, and never open thy mouth any more because of thy shame, when I am pacified toward thee for all that thou hast done" (Ezek. 16:63). Have you this broken heart—broken within sight of the cross? It is not a look into your own heart, or the heart of hell, but into the heart of Christ, that breaks the heart. Oh, pray for this broken heart! Boasting is excluded. To Him be glory. Worthy is the Lamb! All the struggles of a self-righteous soul are to put the crown on your own head.

2. *Broken from love of sin.*—When a man believes on Christ, he then sees sin to be hateful. *First,* It separated between him and God, made the great gulf, and kindled the fires of hell.

Second, It crucified the Lord of Glory; weighed down His soul; made Him sweat, and bleed, and die.

Third, It is the plague of His heart now. All my unhappiness is from my being a sinner. Now he mourns sore like a dove, that he should sin against so much love. "Then shall ye remember your ways, and all your doings wherein ye have been defiled, and shall loathe yourself in your own sight."

IV. *Advantages of a broken heart.*

1. *It keeps you from being offended at the preaching of the cross.*—A natural heart is offended every day at the preaching of the cross. Many of you, I have no doubt, hate it. Many, I have no doubt, are often enraged in their hearts at the preaching of another's righteousness—that you must have it or perish. Many, I doubt not, have left this church on account of it; and many more, I doubt not, will follow. All the offence of the cross is not ceased. But a broken heart cannot be offended. Ministers cannot speak too plainly for a broken heart. A broken heart would sit forever to hear of the righteousness without works.

Many of you are offended when we preach plainly against sin. Many were offended last Sabbath. But a broken heart cannot be offended, for it hates sin worse than ministers can make it. Many are like the worshipers of Baal: "Bring forth thy son that he may die" (Judg. 6:30). But a broken heart loves to see the idol stamped upon and beaten small.

2. *A broken heart is at rest.*—The unconverted heart is like the troubled sea: "Who will show us any good?" It is going from creature to creature. The awakened soul is not at rest; sorrows of death, pains of hell, attend those who are forgetting their resting place. But the broken heart says, "Return unto thy rest, O my soul." The righteousness of Christ takes away every fear, "casts out fear." Even the plague of the heart cannot truly disturb, for he casts his burden on Jesus.

3. *Nothing wrong can happen to it.*—To the unconverted, how dreadful is a sickbed, poverty, death—tossed like a wild beast in a net! But a broken heart is satisfied with Christ. This is enough; he has no ambition for more. Take away all, this remains. He is a weaned child.

Message XVII

"O Ephraim, what shall I do unto thee? O Judah, what shall I do unto thee? for your goodness is as a morning cloud, and as the early dew it goeth away"—Hosea 6:4.

IN THESE WORDS, God complains that He did not know what to do with Israel, their impressions were so fading. He says, (v. 5), that He had hewed them by the prophets, and slain them by the words of His mouth; and their judgments were as the light that goeth forth. At one time He sent them severe awakening messages of coming wrath; then messages of love and grace, as bright and as many as the beams of the sun. They were a little impressed by them; the cloud of distress began to gather on their brow; the dew of grief seemed to start to their cheek, but it soon dried up. It was like the morning cloud and early dew that goeth away. So it is with all the unconverted persons in this congregation, who will finally perish. God has sent them awakening messages; hewed them by the prophets, and slain them by the words of His mouth. He has sent them also sweet encouraging messages; His judgments have been like the light that goeth forth. They think, and are impressed for a little, but it soon dies away. "O Ephraim, what shall I do . . ."

I. *The fact that the impressions of natural men fade away.*

1. *Prove the fact from Scripture.*—The Scriptures abound with examples of it.

First, Lot's wife. She was a good deal awakened. The anxious faces of the two angelic men—their awful words, and

merciful hands—made a deep impression on her. The anxiety
of her husband, too, and his words to his sons-in-law, sank
into her heart. She fled with anxious steps; but as the morning brightened, her anxious thoughts began to wear away. She
looked back, and became a pillar of salt.

Second, Israel at the Red Sea. When Israel had been led
through the deep water in safety, and when they saw their
enemies drowned, then they sang God's praise. Their hearts
were much affected by this deliverance. They sang, "The
Lord is my strength and song, He also is become my salvation." They sang His praise, but soon forgot His works. In
three days they were murmuring against God because of the
bitter waters.

Third, Once *a young man* came running to Jesus, and he
kneeled down, saying, "Good Master, what good thing shall
I do that I may inherit eternal life?" A flash of conviction
had passed over his conscience; he was now kneeling at the
feet of Christ, but he never kneeled there any more; he
went away sorrowful. His goodness was like a morning cloud.

Fourth, Once Paul preached before *Felix,* the Roman gov-
ernor; and as he reasoned of righteousness, temperance, and
judgment to come, Felix trembled. The preaching of the
gospel made the proud Roman tremble on his throne, but did
it save his soul? Ah, no! "Go thy way for this time; when
I have a more convenient season I will send for thee." His
goodness was like the morning cloud.

Fifth, Again, Paul preached before *King Agrippa* and his
beautiful Bernice, with all the captains and chief men of the
city. The word troubled Agrippa's heart, the tear started into
his royal eye, and for a moment he thought of leaving all for
Christ. "Almost thou persuadest me to be a Christian." But
ah! his goodness was like a morning cloud and early dew.
In all these the cloud gathered over them; for a moment the
dew glistened in their eye, but soon it passed away.

2. *Prove the fact from experience.*—Most men under a preached gospel have their times of awakening. If the impressions of natural men were permanent, then most would be saved; but we know that this is not the case. Few there be that find it. Perhaps I would not go far wrong if I were to say that there may not be ten grown-up men in this congregation who have never experienced any concern for their soul, and yet I fear there may be hundreds who will finally perish.

First, How many have had a time of awakening in childhood when they were prayed over by a believing mother, or warned by a believing father, or taught by a faithful Sabbath school teacher; how many have had deep impressions made at the Sabbath school; but they have passed away like the morning cloud and early dew!

Second, At their first communion, when they first spoke to a minister about their soul, and heard his piercing questions and faithful warnings, when they got their token from his hand, when they first received the bread and wine, and sat at the Table of the Lord, they trembled; the tear dimmed their eye; they went home to pray. But soon it wore away. The world—pleasure—cares—involved the mind, and all was gone like the cloud and the dew.

Third, A first sickness. How many, laid down on a bed of sickness, are made to look over the verge of the grave! They tremble as they think how unprepared they are to die; and now they begin to vow and resolve, If the Lord spare me, I will avoid evil companions, I will pray and read my Bible; but no sooner are they better than the resolutions are forgotten, like the cloud and dew.

Fourth, First death in a family. What a deep impression this makes on a feeling heart! That lovely circle is broken round the fire, and never will be whole again. Now they begin to pray, to turn to Him that smites. Perhaps, kneeling beside the cold body, they vow no longer to go back to sin and folly. Or, following the body to the grave, while the big tear stands in the eye, they promise to bury all their sins and follies in the grave of their beloved one. But soon a change comes over them; the tears dry up, and the prayer is forgotten. The world takes its place again and reigns. Their goodness is as the morning cloud.

Fifth, In a time of awakening, many receive deep impressions. Some are alarmed to see others alarmed that are no worse than they. Many have their feelings stirred and their affections moved. Many are brought to desire conversion, to weep and to pray. Mr. Edwards mentions that there was scarcely an individual in the whole town unconcerned; there were tokens of God's presence in every house. So here; and yet, when the time is past, how soon they sink back into former indifference! Their goodness is as the morning cloud.

Dear friends, ye are my witnesses. I do not know, but I believe I am not wrong in stating, that by far the greater number of you have been under remorse at some time or another, and yet God and your own consciences know how fading these impressions have been. Just as the morning cloud passes off the mountain's brow, and the dew is dried up from the rock, and leaves it a rock still, so your impressions have passed away, and left you a rocky heart still. So it is in those that perish. The way to hell is paved with good intentions, and hell is peopled with those who once wept and prayed for their souls. "O Ephraim, what shall I do unto thee?"

3. *Let us show the steps of impressions fading away.*— When a natural man is under concern, he begins to make a very diligent use of the means of grace.

First, Prayer.—When a man is under the fear of hell, he begins to pray, and often he has very melting and sweet affections in prayer. As long as his impressions last, he may be very constant in his duty. But will he always call upon God? When his concern ceases, his praying in secret gradually ceases also. Not all at once, but by degrees he gives up secret prayer. Once he has been out in company, another time kept long at business, another time he is sleeping, and so by degrees he gives it up altogether. "O Ephraim, what shall I do unto thee?"

Second, Hearing the word.—When a man is first awakened, he comes well out to the preaching of the Word. He knows that God blesses especially the preaching of the Word, that it pleases God by the foolishness of preaching to save them that believe. He is an arrested hearer; he drinks in the words of the minister; he is lively in his attendance on the Word; if there be preaching in the week evening, he puts by his work in order to be there. But when his concern wears away, he begins to weary first of the week day service, then of the Sabbath; then perhaps he seeks a more careless ministry, where he may slumber on till death and judgment. Ah! this has been the course of thousands in this place. "O Ephraim, what shall I do unto thee?"

Third, Asking counsel of ministers.—When souls are under remorse, they often ask counsel of the under-shepherds of Christ. "Going and weeping, they come to seek the Lord their God: they ask the way to Zion." They go to the watchman, saying, Saw ye Him whom my soul loveth? This is one of the duties of the faithful pastor, for "the priest's lips should keep knowledge; and they should seek the law at his mouth; for he is the messenger of the Lord of Hosts." But when concern dies away, this dies away. Many come once, that never come again. "O Ephraim!"

Fourth, Avoiding sin.—When a man is under convictions, he always avoids open sin—flees from it with all his might. He reforms his life; his soul is swept and garnished. But when his concern dies away, his lusts revive, and he goes back like a dog to his vomit, and like the sow that was washed to its wallowing in the mire. If there were anything saving in the impressions of natural men, they would turn holier; but, on the contrary, they turn worse and worse. Seven devils enter into that man, and the latter end is worse than the beginning. "O Ephraim, what shall I do unto thee?"

II. *Why the impressions of natural men die away.*

1. *They never are brought to feel truly lost.*—The wounds of natural men are generally skin deep. Sometimes it is just a flash of terror that has alarmed them. Often it is the sense of some one great sin they have committed. Sometimes it is only sympathy with others, fleeing because others flee. They are often brought to say, I am a great sinner; I fear there is no mercy for me. Still they are not brought to feel *undone,* their mouth is not stopped, they do not cover the lip like the leper. They think a little prayer, sorrow, repentance, amendment, will do. If they could only change their way. They are not brought to see that all they do just signifies nothing toward justifying them. If they were brought to feel their utterly lost state, and their need of another's righteousness, they never could rest in the world again.

2. *They never saw the beauty of Christ.*—A flash of terror may bring a man to his knees, but will not bring him to Christ. Ah! no; love must draw. A natural man, under concern, sees no beauty nor desirableness in Christ. He is not brought to look to Him whom he pierced, and to mourn. When once a man gets a sight of the supreme excellence and sweetness of Christ, when he sees His fullness for pardon, peace, holiness, he will never draw back. He may be in distress and in darkness; but he will rise and go about the city to seek Him whom his soul loveth. The heart that has once seen Christ is smitten with the love of Him, and never can rest nor take up with others short of Him.

3. *He never had heart-hatred of sin.*—The impressions of natural men are generally of terror. They feel the danger of sin, not the filthiness of it. They feel that God is just and

true; that the law must be avenged; that the wrath of God
will come. They see that there is hell in their sins; but they
do not feel their sins to be a hell. They love sin; they have
no change of nature. The Spirit of God does not dwell in
them; and therefore the impression wears easily away, like
as on sand. Those that are brought to Christ are brought to
see the turpitude of sin. They cry not, Behold I am undone;
but, Behold I am vile. As long as sin is in their breast, they
are kept fleeing to the cross of Christ.

4. *They have no promises to keep their impressions.*—
Those who are in Christ have sweet promises. "I will put
my fear in their hearts" (Jer. 32:40). "Being confident that
he which hath begun a good work in you will perform it"
(Phil. 1:6). But natural men have no interest in these promises; and so, in the time of temptation, their anxieties easily
wear away.

III. *Sadness of their case.*

1. *God mourns over their case.*—"O Ephraim." It must
be a truly sad case that God mourns over. When Christ wept
over Jerusalem, it showed it was in a desperate case, because
that eye that wept saw plainly what was coming; and, accordingly, in a few years, that lovely city was a ruined heap, and
multitudes of those then living were in hell, and their children vagabonds. When Christ looked round on the Pharisees
with anger, being grieved at the hardness of their hearts, it
showed a desperate case; He would not grieve for nothing.
So here you may be sure the case of natural men who lose
their impressions is very desperate, from these words of God,
"O Ephraim."

2. *God has no new method of awakening.*—God speaks
as even at a loss what to do, to show you that there remaineth
no more sacrifice for sins. You have heard all the awakening
truths in the Bible, and all the winning, comforting truths.
You have been at Sinai, and at Gethsemane, and at Calvary:

what more can I do unto you? These have been pressed home upon you by divine providences, in affliction, by the bed of death, and in a time of wide awakening. You have passed through a season when it was tenfold more likely that you would be truly converted than any other time. You are sunk back! Ah! the harvest is past, the summer is ended, and you are not saved. God has no more arrows in His quiver, no new arguments, no other hell, no other Christ.

3. *No good by your past impressions.*—When the cloud is dried up off the mountain's brow, and the dew off the rock, the mountain is as great as before, and the rock as hard; but when convictions fade away from the heart of a natural man, they leave the mountain of his sins much greater, and his rocky heart much harder. It is less likely that that man will ever be saved. Just as iron is hardened by being melted and cooled again; just as a person recovering from fever relapses, and is worse than before.

First, You are now older, and every day less likely to be saved; your heart gets used to its old ways of thinking and feeling; the old knee cannot easily learn to bend.

Second, You have offended the Spirit; you have missed your opportunity; you have vexed the Holy Spirit; convictions are not in your own power; the Spirit hath mercy on whom He will have mercy.

Third, You have got into the way of putting aside convictions. The eyelid naturally closes when any object is coming against it; so does the heart of a practiced worldling close and shut out convictions.

Fourth, When you come to hell, you will wish you never had had convictions, they will make your punishment so much the greater.

I would now entreat all who have any impressions not to let them slip. It is a great mercy to live under a gospel ministry; still greater to live in a time of revival; still greater to have God pouring the Spirit into your heart, awakening your soul. Do not neglect it, do not turn back; remember Lot's wife. Escape for thy life; look not behind thee; tarry not in all the plain. Escape to the mountain, lest thou be consumed.

MESSAGE XVIII

"She hath done what she could; she is come aforehand to anoint my body to the burying."—MARK 14:8.

FROM the Gospel of John (11:2), we learn that this woman was Mary, the sister of Lazarus and Martha. We have already learned that she was an eminent believer: "She sat at the feet of Jesus, and heard his word." Jesus Himself said of her: "Mary hath chosen the good part, which shall not be taken away from her." Now it is interesting to see this same Mary eminent in another way, not only as a *contemplative believer,* but as an *active believer.*

Many seem to think, that to be a believer is to have certain feelings and experiences; forgetting all the time that these are but the flowers, and that the fruit must follow. The engrafting of the branch is good, the inflowing of the sap good, but the fruit is the end in view. So faith is good, and peace and joy are good, but holy fruit is the end for which we are saved.

I trust many of you, last Sabbath, were like Mary, sitting at the Redeemer's feet, and hearing His Word. Now I would persuade you to be like Mary, in *doing what you can for Christ.* If you have been bought with a price, then glorify God in your body and spirit, which are His. I beseech you by the mercies of God.

I. *These are things which we can do.*

1. *We could love Christ, pray and praise more.*—What this woman did she did to Christ. Jesus had saved her soul,

had saved her brother and sister, and she felt that she could
not do too much for Him. She brought an alabaster box of
ointment, very costly, and broke the box and poured it on His
head. No doubt, she loved His disciples, holy John and frank
Peter, yet still she loved Christ more. No doubt she loved
Christ's poor, and was often kind to them; yet she loved Jesus
more. On His blessed head, that was so soon to be crowned
with thorns, on His blessed feet, that were so soon to be
pierced with nails, she poured the precious ointment. This
is what we should do. If we have been saved by Christ, we
should pour out our best affections on Him. It is well to love
His disciples, well to love His ministers, well to love His poor,
but it is best to love Him. We cannot now reach His
blessed head, nor anoint His holy feet; but we can fall down
at His footstool, and pour out our affections towards Him.
It was not the ointment Jesus cared for—what does the King
of Glory care for a little ointment? But it is the loving heart,
poured out upon His feet; it is the adoration, praise, love,
and prayers of a believer's broken heart, that Christ cares for.
The new heart is the alabaster box that Jesus loves.

Oh, brethren, could you not do more in this way? Could
you not give more time to pouring out your heart to Jesus—
breaking the box, and filling the room with the odor of your
praise? Could you not pray more than you do to be filled
with the Spirit, that the Spirit may be poured down on ministers,
and God's people, and on an unconverted world? Jesus loves
tears and groans from a broken heart.

2. *We could live holier lives.*—The church is thus described in the Song of Solomon: "Who is this that cometh out
of the wilderness like pillars of smoke, perfumed with myrrh
and frankincense, with all powders of the merchant?" The
holiness of the believer is like the most precious perfume.
When a holy believer goes through the world, filled with the
Spirit, made more than conqueror, the fragrance fills the

room; " 'tis as if an angel shook his wings." If the world were full of believers, it would be like a bed of spices. But oh, how few believers carry much of the odor of heaven along with them! How many you might be the means of saving, if you lived a holy, consistent life, if you were evidently a sacrifice bound upon God's altar! Wives might thus, *without the word*, win their husbands, when they see your chaste conversation coupled with fear; parents might in this way save their children, when they saw you holy and happy; children have often thus saved their parents. Servants, adorn the doctrine of God your Saviour in all things; let your light shine before men. The poorest can do this as well as the richest, the youngest as well as the oldest. Oh, there is no argument like a holy life!

3. *You could seek the salvation of others.*—If you have really been brought to Christ and saved, then you know there is a hell. You know that all the unconverted around you are hastening to it; you know there is a Saviour, and that He is stretching out His hands all the day long to sinners. Could you do no more to save sinners than you do? Do you do all you can? You say you *pray for them;* but is it not hypocrisy to pray and do nothing? Will God hear these prayers? Have you no fears that prayers without labors are only provoking God? You say you *cannot speak,* you are not learned. Will that excuse stand in the judgment? Does it require much learning to tell fellow sinners that they are perishing? If their house was on fire, would it require much learning to wake the sleepers?

Begin at home. Could you not do more for the salvation of those at home? If there are children or servants, have you done all you can for them? Have you done all you can to bring the truth before them, to bring them under a living ministry, to get them to pray and give up sin?

Do you do what you can for your neighbors? Can you pass

your neighbors for years together, and see them on the broad way, without warning them? Do you make a full use of tracts, giving suitable ones to those that need them? Do you persuade Sabbath-breakers to go to the house of God? Do you do anything in Sabbath schools? Could you not tell little children the way to be saved? Do you do what you can for the *world?* The field is the world.

4. *Feed Christ's poor.*—I am far from thinking that the wicked poor should be passed over, but Christ's poor are our brothers and sisters. Do you do what you can for them? In the great day, Christ will say to those on His right hand, "Come ye blessed, for I was an hungered, and ye gave me meat." They stand in the place of Christ. Christ does not any more stand in need of Mary's ointment, or Martha's hospitality, or the Samaritan's drink of water. He is beyond the reach of these things, and will never need them more; but He has left many of His brothers and sisters behind in this world, some diseased, some lame, some like Lazarus all covered with sores; and He says, What ye do to them, ye do to me. Do you live plainly, in order to have more to give away? Do you put away vain and gaudy clothes, that you may be able to clothe the naked? Are you thrifty in managing what you have, letting nothing be lost?

II. *Why we should do what we can.*

1. *Christ has done what He could for us.*—"What could have been done more to my vineyard, that I have not done in it?" (Isa. 5:4). He thought nothing too much to do and to suffer for us. While we were yet sinners, Christ died for us. Greater love than this hath no man. *All His life,* between the manger at Bethlehem and the cross of Calvary, was spent in labors and infinite sufferings for us. All that we needed to suffer, He suffered; all that we need to obey, He obeyed. All His life in glory He spends for us. He ever liveth to make intercession for us. He is head over all things for us; makes

everything in all worlds work together for our good. It is all but incredible that each person of the Godhead has made Himself over to us to be ours. The Father says, "I am thy God"; the Son, "Fear not, for I have redeemed thee"; the Holy Ghost makes us a temple, "I will dwell in them, and walk in them." Is it much that we should do all we can for Him, that we should give ourselves up to Him who gave Himself for us?

2. *Satan does all he can.*—Sometimes he comes as a lion: "Your adversary the devil, as a roaring lion, walketh about, seeking whom he may devour"; sometimes as a serpent, "as the serpent beguiled Eve"; sometimes as an angel of light. He does all he can to tempt and beguile the saints, leading them away by false teachers, injecting blasphemies and polluted thoughts into their minds, casting fiery darts at their souls, stirring up the world to hate and persecute them, stirring up father and mother against the children, and brother against brother. He does all he can to lead captive wicked men, blinding their minds, not allowing them to listen to the gospel, steeping them in swinish lusts, leading them into despair. When he knows his time is short, he rages all the more. Oh, should not we do all we can, if Satan does all he can?

3. *We have done all we could the other way.*—This was one of Paul's great motives for doing all he could: "I thank Christ Jesus our Lord for putting me into the ministry; for I was a blasphemer, and persecutor, and injurious." He never could forget how he had persecuted the Church of God, and wasted it; and this made him as diligent in building it up, and haling men and women to Christ. He preached the faith which once he destroyed. So with Peter: "Let us live the rest of our time in the flesh not to the lusts of men, but to the will of God; for the time past of our lives may suffice to have wrought the will of the Gentiles, when we walked in

lasciviousness, lusts, excess of wine, revelings, banquetings,
and abominable idolatries." So with John Newton: "How
can the old African blasphemer be silent?" So with many of
you: you ran greedily after sin; you were at great pains and
cost, and did not spare health, or money, or time, to obtain
some sinful gratification. How can you now grudge anything
for Christ? Only serve Christ as zealously as you once served
the devil.

4. *Christ will own and reward what we do.*—The labor
that Christ blesseth is believing labor. It is not words of
human wisdom, but words of faith, that God makes arrows.
The word of a little maid was blessed in the house of Naaman
the Syrian. "Follow me" was made the arrow to pierce the
heart of Matthew. It is all one to God to save, whether
with many, or with them that have no might. If you would
do all you can, the town would be filled with the fragrance.
Christ will reward it. He defended Mary's work of love, and
said it should be spoken of over all the world, and it will
yet be told in the judgment. A cup of cold water He will not
pass over. "Well done, good and faithful servant."

5. *If you do not do all you can, how can you prove yourself a Christian?*—"Pure religion and undefiled before God and
the Father is this, To visit the fatherless and widows in their
affliction, and to keep himself unspotted from the world."
You are greatly mistaken if you think that to be a Christian
is merely to have certain views, and convictions, and spiritual
delights. This is all well; but if it leads not to a devoted life,
I fear it is all a delusion. If any man be in Christ, he is a new
creature.

III. *Let us answer objections.*

1. *The world will mock at us.*—This is true. They mocked
at Mary; they called it waste and extravagance; and yet,
Christ said it was well done. So, if you do what you can,
the world will laugh at you, but you will have the smile of

Christ. They mocked at Christ when He was full of zeal; they said He was mad and had a devil. They mocked at Paul, and said he was mad; and so with all Christ's living members. "Rejoice, inasmuch as ye are partakers of the sufferings of Christ." "If ye suffer with him, ye shall also reign with him."

2. *What can I do?—I am a woman.*—Mary was a woman, yet she did what she could. Mary Magdalene was a woman, and yet she was first at the sepulchre. Phebe was a woman, yet a succorer of many, and of Paul also. Dorcas was a woman, yet she made coats and garments for the poor at Joppa. *I am a child*—Out of the mouth of babes and sucklings God perfects praise. God has often used children in the conversion of their parents.

3. *I have too little grace to do good.*—"He that watereth others, shall be watered himself." "The liberal soul shall be made fat." "It pleased the Father that in Christ should all fullness dwell." There is a full supply of the Spirit to teach you to pray; a full supply of grace to slay your sins and quicken your graces. If you use opportunities of speaking to others, God will give you plenty. If you give much to God's poor, you shall never want a rich supply. "God is able to make all grace abound toward you; that ye, always having all sufficiency in all things, may abound to every good work." "Bring all the tithes unto my storehouse, and prove me now herewith." "Honor the Lord with thy substance, and with the firstfruits of all thine increase: so shall thy barns be filled with plenty, and thy presses shall burst out with new wine."

April 26, 1842

Message XIX

"It was but a little that I passed from them, but I found him whom my soul
loveth: I held him, and would not let him go, until I had brought him into
my mother's house, and into the chamber of her that conceived me."—Song
of Solomon 3:4.

HAVE YOU found Him whom your soul loveth? Have
you this day seen His beauty, heard His voice, believed
the record concerning Him, sat under His shadow, found fellowship with Him? Then *hold Him,* and *do not let Him go.*

I. *Motives.*

1. *Because peace is to be found in Him.*—Justified by faith,
we have *peace with God—not* peace with ourselves, *not* peace
with the world, with sin, with Satan, but peace with God.
True divine peace is to be found only in believing, only in
keeping fast hold of Christ. If you let *Him* go, you let go
your righteousness; for this is His name. You are then without
righteousness, without a covering from the wrath of God,
without a way to the Father. The law will again condemn
you; God's frown will again overshadow you; you will again
have terrors of conscience. *Hold Him then,* and do not let
Him go. Whatever you let go, *let not Christ go;* for He is
our peace, not in knowledge, not in feeling, but *trust* in *Him*
alone.

2. *Holiness flows from Him.*—No true holiness in this
world, but it springs from Him. A living Christ is the spring
of holiness to all His members. As long as we hold Him,
and do not let Him go, our holiness is secure. He is engaged
to keep us from falling. He loves us too well to let us fall
under the reigning power of sin. His word is engaged: "I
will put my Spirit within you." His honor would be tarnished
if any that cleave to Him were suffered to live in sin. If you
let *Him* go, you will fall into sin. You have no strength, no
store of grace, no power to resist a thousand enemies, no

promises. If Christ be for you, who can be against you? But
if you let go His arms, where are you?

3. *Hope of glory is in Him.*—We rejoice in hope of the
glory of God. If you have found Jesus this day, you have
found a way into glory. A few steps more, you can say, and
I shall be forever with the Lord. I shall be free from pain
and sorrow, free from sin and weakness, free from enemies.
As long as you hold Christ, you can see your way to the
judgment seat. "Thou wilt guide me with thy counsel, and
receive me to thy glory." This gives you such joy, such trans-
porting desires after the heavenly world! But let Christ go,
and this will be gone. Let Christ go, and how can you die?
The grave is covered with clouds of theatening. Let Him go,
and how can you go to the judgment—where can you appear?

II. *Means.*

1. *Christ promises to keep you holding Him.*—If you are
really holding Christ this day, you are in a most blessed condition, for Christ engages to keep you cleaving to Him. "My
soul followeth hard after *thee,* and thy right hand upholdeth
me." He that is the Creator of the world is the upholder of
it, so He that new creates the soul keeps it in being. This
is never to be forgotten. Not only does the Church lean on
her beloved, but He puts His left hand under her head, and
His right hand doth embrace her. "I taught Ephraim how to
go, taking them by their arms." It is good for a child to hold
fast by its mother's neck; but ah! that would be a feeble support, if the maternal arm did not enfold the child, and clasp
it to her bosom. Faith is good; but ah! it is nothing without
the grace that gave it. "I will put my fear in your heart."

2. *Faith in Christ.*—The only way to hold fast is to believe
more and more. Get a larger acquaintance with Christ, with
His person, work, and character. Every page of the gospel
unfolds a new feature in His character, every line of the
epistles discloses new depths of His work. Get more faith,

and you will get a firmer hold. A plant that has a single root may be easily torn up by the hand, or crushed by the foot of the wild beast, or blown down by the wind; but a plant that has a thousand roots struck down into the ground can stand. Faith is like the root. Many believe a little concerning Christ, one fact. Every new truth concerning Jesus is a new root struck downward. Believe more intensely. A root may be in a right direction, but, not striking deep, it is easily torn up. Pray for deep-rooted faith. Pray to be established, strengthened, settled. Take a long intense look at Jesus—often. If you wanted to know a man again, and he was going away, you would take an intense look at his face. Look then at Jesus, deeply, intensely, till every feature is graven on your heart. Thomas Scott overcame the fear of death by looking intensely at his dead child, who had died in the Lord.

3. *Prayer.*—Jacob at Bethel. "Take hold of my strength," (Isa. 27:5). You must begin and pray after another fashion than you have done. Let it be real intercourse with God, like Hezekiah, Jacob and Moses.

4. *By not offending Him.*—*First,* By sloth. When the soul turns sleepy or careless, Christ goes away. Nothing is more offensive to Christ than sloth. Love is an ever-active thing, and when it is in the heart it will keep us waking. Many a night His love to us kept Him waking. Now, can you not watch with Him one hour?

Second, By idols. You cannot hold two objects. If you are holding Christ today, and lay hold of another object to-tomorrow, He cannot stay. He is a jealous God. You cannot keep worldly companions and Christ too. "A companion of fools shall be destroyed." When the ark came into the house of Dagon, it made the idol fall flat.

Third, By being unwilling to be sanctified. When Christ chooses us and draws us to Himself, it is that He may sanctify us. Christ is often grieved by our desiring to reserve *one* sin.

Fourth, By an unholy house. "I brought him into my mother's house." Remember to take Christ home with you, and let Him rule in your house. If you walk with Christ abroad, but never take Him home, you will soon part company forever.

_____

MESSAGE XX

"To whom God would make known what is the riches of the glory of this mystery among the Gentiles; which is Christ in you, the hope of glory."— COLOSSIANS 1:27.

THE GOSPEL is here described as "Christ in you, the hope of glory." There are two distinct senses in which these words may be taken, and I cannot positively determine which is the true one. It is possible that both may be intended. I shall open up both.

I. *Christ in you,* means Christ embraced by faith as our righteousness and strength; and this is the sure ground upon which we hope for glory. In this sense it appears to be used, "That Christ may dwell in your hearts by faith" (Eph. 3:17). When a sinner's heart is opened by the Holy Spirit, when the beauty and excellence of the Saviour is shown to him, the heart inwardly embraces and cleaves to Christ. Every new discovery of Christ to the soul renews this act of inward cleaving to the Lord Jesus. Every reproach, every temptation, every fall into sin, every bereavement, makes the soul more really, firmly, and fully embrace the Lord Jesus; and so, by continual faith, Christ may be said to dwell in the heart, as in Ephesians 3:17, "That Christ may dwell in your hearts by faith." Christ thus embraced is the hope of glory. It is this constant abiding faith, this close embracing of Christ as all our righteousness, which gives a calm, sweet, full, peaceful hope of glory. The soul that can say, Christ is mine, can also say, Glory is mine; for we need nothing but Christ to shelter us in the judgment day. Can you say that Christ is thus in you the hope of glory? If you have not got Christ, you have no good hope of glory.

II. *Christ formed in the soul by the Spirit* (Gal. 4:19).—Christ formed in the soul is also the hope of glory, and this I take to be the full meaning of this verse. So, "Abide in me, and I in you" (John 15:4). "I in them, and thou in me" (John 17:23). "And I in them" (v. 26).

1. *The mind of Christ* is formed in the soul.—"We have the mind of Christ" (I Cor. 2:16). By the mind, I understand the thinking powers of man. Now, every believer has the mind of Christ formed in him. He thinks as Christ does: "This is the spirit of a sound mind" (II Tim. 1:7). This is being of the same mind in the Lord. I do not mean that a believer has the same all-seeing mind, the same infallible judgment concerning everything as Christ has; but up to his light he sees things as Christ does.

He sees *sin* as Christ does. Christ sees sin to be evil and bitter. He sees it to be filthy and abominable, its pleasures all a delusion. He sees it to be awfully dangerous. He sees the inseparable connection between sin and suffering. So does a believer.

He sees the *gospel* as Christ does. Christ sees amazing glory in the gospel, the way of salvation which He Himself has wrought out. It appears a most complete salvation to Him —most free—most glorifying to God and happy for man. So does the believer.

He sees the *world* as Christ does. Christ knows what is in man. He looked on this world as vanity compared with the smile of His Father. Its riches, its honors, its pleasures, appeared not worth a sigh. He saw it passing away. So does the believer.

He sees *time* as Christ did. "I must work the works of him that sent me while it is day; the night cometh." "I come quickly." So does a believer look at time.

He sees *eternity* as Christ does. Christ looked at everything in the light of eternity. "In my Father's house are many
mansions." Everything is valuable in Christ's eyes, only as
it bears on eternity. So with believers.

2. *The heart of Christ is formed in the soul.*—By the heart
I mean the affections, that part of us that loves or hates, hopes
and fears. We have Christ's heart formed in us: "I will put
my Spirit within you." "I in you." "My words abide in you."

First, The same love to God.—What intense delight Jesus
had in His Father! "Righteous Father, the world hath not
known thee, but I have known thee." "I am not alone, for
the Father is with me." "I thank thee, O Father." "Abba,
Father." "Father, into thy hand I commend my spirit." So
with every believer.

Second, The same aversion to God's frown.—"Why hast
thou forsaken me?" (Ps. 22:1). "Thou hast brought me into
the dust of death" (v. 15). "Thy wrath lieth hard upon me"
(Ps. 88:7). "Thou hast lifted me up, and cast me down"
(Ps. 102:10). So with the children of God. "I will say unto
God my rock, Why hast thou forgotten me?" (Ps. 42:9).

Third, The same love to saints.—"To the saints that are
in the earth, and to the excellent, in whom is all my delight"
(Ps. 16:3). "Having loved his own which were in the world,
he loved them to the end" (John 13:1). "Greater love hath
no man than this, that a man lay down his life for his friends"
(John 15:13). "I will come again, and receive you to myself"
(John 14:3). "Saul, Saul, why persecutest thou me?" (Acts
9:4). So it is with all true believers. Every one that loveth
is born of God.

Fourth, Compassion to sinners.—This was the main feature
of Christ's character. This brought Him from heaven to die.
This made Him weep over Jerusalem, and long to gather
her children. This makes Him delay His coming, not willing
that any should perish (II Pet. 3:9). All Christ's own are

like Him in this. The same heart throbs within them.

Fifth, Tenderness to the awakened.—"He will not break the bruised reed." Oh, the tenderness of the lips that said, "Come unto me, all ye that labor and are heavy laden!" Such are all Christians.

3. *The life of Christ is formed in the soul.*—They live the same life in the main that Christ did in the world. Though they have many falls and wax cold, still the main current of their life is Christ living in them. "Christ liveth in me" (Gal. 2:20). "I will dwell in them, and walk in them" (II Cor. 6:16).

First, Bearing reproaches.—"When he was reviled, he reviled not again; when he suffered, he threatened not" (I Pet. 2:23). Christ felt reproach keenly: "Reproach hath broken mine heart." Still He reviled no man, but prayed for them. So believers.

Second, In doing good.—"He went about doing good." He made this His meat and drink. So will all who have Christ formed in them. They do good, and to communicate forget not. They are the almoners of the world. "They parted to all men" (Acts 2:45).

Third, In being separate from sinners.—Christ walked through the midst of sinners undefiled. Like a beam of light piercing into a foul dungeon, or like a river purifying and fertilizing, itself untainted, so did Christ pass through this world; and so do all His own. "I will not know a wicked person" (Ps. 101:4).

III. *But how is it that Christ formed in us is the hope of glory?*

First, Not legally. Christ in the soul is not our title to glory. We must have a complete righteousness to be our title; but Christ in the soul is not complete. Most are sadly deficient in many of the main features of Christ. It is Christ for us, laid hold on by faith, that is our title to glory. Christ our wedding garment—the Lord our righteousness; this, and this alone, can give us boldness in the day of judgment.

Second, Still really it is so. It is evidence that we have believed on Christ. A man may know that he has believed on Christ without any evidences. "He that believes has the witness in himself." But if a man has believed, the effects will soon be seen. Christ will be formed in him, and then he will have double evidence that Christ is his. "He that lacketh these things is blind" (II Pet. 1:9).

It is fitness for glory. A holy believer feels heaven begun. "The kingdom of God is within you." He can say, Now I know I shall soon be in heaven, for it is already begun in me. Christ lives in me. I shall soon be forever with the Lord.

IV. *Improvement.*

1. *Have you the legal title to glory.*—Is Christ dwelling in you by faith? You have heard how those who are enlightened by God embrace Christ, and put Him on abidingly for righteousness. Have you done so? Have you put on Christ? This is the only legal title to glory. If you have not this, your hope is a dream.

2. *Are you fit for glory.*—Is Christ formed in you? Does Christ live in you, and walk in you? "Without holiness no man shall see the Lord."

Dundee, 1843.

MESSAGE XXI

A CASTAWAY

"I therefore so run, not as uncertainly; so fight I, not as one that beateth the air: but I keep under my body, and bring it into subjection; lest that by any means, when I have preached to others, I myself should be a castaway."— I CORINTHIANS 9:26, 27.

OBSERVE how earnestly Paul sought the kingdom of heaven. "I therefore so run, not as uncertainly; so fight I, not as one that beateth the air" (v. 26). It was long after his conversion that Paul writes in this manner. He could say, "To me to live is Christ, and to die is gain." He felt it better to depart and be with Christ. He knew there was a crown laid up for him; and yet see how earnest he was to advance in the divine life. He was like one at the Grecian games running for a prize. This is the way all converted persons should seek salvation. "So run that ye may obtain." It is common for many to sit down after conversion, and say, I am safe, I do not need to strive any more. But Paul pressed toward the mark.

He was very earnest in bringing his body into subjection. He had observed in the Grecian games that those who were to run and fight, were very attentive to this: "And every man that striveth for the mastery is temperate in all things" (v. 25). This was one thing that Paul strove for, to be temperate in all things, especially in eating and drinking: "I keep under my body, and bring it into subjection."

His reason for all this earnestness was his fear that he should be a castaway. Not that Paul had not an assurance of his salvation; but he felt deeply that his high office in the church would not save him although he was one of the apostles, the apostle of the Gentiles, one that had labored more than all the rest. Though many had been converted under his ministry, he knew that still *that* would not keep him from being a castaway. Judas had preached to others, and yet was cast away. Paul felt also, that if he lived a wicked life, he would surely be cast away. He knew there was an indissoluble connection between living in sin and being cast away, and therefore it was a constant motive to him to holy diligence. What he feared was, being "a castaway." The word is frequently translated "reprobate." It is taken from the trying of metals; the dross, or part that is thrown away, is said to be reprobate, or cast away.

What is it to be cast away?

I. *Wicked men shall be cast away from God.*—"Depart from me, ye cursed" (Matt. 25:41). "Who shall be punished with everlasting destruction from the presence of the Lord, and from the glory of his power" (II Thess. 1:9).

1. *Away from Christ.*—At present, ungodly men are often near to Christ. Christ stands at their door and knocks. He stretches out His hands to them all the day long. He speaks to them in the Bible and the preached gospel. He says, "Come unto me . . . and I will give you rest. . . . Him that cometh unto me, I will in no wise cast out." But when Christ pronounces that sentence, "Depart from me, ye cursed," there will not be one knock more, not one invitation more, not one sweet offer more. Christ is the only way to the Father; but it shall be then closed forever. Christ is the only door; but it shall then be shut for evermore. It is the blessedness of the redeemed that they shall be with Christ. "Today shalt thou be *with me.*" Having a desire to be absent from the body and present *with the Lord.* So shall they be ever *with the Lord.* His servants shall serve Him, and they shall see *His face.* It is this that maintains the eternal calm in the bosom of the redeemed. But the ungodly shall be cast away from all this. "Bind him hand and foot, and cast him into outer darkness."

2. *Away from God.*—True, the wicked can never be cast away from the presence of God. "If I make my bed in hell,

behold thou art there!" (Ps. 139:8). Job says, "Hell is
naked before him, and destruction hath no covering" (26:6).
His almighty power creates it; His breath kindles it. "The
breath of the Lord, like a stream of brimstone, doth kindle it"
(Isa. 30:33). But they shall be banished—

First, From the fruition of God.—God said to Abraham, "I
am thy shield, and thine exceeding great reward." God makes
Himself over to the believing soul, saying, I will be thy God.
David says, "God is the strength of my heart, and my portion
forever." Who can tell the joy of those who enjoy God, who
have God, the infinite God, as their portion? From this the
Christless shall be cast away. You will have no portion in
God. God will not be your God. His attributes will be all
against you.

Second, From the favor of God.—"In thy favor is life."
The favor of God is what believers feel on earth. A beam
of God's countenance is enough to fill the heart of a believer
to overflowing. It is enough to light up the pale cheek of a
dying saint with seraphic brightness, and make the heart
of the lone widow sing for joy. From all this the Christless
shall be cast away forever; and instead of it, Jehovah's frown
shall light on them forever. "It is a fearful thing to fall into
the hands of the living God."

Third, Cast away from the blessing of God.—God is the
fountain of all blessing. No creature is good or pleasant
any more than God makes it to be so. The sun warms us,
our food nourishes us, our friends are pleasant to us: because
God makes them so. All the joys in the world are but beams
from that uncreated light; but separate a man from God, and
all becomes dark. God is the fountain of all joy: separate a
man from God finally, and no creature can give him joy. This
is to be cast away, cut off from God forever and ever. Though
there were no lake of fire, this of itself would be hell.

II. *Wicked men shall be cast away by the Holy Spirit.*—It

is not often thought of, but it is true, that the Holy Spirit is now dealing and striving with natural men. All the decency and morality of unconverted men is to be attributed to the restraining grace of the Holy Spirit.

1. *The Holy Spirit works on natural men through the ordinances.*—The ordinance of family worship is often greatly blessed to restrain wicked children, so that they are kept from vicious courses and outbreaking sins. The ordinance of the read and preached Word is also greatly blessed in this way to restrain wicked men. The awful threatenings of the Word, the sweet invitations and promises of the gospel, have this effect on unconverted men, that they are greatly restrained from going to extreme lengths in wickedness.

2. *The Holy Spirit also works through providences in restraining wicked men.*—He places them in such circumstances that they cannot sin as they would otherwise do. He often reduces them to poverty, so that they cannot run into the vices they were inclined unto; or He lays sickness on their body, so that their keen relish for sin is greatly blunted; or He terrifies them by bereavements, so that they are kept in the bondage of fear, and dare not sin with so high a hand as they would otherwise do.

3. *The Holy Spirit also restrains through convictions of sin.*—Many men have deep wounds of conviction who are never saved. Many are pierced with arrows of the Word from time to time, and thus are driven away from their wicked companions, and scared from open sin. Restraining grace is an amazing work of God. It is more wonderful than His setting a bound to the sea that it cannot pass over. Think what a hell every unconverted bosom would become, if the Spirit were to withdraw and give men over to their own hearts' lusts! Think what a hell an unconverted family would become, if the Spirit were to withdraw His bands! What hatreds, strifes, murders, parricides, would take place!

Think what a hell this town would become, if every Christless man were given over to the lusts of his own heart!

Now this is to be a castaway. "My Spirit shall not always strive with man" (Gen. 6:3). The Holy Spirit, I believe, strives with all men: "Ye do always resist the Holy Ghost" (Acts 7:51); but He will not always strive. When the day of grace is done, when the sinner sinks into hell, the Spirit will strive no more.

First, The Spirit will strive no more through ordinances. There will be no family worship in hell, no Bible read, no psalms sung. There will be no Sabbath in hell, no preached gospel, no watchmen to warn you of your sin and danger. The voice of the watchman will be silent; the danger has come; your doom will be past, and no room for repentance.

Second, The Spirit will no more strive through providences. There will be no more poverty or riches, no more sickness or bereavements, no kindly providences restraining the soul from sin, nothing but anguish and despair unutterable.

Third, There will be no more convictions by the Spirit. Conscience will condemn, but it will not restrain. Your hearts will then break out. All your hatred to God, the fountains of contempt and blasphemy in your heart, will be all broken up. You will blaspheme the God of heaven. All your lusts and impurities, that have been pent up and restrained by re-straining grace and the fear of man, will burst forth with amazing impetuosity. You will be as wicked and blasphemous as the devils around you.

Oh, the misery of this! It is an evil thing and bitter. The way of transgressors is hard. Ah! sinners, you will yet find sin the hardest of all masters; you will yet find your groveling lusts to be worse than the worm that never dies. "He that is unjust, let him be unjust still" (Rev. 22:11).

III. *Wicked men shall be cast away by all the creatures.*—The state of unconverted men at present, although a very dreadful one, is yet not hopeless. The angels watch the un-converted, to see if there are any signs of repentance. It is believed that the holy angels are present in the assembly of God's worshipers (I Tim. 5:21). And if so, no doubt they watch your faces, to see if a tear starts into your eye, or a prayer trembles on your lip. There would be joy this day among the angels, if one sinner was to repent.

The redeemed on earth are peculiarly interested in un-converted souls. They pray for them night and day, many of them with tears; many a child of God wets his pillow with tears in behalf of perishing souls. Jeremiah wept in secret places for their pride. David says, "Rivers of water run down mine eyes." They seek your conversion more than any per-sonal benefit. Ministers are set apart to seek after lost and perishing souls. "Go rather to the lost sheep of the house of Israel." If ministers are like their Master, this will be their great errand—that by all means we may save some. But when the day of grace is past, all holy creatures will cast you away. "Reprobate silver shall men call them, for the Lord hath rejected them."

The angels will no longer take any interest in you. They will know that it is not fit they should pity you any more. You will be tormented in the presence of the holy angels, and in the presence of the Lamb.

The redeemed will no longer pray for you, nor shed an-other tear for you. They will see you condemned in the judgment, and not put in one word for you. They will see you depart into everlasting fire, and yet not pray for you. They will see the smoke of your torments going up forever and ever, and yet cry, Alleluia!

Ministers will no more desire your salvation. It will no more be their work. The number of the saved will be com-plete without you; the table will be full. Ministers will bear witness against you in that day.

Even devils will cast you off. As long as you remain on earth, the devil keeps you in his train; he flatters you, and gives you many tokens of his friendship and esteem; but soon he will cast you off. You will be no longer pleasant to him; you will be a part of his torment; and he will hate you and torment you, because you deceived him, and he deceived you.

IV. *Wicked men shall be cast away by themselves.*—It is said they shall wish to die, and shall not be able: they shall seek death, and death shall flee from them. I believe that some suicides experience the beginnings of hell. I believe Judas did: he could not bear himself, and he tried to cast himself away. This will be the feeling of lost souls. They will not be able to bear the sight of themselves; they will be weary of being; they will wish they had never been. At present, unconverted men are often very self-complacent. They love to employ their faculties; the wheels of their life go smoothly; their affections are pleasant. Memory has many pleasant green spots to look back upon. How different when the day of grace is done!

The understanding will be clear and full to apprehend the real nature of your misery. Your mind will then see the holiness of God, His almightiness, His majesty. You will see your own condemned condition, and the depth of your hell.

The will in you will be all contrary to God's will: even though you see it add to your hell, yet you will hate all that God loves, and love all that God hates.

Your conscience is God's vicegerent in the soul. It will accuse you of all your sins. It will set them in order and condemn you.

Your affections will still love your kindred. "I have five brethren," you will say. Earthly fathers who are evil know how to give good gifts to their children. Even in hell you will love your own kindred; but ah! what misery it will cost you, when you hear them sentenced along with you!

Your memory will be very clear. You will remember all your misspent Sabbaths; your sermons heard, as if you did not hear; your place in the house of God; your minister's face and voice; the bell: through millions of ages after this, you will remember these, as if yesterday.

Your anticipations—everlasting despair. Oh, how you will wish you had never been! How you will wish to tear out your memory, these tender affections, this accusing conscience! You will seek death, and it will flee from you. This, this is to be lost! This is everlasting destruction! This is to be a castaway!

Lessons.—1. *Let believers learn Paul's earnest diligence.*— A wicked life will end in being a castaway. These two are linked together, and no man can sunder them.

2. *Hell will be intolerable.*—I have not spoken of the lake of fire, of the utter darkness, and the worm that never dies. I have spoken only of the mental facts of hell; and yet these by themselves are intolerable. Oh, who can tell what it will be when both meet, and meet eternally? "Who knows the power of thine anger?" Oh, do not keep away from Christ now! Now He says, Come; soon, soon He will say, Depart. Oh, do not resist the Holy Spirit now! Now He strives, but He will not always strive with you. Soon, soon He will leave you. Oh, do not despise the word of ministers and godly friends! Now they plead with you, weep for you, pray for you. Soon, soon they will be silent as the grave, or sing hallelujah to see you lost! Oh, do not be proud and self-admiring! Soon you will loathe the very sight of yourself, and wish you had never been!

3. *The amazing love of Christ in bearing all this for sinners.*—Christ is a wrath-bearing Surety. All that is included in being a castaway He bore. Amen.

January, 1843.

———

Message XXII

A COMMUNION SABBATH IN ST. PETER'S

I. SERMON

"Father, I will that they also whom thou hast given me be with me where I
am; that they may behold my glory, which thou hast given me; for thou
lovedst me before the foundation of the world."—John 17:24.

THIS IS the most wonderful prayer that ever rose from
this earth to the throne of God, and this petition is the
most wonderful in the prayer.

I. *The manner of this prayer.*—"Father, I will." No human
lips ever prayed thus before. Abraham was the friend of
God, and got very near to God in prayer; but he prayed as
dust and ashes. "I have taken upon me to speak unto God,
that am but dust and ashes." Jacob had power with God, and
prevailed, yet his boldest word was, "I will not let thee go
except thou bless me." Daniel was a man greatly beloved,
and got immediate answers to prayer, and yet he cried to God
as a sinner: "O Lord, hear! O Lord, forgive! O Lord,
hearken and do!" Paul was a man who got very near to God,
and yet he says, "I bow my knees to the God and Father of
our Lord Jesus Christ." But when Christ prayed, He cried,
"Father, I will." Why did He pray thus? *He was God's
fellow.* "Awake, O sword, against my Shepherd, against the
man that is my fellow." He thought it no robbery to be equal
with God. It was He that said, "Let there be light, and there
was light." So now He says, "Father, I will."

He spoke as the Intercessor with the Father.—He felt as if
His work were already done: "I have finished the work
which thou gavest me to do." He felt as if He had already
suffered the cross, and now claims the crown. "Father, I
will." This is the intercession now heard in heaven.

He had one will with the Father.—"I and my Father are

one." One God, one in heart and will. True, He had a holy
human soul, and therefore a human will; but His human will
was one with His divine will. The human string in His heart
was tuned to the same string as His divine will.

Learn how surely this prayer will be answered, dear children
of God. It is impossible this prayer should be unanswered.
It is the will of the Father and of the Son. If Christ wills it,
and if the Father wills it, you may be sure nothing can hinder
it. If the sheep be in Christ's hand, and in the Father's hand,
they shall never perish.

II. *For whom He prays.*—"They also whom thou hast
given me." Six times in this chapter does Christ call His
people by this name: "They whom thou hast given me." It
seems to have been a favorite word of Christ, especially when
carrying them on His heart before the Father. The reason
seems to be that He would remind the Father that they are as
much the Father's as they are His own; that the Father has
the same interest in them that He has, having given them to
Him before the world was. And so He repeats it in verse 10:
"All mine are thine, and thine are mine." Before the world
was, the Father chose a people out of this world. He gave
them into the hand of Christ, charging Him not to lose one,
to bear their sins on His own body on the tree, to raise Him
up at the last day. And, accordingly, He says, "Of all whom
thou has given me have I lost none."

Is there any mark on those who are given to Christ? They
are no better than others. Sometimes He chooses the worst!
"All that the Father giveth me shall come to me." One
of the sure marks of all that were given to Christ is that
they come to Jesus: "They all come to Jesus the mediator of
the new covenant, and to the blood of sprinkling." Are you
come to Christ? Has your heart been opened to receive
Christ? Has Christ been made precious to you? Then you
may be quite sure you were given to Christ before the world

was. Your name is in the Lamb's Book of Life, and your name is on the breastplate of Christ. It is for you He prays, "Father, I will that that soul be with me." Christ will never lose you. The Father which gave you to Him is greater than all, and none is able to pluck you out of the Father's hand.

III. *The Argument—"For Thou lovedst me."*—He reminds the Father of His love to Him before the world was. When there was no earth, no sun, no man, no angel, when He was by Him, then "Thou lovedst me." Who can understand this love—the love of the uncreated God to His uncreated Son? The love of Jonathan to David was very great, surpassing the love of women. The love of a believer to Christ is very great, for they see Him to be altogether lovely. The love of a holy angel to God is very ardent, for they are like a flame of fire. But these are all creature loves; these are but streams; but the love of God to His Son is an ocean of love. There is everything in Christ to draw the love of His Father. Now discern His argument, If Thou lovest Me, do this for My people.

Just as He said to Paul, "Why persecutest thou me?" He felt Himself one with His afflicted members on earth. Just as He will say at the last day, "Inasmuch as ye did it to one of the least of these my brethren, ye did it unto me." He reckons believers a part of Himself; what is done to them is done to Him. So here, when He carries them to His Father, this is all His argument: "Thou lovedst Me." If Thou lovest Me, love them, for they are part of Me.

See how surely Christ's prayer will be answered for you, beloved. He does not plead that you are good and holy; He does not plead that you are worthy; He only pleads His own loveliness in the eyes of the Father. Look not on them, He says, but look on Me. Thou lovedst Me before the foundation of the world.

Learn to use the same argument with God, dear believers.

This is asking in Christ's name, for the Lord's sake; this is the prayer that is never refused. See that you do not come in your own name, else you will be cast out.

Come thus to His table. Say to the Father, Accept me, for Thou lovedst Him from the foundation of the world.

IV. *The prayer itself.*

1. *"That they may be with me."—What He does not mean.*—He does not mean that we should be presently taken out of this world. Some of you that have come to Christ may, this day, be favored with so much of His presence, and of the love of the Father, so much of the joy of heaven, and such a dread of going back to betray Christ in the world, that you may be wishing that this house were indeed the gate of heaven; you may desire that you might be translated from the table below at once to the table above. "I am in a strait betwixt two, having a desire to depart, and be with Christ." Still Christ does not wish that. "I pray not that thou shouldst take them out of the world, but that thou shouldst keep them from the evil." "Whither I go, thou canst not follow me now." (Like that woman in *Brainerd's Journal*—"O blessed Lord, do come! Oh, do take me away; do let me die and go to Jesus Christ. I am afraid, if I live, I shall sin again.")

What He does mean.—He means, that when our journey is done, we should come to be with Him. Every one that comes to Christ has a journey to perform in this world. Some have a long, and some a short one. It is through a wilderness. Still Christ prays that, at the end, you may be with Him. Every one that comes to Christ hath his twelve hours to fill up for Christ. "I must work the works of him that sent me, while it is day." But when that is done, Christ prays that you may be with Him. He means that you shall come to *His Father's house* with Him. "In my Father's house are many mansions." You shall dwell in the same house with Christ. You are never

very intimate with a person till you see him in his own house,
till you know him at home. This is what Christ wants with
us, that we shall come to be with Him at His own home. He
wants us to come to the same Father's bosom with Him. "I
ascend to my Father and your Father." He wants us to be in
the same smile with Him, to sit on the same throne with Him,
to swim in the same ocean of love with Him.

Learn how certain it is that you shall one day soon be with
Christ. It is the will of the Father, it is the will of the Son.
It is the prayer of Christ. If you have really been brought to
Christ, you shall never perish. You may have *many enemies*
opposing you in your way to glory. Satan desires to have you,
that he may sift you like wheat. Your worldly friends will do
all they can to hinder you. Still you shall be with Christ. We
shall see your face at the table of glory. *You have a hard
heart,* an unbelieving heart, a heart deceitful above all things,
and desperately wicked. You often think your heart will lead
you to betray Christ. Still you shall be with Christ. If you
are in Christ today, you shall be ever with the Lord. You have
lived a wicked life. You have dreadful sins to look back upon.

Still, if you are come to Jesus, this is His word to you,
"Thou shalt be with me in paradise." In truth, Christ cannot
do without you. You are His jewels—His crown. Heaven
would be no heaven to Him, if you were not there. This
may give you courage in coming to the Lord's Table. Some of
you fear to come to this Table, because, though you cleave to
Christ today, you fear you may betray Him tomorrow. But you
need not fear. "He that hath begun a good work in you will
perform it till the day of Jesus Christ." You shall sit at the
Table above, where Christ Himself shall be at the head. You
need not fear to come to this Table.

2. *To "behold my glory which thou hast given me."*—There
are three stages in the glory of Christ. It will be the employ-
ment of heaven to behold them all.

First, The original glory of Christ.—This is His underived, uncreated glory, as the equal of the Father. It is spoken of in Proverbs 8:30: "Then I was by him, as one brought up with him; I was daily his delight, rejoicing always before him." And again, in this prayer, "The glory which I had with thee before the world was" (v. 5). Of this glory no man can speak. no angel, no archangel. One thing alone we know, that we are to honor the Son, even as we honor the Father. He shared with the Father in being the all-perfect One, when there was none to admire, none to adore, no angels with golden harps, no seraphs to hymn His praise, no cherubim to cry, Holy, holy, holy. Before all creatures were, He was—one with the infinitely perfect, good, and glorious God. He was then all that He afterwards showed Himself to be. Creation and redemption did not change Him. They only revealed what He was before. They only provided objects for those beams of glory to rest upon, that were shining as fully before, from all eternity. Eternity will be much taken up with praising God that ever He revealed Himself at all; that ever He came out from the retirement of His lovely and blissful eternity.

Second, When He became flesh.—"The Word was made flesh." Christ did not get more glory by becoming man, but He manifested His glory in a new way. He did not gain one perfection more by becoming man; He had all the perfections of God before. But now these perfections were poured through a human heart. *The almightiness* of God now moved in a human arm. *The infinite love* of God now beat in a human heart. *The compassion* of God to sinners now glistened in a human eye. God was love before, but Christ was love covered over with flesh. Just as you have seen the sun shining through a colored window—sunlight and yet it shines with a mellowed luster—so in Christ dwelt all the fullness of the Godhead bodily. The perfection of the Godhead shone through every pore, through every action, word, and look—

the same perfections—they were only shining with a mellowed brightness. The veil of the Temple was a type of His flesh, because it covered the bright light of the Holiest of all. But just as the bright light of the Shekinah often shone through the veil, so did the Godhead of Christ force itself through the heart of the man Christ Jesus. There were many openings of the veil when the bright glory shone through.

When He turned the water into wine.—He manifested forth His glory, and His disciples believed on Him. Almighty power spoke in a human voice, and the love of God, too, shone in it; for He showed that He came to turn all our water into wine.

When He wept over Jerusalem.—That was a great outlet of His glory. There was much that was human in it. The feet were human that stood upon Mount Olivet. The eyes were human eyes that looked down upon the dazzling city. The tears were human tears that fell upon the ground. But oh, there was the tenderness of God beating benea . that mantle! Look and live, sinners. Look and live. Behold your God! He that hath seen a weeping Christ hath seen the Father. This is God manifest in the flesh. Some of you fear that the Father does not wish you to come to Christ and be saved. But see here, God is manifest in flesh. He that hath seen Christ hath seen the Father. See here the heart of the Father and the heart of the Son laid bare. Oh, wherefore should you doubt? Every one of these tears trickles from the heart of God.

On the cross.—The wounds of Christ were the greatest outlets of His glory that ever were. The divine glory shone more out of His wounds than out of all His life before. The veil was then rent in twain, and the full heart of God allowed to stream through. It was a human body that writhed, pale and racked, upon the accursed tree; they were human hands that were pierced so rudely by the nails; it was human flesh that bore that deadly gash upon the side; it was human blood that streamed from hands, and feet, and side; the eye that meekly turned to His Father was a human eye; the soul that yearned over His mother was a human soul. But oh, there was divine glory streaming through all; every wound was a mouth to speak of the grace and love of God!

Divine holiness shone through. What infinite hatred of sin was there when He thus offered Himself a sacrifice without spot unto God! *Divine wisdom* shone through: all created intelligences could not have devised a plan whereby God would have been just, and yet the justifier. *Divine love:* every drop of blood that fell came as a messenger of love from His heart to tell the love of the fountain. This was the love of God. He that hath seen a crucified Christ hath seen the Father. Oh, look on the broken bread, and you will see this glory still streaming through! Here is the heart of God laid bare—God is manifest in flesh. Some of you are poring over your own heart, examining your feelings, watching your disease. Avert the eye from all within. Behold Me, behold Me! Christ cries. Look to Me, and be ye saved. Behold the glory of Christ! There is much difficulty about your own heart, but no darkness about the heart of Christ. Look in through His wounds; believe what you see in Him.

Third, Christ's glory above.—I cannot speak of this. I trust I shall one day soon see it. He has not laid aside the glory which He had on earth. He is still the Lamb slain from the foundation of the world. But He has more glory now. His humanity is no more a veil to hide any of the beams of His Godhead. God shines all the more plainly through Him. He has many crowns now, the oil of gladness now, the scepter of righteousness now.

Heaven will be spent in beholding His glory.—We shall see the Father eternally in Him. We shall look in His face, and in His human eye shall read the tender love of God to us forever. We shall hear from His holy human lips plainly of the Father. "In that day I shall no more speak to you in parables, but show you plainly of the Father." We shall look on His scars, healed, yet plain and open on His hands, and feet, and side, and heaven-bright brow, and shall read eternally there the hatred of God against sin, and His love to us that made Him die for us. And sometimes, perhaps, we may lean our head where John leaned his, upon His holy bosom. Oh! if heaven is to be spent thus, what will *you* do, who have never seen His glory?

Oh, beloved, if your eternity is to be spent thus, spend much of your time thus! If you are to be thus engaged at the Table above, be thus engaged now at the Table below.

Communion Sabbath, *January 19, 1840.*

II. FENCING THE TABLES.

"But a certain man named Ananias, with Sapphira his wife, sold a possession, and kept back part of the price, his wife also being privy to it, and brought a certain part, and laid it at the apostles' feet. But Peter said, Ananias. why hath Satan filled thine heart to lie to the Holy Ghost, and to keep back part of the price of the land? Whilst it remained, was it not thine own? and after it was sold, was it not in thine own power? Why hast thou conceived this thing in thine heart? Thou hast not lied unto men, but unto God. And Ananias, hearing these words, fell down, and gave up the ghost; and great fear came on all them that heard these things. And the young men arose, wound him up, and carried him out, and buried him. And it was about the space of three hours after, when his wife, not knowing what was done, came in. And Peter answered unto her, Tell me whether ye sold the land for so much? And she said, Yea, for so much. Then Peter said unto her, How is it that ye have agreed together to tempt the Spirit of the Lord? Behold, the feet of them which have buried thy husband are at the door, and shall carry thee out. Then fell she down straightway at his feet, and yielded up the ghost; and the young men came in, and found her dead, and, carrying her forth, buried her by her husband. And great fear came upon all the church, and upon as many as heard these things. And by the hands of the apostles were many signs and wonders wrought among the people; (and they were all with one accord in Solomon's porch. And of the rest durst no man join himself to them; but the people magnified them. And believers were the more added to the Lord, multitudes both of men and women.)"—ACTS 5:1-14.

THERE HAVE BEEN hypocrites in the Church of Christ from the beginning. There was one, Judas, even among the twelve apostles; and in the apostolic church there was an Ananias and a Sapphira. Attend:

1. *To their sin*—a lie. When so much of the Spirit was given, all were of one heart and one soul. Those that had estates, sold them, and brought the price, and laid it at the apostles' feet. It was a lovely sight to see. Among the rest came one Ananias; he was rich. From some worldly motive, he had joined himself to the Christians—husband and wife, both Christless, graceless souls. He sold his possessions to be like the rest, and brought a part, and said it was his all! He pretended to be a Christian—he pretended that grace was in his heart. It was not a lie to man only, but to the Holy Ghost; for he was declaring that God had wrought a change upon his soul, when there was none—he was still old Ananias.

2. *Their punishment.*—They fell down and gave up the Ghost. Oh! it is an awful thing when sinners die in the act of sin—with the lie in their mouth—with the oath on their tongue. So it was with poor Ananias and his wife. In a moment—in the twinkling of an eye—they were in the place where all liars go.

3. *The effect.*—Great fear came upon them all. None durst join themselves to the apostles' company.

Dear friends, these things are written for our learning. Are there none come up here today with Ananias' lie in their heart?

The broken bread and poured-out wine represent the broken body and shed blood of Christ. Oh! it is enough to melt the heart of the stoutest to look at them. To take that bread and that wine is declaring that you do close with Christ—that you take Him to be your Saviour—that God has opened your heart to believe. In marriage, the acceptance of the right hand is a solemn declaration, by sign, that you accept the

bride or bridegroom; and so in the Lord's Supper. If it is not
so with you, then it is *a lie;* and it is *a lie to the Holy Ghost.*
Ananias came declaring that he had the Spirit's work upon
his heart. It was a time when much of God's Spirit had been
given (vv. 31, 32). It is likely he and his wife had some convictions. But since it was false, since he was not really what
he pretended to be, it was said, *"he lied to the Holy Ghost."*
So, dear friends, the Holy Ghost is peculiarly present in this
ordinance. He glorifies Christ. He has converted many in
this place. To sin today is to lie against the Holy Ghost. By
coming to the table you profess that you are under the Spirit's
teaching. If you are not, you lie to the Holy Ghost!

Now, do you know that you have not come to Christ? Do
you know that you are unconverted? And will you sit down
there and take the bread and wine? Take heed, Ananias!
Thou art not lying to a man, but unto God.

Perhaps there is one among you who is secretly addicted to
drinking, to swearing, to uncleanness. Will you come and take
the bread and wine? Take heed, Ananias!

Perhaps there are two of you, husband and wife, who know
that neither of you was ever converted. You never pray together, and yet you agree together to come here. Take heed,
Ananias and Sapphira!

Is there none of you a persecutor? Perhaps you are a father,
whose children have come to Christ, but in your heart you hate
their change; you oppose it with bitter words; and yet, with a
smooth countenance, you come to sit beside them at the same
table! Oh hypocrite, take heed lest you drop down dead!
Draw back that hand lest it wither! If we should see the cup
drop from your hand, and the eye glaze, and the feet become
cold, oh, where would your soul be?

Dear children of God, do not be discouraged from coming
to this holy Table. It is spread for sinners that have come to
Jesus. "Oh, come and dine!" Some of you say, "I do not know

the way to this Table." Jesus says, "I am the way." Some of you say, "I am blind; I cannot see my sins, or my Saviour." Go wash in the Pool of Siloam. Some of you say, "I am naked." Jesus says, "I counsel thee to buy of me white raiment, that thou mayest be clothed." You are polluted in your own blood; but has Christ thrown His skirt over you? Then do not fear; come with His robe on you. Come thus, and you come welcome.

III. TABLE SERVICE.

(The only specimen of his Table Service, found in his own handwriting, but without date.)

"My beloved is mine, and I am his." 1. *In the arms of my faith* He is mine. I was once of the world, cold and careless about my soul. God awakened me, and made me feel I was lost. I tried to make myself good, to mend my life; but I found it in vain: I sat down more lost than before. I was then told to believe on the Lord Jesus. So I tried to make myself believe. I read books on faith, and tried to bend my soul to believe, so that I might get to heaven; but still in vain. I found it written, "Faith is the gift of God." "No man can call Jesus Lord, but by the Holy Ghost." So I sat down more lost than ever. Whilst I was thus helpless, Jesus drew near, His garments dipped in blood. He had waited long at my door, though I knew it not. "His head was filled with dew, and his locks with the drops of the night." He had five deep wounds, and He said, "I died in the stead of sinners; and any *sinner* may have me for a Saviour. You are a helpless sinner, will you have me?" How can I resist Him? He is all I need! I held Him, and would not let Him go. *"My beloved is mine."*

2. *In the arms of my love, He is mine.* Once I did not know what people meant by loving Jesus. I always wished to ask how they could love one whom they had never seen; but was answered, "Whom not having seen, we love." But now that I have hidden in Him—now that I am cleaving to Him—

now I feel that I cannot but love Him; and I long to see
Him, that I may love Him more. Many a time I fall into sin,
and that takes away my feeling of safety in Christ. Darkness
comes, all is clouded, Christ is away. Still even then I am
sick of love. Christ is not light and peace to me; but I follow
hard after Him amid the darkness—He is precious to me; and
even though I be in darkness. He is my Beloved still. "This
is my beloved, and this is my friend."

3. *He is mine in the Sacrament.*—Many a time, have I said
to Him in prayer, "Thou art mine." Many a time, when the
doors were shut, and Jesus came in showing His wounds,
saying, "Peace be unto you," my soul cleaved to Him,
and said, "My Lord and my God!" My Beloved, Thou art
mine! Many a time have I trysted with Him in lonely places,
where there was no eye of man. Many a time have I called to
the rocks and trees to witness that I took Him to be my
Saviour. He said to me, "I will betroth thee unto me forever";
and I said to Him, "My beloved is mine." Many a time have
I gone with some Christian friend, and we poured out our
trembling hearts together, consulting one with another as to
whether we had liberty to close with Christ or no; and both
together we came to this conclusion, that if we were but helpless sinners we had a right to close with the Saviour of sinners.
We cleaved to Him, and called Him ours. And now have we
come to take Him publicly, to call an ungodly world to witness, to call heaven and earth for a record to our soul, that
we do close with Christ. See He giveth Himself to us in
the bread; lo! we accept of Him in accepting this bread. Bear
witness, men and angels, bear witness, all the universe—"My
beloved is mine."

(The communicants then partook of the broken bread and the cup of
blessing.)

(It was his custom, after they had communicated, to speak
briefly on a few suitable texts, before dismissing them from

the Table. On Sabbath, January 19, the texts were, "Love one another"; "Whatsoever ye shall ask the Father in my name, he will give it"; In the world ye shall have tribulation, but in me ye shall have peace.")

IV. ADDRESS AT THE CLOSE OF THE DAY.

"Now unto him that is able to keep you from falling, and to present you fault-less before the presence of his glory with exceeding joy."—JUDE 24.

There is no end to a pastor's anxieties. Our first care is to get you into Christ; and next, to keep you from falling. I have a good hope, dearly beloved, that a goodly number of you have this day joined yourselves to the Lord. But now a new anxiety begins—to get you to walk in Christ, to walk after the Spirit. Here we are to tell you of what God our Saviour is able to do for you: *First,* To keep you from falling all the way; *Second,* To present you faultless at the end.

I. *To keep you from falling.*

1. *We are not able to keep you from falling.*—Those that lean on ministers lean on a reed shaken with the wind. When a soul has received saving good through a minister, he often thinks that he will be kept from falling by the same means. He thinks, "Oh, if I had this friend always beside me to warn me, to advise me!" No; ministers are not always by, nor godly friends. Your fathers, where are they? and the prophets, do they live forever? We may soon be taken from you, and there may come a famine of the bread. And, besides, our words will not always tell. When temptation and passions are strong, *you* would not give heed to us.

2. *You are not able to keep yourselves from falling.*—At present you know little of the weakness or wickedness of your own heart. There is nothing more deceitful than your estimate of your own strength. Oh, if you saw your soul in all its in-firmity; if you saw how every sin has its fountain in your heart; if you saw what a mere reed you are, you would cry, "Lord, hold up my goings." You may be at present strong;

but stop till an inviting company occur; stop till a secret opportunity. Oh, how many have fallen then! At present you feel strong, your feet like hinds' feet. So did Peter at the Lord's Table. But stop till this burst of feeling has passed away; stop till you are asked to join in some unholy game; stop till some secret opportunity of sinning all unseen; till some bitter provocation rouses your anger, and you will find that you are weak as water, and that there is no sin that you may not fall into.

3. *Our Saviour-God is able.*—Christ deals with us as you do with your children. They cannot go alone; you hold them: so does Christ by His Spirit. "I taught Ephraim also to go, taking them by their arms" (Hos. 11:3). Breathe this prayer: "Lord, take me by the arms." John Newton says, "When a mother is teaching her child to walk on a soft carpet, she will sometimes let it go, and it will fall, to teach it its weakness; but not so on the brink of a precipice." So the Lord will sometimes let you fall, like Peter on the waters, though not to your injury. The shepherd layeth the sheep on his shoulder; it matters not how great the distance be; it matters not how high the mountains, how rough the path: our Saviour-God is an almighty Shepherd. Some of you have mountains in your way to heaven; some of you have mountains of lusts in your hearts, and some of you have mountains of opposition: it matters not, only lie on the shoulder. He is able to keep you; even in the dark *valley* He will not stumble.

II. *To present you faultless.*

1. *Faultless in righteousness.*—As long as you live in your mortal body, you will be faulty in yourself. It is a soul-ruining error to believe anything else. Oh, if ye would be wise, be often looking beneath the robe of the Redeemer's righteousness to see your own deformity! It will make you keep faster hold of His robe, and keep you washing in the fountain. Now, when Christ brings you before the throne of God, He

will clothe you with His own fine linen, and present you faultless. Oh, it is sweet to me to think how soon you shall be the righteousness of God in Him. What a glorious righteousness that can stand the light of God's face! Sometimes a garment appears white in dim light: when you bring it into the sunshine you see the spots. Prize, then, this divine righteousness, which is your covering.

2. *Faultless in holiness.*—My heart sometimes sickens when I think upon the defects of believers; when I think of one Christian being fond of company, another vain, another given to evil speaking. Oh, aim to be holy Christians—bright, shining Christians. The heaven is more adorned by the large bright constellations than by many insignificant stars; so God may be more glorified by one bright Christian than by many indifferent ones. Aim at being that one.

Soon we shall be faultless. He that begun will perform it. We shall be like Him, for we shall see Him as He is. When you lay down this body, you may say, Farewell, lust, forever; farewell, my hateful pride; farewell, hateful selfishness; farewell strife and envying; farewell being ashamed of Christ. Oh, this makes death sweet indeed! Oh, long to depart and to be with Christ!

III. *To Him be glory.*

1. Oh, if anything has been done for your soul, give Him *the glory!* Give no praise to others; give all praise to Him. 2. And give Him *the dominion* too. Yield yourselves unto Him, soul and body.

MESSAGE XXIII

THE VOICE OF MY BELOVED.[1]

"The voice of my beloved! behold, he cometh leaping upon the mountains, skipping upon the hills. My beloved is like a roe, or a young hart; behold,

----

[1] August 14, 1836, when he preached as candidate—the first day he preached in St. Peter's.

he standeth behind our wall, he looketh forth at the windows, showing himself through the lattice. My beloved spake, and said unto me, Rise up, my love, my fair one, and come away. For, lo, the winter is past, the rain is over and gone; the flowers appear on the earth; the time of the singing of birds is come, and the voice of the turtle is heard in our land; the fig tree putteth forth her green figs, and the vines with the tender grape give a good smell. Arise, my love, my fair one, and come away. O my dove, that art in the clefts of the rock, in the secret places of the stairs, let me see thy countenance, let me hear thy voice; for sweet is thy voice, and thy countenance is comely. Take us the foxes, the little foxes, that spoil the vines; for our vines have tender grapes. My beloved is mine, and I am his; he feedeth among the lilies. Until the day break, and the shadows flee away, turn, my beloved, and be thou like a roe, or a young hart, upon the mountains of Bether."—SONG OF SOLOMON 2:8-17.

THERE IS no book of the Bible which affords a better test of the depth of a man's Christianity than the Song of Solomon. If a man's religion be *all in his head,* a well-set form of doctrines built like mason-work stone above stone, but exercising no influence upon his heart, this book cannot but offend him; for there are no stiff statements of doctrine here upon which his heartless religion may be built.

Or, if a man's religion be *all in his fancy;* if, like Pliable in *The Pilgrim's Progress,* he be taken with the outward beauty of Christianity; if, like the seed sown upon the rocky ground, his religion is fixed only in the surface faculties of the mind, while the heart remains rocky and unmoved; though he will relish this book much more than the first man, still there is a mysterious breathing of intimate affection in it, which cannot but stumble and offend him.

But if a man's religion be heart religion; if he hath not only doctrines in his head, but love to Jesus in his heart; if he hath not only heard and read of the Lord Jesus, but hath felt his need of Him, and been brought to cleave unto Him, as the chiefest among ten thousand, and the altogether lovely, then this book will be inestimably precious to his soul. It contains the tenderest breathings of the believer's heart towards the Saviour, and the tenderest breathings of the Saviour's heart again towards the believer.

It is agreed among the best interpreters of this book that it consists not of one song, but of many songs; that these songs are in a dramatic form; and that, like the parables of Christ, they contain a spiritual meaning, under the dress and ornaments of some poetical incident.

The passage which I have read forms one of these dramatical songs, and the subject of it is a sudden visit which an Eastern bride receives from her absent lord. The bride is represented to us as sitting lonely and desolate in a kiosk, or Eastern arbor, a place of safety and of retirement in the gardens of the East, described by modern travelers as "an arbor surrounded by a green wall, covered with vines and jessamines, with windows of latticework."

The mountains of Bether (or, as it is on the margin, the mounts of division), the mountains that separate her from her beloved, appear almost impassable. They look so steep and craggy, that she fears he will never be able to come over them to visit her any more. *Her garden* possesses no loveliness to entice her to walk forth. All nature seems to partake in her sadness; winter reigns without and within; no flowers appear on the earth; all the singing birds appear to be sad and silent upon the trees; and the turtle's voice of love is not heard in the land.

It is while she is sitting thus lonely and desolate that the voice of her beloved strikes upon her ear. Love is quick in hearing the voice that is loved; and therefore she hears sooner than all her maidens, and the song opens with her bursting exclamation, "The voice of my beloved!" When she sat in her solitude, the mountains between her and her lord seemed nearly impassable, they were so lofty and so steep; but now she sees with what swiftness and ease he can come over these mountains, so that she can compare him to nothing else but the gazelle, or the young hart, the loveliest and swiftest creatures of the mountains. "My beloved is like a roe, or a young hart."

Yea, while she is speaking, already he has arrived at the garden wall; and now, behold, "he looketh in at the window, showing himself through the lattice." The bride next relates to us the gentle invitation, which seems to have been the song of her beloved as he came so swiftly over the mountains. While she sat alone, all nature seemed dead—winter reigned; but now he tells her that he has brought the springtime along with him. "Arise, my love, my fair one, and come away. For, lo, the winter is past, the rain is over and gone; the flowers appear on the earth; the time of the singing of birds is come, and the voice of the turtle is heard in our land. The fig tree putteth forth her green figs, and the vines with the tender grape give a good smell. Arise, my love, my fair one, and come away."

Moved by this pressing invitation, she comes forth from her place of retirement into the presence of her lord, and clings to him like a timorous dove to the clefts of the rock; and then he addresses her in these words of tenderest and most delicate affection: "O my dove, that art in the clefts of the rock, in the secret places of the precipice, let me see thy countenance, let me hear thy voice; for sweet is thy voice, and thy countenance is comely." Joyfully agreeing to go forth with her lord, she yet remembers that this is the season of greatest danger to her vines, from the foxes which gnaw the bark of the vines; and therefore she will not go forth without leaving this command of caution to her maidens: "Take us the foxes, the little foxes that spoil the vines, for our vines have tender grapes." She then renews the covenant of her espousals with her beloved, in these words of appropriating affection: "My beloved is mine, and I am his; let him feed among the lilies."

And last of all, because she knows that this season of intimate communion will not last, since her beloved must hurry away again over the mountains, she will not suffer him to depart without beseeching him that he will often renew these visits of love, till that happy day dawn when they shall not need to be separated any more: "Until the day break, and the shadows flee away, turn, my beloved, and be thou like a roe or a young hart upon the mountains of Bether."

We might well challenge the whole world of genius to produce in any language a poem such as this—so short, so comprehensive, so delicately beautiful. But what is far more to our present purpose, there is no part of the Bible which opens up more beautifully some of the innermost experience of the believer's heart.

Let us now, then, look at the parable as a description of one of those visits which the Saviour often pays to believing souls, when He manifests Himself unto them in that other way than He doth unto the world.

I. *When Christ is away from the soul of the believer, he sits alone.*—We saw in the parable, that, when her lord was away, the bride sat lonely and desolate. She did not call for the young and the gay to cheer her solitary hours. She did not call for the harp of the minstrel to soothe her in her solitude. There was no pipe, nor tabret, nor wine at her feasts. No, she sat alone. The mountains seemed all but impassable. All nature partook of her sadness. If she could not be glad in the light of her lord's countenance, she was resolved to be glad in nothing else. She sat lonely and desolate.

Just so it is with the true believer in Jesus. Whatever be the mountains of Bether that have come between his soul and Christ, whether he hath been seduced into his old sins, so that his iniquities have separated again between him and his God, and his sins have hid his face from Him, that He will not hear, or whether the Saviour hath withdrawn for a season the comfortable light of His presence for the mere trial of His servant's faith, to see if, when he "walketh in darkness and hath no light, he will still trust in the name of the Lord, and stay himself upon his God"—whatever the

mountains of separation be, it is the sure mark of the believer
that he sits desolate and alone. He cannot laugh away his
heavy care, as worldly men can do. He cannot drown it in
the bowl of intemperance, as poor blinded men can do. Even
the innocent intercourse of human friendship brings no balm
to his wound. Nay, even fellowship with the children of God
is now distasteful to his soul. He cannot enjoy what he enjoyed before, when they that feared the Lord spoke often
one to another. The mountains between him and the Saviour
seem so vast and impassable, that he fears He will never visit
him more. All nature partakes of his sadness—winter reigns
without and within. He sits alone, and is desolate. Being
afflicted, he prays; and the burden of his prayer is the same
with that of an ancient believer: "Lord, if I may not be made
glad with the light of thy countenance, grant that I may be
made glad with nothing else; for joy without thee is death."

Ah! my friends, do you know anything of this sorrow? Do
you know what it is thus to sit alone and be desolate, because
Jesus is out of view? If you do, then rejoice, if it be possible,
even in the midst of your sadness! For this very sadness is
one of the marks that you are a believer—that you find all your
peace and all your joy in union with the Saviour.

But ah, how contrary is the way with most of you! You
know nothing of this sadness. Yes, perhaps you make a mock
at it. You can be happy and contented with the world, though
you have never got a sight of Jesus. You can be merry with
your companions, though the blood of Jesus has never whispered peace to your soul, Ah, how plain that you are hastening on to the place where "there is no peace, saith my God, to
the wicked!"

II. *Christ's coming to the desolate believer is often sudden
and wonderful.*—We saw in the parable, that it was when the
bride was sitting lonely and desolate that she heard suddenly
the voice of her lord. Love is quick in hearing; and she

cried out, "The voice of my beloved!" Before, she thought
the mountains all but impassable; but now she can compare
his swiftness to nothing but that of the gazelle or the young
hart. Yea, while she speaks, he is at the wall—at the window
—showing himself through the lattice. Just so is it oftentimes with the believer. While he sits alone and desolate,
the mountains of separation appear a vast and impassable
barrier to the Saviour, and he fears He may never come again.
The mountains of a believer's provocations are often very
great. "That I should have sinned again, who have been
washed in the blood of Jesus. It is little that other men should
sin against Him; they never knew Him—never loved Him as
I have done. Surely I am the chief of sinners, and have sinned
away my Saviour. The mountain of my provocations hath
grown up to heaven, and He never can come over it any
more."

Thus it is that the believer writes bitter things against himself; and then it is that oftentimes he hears the voice of his
beloved. Some text of the Word, or some word from a Christian friend, or some part of a sermon, again reveals Jesus in
all His fullness, the Saviour of sinners, even the chief. Or it
may be that He makes Himself known to the disconsolate
soul in the breaking of bread, and when He speaks the gentle
words, "This is my body, broken for you; this cup is the new
testament in my blood, shed for the remission of the sins of
many; drink ye all of it"—then he cannot but cry out, "The
voice of my beloved! behold, He cometh leaping upon the
mountains, skipping upon the hills."

Ah! my friends, do you know anything of this joyful sur-
prise? If you do, why should you ever sit down despairingly,
as if the Lord's hand were shortened at all that He cannot
save, or as if His ear were grown heavy that He cannot hear?
In the darkest hour say, "Why art thou cast down, O my
soul? and why art thou disquieted within me? Still trust in

God, for I shall yet praise him, who is the health of my countenance, and my God." Come expectingly to the Word. Do
not come with that listless indifference, as if nothing that a
fellow worm can say were worth your hearing. It is not the
word of man, but the Word of the living God. Come with
large expectations, and then you will find the promise true,
that He filleth the hungry with good things, though He sends
the rich empty away.

III. *Christ's coming changes all things to the believer, and
His love is more tender than ever.*—We saw in the parable
that when the bride sat desolate and alone, all nature was
steeped in sadness. Her garden possessed no charms to draw
her forth, for winter reigned without and within. But when
her lord came so swiftly over the mountains, he brought the
spring along with him. All nature is changed as he advances,
and his invitation is, "For the winter is past, the rain is over
and gone; arise, my love, my fair one, and come away."

Just so it is with the believer when Christ is away; all is
winter to the soul. But when He comes again over the mountains of provocation, He brings a gladsome springtime along
with Him. When that Sun of Righteousness arises afresh
upon the soul, not only do His gladdening rays fall upon the
believer's soul, but all nature rejoices in His joy. The mountains and hills burst forth before Him into singing, and all
the trees of the field clap their hands. It is like a change of
season to the soul. It is like that sudden change from the
pouring rains of a dreary winter to the full blushing spring,
which is so peculiar to the climes of the sun.

The world of nature is all changed. Instead of the thorn
comes up the fir tree, and instead of the brier comes up the
myrtle tree. Every tree and field possesses a new beauty to
the happy soul. *The world of grace* is all changed. *The Bible*
was all dry and meaningless before; now, what a flood of
light is poured over its pages! How full, how fresh, how

rich in meaning, how its simplest phrases touch the heart!
The house of prayer was all sad and dreary before, its services
were dry and unsatisfactory; but now, when the believer sees
the Saviour, as he hath seen Him heretofore within His holy
place, his cry is: "How amiable are thy tabernacles, O Lord
of Hosts! a day in thy courts is better than a thousand." *The
garden of the Lord* was all sad and cheerless before; now tenderness towards the unconverted springs up afresh, and love
to the people of God burns in the bosom—then they that
fear the Lord speak often one to another. The time of singing the praises of Jesus is come, and the turtle voice of love
to Jesus is once more heard in the land; the Lord's vine flour-
ishes, and the pomegranate buds, and Christ's voice to the
soul is, "Arise, my love, my fair one, and come away."

As the timorous dove pursued by the vulture, and well nigh
made a prey, with fluttering anxious wing, hides itself deeper
than ever in the clefts of the rock, and in the secret places
of the precipice, so the backslidden believer, whom Satan
has desired to have that he might sift him as wheat, when
he is restored once more to the all-gracious presence of his
Lord, clings to Him with fluttering, anxious faith, and hides
himself deeper than ever in the wounds of his Saviour.

Thus it was that the fallen Peter, when he had so grievous-
ly denied his Lord, yet, when brought again within sight of
the Saviour, standing upon the shore, was the only one of
the disciples who girt his fisher's coat unto him, and cast
himself into the sea to swim to Jesus; and that backslidden apostle, when again he had hidden himself in the
clefts of the Rock of Ages, found that the love of Jesus was
more tender towards him than ever, when he began that conversation which, more than all others in the Bible, combines
the kindest of reproofs with the kindest of encouragements,
"Simon, son of Jonas, lovest thou me more than these?" Just
so does every backslidden believer find that, when again he is

hidden in the freshly opened wounds of his Lord, the fountain of His love begins to flow afresh, and the stream of kindness and affection is fuller and more overflowing than ever, for His word is, "Oh, my dove, that art in the clefts of the rock, in the secret places of the precipice, let me see thy countenance, let me hear thy voice; for sweet is thy voice, and thy countenance is comely."

Ah, my friends, do you know anything of this? Have you ever experienced such a coming of Jesus over the mountain of your provocations, as made a change of season to your soul? and have you, backslidden believer, found, when you hid yourself again deeper than ever in the clefts of the rock— like Peter girding his fisher's coat unto him, and casting himself into the sea—have you found His love tenderer than ever to your soul? Then, should not this teach you quick repentance when you have fallen? Why keep one moment away from the Saviour? Are you waiting till you wipe away the stain from your garments? Alas! what will wipe it off but the blood you are despising? Are you waiting till you make yourself worthier of the Saviour's favor? Alas! though you wait till all eternity you can never make yourself worthier. Your sin and misery are your only plea. Come, and you will find with what tenderness He will heal your backslidings, and love you freely; and say, "Oh, my dove."

IV. *Observe the threefold disposition of fear, love, and hope, which this visit of the Saviour stirs up in the believer's bosom.* These three form, as it were, a cord in the restored believer's bosom, and a threefold cord is not easily broken.

1. First of all, there is *fear.*—As the bride in the parable would not go forth to enjoy the society of her lord, without leaving the command behind to her maidens to take the foxes, the little foxes, that spoil the vines, so does every believer know and feel that the time of closest communion is also the time of greatest danger. It was when the Saviour had

been baptized, and the Holy Ghost, like a dove, had descended upon Him, and a voice saying, "This is my beloved Son, in whom I am well pleased"—it was then that He was driven into the wilderness to be tempted of the devil. Just so it is when the soul is receiving its highest privileges and comforts, that Satan and his ministers are nearest—the foxes, the little foxes, that spoil the vines. (1.) Spiritual pride is near. When the soul is hiding in the wounds of the Saviour, and receiving great tokens of His love, then the heart begins to say, Surely I am somebody—how far I am above the everyday run of believers! This is one of the little foxes that eats out the life of vital godliness. (2.) There is making a Christ of your comforts—looking to them, and not to Christ —leaning upon them, and not upon your Beloved. This is another of the little foxes. (3.) There is the false notion that now you must surely be above sinning, and above the power of temptation, now you can resist all enemies. This is the pride that goes before a fall—another of the foxes, the little foxes, that spoil the vines. Never forget, I beseech you, that fear is a sure mark of a believer. Even when you feel that it is God that worketh in you, still the Word saith, "Work out your salvation with fear and trembling"; even when your joy is overflowing, still remember it is written, "Rejoice with *trembling*"; and again: "Be not highminded, but fear." Remember the caution of the bride, and say: "Take us the foxes, the little foxes, that spoil the vines, for our vines have tender grapes."

2. But if cautious fear be a mark of a believer in such a season, still more is *appropriating love*. When Christ comes anew over mountains of provocation, and reveals Himself to the soul free and full as ever, in another way than He doth unto the world, then the soul can say, "My beloved is mine, and I am his." I do not say that the believer can use these words at all seasons. In times of darkness and in times of

sinfulness the reality of a believer's faith is to be measured
rather by his sadness than by his confidence. But I do say,
that, in seasons when Christ reveals Himself afresh to the
soul, shining out like the sun from behind a cloud, with the
beams of sovereign, unmerited love—then no other words
will satisfy the true believer but these: "My beloved is mine,
and I am his." The soul sees Jesus to be *so free a Saviour;*
so anxious that all should come to Him and have life; stretching out His hands all the day; having no pleasure in the
death of the wicked; pleading with men: "Turn ye, turn ye,
why will ye die?"

The soul sees Jesus to be *so fitting a Saviour,* the very
covering which the soul requires. When first he hid himself
in Jesus, he found Him suitable to all his need, the shadow
of a great rock in a weary land. But now he finds out a new
fitness in the Saviour, as Peter did when he girt his fisher's
coat unto him, and cast himself into the sea. He finds that
He is a fitting Saviour for the backsliding believer; that his
blood can blot out even the stains of him who, having eaten
bread with Him, has yet lifted up the heel against Him.

The soul sees Jesus to be *so full a Saviour,* giving to the
sinner not only pardons, but overflowing, immeasurable pardons; giving not only righteousness, but a righteousness that
is more than mortal, for it is all divine; giving not only the
Spirit, but pouring water on him that is thirsty, and floods
upon the dry ground. The soul sees all this in Jesus, and
cannot but choose Him and delight in Him with a new and
appropriating love, saying, *"My beloved is mine."* And if
any man ask, How darest thou, sinful worm, to call that divine Savior thine? the answer is here, *For I am His:* He
chose me from all eternity, else I never would have chosen
Him. He shed His blood for me, else I never would have
shed a tear for Him. He cried after me, else I never would
have breathed after Him. He sought after me, else I never

would have sought after Him. He hath loved me, therefore I love Him. He hath chosen me, therefore I evermore choose Him. "My beloved is mine, and I am his."

3. But, lastly, if love be a mark of the true believer at such a season, so also is *prayerful hope.* It was the saying of a true believer, in an hour of high and wonderful communion with Jesus, "Lord, it is good for us to be here!" My friend, you are no believer if Jesus hath never manifested Himself to your soul in your secret devotions, in the house of prayer, or in the breaking of bread, in so sweet and overpowering a manner, that you have cried out, "Lord, it is good for me to be here!" But though it be good and very pleasant, like sunlight to the eyes, yet the Lord sees that it is not wisest and best always to be there. Peter must come down again from the mount of glory, and fight the good fight of faith amid the shame and contumely of a cold and scornful world. And so must every child of God. We are not yet in heaven, the place of open vision and unbroken enjoyment. This is earth, the place of faith, and patience, and heavenward-pointing hope.

One great reason that close and intimate enjoyment of the Saviour may not be constantly realized in the believer's breast is, to give room for hope, the third string that forms the threefold cord. Even the most enlightened believers are walking here in a darksome night, or twilight at most; and the visits of Jesus to the soul do but serve to make the surrounding darkness more visible. But the night is far spent, the day is at hand. The day of eternity is breaking in the east. The Sun of Righteousness is hasting to rise upon our world, and the shadows are preparing to flee away. Till then, the heart of every true believer, that knows the preciousness of close communion with the Saviour, breathes the earnest prayer, that Jesus would often come again, thus sweetly and suddenly, to lighten him in his darksome pilgrimage. Ah! yes, my friends, let every one who loves the Lord Jesus in sincerity, join now in the blessed prayer of the bride: "Until the day break, and the shadows flee away, turn, my beloved, and be thou like a roe or a young hart upon the mountains of Bether."

Message XXIV

OUR DUTY TO ISRAEL.[1]

"To the Jew first."—ROMANS 1:16.

M OST PEOPLE are ashamed of the gospel of Christ. *The wise* are ashamed of it, because it calls men to believe and not to argue; *the great* are ashamed of it, because it brings all into one body; *the rich* are ashamed of it, because it is to be had without money and without price; *the gay* are ashamed of it, because they fear it will destroy all their mirth; and so the good news of the glorious Son of God having come into the world a Surety for lost sinners, is despised, uncared for—men are ashamed of it. Who are not ashamed of it? A little company, those whose hearts the Spirit of God has touched. They were once like the world, and of it; but He awakened them to see their sin and misery, and that Christ alone was a refuge, and now they cry, None but Christ! none but Christ! God forbid that I should glory save in the cross of Christ. He is precious to their heart—He lives there; He is often on their lips; He is praised in their family; they would fain proclaim Him to all the world. They have felt in their own experience that the gospel is the power of God unto salvation, to the Jew first, and also to the Greek. Dear friends, is this your experience? Have you received the gospel not in word only, but in power? Has the power of God been put forth upon your soul along with the Word? Then this word is yours: I am not ashamed of the gospel of Christ.

[1] Preached November 17, 1839, after returning from the Mission to the Jews.

One peculiarity in this statement I wish you to notice. He glories in the gospel as the power of God unto salvation to the Jew first; from which I draw this doctrine—*That the gospel should be preached first to the Jews.*

1. *Because judgment will begin with them.*—"Indignation and wrath, to the Jew first" (Rom. 2:6-10). It is an awful thought, that the Jew will be the first to stand forward at the bar of God to be judged. When the great white throne is set, and He sits down upon it from whose face the heavens and earth flee away; when the dead, small and great, stand before God, and the books are opened, and the dead are judged out of those things that are written in the books; is it not a striking thought, that Israel—poor, blinded Israel— will be the first to stand in judgment before God?

When the Son of Man shall come in His glory, and all the holy angels with Him; when He shall sit upon the throne of His glory, and before Him shall be gathered all nations, and He shall separate them one from another, as a shepherd divideth his sheep from the goats; when the awful sentence comes forth from His lips, Depart, ye cursed; and when the guilty many shall move away from before Him into ever-lasting punishment, is it not enough to make the most care-less among you pause and consider, that the indignation and wrath shall first come upon the Jew? that their faces will gather a deeper paleness, their knees knock more against each other, and their hearts die within them more than others?

Why is this? Because they have had more light than any other people. God chose them out of the world to be His witnesses. Every prophet was sent first to them; every evan-gelist and apostle had a message for them. Messiah came to them. He said, "I am not sent but to the lost sheep of the house of Israel." The Word of God is still addressed to them. They still have it pure and unadulterated in their hand. Yet they have sinned against all this light, against all this love. "O Jerusalem, Jerusalem, thou that killest the prophets, and stonest them which are sent unto thee, how often would I have gathered thy children together, as a hen gathers her chickens under her wings, and ye would not!" Their cup of wrath is fuller than that of other men; their sea of wrath is deeper. On their very faces, you may read in every clime, that the curse of God is over them.

Is not this a reason, then, why the gospel should first be preached to the Jew? They are ready to perish—to perish more dreadfully than other men. The cloud of indignation and wrath that is even now gathering above the lost, will break first upon the head of guilty, unhappy, unbelieving Israel. And have you none of the bowels of Christ in you, that you will not run first to them that are in so sad a case? In an hospital, the kind physician runs first to that bed where the sick man lies who is nearest to die. When a ship is sinking, and the gallant sailors have left the shore to save the sinking crew, do they not stretch out the arm of help first to those that are most apt to perish beneath the waves? And shall we not do the same for Israel? The billows of God's anger are ready to dash first over them—shall we not seek to bring them first to the Rock that is higher than they? Their case is more desperate than that of other men—shall we not bring the good Physician to them, who alone can bring health and cure? For the gospel is the power of God unto salvation, to the Jew first, and also to the Greek.

I cannot leave this head without speaking a word to those of you who are in a situation very similar to that of Israel— to you who have the Word of God in your hands, and yet are unbelieving and unsaved. In many respects, Scotland may be called God's second Israel. No other land has its Sabbath as Scotland has; no other land has the Bible as Scotland has; no other land has the gospel preached, free as the air we breathe, fresh as the stream from the everlasting hills. Oh

then, think for a moment, you who sit under the shade of
faithful ministers, and yet remain unconcerned and unconverted, and are not brought to sit under the shade of Christ,
think how like your wrath will be to that of the unbelieving
Jew! And think, again, of the marvelous grace of Christ,
that the gospel is first to you. The more that your sins are
like scarlet and like crimson, the more is the blood free to
you that washes white as snow; for this is still His word
to all His ministers, Begin at Jerusalem.

2. *It is like God to care first for the Jews.*—It is the chief
glory and joy of a soul to be like God. You remember this
was the glory of that condition in which Adam was created.
"Let us make man in our image, after our likeness." His
understanding was without a cloud. He saw, in some measure, as God seeth; his will flowed in the same channel with
God's will; his affections fastened on the same objects which
God also loved. When man fell, we lost all this, and became children of the devil, and not children of God. But
when a lost soul is brought to Christ, and receives the Holy
Ghost, he puts off the old man, and puts on the new man,
which *after God* is created in righteousness and true holiness.
It is our true joy in this world to be like God. Too many
rest in the joy of being forgiven, but our truest joy is to *be
like Him.* Oh, rest not, beloved, till you are renewed after
His image, till you partake of the divine nature. Long for
the day when Christ shall appear, and we shall be fully *like
Him,* for we shall see Him as He is.

Now, what I wish to insist upon at present is, that we
should be like God, even in those things which are peculiar.
We should be like Him in understanding, in will, in holiness, and also in His *peculiar affections.* "Love is of God,
and every one that loveth is born of God, and knoweth
God. He that loveth not knoweth not God, for God is
love." But the whole Bible shows that God has a peculiar

affection for Israel. You remember when the Jews were in
Egypt, sorely oppressed by their taskmasters, God heard their
cry, and appeared to Moses: "I have seen, I have seen the
affliction of my people, and I have heard their cry, for I
know their sorrows."

And, again, when God brought them through the wilderness, Moses tells them why He did it. "The Lord did not
set his love upon you, nor choose you because ye were more
in number than any people, for ye were the fewest of all
people, but because the Lord loved you" (Deut. 7:7).
Strange, sovereign, most peculiar love! He loved them because He loved them. Should we not be like God in this
peculiar attachment?

But you say, God has sent them into captivity. Now, it
is true God hath scattered them into every land: "The precious sons of Zion, comparable to fine gold, how are they
esteemed as earthen pitchers!" (Lam. 4:2). But what says
God of this? "I have forsaken mine house, I have left mine
heritage, I have given *the dearly beloved of my soul* into the
hand of her enemies" (Jer. 12:7). It is true that Israel is
given for a little moment into the hand of her enemies, but
it is as true that they are still the dearly beloved of His soul.
Should we not give them the same place in our heart which
God gives them in His heart? Shall we be ashamed to cherish
the same affection which our heavenly Father cherishes? Shall
we be ashamed to be unlike the world, and like God in this
peculiar love for captive Israel?

But you say, God has cast them off. Hath God cast away
His people which He foreknew? God forbid! The whole
Bible contradicts such an idea. "Is Ephraim my dear son? is
he a pleasant child? for since I spake against him, I do
earnestly remember him still; therefore my bowels are troubled
for him: I will surely have mercy upon him, saith the Lord"
(Jer. 31:20). "I will plant them again in their own land

assuredly, with my whole heart and with my whole soul."
"Zion saith, The Lord hath forsaken me, and my Lord hath
forgotten me. Can a woman forget her sucking child, that
she should not have compassion on the son of her womb?
Yea, they may forget, yet will I not forget thee" (Isa. 49:14,
15). "And so all Israel shall be saved, as it is written, There
shall come out of Zion the Deliverer, and shall turn away
ungodliness from Jacob." Now the simple question for each
of you is, and for our beloved church, Should we not share
with God in His peculiar affection for Israel? If we are filled
with the Spirit of God, should we not love as He loves?
Should we not grave Israel upon the palms of our hands,
and resolve that through our mercy they also may obtain
mercy?

3. *Because there is peculiar access to the Jews.*—In almost
all the countries we have visited, this fact is quite remarkable;
indeed, it seems in many places as if the only door left open
to the Christian missionary is the door of preaching to the
Jews.

We spent some time in Tuscany, the freest state in the
whole of Italy. There you dare not preach the gospel to the
Roman Catholic population. The moment you give a tract
or a Bible, it is carried to the priest, and by the priest to
the government, and immediate banishment is the certain result. But the door is open to the Jews. No man cares for
their souls; and therefore you may carry the gospel to them
freely.

The same is the case in Egypt and in Palestine.—You dare
not preach the gospel to the deluded followers of Mohammed;
but you may stand in the open market place and preach the
gospel to the Jews, no man forbidding you. We visited every
town in the Holy Land where Jews are found. In Jerusalem
and in Hebron we spoke to them all the words of this life.
In Sychar we reasoned with them in the synagogue, and in

the open bazaar. In Haifa, at the foot of Carmel, we met
with them in the synagogue. In Sidon also we discoursed
freely to them of Jesus. In Tyre we first visited them in the
synagogue and at the house of the rabbi, and then they
returned our visit; for when we had lain down in the khan
for the heat of midday, they came to us in crowds. The Hebrew Bible was produced, and passage after passage explained,
none making us afraid. In Safad, and Tiberias, and Acre,
we had like freedom. There is indeed perfect liberty in
the Holy Land to carry the gospel to the Jew.

In Constantinople, if you were to preach to the Turks, as
some have tried, banishment is the consequence; but to the
Jew you may carry the message. *In Valachia and Moldavia*
the smallest attempt to convert a Greek would draw down
the instant vengeance of the Holy Synod and of the government. But in every town we went freely to the Jews: in Bucharest, in Focsani, in Jassy, and in many a remote Valachian
hamlet, we spoke without hindrance the message to Israel.
The door is wide open.

In Austria, where no missionary of any kind is allowed,
still we found the Jews willing to hear. In their synagogues
we always found a sanctuary open to us; and often, when they
knew they could have exposed us, they concealed that we had
been there.

In Prussian Poland, the door is wide open to nearly 100,000
Jews. You dare not preach to the poor Rationalist Protestants.
Even in Protestant Prussia this would not be allowed; but
you may preach the gospel to the Jews. By the law of the
land every church is open to an ordained minister; and one
of the missionaries assured me that he often preached to
400 or 500 Jews and Jewesses at a time. Schools for Jewish
children are also allowed. We visited three of them, and
heard the children taught the way of salvation by a Redeemer.
Twelve years ago the Jews would not come near a church.

If these things be true—and I appeal to all of you who know these countries if it is not; if the door in one direction is shut, and the door to Israel is so widely open; oh, do you not think that God is saying by His providence, as well as by His word, Go rather to the lost sheep of the house of Israel? Do you think that our church, knowing these things, will be guiltless if we do not obey the call? for the gospel is the power of God unto salvation, to the Jew first, and also to the Greek.

4. *Because they will give life to the dead world.*—I have often thought that a reflective traveler, passing through the countries of this world, and observing the race of Israel in every land, might be led to guess, merely from the light of his natural reason, that that singular people are preserved for some great purpose in the world. There is a singular fitness in the Jew to be the missionary of the world. They have not that peculiar attachment to home and country which we have. They feel that they are outcasts in every land. They are also inured to every clime: they are to be found amid the snows of Russia, and beneath the burning sun of India. They are also in some measure acquainted with all the languages of the world, and yet have one common language—the holy tongue—in which to communicate with one another. All these things must, I should think, suggest themselves to every intelligent traveler as he passes through other lands. *But what says the Word of God?*

"It shall come to pass, that as ye were a curse among the heathen, O house of Judah and house of Israel; so will I save you, and ye shall be a blessing" (Zech. 8:13). To this day they are a curse among all nations, by their unbelief, by their covetousness; but the time is coming when they shall be as great a blessing as they have been a curse.

"And the remnant of Jacob shall be in the midst of many people as a dew from the Lord, as the showers upon the grass, that tarrieth not for man, nor waiteth for the sons of men" (Micah 5:7). Just as we have found, among the parched hills of Judah, that the evening dew, coming silently down, gave life to every plant, making the grass to spring, and the flowers to put forth their sweetest fragrance; so shall converted Israel be when they come as dew upon a dead, dry world.

"In those days it shall come to pass, that ten men shall take hold, out of all languages of the nations, even shall take hold of the skirt of him that is a Jew, saying, We will go with you; for we have heard that God is with you" (Zech. 8:23). This never has been fulfilled; but as the Word of God is true, this is true. Perhaps someone may say, If the Jews are to be the great missionaries of the world, let us send missions to them only. We have got a new light; let us call back our missionaries from India. They are wasting their precious lives there in doing what the Jews are to accomplish. I grieve to think that any lover of Israel should so far pervert the truth as to argue in this way. The Bible does not say that we are to preach *only* to the Jew, but to the Jew *first*. "Go and preach the gospel to *all* nations," said the Saviour. Let us obey His word like little children. The Lord speed our beloved missionaries in that burning clime. The Lord give them good success, and never let one withering doubt cross their pure minds as to their glorious field of labor.

All that we plead for is, that, in sending out missionaries to the heathen, we may not forget to begin at Jerusalem. If Paul be sent to the Gentiles, let Peter be sent to the twelve tribes that are scattered abroad; and let not a bycorner in your hearts be given to this cause; let it not be an appendix to the other doings of our church, but rather let there be written on the forefront of your hearts, and on the banner of our beloved church, "To the Jew first," and "Beginning at Jerusalem."

Lastly, Because there is a great reward. Blessed is he that blesseth thee; cursed is he that curseth thee. Pray for the peace of Jerusalem; they shall prosper that love her. We have felt this in our own souls. In going from country to country, we felt that there was One before us preparing our way. Though we have had perils in the waters, and perils in the wilderness, perils from sickness, and perils from the heathen, still from all the Lord has delivered us; and if it shall please God to restore our revered companions in this mission in peace and safety to their anxious families,[1] we shall then have good reason to say, that in keeping His commandment there is great reward.

But your souls shall be enriched also, and our church too, if this cause find its right place in your affections. It was well said by one who has a deep place in your affections, and who is now on his way to India, that our church must not only be evangelical, but evangelistic also, if she would expect the blessing of God. She must not only have the light, but dispense it also, if she is to be continued as a steward of God. May I not take the liberty of adding to this striking declaration, that we must not only be evangelistic, but evangelistic *as God would have us to be;* not only dispense the light on every hand, but dispense it first to the Jew?

Then shall God revive His work in the midst of the years. Our whole land shall be refreshed as Kilsyth has been. The cobwebs of controversy shall be swept out of our sanctuaries, the jarrings and jealousies of our church be turned into the harmony of praise and our own souls become like a well-watered garden.

---

[1] Drs. Black and Keith were at this time still detained by sickness abroad.

Message XXV

"BLESSED ARE THE DEAD."[2]

"Blessed are the dead which die in the Lord from henceforth: Yea, saith the
  Spirit, that they may rest from their labors; and their works do follow
  them."—REVELATION 14:13.

THERE ARE two remarkable things in the manner in
which these words are given to us.

I. *They are the words of the Father echoed back by the
Spirit.*—"I heard a voice from heaven." "Yea, saith the
Spirit." John's eye had been riveted upon the wondrous sight
mentioned in verse 1. A Lamb stood on Mount Zion, and
one hundred and forty-four thousand redeemed ones following Him whithersoever He goeth, when suddenly a still small
voice broke upon his ear, saying, "Write, Blessed are the
dead;" and then the Holy Spirit breathed, Amen. "Yea, saith
the Spirit."

It is written in the law that the testimony of two witnesses
is true. Now, here are two witnesses—the Father of all, and
the Holy Spirit the Comforter, both testifying that it is a
happy thing to die in the Lord. Are there any of you, God's
children, who tremble at the thought of dying? Does death
appear a monster with a dreadful dart, ready to destroy you?
Here are two sweet and blessed witnesses who declare that
death has lost its sting—that the grave has lost its victory.
Listen, and the frown will disappear from the brow of death,
the valley will be filled with light; the Father and the Holy
Spirit both unite in saying, "Blessed are the dead."

II. *"Write."*—Whatever is written down is more durable,
and less liable to be corrupted, than that which is only spoken
from mouth to mouth. For this reason, God gave the Israelites the Ten Commandments, written with His own finger
on two tables of stone. For the same reason, He commanded
them, on the day they passed over Jordan, to set up great

---

2 Preached in the summer of 1840.

stones, and plaster them with plaster, and *write* upon them all
the words of that law. For the same reason, God commanded
His servants the prophets to *write* their prophecies, and the
apostles to *write* their gospels and epistles, so that we have
a permanent Bible instead of floating tradition. For this reason *did Job wish* his words to be written. "Oh, that my words
were written! Oh, that they were printed in a book! That
they were graven with an iron pen and with lead in the rock
forever! For I know that my Redeemer liveth" (Job 19:25). It
was one of his precious, ever memorable sayings, a saying to
comfort the heart of a drooping believer in the darkest hour,
"I know that my Redeemer liveth." For the same reason did
the voice from heaven say, *"Write,"*—do not hear it only, but
write it—print it in a book—grave it with an iron pen, with
lead in the rock forever.

"Blessed are the dead." Learn the value of this saying. It
is a golden saying—there is gold in every syllable of it. It is
sweeter than honey and the honeycomb, more precious than
gold, yea, much fine gold. It is precious in the eyes of God.
Write it deep in your hearts; it will solemnize your life, and
will keep you from being led away by its vain show. It will
make the siren songs of this world inconvenient and out of tune;
it will sweetly soothe you in the hour of adversity; it will rob
death of its sting, and the grave of its victory. *Write, write*
deep on your heart, "Blessed are the dead which die in the
Lord."

Now, consider the *words* themselves.

1. *"Blessed are the dead."*—*The world* says, Blessed are
the living; but God says, Blessed are the dead. The world
judges of things by sense—as they outwardly appear to men;
God judges of things by what they really are in themselves.
He looks at things in their real color and magnitude. The
world says, "Better is a living dog than a dead lion." The
world looks upon some of their families, coming out like

a fresh blooming flower in the morning, their cheeks covered with the bloom of health, their step bounding with the elasticity of youth, riches and luxuries at their command and long, bright summer days before them. The world says, "There is a happy soul." God takes us into the darkened room, where some child of God lately dwelt. He points to the pale face where death sits enthroned, the cheek wasted by long disease, the eye glazed in death, the stiff hands clasped over the bosom, the friends standing weeping around, and He whispers in our ears, "Blessed are the dead."

Ah, dear friends, think a moment! Does God or you know best? Who will be found to be in the right at last? Alas, what a vain show you are walking in! Disquieted in vain. "Man that is in honor, and understandeth not, is like the beasts that perish." Even God's children sometimes say, "Blessed are the living." It is a happy thing to live in the favor of God, to have peace with God, to frequent the throne of grace, to burn the perpetual incense of praise, to meditate on His Word, to hear the preached gospel, to serve God; even to wrestle, and run, and fight in His service, is sweet. Still God says, *"Blessed are the dead."* If it be happy to have His smile *here,* how much happier to have it without a cloud *yonder!* If it be sweet to be the growing corn of the Lord *here,* how much better to be gathered into His barn! If it be sweet to have an anchor within the veil, how much better *ourselves* to be *there,* where no gloom can come! In "thy presence is *fullness* of joy; at thy right hand are pleasures for evermore." Even *Jesus* felt this—God attests it. *"Blessed are the dead."*

2. *Not all the dead,* but those that *"die in the Lord."* It is truly amazing the multitudes that die. "Thou carriest them away as with a flood." Seventy thousand die every day, about fifty every minute—nearly one every second passing over the verge. Life is like a stream made up of human beings, pouring on, and rushing over the brink into eternity. Are all

these blessed? Ah, no. *"Blessed are the dead who die in the Lord."* Of all that vast multitude continually pouring into the eternal world, a little company alone have savingly believed on Jesus. "Strait is the gate and narrow is the way that leadeth unto life, and *few* there be that find it."

It is not *all* the dead who are blessed. There is no blessing on the Christless dead; they rush into an *undone* eternity, unpardoned, unholy. You may put their body in a splendid coffin; you may print their name in silver on the lid; you may bring the well-attired company of mourners to the funeral, in suits of solemn black; you may lay the coffin slowly in the grave; you may spread the greenest sod above it; you may train the sweetest flowers to grow over it; you may cut a white stone, and grave a gentle epitaph to their memory; still it is but the funeral of a damned soul. You cannot write *blessed* where God hath written *"cursed."* "He that believeth shall be saved; he that believeth not shall be damned."

Consider what is implied in the words "in the Lord."

First, That they were joined to the Lord.—Union to the Lord has a beginning. Every one that is blessed in dying has been converted. You may dislike the word, but that is the truth. They were awakened, began to weep, pray, weep, as they went to seek the Lord their God. They saw themselves lost, undone, helpless, that they could not be just with a holy God. They became babes. The Lord Jesus drew near, and revealed Himself. "I am the bread of life." "Him that cometh unto me, I will in no wise cast out." They believed and were happy, rejoiced in the Lord Jesus, counted everything but loss for Christ. They gave themselves to the Lord. This was the beginning of their being in Christ.

Dear friends, have you had this beginning? Have you undergone conversion—the new birth—grafting into Christ? Call it by any name you will, have you the thing? Has this union to Christ taken place in your history? Some say, I do not know. If at any time of your life you had been saved from drowning, if you were actually drowned and brought to life again, you would remember it to your dying hour. Much more if you had been brought to Christ. If you had been blind, and by some remarkable operation your eyes were opened when you were full-grown, would you ever forget it? So, if you have been truly brought into Christ, you may easily remember it. If not, you will die in your sins. Whither Christ has gone, thither you cannot come. "Except ye repent and be converted, ye shall all likewise perish."

Second, Perseverance is implied.—*Not all* that seem to be branches are branches of the true Vine. Many branches fall off the trees when the high winds begin to blow—all that are rotten branches. So in times of temptation, or trial, or persecution, many false professors drop away. Many that seemed to be believers went back, and walked no more with Jesus. They followed Jesus, they prayed with Him, they praised Him; but they went back, and walked no more with Him. So it is still. Many among us doubtless seem to be converted; they begin well and promise fair, who will fall off when winter comes. Some have fallen off, I fear, already; some more may be expected to follow. These will not be blessed in dying. Oh, of all deathbeds, may I be kept from beholding the deathbed of the false professor! I have seen it before now, and I trust I may never see it again. They are not blessed after death. The rotten branches will burn more fiercely in the flames.

Oh, think what torment it will be, to think that you spent your life in pretending to be a Christian, and lost your opportunity of becoming one indeed! Your hell will be all the deeper, blacker, hotter, that you knew so much of Christ, and were so near Him, and found Him not. Happy are they who endure to the end, who are not moved away from the hope of the gospel, who, when others go away, say, Lord, to whom can we go? In prosperity, they follow the Lord fully; in ad-

versity, they cleave to Him closer still, as trees strike their
roots deeper in storms. Is this your case? Endure it to the end.
"Be not moved away from the hope of the gospel" (Col. 1:23).
"We are made partakers of Christ, if we hold the beginning
of our confidence stedfast unto the end" (Heb. 3:14). Even
in the dark valley you will cling to Him still. Come to Him as
ye came at first—a guilty creature, clinging to the Lord our
Righteousness. Thou wast made my sin. This is to die in the
Lord, and this is to be blessed.

III. *Why they are blessed.*

1. *Because of the time.*—"From henceforth." The time of
the persecutions of Catholicism was coming on. He was to
wear out the saints of the Most High; he was to overcome and
slay the followers of the Lamb. Happy are they that are taken
from the evil to come. The righteous perish, and no man layeth
it to heart. Merciful men are taken away, none considering
that they are taken away from the evil to come. This is one
reason it is better to be with Christ. Persecutions and troubles
are not easy to flesh and blood. If in our day we be called to
them, we must bear them boldly, knowing that a good reward
is provided for those that overcome. See Revelation 2:3—"And
hast borne, and hast patience, and for my name's sake hast labored, and hast not fainted." But if it be the will of God to
call us away before the day of trial come, we must say, "Blessed
are the dead who die in the Lord from henceforth." There
will be no persecutions there. All are friends to Jesus there,
every one contending who shall cast their crowns lowest at His
feet, who shall exalt Him highest in their praise. No discord
there. None to rebuke our song there.

2. *They rest from their labors.*—That which makes everything laborious here is sin—the opposition of Satan and the
world, and the drag of our old nature. Some believers have a
constant struggle with Satan. He is standing at their right
hand to resist them; he is constantly distracting them in prayer,

hurling fiery darts at their soul, tempting to the most horrid sin. Their whole life is labor. But when we die in the Lord, we shall rest from this labor. Satan's work will be done. The accuser of the brethren will no more annoy. No lion shall be there, neither shall any ravenous beast go up thereon, but the redeemed shall walk there. But above all, the wicked heart, the old man, the body of sin, makes this life a dreadful labor. When we wake in the morning, it lies like a weight upon us. When we would run in the way of God's commandments, it drags us back. When we would fly, it weighs us down. When we would pray, it fills our mouth with other things. "O wretched man that I am!"

But to depart and be with Christ, is to be free from this. We shall drop this body of sin altogether. No more any flesh —all spirit, all new man; no more any weight or drag—we shall rest from our labors. Oh, it is this makes death in the Lord blessed! We shall not rest from all work; we shall be as the angels of God—we shall serve Him day and night in His temple. We shall not rest from our work, but from our labors. There will be no toil, no pain, in our work. We shall rest in our work. Oh, let this make you willing to depart, and make death look pleasant, and heaven a home. "We shall rest from our labors." It is the world of holy love, where we shall give free, full, unfettered, unwearied expression to our love forever.

3. *Works follow.*—Our good works done in the name of Jesus shall then be rewarded. *First,* Observe, they shall not go before the soul. It is not on account of them we shall be accepted. We must be accepted *first* altogether on account of *Him* in whom we stand. *Second,* Our evil works shall be forgotten, buried in the depths of the sea—forgotten, no more mentioned. *Third,* All that we have done out of love to Jesus shall then be rewarded. We may forget them, and say to Jesus, "When saw we thee sick, or in prison, and came unto

thee?" But He will not forget them: "Inasmuch as ye have done it unto one of the least of these my brethren, ye have done it unto me." A cup of cold water shall not go unrewarded.

Look to the recompense of reward, dear friends, and it will take the sting from death.

IV. *What followed.*—The Lord Jesus "put in his sickle and reaped." (vv. 14, 15).

1. Learn that the Lord Jesus gathers His sheaves before a storm, just as farmers do; so when you see Him gathering ripe saints, be sure that a storm is near.

2. Learn that Jesus gathers His saints in love. When Jesus gathers His own, He does it in love. Do not mourn for them as those who have no hope. Jesus has gathered them into His bosom. They shall shine as the sun.

MESSAGE XXVI

ON THE CLOSE OF A COMMUNION SABBATH.

"What have I to do any more with idols?"—HOSEA 14:8.

EVERY ONE who has been truly united to Christ, and has this day confessed Him before men, should now take up these words, and solemnly, in the presence of God, declare, "What have I to do any more with idols?" Two reasons are given.

I. *God loves you freely* (v. 4).—If you are this day come to Jesus, God loves you freely. If you believe on Him that justifieth the ungodly, your faith is counted for righteousness. As long as you came to God in yourself, you were infinitely vile, loathsome, condemned—mountains of iniquity covered your soul; but blessed, blessed, blessed be the Holy Spirit who has led you to Jesus. You have come to God's righteous Servant, who by His knowledge justifies many, because He bears their iniquities. Your sins are covered, God sees no iniquity in you; God loves you freely, His anger is turned away from you. What have you to do, then, any more with idols? Is not the love of God enough for thee? The loving and much-loved wife is satisfied with the love of her husband; his smile is her joy, she cares little for any other. So, if you have come to Christ, thy Maker is thine husband; His free love to you is all you need, and all you can care for; there is no cloud between you and God, there is no veil between you and the Father; you have access to Him who is the fountain of happiness, of peace, of holiness—what have you to do any more with idols? Oh! if your heart swims in the rays of God's love, like a little mote swimming in the sunbeam, you will have no room in your heart for idols.

II. *The Spirit, like dew, descends on your souls.*—"I will be like the dew" (v. 5). If you are this day united to Jesus, the Spirit will come like dew upon your soul. The Spirit is given to them that obey Jesus: "I will pray the Father." When all nature is at rest, not a leaf moving, then at evening the dew comes down—no eye to see the pearly drops descending, no ear to hear them falling on the verdant grass: so does the Spirit come to you who believe. When the heart is at rest in Jesus, unseen and unheard by the world the Spirit comes, and softly fills the believing soul, quickening all, renewing all within. "If I go away, I will send Him unto you." Dear little ones, whom God hath chosen out of this world, you are like Gideon's fleece: the Lord will fill you with dew when all around is dry. You are His vineyard of red wine; He says, I will water it every moment—silently, unfelt, unseen, but *surely.* But, ah! that Spirit is a Holy Spirit. "I the Lord thy God am a jealous God." He cannot bear an idol in His temple. When the ark of God was carried into the temple of Dagon, the idol fell flat before it; much more when the Holy Spirit comes into the heart will He cast out the idols.

When Christ came into the temple, He "found those that

sold oxen, and sheep, and doves, and the changers of money, sitting; and when he had made a scourge of small cords, he drove them all out of the temple" (John 2:15). So when the Holy Spirit comes into any heart, He drives out the buyers and sellers. If you have received the Spirit, you will be crying now in your heart, Lord, take these things hence; drive them out of my heart. What have I to do any more with idols? Some of the idols to be cast away are:

1. *Self-righteousness.*—This is the largest idol of the human heart, the idol which man loves most, and God hates most. Dearly beloved, you will always be going back to this idol. You are always trying to be something in yourself, to gain God's favor by thinking little of your sin, or by looking to your repentance, tears, prayers, or by looking to your religious exercises, your feelings, or by looking to your graces—the Spirit's work in your heart. Beware of false Christs. Study sanctification to the utmost, but make not a Christ of it. God hates this idol more than all others, because it comes in the place of Christ; it sits on Christ's throne. Just as the worship of the Virgin Mary is the worst of all kinds of idolatry, because it puts her in the place of Christ, so self-righteousness is the idol God hates most, for it sits on the throne of Christ. Dash it down, dear friends; let it never appear again. It is like Manasseh's carved image in the Holiest of all. When Manasseh came home an altered man to Jerusalem, would not his first visit be to the Holiest of all? With eager hand he would draw the veil aside; and when he found the carved image, he would dash it down from the throne of God. Go and do likewise. If you feel God's love freely by the righteousness without works, then why would you go back to this grim idol? What have I to do any more with idols?

2. *Darling sins.*—Every man has his darling sins. Long they kept you from the Lord Jesus. You have this day declared that you were willing to leave them all for Christ. Go home, then,

and perform your vows. After Hezekiah's Passover, when they had enjoyed much of the love and Spirit of God, "all Israel that were present went home, and broke the images in pieces, and cut down the groves, until they had utterly destroyed them all." You might have seen them entering the shady groves and dashing down the carved images. Go you and do likewise. Dash down family idols, unholy practices that have spread through your family. Dash down secret idols in your own heart. Leave not one. Remember, one Achan in the camp troubled Israel, and they were smitten before their enemies. So, one idol left in your heart may trouble you. Let Achan be slain if you would go on your way rejoicing. What have I to do any more with idols? "If thy right hand offend thee, cut it off."

3. *Unlawful attachments.*—There is not a more fruitful source of sin and misery than unlawful attachments. How much of the poetry and music of our country are given over to the worship of the idols of a foolish heart! How many are given over to worship a piece of clay that will soon be eaten of worms! Oh, my friends, have you felt the love of God? Do you feel the sweet, full beams of His grace shining down upon your soul? Have you received the dew of His Spirit? How can you, then, any more love a creature that is void of the grace of God? What have you to do any more with idols? Dear young persons, abhor the idea of marriage with the unconverted. Be not unequally yoked together with unbelievers. Marry only in the Lord. Remember, if it be otherwise, it is a forbidden marriage. There may be none on earth so kind or faithful as to forbid the banns; earthly friends may be kind and smiling; the marriage circle may be gay and lovely; but God forbids the banns. But may there not be a lawful attachment? I believe there may; but take heed it be not an idol. I believe they are happiest who are living only for eternity, who have no object in this world to divert their hearts from Christ. "The time is

short; it remaineth that they who have wives be as though they had none." What have I to do any more with idols?

4. *Ministers.*—You have good reason to love ministers, and to esteem them highly for their work's sake. They love you; they watch for your souls as they that must give an account; they bear you on their hearts; they travail in birth till Christ be formed in you; they spend and are spent for you; they often endure amazing temptations, agonies, wrestlings for your sake.

Some have been your spiritual fathers. This is a holy tie that will never be broken. You have good reason to love your spiritual father. You may have ten thousand instructors in Christ, but ah, make not an idol of them. The people that would have worshiped Paul, were the very people that stoned him, and left him for dead. Oh, I wish that this day may bring you so near to Christ, and so much under the love of God and the dew of Israel, that you shall no more glory in man! What have I to do any more with idols?

5. *Earthly pleasures.*—This is a smiling, dazzling idol, that has ten thousand worshipers—lovers of pleasure more than lovers of God. What have you to do any more with this idol? Sometimes it is a gross idol. The theater is one of its temples—there it sits enthroned. The tavern is another, where its reeling, staggering votaries sing its praise. What have you to do with these? Have you the love of God in your soul—the Spirit of God in you? How dare you cross the threshold of a theater or a tavern any more! What! the Spirit of God amid the wanton songs of a theater, or the boisterous merriment of a tavern! Shame on such practical blasphemy! No; leave them, dear friends, to be cages of devils and of every unclean and hateful bird. You must never cross their threshold any more. What shall I say of games—cards, dice, dancing? I will only say this, that if you love them, you have never tasted the joys of the new creature. If you feel the love of God and the Spirit, you

will not lightly sin these joys away amid the vain anxieties of cards, or the rattling of senseless dice. What shall I say of simpering tea parties, the pleasures of religious gossiping, and useless calls, without meaning, sincerity, or end? I will only say, they are the happiest of God's children who have neither time nor heart for these things. I believe there cannot be much of the Spirit where there is much of these. What shall I say of dress? A young believer, full of faith and joy, was offered a present of flowers for her hair. She would not take them. She was pressed to accept them; still she refused. Why will you not? Ah, she said, how can I wear roses on my brow, when Christ wore thorns on His? The joy of being in Christ is so sweet, that it makes all other joys insipid, dull, lifeless. In His right hand are riches and honors; in His left are length of days. His ways are ways of pleasantness. What, then, have I to do any more with idols?

6. *Money.*—Dear souls, if you have felt the love of God, the dew, you must dash down this idol. You must not love money. You must be more openhearted, more openhanded, *to the poor.* "He that gives to the poor lends to the Lord." "Inasmuch as ye did it to the least of these, my brethren, ye did it unto me." You must build more churches. God be praised for what has been done: but you must do far more. I have as many in this parish who go nowhere as would fill another church. You must give more to missions, to send the knowledge of Jesus to the Jews, and to the Gentile world. Oh, how can you grasp your money in hand so greedily, while there are hundreds of millions perishing? You that give tens must give your hundreds. You that are poor must do what you can. Remember Mary, and the widow's mite. Let us resolve to give the tenth of all we have to God. God is able to make all grace abound toward you, that ye, always having all sufficiency in all things, may abound to every good work.

7. *Fear of man.*—Grim idol—bloody-mouthed—many souls

he has devoured and trampled down into hell! His eyes are full of hatred to Christ's disciples. Scoffs and jeers lurk in his eye. The laugh of the scorner growls in his throat. Cast down this idol. This keeps some of you from secret prayer, from worshiping God in your family, from going to lay your case before ministers, from openly confessing Christ. You that have felt God's love and Spirit, dash this idol to pieces. Who art thou, that thou shouldst be afraid of a man that shall die? Fear not, thou worm Jacob. What have I to do any more with idols?

Dearly beloved and longed for, my heart's desire for you is, to see you a holy people. How much longer my ministry may be continued among you, God only knows; but if God give me health and grace among you, I here willingly devote my all to Him. No moment, no pleasure, no ease, no wealth, do I wish for myself. I feel that He has bought me, and I am His property. Oh come, give yourselves to the Lord with me! Bind yourself to the horns of God's altar. Time past is enough to have been the devil's, the world's, our own. Now let us be Christ's alone. Are you willing? Lord, bear witness; seal it in heaven; write it in Thy book. Bear witness, angels, devils, scowling world; bear witness, sun and moon; bear witness, stones and timber; bear witness, Jesus, Lamb of God! We are thine now, and thine forever. What have we to do any more with idols?

October 25, 1840.

MESSAGE XXVII

AFTER THE COMMUNION

"But ye, beloved, building up yourselves on your most holy faith, praying in the
Holy Ghost, keep yourselves in the love of God, looking for the mercy of
our Lord Jesus Christ unto eternal life."—JUDE 20, 21.

I F YOU come rightly to this Table, you have been hewn out
of the Rock, and carried and laid on the sure foundation.
Others set at nought that Stone, but to you it is the only name
under heaven. You have been built on Christ alone for righteousness. Think not all is done—forget what is behind. You
have begun salvation, work out your salvation.

I. *Those that have been built on Christ, have need to build
themselves still more on Christ.*—1.—*Build yourselves more
simply on Christ.*—Build on Christ alone—His blood and
righteousness. Some are like a stone resting half on the foundation and half on the sand. Some take half their peace from
Christ's finished work, and half from the Spirit's work within
them. Now the whole of our justification must be from Christ
alone. Other foundation can no man lay.

2. *Build yourselves more surely on Christ.*—Some stones do
not lie smoothly on the foundation, they are apt to totter. Seek,
brethren, to get a sure founding on the Lord Jesus Christ. "If
ye continue in the faith, grounded and settled, and be not
moved away from the hope of the gospel." It is easy to sail
with a gentle sea and the wind in the west, but the gale tries
whether the ship be rightly balanced. It is easy to believe in a
sunny day like this, when broken bread and poured-out wine
have been in your hands; but stop till you are in the wilderness,
or afar at sea alone; stop till fresh guilt lies on the conscience;
stop till a strong temptation blows—oh, then to rely on Christ
alone for righteousness! Under a sight of sin—Satan grappling
with the soul—oh, then to look up into the face of Christ and
say, Thou art my robe, my righteousness, my shield. Thy blood,
Thy obedience is enough for me! This is to believe.

II. *Pray in the Holy Ghost.*—When a believer prays, he is not alone—there are three with him: the Father seeing in secret, His ear open; the Son blotting out sin, and offering up the prayer; the Holy Ghost quickening and giving desires. There can be no true prayer without these three. Some people pray like a parrot, repeating words when the heart is far from God. Some pray without the Father. They do not feel. They are speaking to the back of their chair, or to the world, or to the empty air. Some pray without the Son. They come in their own name—in their own righteousness. That is the sacrifice of fools. Some pray without the Holy Ghost. These are not filled with divine breathings. Dear friends, if you would live, you must pray; and if you would pray with acceptance, you must pray to the Father in the name of Jesus, and by His Spirit quickening.

1. *Get the Holy Ghost.*—Many seem not to know if there be a Holy Spirit. Jesus being raised by the Father, has obtained the Spirit. Ask Him.

2. *Let Him breathe within you.*—Do not vex Him.

3. *Pray without ceasing.*—Whatever you need, ask Him immediately. Have set times of approaching God solemnly. Let nothing interfere with these times. Take your best time.

III. *Keep yourselves in the love of God.*—It is when you are built on Christ, and praying in the Holy Ghost, that you keep yourselves in the love of God. There is one glorious Being whom God loves infinitely. "I am not alone, for the Father is with me." He loved Him from eternity, for the pure, spotless image of Himself. He loved Him for laying down His life. He is well pleased for His righteousness' sake. The eye of the all-perfect One rests with perfect complacency on Him. Have you this day come into Christ—this day come under His shield—are this day found in Him? If you are in the love of God, keep yourselves there.

1. *Care not for the love of the world.*—If you were of the

world, the world would love its own. Its best smiles are little worth. The world is a dying thing—a crucified man to them that are in Christ.

2. *Prize the love of God.*—Oh, it is sweet to be in the garden of spices—to have God for your refuge—God rejoicing over you! *First,* This takes all the sting away from affliction. God is love to me. The hand that wounds is the gentlest and most loving. *Second,* This takes their sting from the world's reproaches. *Third,* This makes death sweet. It is a leap into the arms of infinite love, though to some a leap into a dark eternity. Oh, keep yourselves in the love of God!

IV. *Look for mercy.*—You will be incomplete Christians if you do not look for the coming again of the Lord Jesus. If the Table has been sweet today, what will it be when Jesus comes again to receive us to Himself? If His loveletters and love tokens, sent from a far country, be so sweet, what will the Bridegroom Himself be when He comes and takes us by the hand to present us to Himself, and acknowledge us before an assembled world?

1. *You will get an open acquittal on that day.*—Now He gives us sweet acquittal at the bar of conscience. He says: "Peace be unto you." But when it is open, we shall wear the blood-washed robe. It will need to be mercy even at that day.

2. *Perfect deliverance from sin.*—Now He gives us the victory by faith. He gives us to feel the thorn, and to look up for grace sufficient. Then He will take the thorn away. We shall be like Jesus in soul and body. Oh, be casting sweet looks of love toward that day! When a child is expecting an elder brother's return, when he is to bring some gift, how often he runs to the window and watches for his coming! Your Elder Brother is coming with a sweet gift. Oh, cast your eye often toward the clouds, to see if they will break and let His beautiful feet through! Shorten the time by anticipation.

3. *Jesus no more dishonored.*—Honor to the Lamb is a

sweet mercy to a believing soul. A high day like this, when Jesus gets many a crown cast at His feet, is sweet to a believing soul. How much more the day when He shall wear His full crown, and when the slain Lamb shall be fully praised; and when He shall come to be glorified, who once came to be spit upon! That truly shall be mercy to our poor soul. Our cup shall run over.

January 3, 1841.

MESSAGE XXVIII

"The Spirit of the Lord God is upon me; because the Lord hath anointed me to preach good tidings unto the meek; he hath sent me to bind up the broken-hearted, to proclaim liberty to the captives, and the opening of the prison to them that are bound; to proclaim the acceptable year of the Lord, and the day of vengeance of our God: to comfort all that mourn: to appoint unto them that mourn in Zion, to give unto them beauty for ashes, the oil of joy for mourning, the garment of praise for the spirit of heaviness: that they might be called trees of righteousness, the planting of the Lord, that he might be glorified."—ISAIAH 61:1-3.

IT IS SIX YEARS this day since I first preached to you, as your pastor, from these blessed words. These years have rolled past us like a mighty river. It is a solemn thing to look over them. In climbing a lofty mountain, it is pleasant to come every now and then to a resting place, where you may stand and look back. You can thus see the progress you have made, and you can observe the prospect winding all around you. In like manner, in going up the hill of Zion, it is pleasant to come to such a resting place as this day affords, that we may stand and see what progress we have made, and whether we have a wider, brighter prospect of eternal glory. How many have left our company since these six years began! They have gone to render their last account in the world where time is not measured by years. Of some I trust we can say, "Blessed are the dead, for they died in the Lord." Many, I trust, have been born again—passed from death unto life—begun a new life that shall never have an end.

Some, I hope, have been brought to climb a step higher on Jacob's ladder—to get nearer the top of Pisgah, to see more of Canaan's happy land. Some, I fear, have gone back, and walk no more with Jesus. Ye did run well, who did hinder you? You did put your hand to the plow, but you have turned back, and are not fit for the kingdom of God. Some, I fear, are six years nearer to hell; your ear more deaf to the voice of the charmer; your heart more wedded to its idols—more dead to God. Let us solemnly look back this day, both minister and people, and, oh, let us take warning by the errors of the past, and begin a new and better course from this day.

I. *The anointing of the Holy Spirit makes a successful gospel minister.*—So it was in Christ's ministry. "The Spirit of the Lord God is upon me." So it is in every ministry. The more anointing of the Holy Spirit, the more success will the minister have.

You remember the two olive trees that grew close beside the golden candlestick, and emptied the golden oil out of themselves (Zech. 4:12). These represent successful ministers—"anointed ones that stand by the Lord of the whole earth." Oh, see what need there is that ministers be filled with the Spirit; that, like John, they be "in the Spirit on the Lord's day," that Christ's people may be kept "like a lamp that burneth!" You remember John the Baptist. The angel said of him before he was born, "He shall be filled with the Holy Ghost, even from his mother's womb." What then will his success be? "And many of the children of Israel shall he turn to the Lord their God." Oh, learn what need there is that ministers be filled with the Holy Ghost, that they may be converting ministers; that, like John, they may "turn the hearts of the fathers to the children, and the disobedient to the wisdom of the just."

You remember the apostles. Before the day of Pentecost they were dry, sapless trees. They went over the cities of Israel preaching the glad tidings of the kingdom, and yet it would seem they had little or no success. They could not number many spiritual children. But when the day of Pentecost was fully come, when the Spirit came on them like a mighty rushing wind—then behold what a change! Under the first sermon three thousand men were pricked in their heart, and said, "Men and brethren, what must we do?" Oh, see what need we have of a day of Pentecost to begin in the hearts of ministers, that our words may be like fire, and the hearts of the people like wood!

In looking back upon my ministry, I am persuaded that this has been the great thing wanting. We have not been like the green olive trees; we have not been like John the Baptist, filled with the Holy Ghost; we have not been like the apostles on the day of Pentecost, filled as with a mighty rushing wind; we have not been able to say, like the Saviour, "The Spirit of the Lord God is upon me," or you would not be as you are this day. There would not be so many dead sinners among you —slumbering under the voice of gospel mercy, on the very brink of hell. There would not be so many laboring and heavy-laden souls going from mountain to hill, forgetting your resting place. There would not be so many children of light walking in darkness, dull, heavy, beclouded Christians. That is a piercing word: "If they had stood in my counsel, and had caused my people to hear my words, then they should have turned from their evil way, and from the evil of their doings" (Jer. 23:22).

Success is the rule under a living ministry. Want of success is the exception. Oh, pray that if God spare us another year, we may be more like the high priest, who first went into the Holiest of all, and then came out and lifted up his hands and blessed the people! Pray that we may be more like the angels, who always behold the face of our Father, and therefore are like a flame of fire. "He maketh his angels spirits, his minis-

ters a flame of fire." You know that a heated iron, though
blunt, will pierce its way, even where a much sharper instrument, if it be cold, cannot penetrate. So, if only our ministers
be filled with the Spirit, who is like fire, they will pierce into
the hardest hearts, where the sharpest wits cannot find their
way. It was thus with Whitefield: that great man lived so
near to God, he was so full of heavenly joy and of the Spirit
of God, that souls were melted under him like snow in a thaw.
John Newton mentions it as a fact, that, in a single week,
Whitefield received no fewer than a thousand letters from persons distressed in conscience under his preaching. Oh, pray that
we may not be "clouds without water," which indeed have all
the appearance of clouds, but have no rain in them! Pray that
we may come to you as Paul came to the Corinthians, "in
weakness, and in fear, and in much trembling; and that our
speech and our preaching may not be with enticing words of
man's wisdom, but in demonstration of the Spirit and of
power" (I Cor. 2:2-4).

II. *The subject matter of all faithful preaching.*

1. *A faithful minister preaches good tidings to all distressed
consciences.*—This was one great object of Christ's ministry.
"The Lord hath anointed me to preach good tidings unto the
meek." Jesus came to be a Saviour *to the meek*—not the naturally gentle and sweet-tempered, but those who are concerned
about their souls. Men naturally say, "I am rich and increased
with goods, and have need of nothing"; therefore they are
proud, and their tongue walketh through the earth. But
when God begins a work of grace in their heart, He convinces of sin, He humbles them to the dust, and makes them
feel "wretched, and miserable, and poor, and blind, and
naked." Jesus always offered Himself as a Saviour to such.
One poor leper said, "Lord, if thou wilt, thou canst make me
clean." Jesus said, "I will, be thou clean." Nay, He left an
invitation which will be precious to burdened souls even to the

end of the world: "Come unto me, all ye that labor and are heavy laden, and I will give you rest" (Matt. 11:28).

Jesus came *"to bind up the brokenhearted."* There is many a wounded heart that is not broken. The brokenhearted are those who have lost all hope of saving themselves by their own righteousness. As long as a person has hope, the heart remains whole and unbroken. As long as a sailor's wife has hope that her husband's vessel may outride the storm, her heart is calm within her; but when the fatal news comes—when an eyewitness tells that he saw the lifeless body sinking in the waves—the thread of hope is cut asunder, her heart dies within her, she droops, she sits down brokenhearted. As long as an awakened sinner has hope of saving himself, as long as he thinks that self-reformation, weeping over past sins, and resolving against future ones, will clear him before God—so long his heart is calm; but when the fatal news comes, that all he does is done out of a sinful heart, that even "his right- eousnesses are as filthy rags," that "by the deeds of the law no flesh can be justified," then does the heart of the sinner die within him. He says, "It is done now, it is all done now, I never can do anything to justify myself."

Is this the state of your soul? This is a case for Christ. He justifieth the ungodly; He imputes righteousness without works; His blood and righteousness are ready for poor broken- hearted sinners. They are the very souls that answer Him; He is the very Saviour that answers them. Once a broken-hearted woman, who had spent her all upon physicians, and was noth- ing better, but rather worse, came behind Jesus, and touched the hem of His garment. Did He show Himself the Saviour of the brokenhearted? Yes; He said, "Daughter, be of good comfort; thy faith hath made thee whole."

Jesus came *"to proclaim liberty to the captives."* All natural men are slaves. Some are bound, and know it not, like the slave in the West Indies, who could not comprehend what liberty meant. They are corded by their sins, yet say, I am free. Some are bound and know it. They are awakened to feel the galling chains of lust; they feel their feet sinking in miry clay. Some of you know what it is to sin and weep, and sin and weep again. "The way of transgressors is hard." Jesus came to be a Saviour to such. He came not only to be our righteousness, but to be a fountain of life. "In the Lord have I righteousness and strength." Once there was a man possessed by a legion of devils, exceeding fierce, who wore no clothes, and dwelt among the tombs. But Jesus commanded the unclean spirit to go out of him, and "he sat down at the feet of Jesus, clothed and in his right mind."

One great object of our ministry among you has been to bring good tidings to distressed consciences. Blessed be God, there have always been some distressed consciences among you from the first day until now. In almost all our parishes, in these remarkable times, there are many souls under conviction of sin. There are always some who feel uneasy under the Word—who feel that their heart is not right with God, that they are slaves of sin, and who go on from day to day carrying a heavy burden. I have always tried to speak to such souls. I have shown you plainly that you are not safe because you are anxious; that you need to be *in* Christ Jesus; that these convictions may die away. I have tried to let down the gospel cord within your reach. I have showed you that Christ offers Himself in a peculiar manner to such as you. "The whole have no need of a physician, but they who are sick."

How often Brainerd records it in his journal, that a heavy-laden soul was brought to true and solid comfort in Christ this day! Why have I so seldom to record the same thing of weary souls among you? For years I have gone among you preaching the only foundation of a sinner's peace. Yet how few have had a lively and soul-refreshing view of Christ! How few can say, "What things were gain to me, these I count loss for Christ!" Ah! my friends, the fault lies with you or with me, for God has no pleasure in a burdened soul. "Oh, that ye had hearkened to my commandments, for then had your peace been like a river, and your righteousness like the waves of the sea!"

2. *A faithful pastor comforts mourners in Zion.*—This was another great object of Christ's ministry—"to comfort all that mourn." There are many things to bring a cloud over the brow of a Christian. There are outward troubles. "Many are the afflictions of the righteous." Persecutions will come: "a man's foes shall be they of his own household." Temptations will come; they are common to man. Sloth and want of watchfulness often bring into darkness (S.S. 5:2-8). The body of sin often makes us cry, "O wretched man!" But the Lord Jesus has the tongue of the learned, to speak a word in season to them that are weary. The religion of Jesus is eminently the religion of joy. He does not love to see His church sitting in ashes, mourning, and heavy with sorrow. He loves to see her putting on His beautiful righteousness, filled with the Holy Spirit of joy, and covered with the garment of praise, waving like green trees of righteousness to His glory.

Once "Peter walked on the water to go to Jesus; but when he saw the wind boisterous, he began to sink, and cried, Lord, save me. And immediately Jesus stretched forth his hand and caught him, and said unto him, O thou of little faith, wherefore didst thou doubt?" Christ has an almighty arm for sinking disciples to cling to. Once two disciples were walking towards a village north of Jerusalem. They talked earnestly together to beguile the way, and they were sad. A stranger drew near, and went with them; and as He went He expounded to them, in all the Scriptures, the things concerning Jesus. In breaking of bread He was revealed to them, and left them exclaiming, "Did not our hearts burn within us?" So Jesus reveals Himself to His own to this day, and makes the sad bosom burn with holy joy.

This has been one of the chief objects of my ministry among you. That scripture has been for some time deeply engraved upon my memory and heart, "He gave some pastors and teachers, for the perfecting of the saints, for the work of the ministry, for the edifying of the body of Christ" (Eph. 4:11, 12); and, accordingly, it has been my endeavor to lead mourners in Zion to a meeting with Christ, who alone can restore comfort to them. What has been our success? I fear there are not many of you as happy as you might be. Are not most, like Peter, sinking; or sad, like the two going to Emmaus? Are not most in all our parishes rather seeking than finding rest? How little is there among you of the "beauty—the oil of joy, and the garment of praise!" How few can truly sing the One Hundred and Third Psalm; how few feel their sins removed, as far as east is from the west; how few keep themselves in the love of God; how few have Christ dwelling in their hearts by faith; how few are filled with all the fullness of God, and rejoice with joy unspeakable, and full of glory!

How often Brainerd mentions in his journal: "Numbers wept affectionately, and to appearance unfeignedly, so that the Spirit of God seemed to be moving on the face of the assembly." And again, "They seemed willing to have their ears bored to the doorposts of God's house, and to be His servants forever!" How little is there of this divine presence and holy impression in our assemblies! How many a meeting for prayer has lost the fervency which once it had! Ah! surely the fault lies with you or with me. Immanuel is still in the midst of us. He is still "full of grace and truth"; He is "the same yesterday, to-day, and for ever." Oh, that the little flock in this place were covered with His beauty, filled with His holy joy, and clothed with His garment of praise!

3. *A faithful watchman preaches a free Saviour to all the world.*—This was the great object of Christ's ministry—"To proclaim the acceptable year of the Lord." "Unto you, O men,

I call," was the very motto of His life. On the year of jubilee the silver trumpet was made to sound throughout the whole land. Every man might return to his possession; every slave might go free. Christ felt that the trumpet of the true jubilee was committed to Him; and therefore His feet were beautiful upon the mountains, and He went about continually publishing glad tidings of peace. Once He stood among a crowd of un-believing Jews. His word was, "Him that cometh unto me I will in no wise cast out"; and again, to a similar crowd He said, "I am the door; by me if any man enter in, he shall be saved." When He died upon the cross, the priests scoffed at Him, the people wagged their heads at Him, the soldiers cast lots for His garment; but "the veil of the temple was rent from the top to the bottom," signifying that the way into the Holiest was now made manifest, that any sinner might enter in and be saved.

When He arose from the dead, there were but five hundred brethren who believed on His name: the whole world was lying in the wicked one; every creature under the frown of an angry God. "Go ye," said He, "into all the world, and preach the gospel to every creature." When Laodicea became a dead and lukewarm church, fit only to be spued out of Christ's mouth, you would have expected a message of judgment. No, He sends one of free, boundless, glorious grace. "If any man will hear my voice and open the door, I will come in to him."

This has been the great object of our ministry. In all our parishes, at the present day, the great mass of the people are living without Christ, and without God, and without hope in the world. The most, even of church-going people, it is to be feared, are "dead in trespasses and sins." Ever since coming among you, our great object has been to awaken such. We have proclaimed the acceptable year of the Lord, and the day of vengeance of our God. We have told you that Christ is freely offered to you in your present condition, whatever that may be; that though you have lived in sin, and are now living in sin, and God is angry with you every day, still Christ is free to you every day. We have told you that though you do not care for your soul, still Christ cares for it; though you are lost, still Christ is seeking the lost; though you are loving your simplicity, delighting in scorning, and hating knowledge, still Christ is crying after you; that before you repent, and before you believe, Christ is freely offered unto you: "All day long have I stretched out my hands to a disobedient and gainsaying people."

What has been our success? Blessed be God, there are some of you who have fled for refuge to the hope set before you; but the most sleep on. Six acceptable years have passed over you. A year of gospel preaching is an acceptable year; a year of revival, when many have been pressing into the kingdom of God, is still more an acceptable year: both these have passed over you. The door has stood open all this time, and any sinner among you might have entered in. Bibles, ministers, Providence, the Spirit striving—all have been pressing you to enter in. But you are still without—Christless, unpardoned, unsaved.

What can you look for but "the day of vengeance?" *A year* of mercy is past, *a day* of vengeance is coming. God pleads long, but judgment will be the work of a day. How many among you will never see such another season of grace as that which lately passed over you! You will probably never again have such an opportunity to be saved. "The harvest is past, the summer is ended, and you are not saved." Many of you will one day wish you had never heard of the acceptable year; many of you will wish that you had never heard the preached gospel—that you had perished before the glorious work of God began. "Oh that ye were wise, that ye understood this: that ye would consider your latter end."

St. Peter's, Dundee, November 27, 1842.

Message XXIX

WHY CHILDREN SHOULD FLY TO CHRIST WITHOUT DELAY.

"O satisfy us early with thy mercy; that we may rejoice and be glad all our days."—Psalm 90:14.

THE late Countess of Huntingdon was not only rich in this world, but rich in faith, and an heir of the kingdom. When she was about nine years of age she saw the dead body of a little child of her own age carried to the grave. She followed the funeral; and it was there that the Holy Spirit first opened her heart to convince her that she needed a Saviour. My dear little children, when you look upon the year that has come to an end, may the Holy Spirit bring you to the same conviction; may the still small voice say in your heart, Flee now from the wrath to come. Fly to the Lord Jesus without delay. "Escape for thy life: look not behind thee."

I. *Because life is very short.*—"The days of our years are three-score years and ten; and if by reason of strength they be four-score years, yet is their strength labor and sorrow, for it is soon cut off, and we fly away." Even those who live longest, when they come to die, look back on their life as upon a dream. It is "like a sleep." The hours pass rapidly away during sleep; and when you awake, you hardly know that any time is passed. Such is life. It is like "a tale that is told." When you are listening to an entertaining tale, it fills up the time, and makes the hours steal swiftly by. Even so "we spend our years as a tale that is told."

You have seen a ship upon the river, when the sailors were all on board, the anchor heaved, and the sails spread to the wind, how it glided swiftly past, bounding over the billows; so is it with your days: "They are passed away as the swift ships." Or perhaps you have seen an eagle, when from its nest in the top of the rocks it darts down with quivering wing to seize upon some smaller bird, how swiftly it flies; so is it

with your life. It flies "as the eagle hasteth to the prey." You
have noticed the mist on the brow of the mountain early in the
morning, and you have seen, when the sun rose with his warm,
cheering beams, how soon the mist melted away. And "what is
your life? It is even a vapor that appeareth for a little time,
and then vanisheth away."

Some of you may have seen how short life is in those
around you. "Your fathers, where are they? And the prophets,
do they live forever?" How many friends have you lying in the
grave! Some of you have more friends in the grave than in
this world. They were carried away "as with a flood," and we
are fast hastening after them. In a little while the church
where you sit will be filled with new worshipers, a new voice
will lead the psalm, a new man of God fill the pulpit. It is an
absolute certainty that, in a few years, all of you who read this
will be lying in the grave. Oh, what need, then, to fly to Christ
without delay! How great a work you have to do! How short
the time you have to do it in! You have to flee from wrath,
to come to Christ, to be born again, to receive the Holy Spirit,
to be made meet for glory. It is high time that you seek the
Lord. The longest lifetime is short enough. Seek conviction of
sin and an interest in Christ. "Oh, satisfy me early with thy
mercy, that I may rejoice and be glad all my days."

II. *Because life is very uncertain.*—Men are like grass:
"In the morning, it groweth up and flourisheth: in the evening, it is cut down and withereth." Most men are cut down
while they are green. More than one-half of the human race
die before they reach manhood. In the city of Glasgow alone,
more than one-half of the people die before the age of twenty.
Of most men it may be said, "He cometh forth as a flower,
and is cut down." Death is very certain, but the time is
very uncertain. Some may think they shall not die because
they are in good health; but you forget that many die in
good health by accidents and other causes. Again, riches

and ease and comforts, good food and good clothing, are no safeguards against dying. It is written, "The rich man also died, and was buried." Kind physicians and kind friends cannot keep you from dying. When death comes, he laughs at the efforts of physicians, he tears you from the tenderest arms. Some think they shall not die because they are not pre-pared to die; but you forget that most people die unprepared, unconverted, unsaved. You forget that it is written of the strait gate, "Few there be that find it." Most people lie down in a dark grave, and a darker eternity.

Some of you may think you shall not die because you are young. You forget that one-half of the human race die be-fore they reach manhood. The half of the inhabitants of this town die before they are twenty. Oh, if you had to stand as often as I have beside the dying bed of little children, to see their wild looks and outstretched hands and to hear their dying cries, you would see how needful it is to fly to Christ now. It may be your turn next. Are you prepared to die? Have you fled for refuge to Jesus? Have you found forgiveness? "Boast not thyself of tomorrow; for thou knowest not what a day may bring forth."

III. *Most that are ever saved fly to Christ when young.*— It was so in the days of our blessed Saviour. Those that were come to years were too wise and prudent to be saved by the blood of the Son of God, and He revealed it to those that were younger and had less wisdom. "I thank thee, O Father, Lord of heaven and earth, because thou hast hid these things from the wise and prudent, and revealed them unto babes. Even so, Father, for so it seemed good in thy sight." "He gathers the lambs with his arm, and carries them in his bosom." So it has been in almost all times of the revival of religion. If you ask aged Christians, the most of them will tell you that they were made anxious about their souls when young.

Oh, what a reason is here for seeking an early inbringing to Christ! If you are not saved in youth, it is likely you never will be. There is a tide in the affairs of souls. There are times which may be called converting times. All holy times are peculiarly converting times. The Sabbath is the great day for gathering in souls—it is Christ's market day. It is the great harvest day of souls. I know there is a generation rising up that would fain trample the Sabbath beneath their feet; but prize you the Sabbath day. The time of affliction is converting time. When God takes away those you love best, and you say, "This is the finger of God," remember it is Christ wanting to get in to save you: open the door and let Him in. The time of the striving of the Holy Spirit is converting time. If you feel your heart pricked in reading the Bible, or in hearing your teacher, "quench not the Spirit"; "resist not the Holy Ghost"; "grieve not the Holy Spirit of God." Youth is converting time. "Suffer little children to come unto me, and forbid them not." Oh, you that are lambs, seek to be gathered with the arm of the Saviour, and carried in His gentle bosom. Come to trust under the Saviour's wings. "Yet there is room."

IV. *Because it is happier to be in Christ than out of Christ.* —Many that read these words are saying in their heart, It is a dull thing to be religious. Youth is the time for pleasure—the time to eat, drink, and be merry; to rise up to play. Now, I know that youth is the time for pleasure; the foot is more elastic then, the eye more full of life, the heart more full of gladness. But that is the very reason I say youth is the time to fly to Christ. It is far happier to be in Christ than to be out of Christ.

1. *It satisfies the heart.*—I never will deny that there are pleasures to be found out of Christ. The song and the dance, and the exciting game, are most engaging to young hearts. But ah! think a moment. Is it not an awful thing to be happy

when you are unsaved? Would it not be dreadful to see a
man sleeping in a house all on fire? And is it not enough
to make one shudder to see you dancing and making merry
when God is angry with you every day?

Think again. Are there not infinitely sweeter pleasures to
be had in Christ? "Whoso drinketh of this water shall thirst
again; but whoso drinketh of the water that I shall give him
shall never thirst." "In thy presence is fullness of joy: at thy
right hand are pleasures for evermore." To be forgiven, to
be at peace with God, to have Him for a Father, to have Him
loving us and smiling on us, to have the Holy Spirit coming
into our hearts, and making us holy, this is worth a whole
eternity of your pleasures. "A day in thy courts is better than
a thousand." Oh, to be "satisfied with favor, and full with
the blessing of the Lord!" Your daily bread becomes sweeter.
You eat your meat "with gladness and singleness of heart,
praising God." Your foot is more light and bounding, for
it bears a ransomed body. Your sleep is sweeter at night, for
"so he giveth his beloved sleep." The sun shines more
lovingly, and the earth wears a pleasanter smile, because you
can say, "My Father made them all."

2. *It makes you glad all your days.*—The pleasures of sin
are only "for a season"; they do not last. But to be brought
to Christ is like the dawning of an eternal day; it spreads
the serenity of heaven over all the days of our pilgrimage.
In suffering days, what will the world do for you? "Like
vinegar upon niter, so is he that singeth songs to a heavy
heart." Believe me, there are days at hand when you will
"say of laughter, It is mad; and of mirth, What doeth it?"
But if you fly to Jesus Christ now, He will cheer you in the
days of darkness. When the winds are contrary and the waves
are high, Jesus will draw near, and say, "Be not afraid; it is
I." That voice stills the heart in the stormiest hour. When
the world reproaches you, and casts out your name as evil,

when the doors are shut, Jesus will come in, and say, "Peace be unto you." Who can tell the sweetness and the peace which Jesus gives in such an hour? One little girl that was early brought to Christ felt this when long confined to a sickbed. "I am not weary of my bed," she said, "for my bed is green, and all that I meet with is perfumed with love to me. The time, night and day, is made sweet to me by the Lord. When it is evening, it is pleasant; and when it is morning, I am refreshed."

Last of all, in a dying day, what will the world do for you? The dance, and the song, and the merry companion, will then lose all their power to cheer you. Not one jest more; not one smile more. "Oh, that you were wise, that you would understand this, and consider your latter end!" But that is the very time when the soul of one in Christ rejoices with a joy unspeakable and full of glory. "Jesus can make a dying bed softer than downy pillows are." You remember, when Stephen came to die, they battered his gentle breast with cruel stones; but he kneeled down and said, "Lord Jesus, receive my spirit." John Newton tells us of a Christian girl who, on her dying day, said, "If this be dying, it is a pleasant thing to die." Another little Christian, of eight years of age, came home ill of the malady of which he died. His mother asked him if he were afraid to die. "No," said he, "I wish to die, if it be God's will: that sweet word, Sleep in Jesus, makes me happy when I think on the grave."

"My little children, of whom I travail in birth again till Christ be formed in you," if you would live happy and die happy, come now to a Saviour. The door of the ark is wide open. Enter now, or it may be never.

———

Message XXX

WHY IS GOD A STRANGER IN THE LAND?

"O the hope of Israel, the Saviour thereof in time of trouble, why shouldest thou
be as a stranger in the land, as a wayfaring man that turneth aside to tarry
for a night? Why shouldest thou be as a man astonished, as a mighty man
that cannot save? Yet thou, O Lord, art in the midst of us, and we are
called by thy name; leave us not."—JEREMIAH 14:8, 9.

IN MANY PARTS of Scotland there is good reason to
think that God is not a stranger, but that the Lord Jesus
has been making Himself known, and that the Holy Spirit
has been quickening whom He will. Still, in most parts of
our land, it is to be feared that God is a stranger, and like
a wayfaring man who turneth aside to tarry for a night.

1. How few conversions are there in the midst of us!
When God is present with power in any land, then there are
always many awakened to a sense of sin, and flocking to
Christ. One godly minister, speaking of such a time, says,
"There were tokens of God's presence in almost every house.
It was a time of joy in families, on account of salvation
being brought unto them. Parents were rejoicing over their
children as newborn, husbands over their wives, and wives
over their husbands. The town seemed to be full of the
presence of God. It never was so full of love nor of joy,
and yet never so full of distress, as it was then." We have
nothing of the kind amongst us. Alas! what a dismal contrast do most of our families present! How many families
where there is not one living soul!

2. How much deadness there is among true Christians!
In times of reviving, when God is present with power in
any land, not only are unconverted persons awakened and
made to flee to Christ, but those who were in Christ before,
receive new measures of the Spirit; they undergo, as it were,
a second new birth; they are brought into the palace of the
King, and say, "Let him kiss me with the kisses of his

mouth, for thy love is better than wine." A dear Christian in such a time says, "My wickedness, as I am in myself, has long appeared to me perfectly ineffable—like an infinite deluge, or mountains over my head. I know not how to express better what my sins appear to me to be, than by heaping infinite upon infinite, and multiplying infinite by infinite. Very often these expressions are in my mind, and in my mouth— infinite upon infinite, infinite upon infinite." How little of this feeling is there amongst us! How few seem to feel sin as an infinite evil! How plain that God is a stranger in the land!

3. How great is the boldness of sinners in sin! As in Jeremiah's day, so in ours, many seem as if "their neck were an iron sinew, and their brow brass." When God is present with power, then open sinners, though they may remain unconverted, are often much restrained. There is an awe of God upon their spirits. Alas! it is not so amongst us. The floodgates of sin are opened. "They declare their sin as Sodom, they hide it not." Is it not, then, a time to cry, "Oh, the hope of Israel, the Saviour thereof"?

Should we not solemnly ask this question, What are the reasons God is such a stranger in this land?

I. *In ministers.*—Let us begin with those who bear the vessels of the sanctuary.

1. It is to be feared *there is much unfaithful preaching to the unconverted.* Jeremiah complained of this in his day: "They have healed the hurt of the daughter of my people slightly, saying, Peace, peace, when there is no peace." Is there no reason for the same complaint in our own day? The great part of all our congregations are out of Christ, and lying night and day under the wrath of the Lord God Almighty; and yet it is to be feared that the most of the minister's anxiety and painstaking is *not* taken up about them, that his sermons are *not* chiefly occupied with their case.

All the words of men and angels cannot describe the dreadfulness of being Christless; and yet, it is to be feared, we do not speak to those who are so with anything like sufficient plainness, frequency, and urgency. Alas! how few ministers are like the angels at Sodom, mercifully bold to lay hands on lingering sinners! How few obey that word of Jude, "Save with fear, pulling them out of the fire!"

Many of those who deal faithfully, do not deal tenderly. We have more of the bitterness of man than of the tenderness of God. We do not *yearn over* men in the bowels of Jesus Christ. Paul wrote of "the enemies of the cross of Christ" with tears in his eyes! There is little of his weeping among ministers now. "Knowing the terrors of the Lord," Paul persuaded men. There is little of this persuading spirit among ministers now. How can we wonder that the dry bones are very, very dry—that God is a stranger in the land?

2. It is to be feared *there is much unfaithfulness in setting forth Christ as a refuge for sinners.* When a sinner is newly converted, he would fain persuade every one to come to Christ; the way is so plain, so easy, so precious. He thinks, Oh, if I were but a minister, how I would persuade men! This is a true feeling and a right feeling. But oh, how little is there of this among ministers! David said, "I believed, therefore have I spoken." Few are like David in this. Paul said he was "determined to know nothing among men but Jesus Christ, and Him crucified." Few are like Paul in this. Many do not make it the end of their ministry to testify of Jesus as the hidingplace for sinners. It is to be feared that many are like the scribes and Pharisees: they hold the door in their hand; they enter not in themselves, and them that are entering in they hinder. Some set forth Christ plainly and faithfully, but where is Paul's *beseeching* men to be reconciled? We do not invite sinners tenderly; we do not gently woo them to Christ; we do not authoritatively bid them to the

marriage; we do not *compel* them to come in; we do not travail in birth till Christ be formed in them the hope of glory. Oh, who can wonder that God is such a stranger in the land?

II. *In Christian people.*

1. *In regard to the Word of God.* There seems *little thirst for hearing the Word of God among Christians now.* As a delicate stomach makes a man eat sparingly, so must Christians seem sparing in their diet in our day. Many Christians seem to mingle pride with the hearing of the Word. They come rather as judges than as children. Few behave themselves as a weaned child. Most seem to prefer the seat of Moses to the seat of Mary at the feet of Christ. Many come to hear the word of a man that shall die, and not the Word of the living God. Oh, should not Christians be taught this prayer: "Oh, the hope of Israel, why shouldest thou be a stranger in the land?"

2. *In regard to prayer.* There is much ploughing and much sowing, but *very little harrowing in of the seed by prayer.* God and your conscience are witnesses how little you pray. You know you would be men of power if you were men of prayer, and yet ye will not pray. Unstable as water, you do not excel. Luther set apart his three best hours for prayer. How few Luthers we have now! John Welch spent seven hours a day in prayer. How few Welches we have now!

It is to be feared *there is little intercession among Christians now.* The high priest carried the names of the children of Israel upon his shoulders and breast when he drew near to God—a picture of what Christ now does, and all Christians should do. God and your conscience are witnesses how little you intercede for your children, your servants, your neighbors, the church of your fathers, and the wicked on every side of you; how little you pray for ministers, for the gift of the Spirit, for the conversion of the world.

It is to be feared *there is little union in prayer.* Christians are ashamed to meet together to pray. Christ has promised, "If two of you shall *agree* on earth, touching something that ye shall ask, it shall be done for you of my Father." Many Christians neglect this promise. In the Acts, we find that when the apostles and disciples were praying together, "the place was shaken where they were assembled *together,* and they were all filled with the Holy Ghost, and they spake the word of God with boldness." Oh, how often and how long have we despised this way of obtaining the outpouring of the Spirit! Do not some persons speak slightingly of united prayer? Here is one reason God commands the clouds that they rain no rain on us. He waits till we seek Him *together,* and *then* He will open the windows of heaven and pour down a blessing. Oh, that all Christians would lift up the cry, "Oh, the hope of Israel!"

III. *In unconverted souls.*—There is much to blame in ministers, and much in the people of God, but most of all to blame in unconverted souls.

1. *Sinners in our day have great insensibility as to their lost condition.* Many know that they never believed on the Son of God, and yet they are smiling and happy. Many know that they were never born again, and that the Bible says they cannot see the kingdom of God; and yet their step is as light, and their laugh as loud, as if they were heirs of the kingdom of God, instead of heirs of hell! It is this that keeps God away, and makes Him a stranger in the land.

2. *Sinners in our day have great insensibility as to their need of Jesus Christ.* The Bible declares Him to be the Friend of sinners; yet how many read this who are contented to live without knowing Him! Though Christians are always speaking of the excellency of Christ, that He is the chiefest among ten thousand, and altogether lovely; yet most see no form nor comeliness in Christ, no beauty that they should

desire Him. They are willing to hear of heaven or hell rather than of Christ. Ah! this is the crowning sin of Scotland, contempt of Christ, rejection of a freely offered Saviour! Oh, ye deaf adders, that will not hear the voice of the charmers, it is *you* that make God a stranger in the land, and like a wayfaring man that turneth aside to tarry for a night!

3. *There has been much resisting of the Spirit in our day.* In some parts of Scotland this is eminently true. Many have been pricked to the heart, and yet have smothered their convictions. Some have been brought to intense anxiety about their souls, but have looked back, like Lot's wife, and become pillars of salt! Oh, it is this that keeps God away!

Dear unconverted sinners, ye little know how concerned you should be that this be a time of reviving from the presence of the Lord. It is not our part to tell of coming judgments, of fire from heaven or fire from hell; but this we can plainly see, that unless the Spirit of God shall come down on our parishes like rain on the mown grass, many souls that are now in the land of peace shall soon be in the world of tossing and anguish! There may be no sudden judgments; hell may not be rained down from heaven, as upon Sodom; the earth may not yawn to receive her prey, as in the camp of Israel; but Sabbath-breakers, liars, swearers, drunkards, unclean persons, formalists, worldlings, and hypocrites, yea, all Christless souls, will quietly slip away, one by one, into an undone eternity! Come, then, and let every believer, and, above all, every minister, stir up his heart to lay hold on God and cry, "Oh, the hope of Israel, the Saviour thereof in time of trouble, *why* shouldest thou be as a stranger in the land, and as a wayfaring man that turneth aside to tarry for a night?"

It has been the practice of many ministers in England and Scotland to hold a concert for prayer every Saturday morning, from seven to eight o'clock. Several ministers of our own church have been meeting at the throne of grace on Saturday evening, at seven o'clock. Many congregations in different parts of Scotland have agreed to a concert for prayer in secret, and in the family, from eight to nine on Sabbath mornings.

Might not the Christian ministers and people of Scotland, while separated in body, in this manner maintain union in prayer so that the cloud of blessing, now like a man's hand, might spread over the whole sky, and bring times of refreshing from the presence of the Lord?

MESSAGE XXXI

I LOVE THE LORD'S DAY

"The Sabbath was made for man."

DEAR FELLOW COUNTRYMEN, as a servant of God in this dark and cloudy day, I feel constrained to lift up my voice in behalf of the entire sanctification of the Lord's Day. The daring attack that is now made by some of the directors of the Edinburgh and Glasgow Railway on the law of God and the peace of our Scottish Sabbath, the blasphemous motion which they mean to propose to the shareholders next February, and the wicked pamphlets which are now being circulated in thousands, full of all manner of lies and impieties, call loudly for the calm, deliberate testimony of all faithful ministers and private Christians in behalf of God's holy day. In the name of all God's people in this town and in this land, I commend for your consideration the following reasons for loving the Lord's day:

I. *Because it is the Lord's Day.*—"This is the day which the Lord hath made; we will rejoice, and be glad in it." (Ps. 118:24). "I was in the Spirit on the Lord's day" (Rev. 1:10). It is His, by example. It is the day on which He rested from

His amazing work of redemption. Just as God rested on the seventh day from all His works, wherefore God blessed the Sabbath day, and hallowed it; so the Lord Jesus rested on this day from all His agony, and pain, and humiliation. "There remaineth therefore the keeping of a sabbath to the people of God" (Heb. 4:9). The Lord's Day is His property, just as the Lord's Supper is the supper belonging to Christ. It is His table. He is the bread. He is the wine. He invites the guests. He fills them with joy and with the Holy Ghost. So it is with the Lord's Day. All days of the year are Christ's, but He hath marked out one in seven as peculiarly His own. "He hath made it" or marked it out. Just as He planted a garden in Eden, so He hath fenced about this day and made it His own.

This is the reason we love it, and would keep it entire. We love everything that is Christ's. We love *His Word*. It is better to us than thousands of gold and silver. "O how we love His law! it is our study all the day." We love *His house*. It is our trysting-place with Christ, where He meets with us and communes with us from off the mercy seat. We love *His table*. It is His banqueting-house, where His banner over us is love—where He looses our bonds, and anoints our eyes, and makes our hearts burn with holy joy. We love *His people*, because they are His, members of His body, washed in His blood, filled with His Spirit, our brothers and sisters for eternity. And we love the *Lord's Day*, because it is His. Every hour of it is dear to us—sweeter than honey, more precious than gold. It is the day He rose for our justification. It reminds us of His love, and His finished work, and His rest. And we may boldly say that that man does not love the Lord Jesus Christ who does not love the entire Lord's Day.

Oh, Sabbath-breaker, whoever you are, you are a sacrilegious robber! When you steal the hours of the Lord's Day for business or for pleasure, you are robbing Christ of the precious

hours which He claims as His own. Would you not be
shocked if a plan were deliberately proposed for breaking
through the fence of the Lord's Table, and turning it into a
common meal, or a feast for the profligate and the drunkard?
Would not your best feelings be harrowed to see the silver
cup of communion made a cup of revelry in the hand of
the drunkard? And yet what better is the proposal of our
railway directors? *"The Lord's Day" is as much His day as
"the Lord's Table" is His table.* Surely we may well say, in
the words of Dr. Love, that eminent servant of Christ, now
gone to the Sabbath above, "Cursed is that gain, cursed is
that recreation, cursed is that health, which is gained by
criminal encroachments on this sacred day."

II. *Because it is a relic of paradise and type of heaven.*—
The first Sabbath dawned on the bowers of a sinless paradise.
When Adam was created in the image of his Maker, he was
put into the garden to dress it and to keep it. No doubt this
called forth all his energies. To train the luxuriant vine, to
gather the fruit of the fig tree and palm, to conduct the
water to the fruit trees and flowers, required all his time and
all his skill. Man was never made to be idle. Still, when the
Sabbath day came round, his rural implements were all laid
aside; the garden no longer was his care. His calm, pure
mind looked beyond things seen into the world of eternal
realities. He walked with God in the garden, seeking deeper
knowledge of Jehovah and His ways, his heart burning more
and more with holy love, and his lips overflowing with seraphic praise. *Even in paradise man needed a Sabbath.* Without it Eden itself would have been incomplete. How little
they know the joys of Eden, the delight of a close and holy
walk with God, who would wrest from Scotland this relic
of a sinless world!

It is also the type of heaven. When a believer lays aside
his pen or loom, brushes aside his worldly cares, leaving

them behind him with his weekday clothes, and comes up
to the house of God, it is like the morning of the resurrection,
the day when we shall come out of great tribulation into the
presence of God and the Lamb. When he sits under the
preached Word, and hears the voice of the shepherd leading
and feeding his soul, it reminds him of the day when the
Lamb that is in the midst of the throne shall feed him and
lead him to living fountains of waters. When he joins in
the psalm of praise, it reminds him of the day when his
hands shall strike the harp of God—

> "Where congregations ne'er break up,
> And Sabbaths have no end."

When he retires, and meets with God in secret in his closet,
or, like Isaac, in some favorite spot near his dwelling, it reminds him of the day when "he shall be a pillar in the house
of our God, and go no more out."

This is the reason we love the Lord's Day. This is the reason we "call the Sabbath a delight." A well-spent Sabbath
we feel to be a day of heaven upon earth. For this reason we
wish our Sabbaths to be wholly given to God. We love to
spend the whole time in the public and private exercises of
God's worship, except so much as is taken up in the works of
necessity and mercy. We love to rise early on that morning,
and to sit up late, that we may have a long day with God.

How many may know from this that they will never be in
heaven! A straw on the surface can tell which way the
stream is flowing. Do you abhor a holy Sabbath? Is it a
kind of hell to you to be with those who are strict in keeping
the Lord's Day? The writer of these lines once felt as you do.
You are restless and uneasy. You say, "Behold, what a weariness is it!" "When will the Sabbath be gone, that we may
sell corn?" Ah! soon, very soon, and you will be in hell.
Hell is the only place for you. Heaven is one long, never-
ending, holy Sabbath day. There are no Sabbaths in hell.

III. *Because it is a day of blessings.*—When God instituted the Sabbath in paradise, it is said, "God blessed the Sabbath day, and sanctified it" (Gen. 2:3). He not only set it apart as a sacred day, but made it a day of blessing. Again, when the Lord Jesus rose from the dead on the first day of the week before dawn, He revealed Himself the same day to two disciples going to Emmaus, and made their hearts burn within them (Luke 24:13). The same evening He came and stood in the midst of the disciples, and said, "Peace be unto you"; and He breathed on them and said, "Receive ye the Holy Ghost" (John 20:19). Again, after eight days, that is, *the next Lord's Day,* Jesus came and stood in the midst, and revealed Himself with unspeakable grace to unbelieving Thomas (John 20:26). It was on the Lord's Day, also, that the Holy Spirit was poured out at Pentecost (Acts 2:1; cf. Lev. 23:15, 16). That beginning of all spiritual blessings, that first revival of the Christian Church, was on the Lord's Day. It was on the same day that the beloved John, an exile on the seagirt isle of Patmos, far away from the assembly of the saints, was filled with the Holy Spirit, and received his heavenly revelation.

So that in all ages, from the beginning of the world, and in every place where there is a believer, the Sabbath has been a day of double blessing. It is so still, and will be, though all God's enemies should gnash their teeth at it. True, God is a God of free grace, and confines His working to no time or place; but it is equally true, and all the scoffs of the infidel cannot alter it, that it pleases Him to bless His Word most on the Lord's Day. All God's faithful ministers in every land can bear witness that sinners are converted most frequently on the Lord's Day—that Jesus comes in and shows Himself through the lattice of ordinances oftenest on His own day. Saints, like John, are filled with the Spirit on the Lord's Day, and enjoy calm, deep views into eternity.

Unhappy men, who are striving to rob our beloved Scotland of this day of double blessing, "ye know not what you do." You would wrest from our dear countrymen the day when God opens the windows of heaven and pours down a blessing. You want to make the heavens over Scotland like brass, and the hearts of our people like iron. Is it the sound of the golden bells of our everliving High Priest on the mountains of our land, and the breathing of His Holy Spirit over so many of our parishes, that has roused up your satanic exertions to drown the sweet sound of mercy by the deafening roar of railway carriages? Is it the returning vigor of the revived and chastened Church of Scotland that has opened the torrents of blasphemy which you pour forth against the Lord of the Sabbath? Have your own withered souls no need of a drop from heaven? May it not be the case that some of you are blaspheming the very day on which your own soul might have been saved? Is it not possible that some of you may remember, with tears of anguish in hell, the exertions which you are now making, against light and against warning, to bring down a withering blight on your own souls and on the religion of Scotland?

To those who are God's children in this land, I would now, in the name of our common Saviour, who is Lord of the Sabbath day, address a word of exhortation.

I. *Prize the Lord's Day.*—The more that others despise and trample on it, love you it all the more. The louder the storm of blasphemy howls around you, sit the closer at the feet of Jesus. "He must reign till he has put all enemies under his feet." Diligently improve all holy time. It should be the busiest day of the seven; but only in the business of eternity. Avoid sin on that holy day. God's children should avoid sin every day, but most of all on the Lord's Day. It is a day of double cursing as well as of double blessing. The world will have to answer dreadfully for sins committed in holy time. Spend the Lord's Day in the Lord's presence. Spend it as a day in heaven. Spend much of it in praise and in works of mercy, as Jesus did.

II. *Defend the Lord's Day.*—Lift up a calm, undaunted testimony against all the profanations of the Lord's Day. Use all your influence, whether as a statesman, a magistrate, a master, a father, or a friend, both publicly and privately, to defend the entire Lord's Day. This duty is laid upon you in the Fourth Commandment. Never see the Sabbath broken without reproving the breaker of it. Even worldly men, with all their pride and contempt for us, cannot endure to be convicted of Sabbath breaking. Always remember God and the Bible are on your side, and that you will soon see these men cursing their own sin and folly when too late. Let all God's children in Scotland lift up a united testimony especially against these three public profanations of the Lord's Day:

1. *The keeping open of reading rooms.*—In this town, and in all the large towns of Scotland, I am told, you may find in the public reading rooms many of our men of business turning over the newspapers and magazines at all hours of the Lord's Day; and especially on Sabbath evenings, many of these places are filled like a little church. Ah, guilty men! how plainly you show that you are on the broad road that leadeth to destruction. If you were a murderer or an adulterer, perhaps you would not dare to deny this. Do you not know, and all the sophistry of hell cannot disprove it, that the same God who said, "Thou shalt not kill," said also, "Remember the Sabbath day to keep it holy?" The murderer who is dragged to the gibbet, and the polished Sabbath breaker, are one in the sight of God.

2. *The keeping open of public houses.*—Public houses are the curse of Scotland. I never see a sign, "Licensed to sell spirits," without thinking that it is a license to ruin souls. They are the yawning avenues to poverty and rags in this life, and,

as another has said, *"the short cut to hell."* Is it to be tamely
borne in this land of light and reformation, that these pest-
houses and dens of iniquity—these man-traps for precious
souls—shall be open on the Sabbath, nay, that they shall be
enriched and kept afloat by this unholy traffic, many of them
declaring that they could not keep up their shop if it were
not for the Sabbath market day? Surely we may well say,
"Cursed is the gain made on that day." Poor wretched men!
Do you not know that every penny that rings upon your
counter on that day will yet eat your flesh as if it were fire—
that every drop of liquid poison swallowed in your gaslit
palaces will only serve to kindle up the flame of "the fire
that is not quenched?"

3. *Sunday trains upon the railway.*—A majority of the directors of the Edinburgh and Glasgow Railway have shown
their determination, in a manner that has shocked all good
men, to open the railway on the Lord's Day. The sluices
of infidelity have been opened at the same time, and floods
of blasphemous tracts are pouring over the land, decrying
the holy day of the blessed God, as if there were no eye in
heaven, no King on Zion Hill, no day of reckoning.

Christian countrymen, awake! and, filled by the same spirit
that delivered our country from the dark superstitions of
Rome, let us beat back the incoming tide of infidelity and
enmity to the Sabbath.

Guilty men who, under Satan, are leading on the deep,
dark phalanx of Sabbath-breakers, yours is a solemn position.
You are *robbers.* You rob God of His holy day. You are
murderers. You murder the souls of your servants. God said,
"Thou shalt not do any work, thou, nor thy servant"; but
you compel your servants to break God's law, and to sell
their souls for gain. You are *sinners against light.* Your
Bible and your catechism, the words of godly parents, perhaps now in the Sabbath above, and the loud remonstrances of

God-fearing men, are ringing in your ears, while you perpe-
trate this deed of shame, and glory in it. You are *traitors to
your country*. The law of your country declares that you
should "observe a holy rest all that day from your own words,
works, and thoughts"; and yet you scout it as an antiquated
superstition. Was it not Sabbath-breaking that made God
cast away Israel? And yet you would bring the same curse
on Scotland now. You are *moral suicides,* stabbing your
own souls, proclaiming to the world that you are not the
Lord's people, and hurrying on your souls to meet the Sabbath-breaker's doom.

In conclusion, I propose, for the calm consideration of all
soberminded men, the following serious questions:

1. Can you name one godly minister, of any denomination
in all Scotland, who does not hold the duty of the entire sanctification of the Lord's Day?

2. Did you ever meet with a lively believer in any country
under heaven—one who loved Christ, and lived a holy life—
who did not delight in keeping holy to God the entire Lord's
Day?

3. Is it wise to take the interpretation of God's will concerning the Lord's Day from "men of the world," from in-
fidels, scoffers, men of unholy lives, men who are sand-blind
in all divine things, men who are the enemies of all righteousness, who quote Scripture freely, as Satan did, to deceive
and betray?

4. If, in opposition to the uniform testimony of God's
wisest and holiest servants, against the plain warnings of
God's Word, against the very words of your catechism, learned
beside your mother's knee, and against the voice of your out-
raged conscience, you join the ranks of the Sabbath-breakers,
will not this be *a sin against light,* will it not lie heavy on
your soul upon your deathbed, will it not meet you in the
judgment day?

I am praying that these words of truth and soberness may be owned of God, and carried home to your hearts with divine power.

December 18, 1841.

———

SCRIPTURES TO BE MEDITATED ON

1. Sabbath commanded.—Exodus 16:22-30; 20:8-11; 35:1-3; Leviticus 19:3-30; Deuteronomy 5:12-15; Nehemiah 9:14.

2. A sign of God's people.—Exodus 31:12-17; II Kings 4:23; Ezekiel 20:12; Lamentations 1:7; Hebrews 4:9.

3. Sabbath-breaking punished.—Numbers 15:32-36; Leviticus 26:33-35; II Chronicles 36:21; Jeremiah 17:19 to the end. Lamentations 2:6; Ezekiel 20:12-26; Amos 8:4-14.

4. Day of blessing.—Genesis 2:2, 3; Exodus 16:24; Leviticus 24:8; Numbers 28:9, 10; Isaiah 56:1-8; 58:13, 14; John 20:1, 19, 26; Acts 2:1 with Leviticus 23:15; Revelation 1:10.

5. Rulers should guard the Sabbath.—Exodus 20:10; Nehemiah 13:15-22.

6. Sabbath in gospel times.—Psalm 118:24; Isaiah 66:23; Ezekiel 46:1; Mark 2:27, 28; Acts 2:1; 20:6, 7; I Corinthians 16:2; Revelation 1:10.

———

MESSAGE XXXII

"He shall feed his flock like a shepherd; he shall gather the lambs with his arm, and carry them in his bosom."—ISAIAH 40:11.

BELOVED CHILDREN, Jesus is the Good Shepherd. His arm was stretched out on the cross, and His bosom was pierced with the spear. That arm is able to gather you, and that bosom is open to receive you. I pray for you every day that you may be saved by Christ. He said to me, "Feed my lambs," and I daily return the word to Him, "Lord, feed my lambs." In the bowels of Jesus Christ, I long after you all.

I believe Christ has gathered some of you. But are no more
to be gathered? Are no more green brands to be plucked from
the burning? Will no more of you hide beneath the white
robe of Jesus? Oh, come! for "yet there is room." Lift up
your hearts to God while I tell you something more of the
Good Shepherd.

I. *Jesus has a flock.*—"He shall feed his flock like a shepherd." Every shepherd must have a flock, and so has Christ.
I once saw a flock in a valley near Jerusalem; and the shepherd
went before them and called the sheep, and they knew his
voice and followed him. I said, This is the way Jesus leads
His sheep. Oh, that I may be one of them!

1. Christ's flock is a little flock.—Hear what Jesus says:
"Fear not, little flock, for it is your Father's good pleasure
to give you the kingdom" (Luke 12:32). Pray to be among
the little flock. Look at the world—eight hundred millions of
men, women, and children, of different countries, color and
language, all journeying to the judgment seat! Is this Christ's
flock? Ah, no! Five hundred millions never heard the sweet
name of Jesus, and of the rest the most see no beauty in
the Rose of Sharon. Christ's is a little flock. Look at this
town. What large crowds press along the streets on a market
day! What a large flock is here! Is this the flock of Christ?
No. It is to be feared that most of these are not the brothers
and sisters of Christ; they do not bear His likeness; they do
not follow the Lamb now, and will not follow Him in eternity.
Look round the Sabbath schools. What a number of young
faces are there! How many beaming eyes! How many precious
souls! Is this the flock of Christ? No, no. The most of you
have hard and stony hearts; the most of you love pleasure more
than God; the most of you love sin, and lightly esteem Christ.
"What a pity it is that they do not all come to Christ, for they
would be so happy!" said one of yourselves. I could weep
when I think how many of you will live lives of sin, and die

deaths of horror, and spend an eternity in hell. Beloved children, pray that you may be like the one lily among many thorns—that you may be the few lambs in the midst of a world of wolves.

2. *Christ's sheep are marked sheep.*—In almost every flock the sheep are all marked in order that the shepherd may know them. The mark is often made with tar on the woolly back of the sheep. Sometimes it is the first letter of the owner's name. The use of the mark is that they may not be lost when they wander among other sheep. So it is with the flock of Jesus. Every sheep of His has two marks. *One mark is made with the blood of Jesus.* Every sheep and lamb in Christ's flock was once guilty and defiled with sin, altogether become filthy. But every one of them has been drawn to the blood of Jesus and washed there. They are all like sheep "come up from the washing." They can all say, "Unto him that loved us, and washed us from our sins in his own blood" (Rev. 1:5). Have you this mark? Look and see. You can never be in heaven unless you have it. Every one there has washed his robes and made them white in the blood of the Lamb (Rev. 7:14). *Another mark is made by the Holy Spirit.* This is not a mark which you can see outside, like the mark on the white wool of the sheep. It is deep, deep in the bosom, where the eye of man cannot look. It is a new heart. "A new heart also will I give you" (Ezek. 36:26). This is a seal of the Holy Spirit, which He gives to all them that believe. With infinite power He puts forth His unseen hand, and silently changes the heart of all that are truly Christ's. Have you got the new heart? You never will go to heaven without it. "If any man have not the Spirit of Christ, he is none of his." Beloved children, pray for these two marks of the sheep of Jesus—forgiveness through blood and a new heart. Oh, be in earnest to get them, and to get them *now*. Soon the Chief Shepherd will come, and set the sheep on His right

hand, and the goats on His left. Where will you be in that day?

3. *Christ's sheep all flock together.*—Sheep love to go together. A sheep never goes with a wolf or with a dog, but always with the flock. Especially when a storm is coming down, they keep near one another. When the sky turns dark with clouds, and the first drops of a thundershower are coming on, the shepherds say that you will see the sheep flocking down from the hills, and all meeting together in some sheltered valley. They love to keep together. So it is with the flock of Jesus. They do not love to go with the world, but always one with another. Christian loves Christian. They have the same peace, the same Spirit, the same Shepherd, the same fold on the hills of immortality. Especially in the dark and cloudy day, such as our day is likely to be, the sheep of Christ are driven together, to weep together. They love to pray together, to sing praise together, to hide in Christ together.

"Little children, love one another." Make companions of those that fear God. Flee from all others. Who can take fire into his bosom, and not be burned? I remember of one little boy who was indeed a lamb of Christ's fold. He could not bear a lie; and whenever he found any of his companions telling a falsehood, he left their company altogether. There was one boy with whom he was very intimate. This boy one day began to boast of something he had done, which boast our little Christian saw at once to be a lie. Upon this he told him that he must never again come to his house, and that he would have nothing more to do with him till he was a better boy. His mother asked him how he would soon know when he was a better boy. He said that he would see some marks which would show him that he was better. "And what marks will you know it by?" "I think," said he, "the biggest mark will be that he loves God."

II. *What Jesus does for His flock.*

1. *He died for them.*—"I am the good Shepherd: the good Shepherd giveth his life for the sheep." This is the chief beauty in Christ. The wounds that marred His fair body make Him altogether lovely in a needy sinner's eye. All that are now and ever shall be the sheep of Christ, were once condemned to die. The wrath of God abode upon them. They were ready to drop into the burning lake. Jesus had compassion upon them, left His Father's bosom, emptied Himself, became a worm and no man, and died under the sins of many. "While we were yet sinners, Christ died for us." This is the grace of the Lord Jesus.

2. *He seeks and finds them.*—We would never seek Christ if He did not seek us first. We would never find Christ if He did not find us. "The Son of man is come to seek and to save that which was lost." I once asked a shepherd, "How do you find sheep that are lost in the snow?" "Oh," he said, "we go down into the deep ravines, where the sheep go in storms; there we find the sheep huddled together beneath the snow." "And are they able to come out when you take away the snow?" "Oh, no; if they had to take a single step to save their lives, they could not do it. So we just go in and carry them out." Ah, this is the very way Jesus saves lost sheep. He finds us frozen and dead in the deep pit of sin. If we had to take a single step to save our souls, we could not do it; but He reaches down His arm and carries us out. This He does for every sheep He saves. Glory, glory, glory be to Jesus, the Shepherd of our souls. Oh, children, let Jesus gather you. Feel your helpless condition, and look up and say, Lord, help me.

3. *He feeds them.*—"By me if any man enter in, he shall be saved, and shall go in and out and find pasture." If Jesus has saved you, He will feed you. He will feed your body. "I have been young, and now am old; yet never saw I the righteous forsaken, nor his seed begging bread."

> The birds without barn or storehouse are fed;
> From them let us learn to trust for our bread:
> His saints what is fitting shall ne'er be denied,
> So long as 'tis written—The Lord will provide.

He will feed your soul. He that feeds the little flower in the cleft of the craggy precipice, where no hand of man can reach it, will feed your soul with silent drops of heavenly dew. I shall never forget the story of a little girl in Belfast, Ireland. She was at a Sabbath school, and gained a Bible as a prize for her good conduct. It became to her a treasure indeed. *She was fed out of it.* Her parents were wicked. She often read to them, but they became worse and worse. This broke Eliza's heart. She took to her bed and never rose again. She desired to see her teacher. When he came he said, "You are not without a companion, my dear child," taking up her Bible. "No," she replied—

> "Precious Bible! what a treasure
> Does the Word of God afford!
> All I want for life or pleasure,
> Food and med'cine, shield and sword.
> Let the world account me poor,
> Having this, I ask no more."

She had scarcely repeated the lines when she hung back her head and died. Beloved children, this is the way Jesus feeds His flock. He is a tender, constant, almighty Shepherd. If you become His flock, He will feed you all the way to glory.

III. *Jesus cares for lambs.* "He shall gather the lambs with his arms, and carry them in his bosom." Every careful shepherd deals gently with the lambs of the flock. When the flocks are traveling, the lambs are not able to go far: they often grow weary and lie down. Now, a kind shepherd stoops down and puts his gentle arm beneath them, and lays them in his bosom. Such a shepherd is the Lord Jesus, and saved children are His lambs. He gathers them with His arm, and carries them in His bosom. Many a guilty lamb He has gathered and carried to His Father's house. Some He has gathered out of this place whom you and I once knew well.

Before He came into the world, Jesus cared for lambs. Samuel was a very little child, no bigger than the least of you, when he was converted. He was girded with a linen ephod, and his mother made him a little coat, and brought it to him every year. One night as he slept in the Holy Place, near where the ark of God was kept, he heard a voice cry, "Samuel!" He started up and ran to old Eli, whose eyes were dim, and said, "Here am I, for thou calledst me." And Eli said, "I called not, lie down again." He went and lay down, but a second time the voice cried, "Samuel!" He rose and went to Eli, saying, "Here am I, for thou didst call me." And Eli said, "I called not, my son, lie down again." A third time the holy voice cried, "Samuel!" And he arose and went to Eli with the same words. Then Eli perceived that the Lord had called the child; therefore Eli said, "Go, lie down; and it shall be if He call thee, thou shalt say, Speak, Lord, for thy servant heareth!" So he went and lay down. A fourth time (how often Christ will call on little children!) the voice cried, "Samuel! Samuel!" Then Samuel answered, "Speak, Lord, for thy servant heareth!" Thus did Jesus gather this lamb with His arm and carried him in His bosom. For "Samuel grew, and the Lord was with him; and the Lord revealed himself to Samuel in Shiloh" (I Sam. 3).

Little children, of whom I travail in birth till Christ be formed in you, pray that the same Lord would reveal Himself to you. Some people say, you are too young to be converted and saved. But Samuel was not too young. Christ can open the eyes of a child as easily as of an old man. Yea, youth is the best time to be saved in. You are not too young to die, not too young to be judged, and therefore not too young to be brought to Christ. Do not be contented to hear about Christ from your teachers; pray that He would *reveal Himself* to you. God grant there may be many little Samuels amongst you.

Jesus cares for lambs still. The late Duke of Hamilton had

two sons. The eldest, when a boy, fell into consumption which ended in his death. Two ministers went to see him at the family seat, near Glasgow, where he lay. After prayer, the youth took his Bible from under his pillow, and turned to II Timothy 4:7, "I have fought a good fight, I have finished my course, I have kept the faith; henceforth there is laid up for me a crown of righteousness"; and added, "This, sirs, is all my comfort!" When his death approached, he called his younger brother to his bed, and spoke to him with great affection. He ended with these remarkable words: "And now, Douglas, in a little time you will be a duke, but I *shall be a king.*"

Let me tell you a word of another gentle lamb, whom Jesus gathered, and whom I saw on her way from grace to glory. She was early brought to Christ, and early taken to be with Him where He is. She told her companions that she generally fell asleep on these words, "His left hand is under my head, and his right hand doth embrace me"; and sometimes on these, "Underneath are the everlasting arms." She said she did not know how it was, but somehow she felt that Christ was always near her. Another time she said, "I think it's the best way to make myself as loathsome as I can before Him, and then to look to Jesus." When seized with her last illness, and told that the doctors thought she would not live long, she looked quite composed, and said, "I am very happy at that." She said she could not love Jesus enough here; that she would like to be with Him, and then she would love Him as she ought. To her tender, watchful relative she said, "I wonder at your often looking so grave. I'm surprised at it, for I think I am the happiest person in the house. I have every temporal comfort, and then I am going to Jesus." After a companion had been with her, she said, "Margaret quite entered into my happiness; she did not look grave, but smiled; that showed how much she loves me." When sitting one evening, her head resting on a pillow, she was asked, "Is there anything the matter, my darling?" "Oh," she said, "I am only weak. I am quite happy. Jesus has said, 'Thou art mine.' " Another day, when near her last, one said to her, "Have you been praying much today?"

"Yes," she replied, "and I have been trying to praise too." "And what have you been praising for?" "I praise God," she said, "for all the comforts I have. I praise Him for many kind friends—you know He is the foundation of *all;* and I praise Him for taking a sinner to glory."

These are a few of the many golden sayings of this lamb of Christ, now, I trust, safe in the fold above. Would you wish to be gathered thus? Go now to some lonely place—kneel down, and call upon the Lord Jesus. Do not leave your knees until you find Him. Pray to be gathered with His arm, and carried in His bosom. Take hold of the hem of His garment, and say, "I must not—I dare not—I will not let Thee go except Thou bless me."

> O seek Him in earnest, and seek Him in time,
> For they that seek early shall find;
> While they that neglect Him are hardened in crime,
> And never can come to this pure blessed clime—
> They perish in anguish of mind.

Message XXXIII

DAILY BREAD

READING THROUGH THE WORD OF GOD IN A YEAR.

"Thy word is very pure; therefore thy servant loveth it."—Psalm 119:141

THE APPROACH of another year stirs up within me new desires for your salvation, and for the growth of those of you who are saved. "God is my record how greatly I long after you all in the bowels of Jesus Christ." What the coming year is to bring forth, who can tell? There is plainly a weight lying on the spirits of all good men, and a looking for some strange work of judgment coming upon this land. There is need now to ask that solemn question: "If in the land of peace, wherein thou trustedst, they wearied thee, then how wilt thou do in the swelling of Jordan?"

Those believers will stand firmest who have no dependence upon self or upon creatures, but upon Jehovah our Righteousness. We must be driven more to our Bibles, and to the mercy-seat, if we are to stand in the evil day. Then we shall be able to say, like David, "The proud have had me greatly in derision, yet have I not declined from thy law." "Princes have persecuted me without a cause, but my heart standeth in awe of thy word."

It has long been in my mind to prepare a scheme of Scripture reading, in which as many as were made willing by God might agree, so that the whole Bible might be read once by you in the year, and all might be feeding in the same portion of the green pasture at the same time.

I. *Dangers of such a plan.*

1. *Formality.*—We are such weak creatures that any regularly returning duty is apt to degenerate into a lifeless form. The tendency of reading the Word by a fixed rule may, in some minds, be to create this skeleton religion. This is to be the peculiar sin of the last days: "Having the form of godliness, but denying the power thereof." Guard against this. Let the calendar perish rather than this rust eat up your souls.

2. *Self-righteousness.*—Some, when they have devoted their set time to reading the Word, and accomplished their prescribed portion, may be tempted to look at themselves with self-complacency. Many, I am persuaded, are living without any divine work on their soul—unpardoned and unsanctified, and ready to perish—who spend their appointed times in secret and family devotion. This is going to hell with a lie in the right hand.

3. *Careless reading.*—Few *tremble* at the Word of God.

Few, in reading it, hear the voice of Jehovah, which is full of majesty. Some, by having so large a portion, may be tempted to weary of it, as Israel did of the daily manna, saying, "Our soul loatheth this light bread!" and to read it in a slight and careless manner. This would be fearfully provoking God. Take heed lest that word be true of you: "Ye said also, Behold, what a weariness is it! and ye have snuffed at it, saith the Lord of Hosts."

4. *A yoke too heavy to bear.*—Some may engage in reading with alacrity for a time, and afterwards feel it a burden, grievous to be borne. They may find conscience dragging them through the appointed task without any relish of the heavenly food. If this be the case with any, throw aside the fetter, and feed at liberty in the sweet garden of God. My desire is not to cast a snare upon you, but to be a helper of your joy.

If there be so many dangers, why propose such a scheme at all? To this I answer, that the best things are accompanied with danger, as the fairest flowers are often gathered in the clefts of some dangerous precipice.

II. *The advantages.*

1. *The whole Bible will be read through in an orderly manner in the course of a year.*—The Old Testament once, the New Testament and Psalms twice. I fear many of you never read the whole Bible; and yet it is all equally divine: "All scripture is given by inspiration of God, and is profitable for doctrine, for reproof, for correction, and instruction in righteousness, that the man of God may be perfect." If we pass over some parts of Scripture, we shall be incomplete Christians.

2. *Time will not be wasted in choosing what portions to read.*—Often believers are at a loss to determine towards which part of the mountains of spices they should bend their steps. Here the question will be solved at once in a very simple manner.

3. *Parents will have a regular subject upon which to ex-*

amine their children and servants.—It is much to be desired that family worship were made more instructive than it generally is. The mere reading of the chapter is often too like water spilt on the ground. Let it be read by every member of the family beforehand, and then the meaning and application drawn out by simple question and answer. The calendar will be helpful in this. Friends, also, when they meet, will have a subject for profitable conversation in the portions read that day. The meaning of difficult passages may be inquired from the more judicious and ripe Christians, and the fragrance of simpler scriptures spread abroad.

4. *The pastor will know in what part of the pasture the flock are feeding.*—He will thus be enabled to speak more suitably to them on the Sabbath; and both pastor and elders will be able to drop a word of light and comfort in visiting from house to house, which will be more readily responded to.

5. *The sweet bond of Christian love and unity will be strengthened.*—We shall be often led to think of those dear brothers and sisters in the Lord, here and elsewhere, who agree to join with us in reading these portions. We shall oftener be led to agree on earth, touching something we shall ask of God. We shall pray over the same promises, mourn over the same confessions, praise God in the same songs, and be nourished by the same words of eternal life.

MISCELLANEOUS PAPERS

MISCELLANEOUS PAPERS

~~~~~~~

EVIDENCE ON REVIVALS

ANSWERS TO QUERIES ON THE SUBJECT OF THE REVIVAL OF

RELIGION IN ST. PETER'S PARISH, DUNDEE

Submitted to a Committee of the Presbytery of Aberdeen.

IN December 1840, the Presbytery of Aberdeen appointed a committee to inquire into the revivals which had recently occurred in different parts of the country, or were taking place at that time. The committee, besides hearing evidence *viva voce,* issued queries which were sent, among other ministers, to Mr. McCheyne. The following are copies of these queries, and of his answers:

"1. Have revivals taken place in your parish or district; and if so, to what extent, and by what instrumentality and means?

"2. Do you know what was the previous character and habits of the parties?

"3. Have any who are notorious for drunkenness, or other immoralities, neglect of family duties or public ordinances, abandoned their evil practices, and become remarkable for their diligence in the use of the means of grace?

"4. Could you condescend on the number of such cases?

"5. Has the conduct of any of the parties been hitherto consistent; and how long has it lasted?

"6. Have the means to which the revivals are ascribed been attended with beneficial effects on the religious condition of the people at large?

"7. Were there public manifestations of physical excitement, as in audible sobs, groans, cries, screams?

"8. Did any of the parties throw themselves into unusual postures?

"9. Were there any who fainted, fell into convulsions, or were ill in other respects?

"10. How late have you ever known revival meetings to last?

"11. Do you approve or disapprove of these meetings upon the whole? In either case, have the goodness to state why.

"12. Was any death occasioned, or said to be occasioned, by overexcitement in any such case? If so, state the circumstances, insofar as you know them.

"13. State any other circumstances connected with revivals in your parish or district, which, though not involved in the foregoing queries, may tend to throw light upon the subject."

ADDITIONAL QUERIES

"14. What special circumstances in the preaching or ministrations of the instruments appear to have produced the results in each particular case which may have come under your notice?

"15. Did the person or persons whom you described as the instruments in producing the effects above adverted to address children? At what hour? In what special terms? And what might be the age of the youngest of them?"

MR. McCHEYNE'S ANSWERS

Answer to Query 1.—It is my decided and solemn conviction, in the sight of God, that a very remarkable and glorious work of God, in the conversion of sinners and edifying of saints, has taken place in this parish and neighborhood. This work I have observed going on from the very beginning of my ministry in this place in November 1836, and it has continued to the present time; but it was much more remarkable in the autumn of 1839, when I was abroad on a Mission of Inquiry to the Jews, and when my place was occupied by the Rev. W. C. Burns. Previous to my going abroad, and for several months afterwards, the means used were of the ordinary kind. In addition to the services of the Sabbath, in the summer of 1837, a meeting was opened in the church, on Thursday evenings, for prayer, exposition of Scripture, reading accounts of missions, revivals of religion, and so forth; Sabbath schools were formed, private prayer meetings were encouraged, and two weekly classes for young men and young women were instituted, with a very large attendance. These means were accompanied with an evident blessing from on high in many instances.

But there was no visible or general movement among the people until August 1839, when, immediately after the beginning of the Lord's work at Kilsyth, the Word of God came with such power to the hearts and consciences of the people here, and their thirst for hearing it became so intense, that the evening classes in the schoolroom were changed into densely crowded congregations in the church, and for nearly four months it was found desirable to have public worship almost every night. At this time, also, many prayer meetings were formed, some of which were strictly private or fellowship meetings, and others, conducted by persons of some Christian experience, were open to persons under concern about their souls. At the time of my return from the Mission to the Jews, I found thirty-nine such meetings held weekly in connection with the congregation, and five of these were conducted and attended entirely by little children. At present, although many changes have taken place, I believe the number of these meetings is not much diminished. Now, however, they are nearly all of the more private kind—the deep and general anxiety, which led to many of them being open, having in a great degree subsided. Among the many ministers who have assisted here from time to time, and especially in the autumn of 1839, I may mention Mr. Macdonald of Urquhart, Mr. Cumming of Dumbarney, Mr. Bonar of Larbert, Mr. Bonar of Kelso, and Mr. Somerville of Anderston. Some of these were present here for a considerable time, and I have good reason for believing that they were eminently countenanced by God in their labors.

As to the extent of this work of God, I believe it is impossible to speak decidedly. The parish is situated in the suburb of a city containing 60,000 inhabitants. The work extended to individuals residing in all quarters of the town, and belonging to all ranks and denominations of the people. Many hundreds, under deep concern for their souls, have come, from first to last, to converse with the ministers; so that I am deeply persuaded, the number of those who have received saving benefit is greater than any one will know till the judgment day.

2, 3. The previous character of those who seem to have

been converted was various. I could name not a few in the higher ranks of life that seem evidently to have become new creatures, who previously lived a worldly life, though unmarked by open wickedness. Many, again, who were before nominal Christians, are now living ones. I could name, however, far more, who have been turned from the paths of open sin and profligacy, and have found pardon and purity in the blood of the Lamb, and by the Spirit of our God; so that we can say to them, as Paul said to the Corinthians, "Such were some of you; but ye are washed, but ye are sanctified, but ye are justified." I often think, when conversing with some of these, that the change they have undergone might be enough to convince an atheist that there is a God, or an infidel that there is a Saviour.

4. It is not easy for a minister, in a field like this, to keep an exact account of all the cases of awakening and conversion that occur; and there are many of which he may never hear. I have always tried to mark down the circumstances of each awakened soul that applied to me, and the number of these, from first to last, has been very great. During the autumn of 1839 not fewer than from 600 to 700 came to converse with the ministers about their souls; and there were many more, equally concerned, who never came forward in this way. I know many who appear to have been converted, and yet have never come to me in private; and I am every now and then meeting with cases of which I never before heard. Indeed, eternity alone can reveal the true number of the Lord's hidden ones among us.

5. With regard to the consistency of those who are believed to have been converted, I may first of all remark, that it must be acknowledged, and should be clearly understood, that many who came under concern about their souls, and seemed for a short time to be deeply convinced of sin, have gone back to the world. I believe that, at that remarkable season in 1839, there were very few persons who attended the meetings without being more or less affected. It pleased God at that time to

bring an awfully solemn sense of divine things over the minds of men. It was, indeed, the day of our merciful visitation. But many allowed it to slip past them without being saved; and these have sunk back, as was to be expected, into their former deadness and impenitence. Alas! there are some among us, whose very looks remind you of that awful warning, "Quench not the Spirit."

Confining our view, however, to those who, as far as ministers could judge by the rules of God's Word, seemed to be savingly converted, I may with safety say, that I do not know of more than two who have openly given the lie to their profession. Other cases of this kind may have occurred, but they are unknown to me. More, I have little doubt, will eventually occur; for the voice of God teaches us to expect such things. Some of those converted have now walked consistently for four years; the greater part from one to two years. Some have had their falls into sin, and have thus opened the mouths of their adversaries; but the very noise that this has made, shows that such instances are very rare. Some have fallen into spiritual darkness; many, I fear, have left their first love; but yet I see nothing in all this but what is incident in the case of every Christian church. Many there are among us, who are filled with light and peace and are examples to believers in all things.

We had an additional communion season at my return from the Continent, which was the happiest and holiest that I was ever present at. The Monday was entirely devoted to thanksgiving, and a thank offering was made among us to God for His signal mercies. The times were hard, and my people are far from wealthy, yet the sum contributed was £71. This was devoted to missionary purposes. It is true that those whom I esteem as Christians do often grieve me by their inconsistencies; but still I cannot help thinking that, if the world were full of such, the time would be come when "they shall neither hurt nor destroy in all God's holy mountain."

6. During the progress of this work of God, not only have many individuals been savingly converted, but important effects have also been produced upon the people generally. It is indeed amazing, and truly affecting to see, that thousands living in the immediate vicinity of the spot where God has been dealing so graciously, still continue sunk in deep apathy in regard to spiritual things, or are running on greedily in open sin. While many from a distance have become heirs of glory, multitudes, I fear, of those who live within the sound of the Sabbath bell continue to live on in sin and misery. Still, however, the effects that have been produced upon the community are very marked. It seems now to be allowed, even by the most ungodly, that there *is* such a thing as conversion. Men cannot any longer deny it.

The Sabbath is now observed with greater reverence than it used to be; and there seems to be far more of a solemn awe upon the minds of men than formerly. I feel that I can now stop sinners in the midst of their open sin and wickedness, and command their reverent attention, in a way that I could not have done before. The private meetings for prayer have spread a sweet influence over the place. There is far more solemnity in the house of God; and it is a different thing to preach to the people now from what it once was. Any minister of spiritual feeling can discern that there are many praying people in the congregation. When I came first here, I found it impossible to establish Sabbath schools on the local system; while, very lately, there were instituted with ease nineteen such schools, that are well taught and well attended.

7, 8, 9. As I have already stated, by far the most remarkable season of the working of the Spirit of God in this place was in 1839, when I was abroad. At that time there were many seasons of remarkable solemnity, when the house of God literally became "a Bochim, a place of weepers." Those who were privileged to be present at these times will, I believe, never forget them. Even since my return, however, I have myself frequently seen the preaching of the Word attended with so much power, and eternal things brought so near, that the feelings of the people could not be restrained. I have observed at such times an awful and breathless stillness pervading the assembly; each hearer bent forward in the posture of rapt attention; serious men covered their faces to pray that the arrows of the King of Zion might be sent home with power to the hearts of sinners.

Again, at such a time, I have heard a half-suppressed sigh rising from many a heart, and have seen many bathed in tears. At other times I have heard loud sobbing in many parts of the church, while a deep solemnity pervaded the whole audience. I have also, in some instances, heard individuals cry aloud, as if they had been pierced through with a dart. These solemn scenes were witnessed under the preaching of different ministers, and sometimes occurred under the most tender gospel invitations. On one occasion, for instance, when the minister was speaking tenderly on the words, "He is altogether lovely," almost every sentence was responded to by cries of the bitterest agony. At such times I have seen persons so overcome, that they could not walk or stand alone.

I have known cases in which believers have been similarly affected through the fullness of their joy. I have often known such awakenings to issue in what I believe to be real conversion. I could name many of the humblest, meekest believers, who at one time cried out in the church under deep agony. I have also met with cases where the sight of souls thus pierced has been blessed by God to awaken careless sinners who had come to mock.

I am far from believing that these signs of deep alarm always issue in conversion, or that the Spirit of God does not often work in a more quiet manner. Sometimes, I believe, He comes like the pouring rain; sometimes like the gentle dew. Still I would humbly state my conviction, that it is the duty of all who seek the salvation of souls, and especially the duty of ministers, to long and pray for such solemn times, when the arrows shall be sharp in the heart of the King's enemies, and our slumbering congregations shall be made to cry out, "Men and brethren, what shall we do?"

10, 11. None of the ministers who have been engaged in the work of God here have ever used the name "revival meeting"; nor do they approve of its use. We are told in the Acts that the apostles preached and taught the gospel daily; yet their meetings are never called revival meetings. No other meetings have taken place here, but such as were held for the preaching and teaching of the gospel, and for prayer. It will not be maintained by any one, that the meetings in the sanctuary every Lord's Day are intended for any other purpose than the revival of genuine godliness, through the conversion of sinners and the edification of saints. All the meetings in this place were held, I believe, with a single eye to the same object. There seems, therefore, to be no propriety in applying the name peculiarly to any meetings that have been held in this place. It is true, indeed, that on week evenings there is not generally the same formality as on Sabbaths; the congregation are commonly dressed in their working clothes, and the minister speaks with less regular preparation.

During the autumn of 1839 the meetings were in general dismissed at ten o'clock; although in several instances the state of the congregation seemed to be such as to demand that the ministers should remain still longer with them, that they might counsel and pray with the awakened. I have myself once or twice seen the service in the house of God continue till about midnight. On these occasions the emotion during the preaching of the Word was so great, that after the blessing had been pronounced at the usual hour, the greater part of the people remained in their seats or occupied the passages, so that it was impossible to leave them. In consequence of this, a few words more were spoken suited to the state of awakened souls; singing and prayer filled up the rest of the time. In this way the meeting was prolonged by the very necessity of the case.

On such occasions I have often longed that all the ministers in Scotland were present, that they might learn more deeply what the true end of our ministry is. I have never seen or heard of anything indecorous at such meetings; and on all such occasions, the feelings that filled my soul were those of the most solemn awe, the deepest compassion for afflicted souls, and an unutterable sense of the hardness of my own heart. I do entirely and solemnly approve of such meetings, because I believe them to be in accordance with the Word of God, to be pervaded by the Spirit of Christ, and to be ofttimes the birthplaces of precious, never-dying souls. It is my earnest prayer that we may yet see greater things than these in all parts of Scotland.

12. There was one death that took place in very solemn circumstances at the time of the work of God in this place, and this was ascribed by many of the enemies to religious excitement. The facts of the case, however, which were published at the time, clearly show that this was a groundless calumny.

13. I have been led to examine with particular care the accounts that have been left us of the Lord's marvelous works in the days that are past, both in our own land and in other parts of the world, in order that I might compare these with what has lately taken place at Dundee, and in other parts of Scotland. In doing this, I have been fully convinced that the outpouring of the Holy Spirit at the Kirk of Shotts, and again, a century after, at Cambuslang, in Scotland, and under the ministry of President Edwards in America, was attended by the very same appearances as the work in our own day. Indeed, so completely do they seem to agree, both in their nature and in the circumstances that attended them, that I have not heard a single objection brought against the work of God now which was not

urged against it in former times, and that has not been most scripturally and triumphantly removed by Mr. Robe in his *Narrative,* and by President Edwards in his invaluable *Thoughts on the Revival of Religion in New England:* "And certainly we must throw by all talk of conversion and Christian experience; and not only so, but we must throw by our Bibles, and give up revealed religion, if this be not in general the work of God."

14. I do not know of anything in the ministrations of those who have occupied my pulpit that may with propriety be called peculiar, or that is different from what I conceive ought to characterize the services of all true ministers of Christ. They have preached, so far as I can judge, nothing but the pure gospel of the grace of God. They have done this fully, clearly, solemnly; with discrimination, urgency, and affection. None of them read their sermons.

They all, I think, seek the *immediate* conversion of the people, and they believe that, under a living gospel ministry, success is more or less the rule, and want of success the exception. They are, I believe, in general, peculiarly given to secret prayer; and they have also been accustomed to have much united prayer when together, and especially before and after engaging in public worship. Some of them have been peculiarly aided in declaring the terrors of the Lord, and others in setting forth the fullness and freeness of Christ as the Saviour of sinners; and the same persons have been, at different times, remarkably assisted in both these ways. So far as I am aware, no unscriptural doctrines have been taught, nor has there been a keeping back of any part of "the whole counsel of God."

15. The ministers engaged in the work of God in this place, believing that children are lost, and may through grace be saved, have therefore spoken to children as freely as to grown persons; and God has so greatly honored their labors, that

many children, from ten years old and upwards, have given full evidence of their being born again. I am not aware of any meetings that have been held peculiarly for children, with the exception of the Sabbath schools, the children's prayer meetings, and a sermon to children on the Monday evening after the Communion. It was commonly at the public meetings in the house of God that children were impressed; often also in their own little meetings, when no minister was present.

March 26, 1841.

This Do in Remembrance of Me

THE LORD'S SUPPER is the sweetest of all ordinances:
1. *Because of the time when it was instituted.*—"The Lord Jesus, the same night in which he was betrayed, took bread." It was the darkest night that ever was in this world, and yet the brightest—the night when His love to sinners was put to the severest test. How amazing that He should remember our comfort at such a time!

2. *Because it is the believer's ordinance.*—It is the duty of all men to pray. God hears even the ravens when they cry, and so He often hears the prayers of unconverted men (Ps. 107; Acts 8:22). It is the duty of all men to hear the preached gospel. "Unto you, O men, I call, and my voice is to the sons of men." But the Lord's Supper is the children's bread; it is intended only for those who know and love the Lord Jesus.

3. *Because Christ is the beginning, middle, and end of it.*— "This do in remembrance of me." "Ye do show the Lord's death till he come." There are many sermons in which Christ is not from beginning to end; many books where you cannot find the fragrance of His name: but there cannot be a sacrament where Christ is not from beginning to end. Christ is the Alpha and Omega of the Lord's Supper; it is all Christ and Him crucified. These give a sweetness to the bread and wine.

I fear the Lord's Supper is profaned in a dreadful manner among you. Many come who are living in positive sins, or in the neglect of positive duties. Many come who know that they were never converted; many who in their hearts ridicule the very thoughts of conversion. Unworthy communicating is a fearful sin; on account of it God is greatly provoked to withdraw His Spirit from you, to visit you with frowns of Providence, and to seal you to the day of perdition. Am I become your enemy because I tell you the truth? Deal honestly with your soul, and pray over what I am now writing; and may He who opened the heart of Lydia open your heart while I explain.

THE ACTIONS OF THE 'COMMUNICANT

I. *He takes the bread and the wine.*—When the minister offers the bread and wine to those at the table, this represents Christ freely offered to sinners, even the chief. The receiving of the bread and wine means, I do thankfully receive the broken, bleeding Saviour as my Surety. The act of taking that bread and wine is an appropriating act; it is saying before God, and angels, and men, and devils, "I do flee to the Lord Jesus Christ as my refuge." Noah's entering into the ark was an appropriating act. Let others fly to the tops of their houses, to their castles and towers, to the rugged rocks, to the summits of the highest mountains. As for me, I believe the word of God, and flee to the ark as my only refuge (Heb. 11:7). When the manslayer fled into the city of refuge, it was an appropriating act. As he entered breathless at the gates of Hebron, his friends might cry to him, Flee unto the wilderness! or, Flee beyond Jordan! But no, he would say, I believe the Word of God, that I shall be safe only within these walls; this is my refuge city, here only will I hide! (Josh. 20).

When an Israelite brought an offering of the herd or of the flock, when the priest had bound it with cords to the horns of the altar, the offerer laid his hands upon the head of the lamb: this was an appropriating act, as much as to say, I take this lamb as dying for me. The world might say, How will this save you? Mend your life, give alms to the poor. I believe the Word of God, he would say; I do not wish to bear my own sins, I lay them on the Lamb of God (Lev. 1:4). When the woman, trembling, came behind Jesus and touched the hem of His garment, this also was an appropriating act. Her friends might say to her, Come and try some more physicians, or wait till you are somewhat better. No, said she, "If I may but touch His garment, I shall be made whole" (Mark 5:28). In the Forty-second Psalm, David's enemies said to him continually, "Where is thy God?" This made tears his meat night and day. It was like a sword in his bones. But in the Forty-third Psalm he gathers courage, and says, "I will go unto the altar of God," where the lamb was slain; and then he says, "Unto God, my exceeding joy." You say, I have no God: behold, I take this lamb as slain for me, and therefore God is my God. In the Song of Solomon, when the bride found him whom her soul loved, she says, "I held him, and would not let him go." This was true appropriating faith. The world might say to her, "Come this way, and we will show thee other beloveds, fairer than thy beloved." Nay, saith she, "I held him, and would not let him go. This is my beloved, and this is my friend" (S. S. 3:4).

Just such, beloved, is the meaning of receiving broken bread and poured out wine at the Lord's Table. It is the most solemn appropriating act of all your lives. It is declaring by signs, "I do enter into the ark; I flee into the city of refuge; I lay my hand on the head of the Lamb; I do touch the hem of His garment; I do take Jesus to be my Lord and my God; I hold Him, and by grace I will never let Him go." It is a deliberate closing with Christ, by means of signs, in the presence of witnesses. When the bride accepts the right hand in marriage before many witnesses, it is a solemn declaration to all the world that she does accept the bridegroom to be her only husband. So, in the Lord's Supper, when you receive that bread and wine, you solemnly declare, that, forsaking all others, you heartily do receive the Lord Jesus as your only Lord and Saviour.

If these things be true, should not many stay away from this holy Table? Many of you know that a work of grace has never been begun in your heart; you never were made to tremble for your soul; you never were made to pray, "God be merciful to me a sinner"; you never were brought to "rejoice, believing in God." Oh, beloved, let me say it with all tenderness, this table is not for you. Many of you know you are not in a state you would do to die in. You say, "I hope to turn yet before I die." Does not this show that your sins are not covered—that you are not born again—that you are not fled to the hope set before you? This table is not for you.

Some of you know well that you have had convictions of sin, but they have passed away. The walls of the house of God have seen you trembling on the brink of eternity, but you were never brought to "peace in believing"—to "peace with God." You have drowned your anxieties in the whirl of business or of pleasure. You have drawn back. Your goodness is like the "morning cloud and early dew, it goeth away." This table is not for you. I speak to your sense of honor and common honesty. In worldly things, would you tell a lie either by word of mouth or by signs? And is it a light matter to tell a lie in eternal things? Will you deliberately declare, by taking the broken bread and poured out wine, what you know to be a lie? Oh, pray over the story of Ananias and Sapphira, and tremble (Acts 5:1-11). May it not be said in heaven of many, "Thou hast not lied unto men, but unto God"?

A word to trembling, believing souls. This feast is spread for you. "Eat, O friends; drink, yea, drink abundantly, O beloved." If you have faith as a grain of mustard seed, come. If you are "weak in the faith," ministers are commanded to receive you. If on the morning of the communion Sabbath, even for the first time in your life, Christ appear full and free to you, so that you cannot but believe on Him, do not hesitate to come. Come to the table, leaning on the Beloved, and you will have John's place there. You will lean peacefully upon His breast.

II. *He eats the bread and drinks the wine.*—"Take, eat." "Drink ye all of it." Eating and drinking in this ordinance imply feeding upon Christ. It is said of bread that it "strengtheneth man's heart," and of wine, that it "maketh glad the heart of man." Bread is the staff of life, and wine is very reviving to those who, like Timothy, have often infirmities. They are the greatest nutritive blessings which man possesses. To feed on them in the Lord's Supper is as much as to say, I do feed on Jesus, as my only strength; in the Lord have I righteousness and strength. To take the bread into the hand is saying by signs, "He is made of God unto me righteousness." To feed upon it is saying, "He is made unto me sanctification."

When Israel fed on manna for forty years, and drank water from the rock, they were strengthened for their journey through the howling wilderness. This was a picture of believers journeying through this world. They feed every day on Christ their strength; He is their daily manna; He is the rock that follows them. When the bride sat under the shadow of the apple tree, she says, "His fruit was sweet to my taste"; and again, "Stay me with flagons, comfort me with apples, for I am sick of love." Believers, this is a picture of you. No sooner are you sheltered by the Saviour, than you are nourished and renewed by Him. He comforts your hearts, and stablishes you in every good word and work.

In the Thirty-sixth Psalm, when David speaks of men trusting under the wings of the Lord Jesus, he adds, "They shall be abundantly satisfied with the fatness of thy house, and thou shalt make them drink of the river of thy pleasures." Little children, you know by experience what this means. When you were brought to believe on the Son of God, you were adopted into His family, fed with the children's bread, and your heart filled with the holy pleasures of God. The same thing is represented in feeding on the bread and wine. It is a solemn declaration in the sight of the whole world, that you have been put into the clefts of the smitten rock, and that you are feeding on the honey treasured there. It is declaring that you have sat down under Christ's shadow, and that you are comforted and nourished by the fruit of that tree of life. It is saying, "I have come to trust under the shadow of His wings, and now I drink of the river of His pleasures." It is a sweet declaration of your own helplessness and that Christ is all your strength.

If this be true, should not many stay away from the Lord's Table? Many of you know that you were never really grafted into the true vine, that you never received any nourishment from Christ, that you never received the Holy Spirit. Many of you know that you are dead branches—that you only *seem* to be united to the vine—that you are the branches that bear no fruit, which He taketh away. Why should you feed on that bread and wine? Some of you may know that you are dead in sins, unconverted, not born again, that you never experienced any change of heart like that spoken of (Ezek. 36:26). This bread and wine are not for you. Some of you know that you are living under the power of sins that you could name: some of you, perhaps, in secret profanation of the holy Sabbath, "doing your own ways, finding your own pleasures, speaking your own words." Some, perhaps, in secret swearing, or lying, or dishonesty, or drinking, or uncleanness! Ah! why should you feed on this bread and wine? It will do you no good. Can you for a moment doubt that you will eat and drink *unworthily?* Dare you do this? Pray over these awful words and tremble: "He that eateth and drinketh unworthily, eateth and drinketh damnation to himself."

All who are really "looking unto Jesus" are invited to come to the Lord's Table. Some feel like a sick person recovering from a fever: you are without strength, you cannot lift your hand or your head. Yet you look unto Jesus as your strength: He died for sinners, and He lives for them. You look to Him day by day. You say, He is my bread, He is my wine; I have no strength but what comes from Him. Come you and feed at the Lord's Table, and welcome. Some feel like a traveler when he arrives at an inn, faint and weary: you have no strength to go farther, you cannot take another step; but you lean on Jesus as your strength; you believe that word: "Because I live, ye shall live also." Come you and feed on this bread and wine, with your staff in your hand and shoes on your feet, and you will "go on your way rejoicing." Feeble branches need most nourishment. The more you feel your weakness, the amazing depravity of your heart, the power of Satan, and the hatred of the world, the more need have you to lean on Jesus, to feed on this bread and wine—you are all the more welcome.

III. *He shares the bread and wine with others.*—The Lord's Table is not a selfish, solitary meal. To eat bread and wine alone is not the Lord's Supper. It is a family meal of that family spoken of in Ephesians 3:15. You do not eat and drink by yourself; you share the bread and wine with all at the same table. Jesus said, "Drink ye all of it."

This expresses *love to the brethren,* a sweet feeling of oneness with "all those who love the Lord Jesus in sincerity," a heart-filling desire that all should have the same peace, the same joy, the same spirit, the same holiness, the same heaven with yourself. You remember the golden candlestick in the temple, with its seven lamps. It was fed out of one golden bowl on the top of it, which was constantly full of oil. The oil ran down the shaft of the candlestick, and was distributed to each lamp by seven golden pipes or branches. All the lamps shared the same oil. It passed from branch to branch.

None of the lamps kept the oil to itself; it was shared among them all. So it is in the vine. The sap ascends from the root, and fills all the branches. When one branch is satisfied, it lets the stream pass on to the next; nay, it carries the rich juice to the smaller twigs and tendrils, that all may have their share, that all may bear their precious fruit. So it is with the body. The blood comes from the heart in full and nourishing streams; it flows to all the members and one member conducts it to another, that all may be kept alive, and all may grow.

So it is in the Lord's Supper. The bread and wine are passed from hand to hand, to show that we are members one of another. "For we being many, are one bread and one body, for we are all partakers of that one bread" (I Cor. 10: 17). It is a solemn declaration that you are one with all true Christians, one in peace, one in feeling, one in holiness; and that if one member suffer, you will suffer with it, or if one member be honored, you will rejoice with it. You thereby declare that you are branches of the true Vine, and are vitally united to all the branches, that you wish the same Holy Spirit to pervade every bosom. You declare that you are lamps of the same golden candlestick, and that you wish the same golden oil to keep you and them burning and shining as lights in a dark world.

Learn, once more, that most should stay away from this table. Some of you know that you have not a spark of love to the Christians. You persecute them, or despise them. Your tongue is like a sharp razor against them; you ridicule their notions of grace, and conversion, and the work of the Spirit. You hate their conversation; you call it cant and hypocrisy. When they are speaking on divine things with a full heart, and you come in, they are obliged to stop because you dislike it. Why should you come to this holy Table? What is hypocrisy, if this is not? You put on a serious face and air; you press eagerly in to the table; you sit down, and look deeply solemnized; you take the bread into your hand, pretending to declare that you have been converted, and brought to accept of a crucified Christ. You then eat of the broken bread and drink of that cup with evident marks of emotion, pretending that you are one of those who live upon Jesus, who are filled with the Spirit. You then pass the bread and wine to others, pretending that you love the Christians, that you wish all to be partakers with you in the grace of the Lord Jesus; and yet all the while you hate and detest them, their thoughts, their ways, their company. You would not for the world become a man of prayer. Beloved souls, what is hypocrisy, if this is not? I solemnly declare, that I had rather see you "breathing out threatenings and slaughter against the disciples of the Lord," than come to be a wolf in sheep's clothing. Are you not afraid, lest, while you are sitting at the table, you should hear the voice of the Lord Jesus saying, "Judas, betrayest thou the Son of man with a kiss?"

Dear believer, you "know that you are passed from death unto life, because you love the brethren." This pure and holy life is one of the first feelings in the converted bosom. It is divine and imperishable. You are a companion of all that fear God. It would be hell to you to spend eternity with wicked men. Come and show this love at the feast of love. The table in the upper room at Jerusalem was but a type and earnest of the table in the upper room of glory. Soon we shall exchange the table below for the table above, where we shall give full expression to our love to all eternity. There no betrayers can come—"no unclean thing can enter." Jesus shall be at the head of the table, and God shall wipe away all tears from our eyes.

———

COMMUNION WITH BRETHREN OF OTHER
DENOMINATIONS

To the Editor of the Dundee Warder

ALLOW ME, for the first time in my life, to ask a place in your columns. My object in doing so is not to defend myself, which we are all perhaps too ready to do, but to state simply and calmly what appear to me to be the scriptural grounds of Free Ministerial Communion among all who are faithful ministers of the Lord Jesus Christ, by whatever name known among men. These views I have long held: they were maintained by the early Reformers, and by the Church of Scotland in her best days; and I bless God that, by the decision of the last General Assembly, they are once more declared to be the principles of our beloved church. I am anxious to do this, because the question is one of great difficulty, requiring deeper thought than most have bestowed upon it; and it is of vast importance, in this day of conflicting opinions, to be firmly grounded on the Lord's side.

Of the respectable ministers, who so lately officiated for me during my illness, I shall say nothing, except that they agreed to assist me in a time of need in the kindest manner, and that, however much I differ from them on several points of deepest interest, I, along with many in the church, do regard them as faithful ministers of Christ; and I trust they will utterly disregard the poor insinuations as to their motives (contained in the letters of your correspondents), which, I regret to say, disfigure your last paper.

In order to clear our way in this subject, allow me to open up, first, the subject of Free Communion among private Christians, and then that of Free Communion among Christian ministers.

1. I believe it to be the mind of Christ, that all who are

vitally united to Him, should love one another, exhort one another daily, communicate freely of their substance to one another when poor, pray with and for one another, and sit down together at the Lord's Table. Each of these positions may be proved by the Word of God. It is quite true that we may be frequently deceived in deciding upon the real godliness of those with whom we are brought into contact. The apostles themselves were deceived, and we must not expect to do the work of the ministry with fewer difficulties than they had to encounter. Still I have no doubt from Scripture that, where we have good reason for regarding a man as a child of God, we are permitted and commanded to treat him as a brother; and, as the most sacred pledge of heavenly friendship, to sit down freely at the table of our common Lord, to eat bread and drink wine together in remembrance of Christ.

The reason of this rule is plain. If we have solid ground to believe that a fellow sinner has been, by the Holy Spirit, grafted into the true vine, then we have ground to believe that we are vitally united to one another for eternity. The same blood has washed us, the same Spirit has quickened us, we lean upon the same pierced breast, we love the same law, we are guided by the same sleepless eye, we are to stand at the right hand of the same throne, we shall blend our voices eternally in singing the same song: "Worthy is the Lamb!" Is it not reasonable, then, that we should own one another on earth as fellow travelers to our Father's house, and fellow heirs of the incorruptible crown? Upon this I have always acted, both in sitting down at the Lord's Table and in admitting others to that blessed privilege.

I was once permitted to unite in celebrating the Lord's Supper in an upper room in Jerusalem. There were fourteen present, the most of whom, I had good reason to believe, knew and loved the Lord Jesus Christ. Several were godly Episcopalians, two were converted Jews, and one a Christian from Nazareth,

converted under the American missionaries. The bread and
wine were dispensed in the Episcopal manner, and most were
kneeling as they received them. Perhaps your correspondents
would have shrunk back with horror, and called this the
confusion of Babel. We felt it to be sweet fellowship with
Christ and with the brethren; and as we left the upper room,
and looked out upon the Mount of Olives, we remembered
with calm joy the prayer of our Lord that ascended from one
of its shady ravines, after the first Lord's Supper: "Neither
pray I for these alone, but for them also which shall believe
in me through their word, that they all may be ONE."

The Table of Christ is a family table spread in this wilderness, and none of the true children should be absent from it,
or be separated while sitting at it. We are told of Rowland
Hill that, upon one occasion, "when he had preached in a
chapel where none but baptized adults were admitted to the
sacrament, he wished to have communicated with them, but
was told respectfully, "You cannot sit down at our table." He
only calmly replied, "I thought it was the Lord's Table."

The early Reformers held the same view. Calvin wrote to
Cranmer that he would cross ten seas to bring it about.
Baxter, Owen, and Howe, in a later generation, pleaded for
it; and the Westminster Divines laid down the same principle
in few but solemn words: "Saints, by profession, are bound
to maintain an holy fellowship and communion in the worship of God—which communion, as God offereth opportunity,
is to be extended unto all those who in every place call upon
the name of the Lord Jesus." These words, embodied in our
standards, show clearly that the views maintained above are
the very principles of the Church of Scotland.

2. The second scriptural communion is Ministerial Communion. Here also I believe it to be the mind of Christ, that
all who are true servants of the Lord Jesus Christ, sound in
the faith, called to the ministry, and owned of God therein,

should love one another, pray one for another, bid one another Godspeed, own one another as fellow soldiers, fellow servants, and fellow laborers in the vineyard, and, so far as God offereth opportunity, help one another in the work of the ministry. Each of these positions also may be proved by the Word of God. I am aware that, practically, it is a point of far greater difficulty and delicacy than the communion of private Christians, because I can own many a one as a fellow Christian, and can joyfully sit down with him at the Lord's Table, while I may think many of his views of divine truth defective, and could not receive him as a sound teacher. But although caution and sound discretion are no doubt to be used in applying this or any other Scripture rule, yet the rule itself appears to be simple enough—that, where any minister of any denomination holds the Head, is sound in doctrine and blameless in life, preaches Christ and Him crucified as the only way of pardon and the only source of holiness, especially if he has been owned of God in the conversion of souls and upbuilding of saints, we are bound to hold ministerial communion with him, whenever Providence opens the way.

What are we that we should shut our pulpits against such a man? True, he may hold that Prelacy is the scriptural form of church government; he may have signed the thirty-seventh article of the Church of England, giving the Queen the chief power in all causes, whether ecclesiastical or civil: still, if he be a Berridge or a Rowland Hill, he is an honored servant of Christ. True, he may hold Establishments to be unscriptural—he may not see, as I do, that the Queen is the minister of God, and ought to use all her authority in extending, defending, and maintaining the Church of Christ: still, if he be like some I could name, he is a faithful servant of Christ. True, he may have inconsistencies of mind which he cannot account for—he may have prejudices of sect and education which destroy much of our comfort in meeting him—and can we plead exemption from these? He may sometimes have spoken rashly and uncharitably—I also have done the same. Still, I cannot but own him as a servant of Christ. If the Master owns him in His work, shall the sinful fellow servant disown him? Shall we be more cautious than our Lord? True, he may have much imperfection in his views; so had Apollos. He may be to be blamed in some things, and withstood to the face; so it was with Peter. He may have acted a cowardly part at one time; so did John Mark. Still I maintain that unless he has shown himself a Demas, "a lover of this present world," or one of those who have a "form of godliness, denying the power thereof," we are not allowed to turn away from him, nor to treat him as an adversary.

Such were the principles of the Reformers. Calvin says of Luther, when he was loading him with abuse, "Let him call me a dog or a devil, I will acknowledge him as a servant of Christ." The devoted Usher preached in the pulpit of Samuel Rutherford; and at a later date, before the unscriptural Act of 1799 was passed, to hinder faithful English ministers from carrying the light of divine truth into the deathlike gloom of our Scottish parishes, a minister of the Synod of Glasgow defended himself for admitting Whitefield into his pulpit in these memorable words: "There is no law of Christ, no Act of Assembly, prohibiting me to give my pulpit to an Episcopal, Independent, or Baptist minister, *if of sound principles in the fundamentals of religion, and of sober life.*"

The same truth is clearly to be deduced from the twenty-fifth chapter of the Confession of Faith, where it is declared that "the visible Church consists of all those throughout the world that profess the true religion, together with their children." And then it is added, "Unto this catholic, visible Church, Christ hath given the ministry." From which it plainly follows, that faithful ministers belonging to all parts of the visible

Church are to be recognized *as ministers whom Christ hath given.* Such I believe to be the principles of God's Word; such are clearly the views of the standards of our Church; and I do hail it as a token that the Spirit of God was really poured down upon the last General Assembly, that they so calmly and deliberately swept away the unchristian Act of 1799 from the statute book, and returned to the good old way.

It has often been my prayer, that no unfaithful minister might ever be heard within the walls of St. Peter's. My elders and people can bear witness that they have seldom heard any voice from its pulpit that did not proclaim "ruin by the Fall, righteousness by Christ, and regeneration by the Spirit." Difficult as it is in these days to find supply, I had rather that no voice should be heard there at all than "the voice of strangers," from whom Christ's sheep will flee. Silence in the pulpit does not edify souls, but it does not ruin them. But the living servant of Christ is dear to my heart, and welcome to address my flock, let him come from whatever quarter of the earth he may. I have sat with delight under the burning words of a faithful Lutheran pastor. I have been fed by the ministrations of American Congregationalists and devoted Episcopalians, and all of my flock who know and love Christ would have loved to hear them too. If dear Martin Boos were alive, pastor of the Church of Rome though he was, he would have been welcome too; and who that knows the value of souls and the value of a living testimony would say it was wrong?

Had I admitted to my pulpit some frigid Evangelical of our own church—I allude to no individual, but I fear it is a common case—one whose head is sound in all the stirring questions of the day, but whose heart is cold in seeking the salvation of sinners, would any watchful brother of sinners have sounded an alarm in the next day's gazette to warn me and my flock of the sin and danger? I fear not. And yet Baxter says of such a man, "Nothing can be more indecent than to hear a dead preacher speaking to dead sinners the living truth of the living God." With such ministers I have no communion. "O my soul, come not thou into their secret; unto their assembly, mine honor, be not thou united."

In conclusion, let me notice the effect of this Free Ministerial Communion upon our glorious struggle for Christ's kingly office in Scotland. I believe, with many of my brethren, that the Church of Scotland is at this moment a city set upon a hill that cannot be hid. I believe she is a spectacle to men and to angels, contending in the sight of the universe for Christ's twofold crown—His crown over nations, and His crown over the visible, catholic Church. She stands between the Voluntary on the one side, and the Erastian on the other, and with one hand on the Word of God, and the other lifted up to heaven, implores her adorable Head to uphold her as a faithful witness unto death, in a day of trouble, and rebuke, and blasphemy. In generations past this cause has been maintained in Scotland at all hands, and against all enemies; and if God calls us to put our feet in the blood-stained footsteps of the Scottish worthies, I dare not boast, but I will pray that the calm faith of Hugh Mackail, and the cheerful courage of Donald Cargill, may be given me.

But is this a reason we should not live up to the spirit of the New Testament, in our dealing with Christians and Christian ministers of other denominations? Is this a reason we should not wipe off every stain from the garments of our beloved church? Is it not the very thing that demands that each member of our church should set his house in order, purging out all the old leaven of carnal division, reforming his own spirit and family, according to the rule of God's Word; that elders and ministers should seek revival and reformation in their private and public walk, and pant after more of the spirit of our suffering Head and Elder Brother? If a faithful Episcopal minister be wrong in his views of church government, as I believe he is; if many of our faithful Dissenting brethren are wrong in opposing Christ's headship over nations, as I believe they are, what is the scriptural mode of seeking to set them right? Is it to set up unscriptural barriers between us and them? Is it to count them as enemies, however much Christ acknowledges them as good and faithful servants? Is it to call them by opprobrious epithets, to impute mean and wicked motives for their undertaking the holiest services, to rake among the ashes for their hard sayings? I think not. Christ's way is a more excellent way, however unpleasant to the proud, carnal heart. "Let us, therefore, as many as be perfect, be thus minded; and if in anything ye be otherwise minded, God shall reveal even this unto you."

I have looked at this question from the brink of eternity, and in such a light, I can assure your correspondents that, if they know the Lord, they will regret, as I have done, the want of more caution in speaking of the doings and motives of other men. Let us do our part towards our Dissenting brethren according to the Scriptures, however they may treat us. We shall be no losers. Perhaps we may gain those who are brethren indeed to think more as we do. At least they will love us, and cease to speak evil of us.

If our church is to fall under the iron foot of despotism, God grant that it may fall reformed and purified; pure in its doctrine, government, discipline, and worship; scriptural in its spirit; missionary in its aim, and holy in its practice; a truly golden candlestick; a pleasant vine. If the daughter of Zion must be made a widow, and sit desolate on the ground, grant her latest cry may be that of her once suffering, now exalted Head: "Father, forgive them, for they know not what they do."

St. Peter's, Dundee, *July 6, 1842.*

JEHOVAH TSIDKENU

"THE LORD OUR RIGHTEOUSNESS"

(The watchword of the Reformers.)

I once was a stranger to grace and to God,
I know not my danger, and felt not my load;
Though friends spoke in rapture of Christ on the tree,
Jehovah Tsidkenu was nothing to me.

I oft read with pleasure, to soothe or engage,
Isaiah's wild measure and John's simple page;
But e'en when they pictured the blood-sprinkled tree,
Jehovah Tsidkenu seemed nothing to me.

Like tears from the daughters of Zion that roll,
I wept when the waters went over His soul;
Yet thought not that my sins had nailed to the tree,
Jehovah Tsidkenu—'twas nothing to me.

When free grace awoke me, by light from on high,
Then legal fears shook me, I trembled to die;
No refuge, no safety in self could I see—
Jehovah Tsidkenu my Saviour must be.

My terrors all vanished before the sweet name;
My guilty fears banished, with boldness I came
To drink at the fountain, life-giving and free—
Jehovah Tsidkenu is all things to me.

Jehovah Tsidkenu! my treasure and boast,
Jehovah Tsidkenu! I ne'er can be lost;
In Thee I shall conquer by flood and by field—
My cable, my anchor, my breastplate and shield!

Even treading the valley, the shadow of death,
This "watchword" shall rally my faltering breath;
For while from life's fever my God sets me free,
Jehovah Tsidkenu my death-song shall be.

November 18, 1834

———

"THEY SING THE SONG OF MOSES"

Dark was the night, the wind was high,
The way by mortals never trod;
For God had made the channel dry,
When faithful Moses stretched the rod.

The raging waves on either hand
Stood like a massy tott'ring wall,
And on the heaven-defended band
Refused to let the waters fall.

With anxious footsteps, Israel trod
The depths of that mysterious way;
Cheered by the pillar of their God,
That shone for them with fav'ring ray.

But when they reached the opposing shore,
As morning streaked the eastern sky,
They saw the billows hurry o'er
The flower of Pharaoh's chivalry.

Then awful gladness filled the mind
Of Israel's mighty ransomed throng;
And while they gazed on all behind,
Their wonder burst into a song.

Thus, thy redeemed ones, Lord, on earth,
While passing through this vale of weeping,
Mix holy trembling with their mirth,
And anxious watching with their sleeping.

The night is dark, the storm is loud,
The path no human strength can tread;
Jesus, be Thou the pillar-cloud,
Heaven's light upon our path to shed.

And oh! when, life's dark journey o'er,
And death's enshrouding valley past,
We plant our foot on yonder shore,
And tread yon golden strand at last.

Shall we not see with deep amaze,
How grace hath led us safe along;
And whilst behind—before, we gaze,
Triumphant burst into a song!

And even on earth, though sore bested,
Fightings without, and fears within;
Sprinkled today from slavish dread,
Tomorrow captive led by sin:

Yet would I lift my downcast eyes
On Thee, Thou brilliant tower of fire—
Thou dark cloud to mine enemies—
That hope may all my breast inspire.

And thus the Lord, my strength, I'll praise,
Though Satan and his legions rage;
And the sweet song of faith I'll raise,
To cheer me on my pilgrimage.

EDINBURGH, 1835

"I AM DEBTOR."

When this passing world is done,
When has sunk yon glaring sun,
When we stand with Christ in glory,
Looking o'er life's finished story,
Then, Lord, shall I fully know—
Not till then—how much I owe.

When I hear the wicked call
On the rocks and hills to fall,
When I see them start and shrink
On the fiery deluge brink,
Then, Lord, shall I fully know—
Not till then—how much I owe.

When I stand before the throne
Dressed in beauty not my own,
When I see Thee as Thou art,
Love Thee with unsinning heart,
Then, Lord, shall I fully know—
Not till then—how much I owe.

When the praise of heaven I hear
Loud as thunders to the ear,
Loud as many waters' noise,
Sweet as harp's melodious voice,
Then, Lord, shall I fully know—
Not till then—how much I owe.

Even on earth, as through a glass
Darkly, let thy glory pass,
Make forgiveness feel so sweet,
Make Thy Spirit's help so meet,
Even on earth, Lord, make me know
Something of how much I owe.

Chosen not for good in me,
Wakened up from wrath to flee,
Hidden in the Saviour's side,
By the Spirit sanctified,
Teach me, Lord, on earth to show,
By my love, how much I owe.

Oft I walk beneath the cloud,
Dark as midnight's gloomy shroud;
But, when fear is at the height,
Jesus comes, and all is light:
Blessed Jesus! bid me show
Doubting saints how much I owe.

When in flowery paths I tread,
Oft by sin I'm captive led;
Oft I fall, but still arise;
The Spirit comes—the tempter flies:
Blessed Spirit! bid me show
Weary sinners all I owe.

Oft the nights of sorrow reign—
Weeping, sickness, sighing, pain,
But a night thine anger burns—
Morning comes, and joy returns:
God of comforts! bid me show
To Thy poor, how much I owe.

May 1837.

"THY WORD IS A LAMP UNTO MY FEET, AND A LIGHT UNTO MY PATH."

When Israel knew not where to go,
God made the fiery pillar glow;
By night, by day, above the camp
It led the way—their guiding lamp:
Such is Thy holy Word to me
In day of dark perplexity.
When devious paths before me spread,
And all invite my foot to tread,
I hear Thy voice behind me say—
"Believing soul, this is the way;
Walk thou in it." O gentle Dove,
How much thy holy law I love!
        My lamp and light
        In the dark night.

When Paul amid the seas seemed lost,
By Adrian billows wildly tossed,
When neither sun nor star appeared,
And every wave its white head reared
Above the ship, beside his bed
An angel stood, and "Fear not" said.
Such is Thy holy Word to me
When tossed upon affliction's sea:
When floods come in unto my soul,
And the deep waters o'er me roll,
With angel voice Thy Word draws near
And says, " 'Tis I, why shouldst thou fear?
Through troubles great my saints must go
Into their rest, where neither woe

Nor sin can come; where every tear
From off the cheek shall disappear,
Wiped by God's hand." O gentle Dove,
Thy holy law how much I love?
　　My lamp and light
　　In the dark night.

When holy Stephen dauntless stood
Before the Jews, who sought his blood,
With angel face he looked on high,
And wondering, through the parted sky,
Saw Jesus risen from His throne
To claim the martyr as His own.
Angelic peace that sight bestowed,
With holy joy his bosom glowed;
And while the murderous stones they hurled,
His heaven-wrapt soul sought younder world
Of rest. "My spirit, Saviour, keep,"
He cried, he kneeled, he fell asleep.
Such be Thy holy Word to me
In hour of life's extremity!
Although no more the murdering hand
Is raised within our peaceful land—
The church has rest, and I may ne'er
Be called the martyr's crown to wear:
Yet still, in whatsoever form
Death comes to me—in midnight storm
Whelming my bark, or in my nest,
Gently dismissing me to rest—
O grant me in thy Word to see
A risen Saviour beckoning me.
No evil then my heart shall fear
In the dark valley. Thou art near!
My trembling soul and Thou, my God,
Alone are there; Thy staff and rod
Shall comfort me. O gentle Dove,
How much Thy holy law I love!
　　My lamp and light
　　In the dark night.

1838

Moody Press, a ministry of the Moody Bible Institute, is
designed for education, evangelization, and edification.
If we may assist you in knowing more about Christ and
the Christian life, please write us without obligation:
Moody Press, c/o MLM, Chicago, Illinois 60610.